# English for Law

# English for Law

Alison Riley, LL.B.

MACMILLAN PUBLISHERS

First published 1991
Reprinted 1992, 1993 (twice), 1994

Published by MACMILLAN PUBLISHERS LTD
London and Basingstoke

Photoset by Parker Typesetting Service, Leicester
Printed in Singapore


**British Library Cataloguing in Publication Data**
Riley, Alison
English for Law
1. Law, Terminology
1. Title
340.014

ISBN 0 – 333 – 49387 – 7

# Contents

**Introductory Unit: The Study and Classification of Law**

(pp. 1–12)

■ **Themes and materials**

Reading a university Law Faculty list of subjects and course description

*The Study and Classification of Law:* subjects studied in the Law Faculty at an English university; the style, method and contents of an English university Law degree course; the contents of a single university Law course.

Extracts from:
Cambridge University Law Faculty Schedule;
Cambridge University Prospectus.

■ **Skills**

Reading to understand the general contents of a text; reading for detail; reading to confirm expectations.
Reader autonomy: choosing a section of text to read in detail according to personal interest.

■ **Vocabulary**

Using the reader's mother-tongue or other known languages to understand new words: recognising true cognates and false friends.
Contextual deduction.
Personal vocabulary research: selecting vocabulary of interest and using all available resources to understand meaning.

*Theme:* branches of law.

**Unit 1: English Law**

(pp. 13–33)

■ **Themes and materials**

Reading a law textbook; reading extracts from law dictionaries and works of reference.

**Section One. Sources of English Law:** The role and importance of legislation, judicial decision, custom and authoritative writings in English law, including elements of comparison with civil-law legal systems; how law develops in the case-law system and the basic method and principles of the common law.

Extracts from:
Philip S. James, *Introduction to English Law*.

**Section Two. Common Law:** The various meanings of common law in the English and US legal systems; common law and Equity.

Short extracts from:
Roger Bird, *Osborne's Concise Law Dictionary*; Gavin McFarlane, *The Layman's Dictionary of English Law*; David M. Walker, *The Oxford Companion to Law*; *Black's Law Dictionary*; *Encyclopaedia Britannica*.

## ■ Skills

Using previous knowledge: thinking about a topic before you read.
Introduction to different reading purposes: reading for gist, reading for specific information, reading for detailed understanding. Suiting reading style to reading purpose.
Reformulation: matching a brief summary to the text to aid and check comprehension; completing a simple chart.
Reader autonomy: choosing a section of text for personal study.

## ■ Vocabulary

Recognising that it is not necessary to understand every word in a text; defining which unknown vocabulary it is necessary to understand, depending on your reading purpose.
Realising that the proportion of completely unknown vocabulary in a text is limited and that it's often possible to work out the meaning of new words using the context and logical reasoning, word families and cognates.

Identifying law terms.
Remembering vocabulary: classifying words in groups.
Word families: compounds of known words and simple word-building, negative prefixes in un-, people in -ist.

*Themes:* Expressions with 'law' (e.g. Roman law, source of law). Legislation.

## ■ Language and structure

Understanding past participle phrases where noun and past participle are used to substitute a relative clause.
Attending to detail: understanding pronouns.
The language of contrast and comparison.
Connectives – understanding the meaning and function of thus, therefore, however, further, for.

## Unit 2: State and Government
(pp. 34–57)

## ■ Themes and materials

Reading a descriptive legal report.

**Section One. The UK:** composition and brief history of the UK.

Extract from:
Kenneth R. Simmonds, *International Encyclopaedia of Comparative Law, National Report: the U.K.*

**Section Two. The UK System of Government:** composition, role and powers of the monarchy, legislature and executive, including Law Officers of the Crown.

Ibid.

## ■ Skills

Reading for gist; reading for detail.
Using previous knowledge of text topic and creating a personal purpose for reading; reading for confirmation.
Reformulation: matching a reformulated version of the text to original; summarising the text from notes provided; reformulating the text information to focus on main points and keep them available for easy future reference: identifying the main points of the text and guided note-taking in chart form.

## ■ Vocabulary

Contextual deduction: looking for information in the text to suggest the probable meaning of unknown words.
Word-building: learning to recognise root words and word families; prefixes re-, non-.
Remembering vocabulary: categorising words in groups to help remember and recall.
Translating national institutional terms.
Guided dictionary use: selecting the correct definition of words with more than one meaning using monolingual dictionary definitions.

*Themes:* State and government. State systems of the world. Giving details of a law or rule (the . . . Act provided that . . .). More expressions with 'law'; law and laws.

## ■ Language and structure

The passive: function and form.
Relative clauses: finding basic subject–verb–object pattern in the presence of relatives.
Further practice in understanding relative pronouns.
Expressing obligation and capacity.

## Unit 3: The Constitution
(pp. 58–72)

## ■ Themes and materials

Reading a critical analysis.

**Section One. Parliamentary Sovereignty:** from Dicey to Lord Hailsham – the changing face of parliamentary sovereignty in modern Britain.

Extract from:
Gabriele Ganz, *Understanding Public Law* from the series Understanding Law, series editor J. A. G. Griffiths.

**Section Two. The UK electoral system:** a description and critical analysis of UK electoral law viewed in relation to Britain's political parties.

Ibid.

## ■ Skills

Reading for gist; reading for rapid information; reading for detail.

Reformulation: completing a diagram.
Understanding the author's attitude to information presented in the text.

## ■ Vocabulary

Prediction: using key vocabulary to predict what a text is about.
Selecting which unknown words in a text it is necessary to understand for a particular reading purpose.
Word families: recognising word families: verb/noun/adjective relationships, people in -or and -er; using word-building to deduce meaning by breaking a word down into its component parts; affixes un-, -ship and re-.

*Themes:* Titles of cases (R v..../*ex parte*...). Electoral law.

## ■ Language and structure

Understanding complex sentences: relative clauses with 'whose' and conditionals.
Understanding the function of basic connectives in the text (although, thus, etc.).
'Whichever'.

## Unit 4: Revision and Consolidation, Units 1–3

(pp. 73–82)

## ■ Themes and materials

Reading a work of legal reference.
*Constitutional conventions*: their legal status, and an outline of the principal conventions concerning the legislature, executive and judiciary.

Extract from:
Lord Hailsham of St Marylebone, *Halsbury's Laws of England*, 4th edition.

Factual quiz on English law, Units 1–3.

## ■ Skills

Using previous knowledge and prediction: thinking about the text topic before you read.
Reading for gist.
Reading for specific information.
Reading for detailed understanding.
Reformulation: identifying the main points of a text and guided note-taking in chart form.

## ■ Vocabulary

Contextual deduction: using the general context to decide the meaning of unknown words.
Word families: using the root word and component parts to deduce the meaning of unknown words.
Testing some key words and phrases from Units 1–3.

## ■ Language and structure

Testing the understanding of pronouns and relative clauses.

## Unit 5: Statutory Interpretation and EC Law

(pp. 83–99)

### ■ Themes and materials

Reading a law textbook; reading a statute; reading a case.

**Section One. Statutory Interpretation:** the interpretation of statutes by the English courts; comparing judicial interpretation in other legal systems.

Extracts from:
Philip S. James, *Introduction to English Law.*
The Public Order Act 1986.

**Section Two. EC Law:** the interpretation and application of the law of the European Community in the UK, and its effect on the interpretation and validity of UK law.

Extract from the case:
*Macarthys Ltd v. Smith* (Case 129/79)
All E.R. [1981] 1 111

### ■ Skills

Using prediction to create a personal purpose for reading.
Selective reading: finding the section of a text relevant to your reading purpose.
Reading for rapid information; reading to understand the organisation of themes in a text; reading for general understanding; reading for detail.
Reformulation: writing brief written notes and using them to describe a case.
Legal reasoning: applying law from the text to example situations and cases.

### ■ Vocabulary

Contextual deduction; using specific context clues to work out the probable meaning of unknown words in a text.
Personal vocabulary study and research.
Techniques for storing, memorising and revising vocabulary: making vocabulary cards, storing related groups of words in lists, tables and vocabulary networks.
Word families: using word-building to understand new words.
The interpretation of words and their literal meaning.
Positive and negative forms of adjectives.

*Themes:* abbreviations in a court case. UK law and EC law.

### ■ Language and structure

Expressing purpose: so as to . . . in order to . . . .
Obligation and possibility: further study.
The passive: use of the passive with modal verbs (must, should, may, etc.).

## Unit 6: The Judicial System

(pp. 100–115)

### ■ Themes and materials

Reading works of legal reference and a House of Lords statement.

**Section One. The Courts:** the hierarchy and jurisdiction of civil and criminal courts in England and Wales.

Extract from:
David M. Walker, *The Oxford Companion to Law.*

**Section Two. Judicial Precedent:** the nature and operation of the doctrine of precedent in English law, with regard to decisions of courts in the UK and in other common-law jurisdictions and including the notions of *ratio decidendi* and *dicta*.

House of Lords 1966 Practice Statement, All England Law Reports, and extracts from:
Lord Hailsham of St Marylebone, *Halsbury's Laws of England*, 4th edition.

### ■ Skills

Understanding the organisation and contents of the text; reading for general understanding; reading for specific information; reading for detailed understanding.
Personal reading comprehension: making predictions and formulating personal questions on the text.
Reformulation of text information in diagram form: completing and designing diagrams; taking notes.
Legal reasoning: applying legal principles in the text to solve practical problems.

### ■ Vocabulary

Cognates: distinguishing true cognates and false friends.
Dictionary use: using a dictionary efficiently and selecting the correct definition from a mono- or bilingual dictionary.
Word families: the prefix mis-; related verb and noun forms; related adjective and noun forms.
Remembering vocabulary: completing and creating vocabulary networks to store and recall words.

*Themes:* The courts and judiciary. Legal phrases in Latin (*stare decisis, per incuriam . . .*)

### ■ Language

Obligation: phrases with 'bind', 'bound' and 'binding'; modal verbs – should and ought to.

## Unit 7: Private Law — Contract
(pp. 116–32)

### ■ Themes and materials

Reading the judgment of an English court case.
The formation of a contract: agreement.

**Section One. The Facts of the Case; the Defence:** presentation of the facts and arguments for the defence.

Extracts from:
*Carlill v. Carbolic Smoke Ball Co. [1893] 1 Q. B. 256*

**Section Two. The Decision:** analysis of the facts and decision from Bowen L.J's judgment.

Ibid.

### ■ Skills

Understanding the organisation of material in the text; reading for general understanding; reading to find specific information; reading for very detailed understanding.

Reformulation: summarising the main points of the text briefly in your own words.
Using prediction while reading to understand the organisation and development of ideas in the text.
Comparing English substantive law with the reader's own system.
Legal reasoning: applying legal principles from the text to solve example cases; presentation of legal arguments: a moot.

## ■ Vocabulary

Predicting vocabulary before reading a text to encourage active vocabulary research and as an aid to understanding.
Contextual deduction – context clues: finding and using specific clues in the text that indicate the meaning of unknown words.
Word families: the suffixes -er and -or.

*Themes:* The language of a court case. People in private law. Abbreviations.

## ■ Language and structure

Understanding very complex sentences. Learning the technique of analysing a sentence phrase by phrase to understand its overall meaning.

**Unit 8: Revision and Consolidation, Units 5–7**

(pp. 133–42)

## ■ Themes and materials

Reading an offer and the terms and conditions of a contract.
*Contract:* Invitation to treat, offer and acceptance; the terms of the agreement.

Extract from:
The Rolls Royce share offer, 1987.

Factual quiz on English law, Units 5–7.

## ■ Skills

Reading for specific information
Reading to understand the themes and organisation of material in the text.
Reading for detail and using text information to solve legal problems.

## ■ Vocabulary

Dictionary use: selecting the correct definition of words with more than one meaning from a mono-lingual dictionary.
Contextual deduction: using specific context clues and the general context to deduce the meaning of new words in the text.
Word families: using root words and word families to work out the meaning of new words.
Testing key words and expressions from Units 5–7.

## ■ Language and structure

Expressing obligation, possibility, necessity and duty.

**Unit 9: Public Law – Criminal Law**

(pp. 143–59)

## ■ Themes and materials

Reading a European Court of Human Rights case; reading a statute; reading newspaper crime reports.

**Section One. The Facts of the Case:** conviction and punishment for a crime of violence under Isle of Man law.

Extracts from:
European Court of Human Rights, *Tyrer case*, judgment of 25 April 1978, Series A, No. 26, including extracts from the Petty Sessions and Summary Jurisdiction Act 1927 and the Summary Jurisdiction Act 1960.

**Section Two. The Background to the Case:** the constitutional position of the Isle of Man in relation to the UK as regards domestic legislation and International Law; the use and legal status of judicial corporal punishment in the UK and Isle of Man.

Ibid.

**Section Three. Reading Newspaper Crime Reports:** reports of arrests and charges; trial, conviction and sentencing of offenders.

Articles from the *Independent*, *Guardian*, and *The Sunday Times* newspapers.

## ■ Skills

Finding out as much as possible about a text from external information, skimming and scanning: using the title, subtitles, publication information, key words and gist.
Reading for detailed understanding.
Reformulation: guided summary: method for creating a personal summary independently; checking the quality of a summary.
Independent personal study of a text: creating and correcting personal comprehension questions on the text.

## ■ Vocabulary

Selective vocabulary study: choosing which unknown words are necessary to understand the main points of the text; studying vocabulary of personal interest.
Independent dictionary use.
Independent contextual deduction.
Independent use of word families and root words to understand new vocabulary.
Storing and processing vocabulary on a word-ladder.

*Theme:* Crime, the criminal process and punishment.

## ■ Language and structure

'Unless'. 'So' and 'Such'.
Independent selection and study of language points of interest in a text.

## Unit 10: International Law – Human Rights
(pp. 160–75)

## ■ Themes and materials

Reading a European Court of Human Rights judgment.

**Section One. Proceedings before the Commission:** case against the UK for the use of corporal punishment; decision of the European Commission of Human Rights.

Extract from:
European Court of Human Rights, *Tyrer case*, idem.

**Section Two. Judgment and Decision:** the Court's judgement on Article 3 of the European Convention on Human Rights (regarding torture, inhuman or degrading treatment or punishment) and its decision on the whole case.

Extracts from ibid.

## ■ Skills

Reformulation: completing and designing a chart.
Introduction to an independent reading strategy, bringing together the skills of: using previous knowledge and all available information about the text before reading, prediction, skimming, scanning, creating personal questions on a text, reading for confirmation, identifying and reformulating the main points of the text, detailed understanding.
Using prediction while reading to understand the development of a text.
Reading to understand the general themes of a text; reading for specific information.
Understanding the writer's attitude to information in the text.

## ■ Vocabulary

Identifying law terms: International Law and domestic law.
Cognates: distinguishing false friends from true cognates.
Selective vocabulary study: deciding which words it is necessary to understand for a particular reading purpose; choosing which vocabulary skills to apply to understand key words from the text.
Word-building: verb and noun relationships, including nouns in -tion, -ation, -ication and -ment.

*Themes:* International Law terms. The violation or respect of legal rules (e.g. in breach of Art. 3, pursuant to . . .). Verbs in legal proceedings.

## ■ Language and structure

Connectives: using connectives to predict and understand the development of the text and as context clues; recognising the function of connectives and using them to understand the writer's attitude (nevertheless, accordingly, indeed, furthermore, admittedly, etc.).
'Shall' for obligation.

## Unit 11: International Law — Use of Force and Espionage
(pp. 176–191)

## ■ Themes and materials

Reading a law review article.
The *Rainbow Warrior* Affair

**Section One. The Facts:** the full facts of the *Rainbow Warrior* affair.

Extracts from:
Michael Pugh, 'Legal Aspects of the *Rainbow Warrior* Affair', *International and Comparative Law Quarterly*, Volume 36, July 1987, Part 3.

**Section Two. The Law:** an analysis of the principles of International Law governing individual and State responsibility for criminal acts of agents abroad.

Ibid.

## ■ Skills

Analysing the development of themes in the text.
Independent summary of the text in a personally designed format.
Completely independent application of the reading strategy brought together and presented in Unit 10.
Distinguishing statements of fact and opinion.
Applying legal principles from the text to practical cases; presenting legal arguments: a moot.

## ■ Vocabulary

Independent vocabulary study; personal selection of words to study from the text; selection and application of all vocabulary skills (cognates; root words and word families; logical reasoning and contextual deduction; dictionary use) to understand words in context.
Understanding words that remain unchanged as different parts of speech.
Independent vocabulary consolidation: storing vocabulary in a format of your choice and personalised vocabulary consolidation activities.

*Themes:* Holders of high office in the UK and international organisations.
Abbreviations in International Law (ICJ, POW, UN, etc.). The language of war and force.

## ■ Language and structure

Understanding descriptive phrases: noun/noun and adjective/noun combinations; noun + 's or s'; clauses; prepositional phrases.

**Unit 12: Revision and Consolidation, Units 9–11**

(pp. 192–202)

## ■ Themes and materials

Reading an International Court of Justice judgment.
*Diplomatic relations:* responsibility for the protection of diplomatic and consular staff and premises and the use of force to remedy breaches of International Law.

Extracts from:
*United States of America v. Iran*, International Court of Justice, judgment in the case concerning United States diplomatic and consular staff in Tehran, 24 May 1980.

Factual quiz on English and International Law, Units 9–11.

## ■ Skills

Reading for gist and understanding the development of themes in a text.
Reading for general understanding.
Reformulation: identifying and summarising the main points of a text.
Reading for detailed understanding.
Understanding the author's attitude to information presented in a text.

## ■ Vocabulary

Selecting which unknown vocabulary to study for a particular reading purpose.
Contextual deduction: using the context to work out the probable meaning of unknown words in a text.

Word families: using root words and word families to work out the meaning of new words in a text.
Testing key words and expressions from Units 9–11.

## ■ Language and structure

Understanding the logical development of arguments in a text and interpreting connectives.

# Acknowledgements

Thank you very much to everyone who has helped in the production of this book.

I would like to thank all the writers whose ideas on design, methodology and language activities have influenced my work, including in particular Ruth Gairns, John Morgan, Stuart Redman, Mario Rinvolucri, Michael Swan, Catherine Walter, and Peter Watcyn-Jones on teaching vocabulary; Christine Nuttall, Wilga M. Rivers and Mary S. Temperley on teaching reading skills, and Fraida Dubin and Elite Olshtain on course design.

Thank you to all my students and colleagues at Ferrara University, Italy, for their help in encouraging and developing the project, and especially Giovanni Battaglini, Lorenza Carlassare and Laura Forlati.

For help with foreign-language law terms, thanks to Bożena Gronowska (Polish), Thomas Dürbeck (German) and Ylva Cannizzo-Wadén (Swedish) and, for checking the legal content of the text, Elaine Sutherland. Thanks to Simon Nugent for many helpful suggestions.

Special thanks for all kinds of help to my friends and family – to my husband Riccardo Cannizzo, to Cecilia Reynolds, Catherine and Ken Riley, Carolyn and Sue Riley, Salah Troudi and Martina Ward.

# References

**Introductory Unit**   Cambridge University Prospectus, 1988-89; Cambridge University Law Faculty Schedule, 1988–89.

**Unit 1**   *Introduction to English Law*, 11th edition, by Philip S. James (London: Butterworth, 1985); *Osborne's Concise Law Dictionary*, 7th edition, by Roger Bird (London: Sweet & Maxwell, 1983); *The Layman's Dictionary of English Law*, by Gavin McFarlane (London: Waterlow, 1984); *The Oxford Companion to Law*, by David M. Walker (Oxford: Oxford University Press, 1980); *Black's Law Dictionary*, by Henry Campbell Black, 5th edition (St Paul, Minnesota, USA: West Publishing Company, 1979); *The New Encyclopaedia Britannica*, Encyclopaedia Britannica Inc., 1981.

**Unit 2**   *International Encyclopaedia of Comparative Law, Volume 1, National Reports: the U.K.* by Kenneth R. Simmonds, under the auspices of the International Association of Legal Science, Victor Knapp, chief editor (Mouton, the Hague and J. C. B. Mohr [Paul Siebeck], Tubingen, 1976).

**Unit 3**   *Understanding Public Law*, by Gabriele Ganz, from the series Understanding Law, series editor J. A. G. Griffiths (London: Fontana, 1987).

**Unit 4**   *Halsbury's Laws of England*, 4th edition, Lord Hailsham of St Marylebone (London: Butterworth, 1979).

**Unit 5**   *Introduction to English Law*, 11th edition, by Philip S. James (see Unit 1); The Public Order Act 1986, available from HMSO, London; Case 129/79 Macarthys Ltd v. Smith, All England Law Reports, All E R [1981] 1 111 (London: Butterworth).

**Unit 6**   *The Oxford Companion to Law*, by David M. Walker (see Unit 1); House of Lords 1966 Practice Statement, All England Law Reports, All E R [1966] 3, (London: Butterworth); *Halsbury's Laws of England*, 4th edition, Lord Hailsham of St Marylebone (see Unit 4).

**Unit 7**   *Carlill v. Carbolic Smoke Ball Co.* [1893] 1 Q.B. 256, from *Cases on the Law of Contract*, 3rd edition, by G. C. Cheshire and C. H. S. Fifoot (London: Butterworth, 1959).

**Unit 8**   Rolls Royce share offer, from the *Observer*, Sunday, 3 May 1987.

**Unit 9**   *European Court of Human Rights, Tyrer case*, judgment of 25 April 1978, Series A, No 26, European Court of Human Rights, Strasbourg; The Petty Sessions and Summary Jurisdiction Act 1927; The Summary Jurisdiction Act 1960, available from HMSO.

**Unit 10**   *Tyrer case* (see Unit 9).

# Introduction to the Reader

### The purpose of *English for Law*

The purpose of this book is to teach native speakers of other languages to understand and use the language of the law in English. In particular it aims to teach foreign law students and lawyers how to choose, read and use original legal materials of any kind in English in the course of their studies, research or work. Through a wide variety of exercises based on authentic legal texts, readers will gradually learn the reading, vocabulary and study skills (abilities) necessary to work independently on legal materials of their own choice. The book presents about 400 general and specialised law terms, and teaches techniques for building up systematically a wide legal vocabulary in fields of special interest to the reader. Readers are encouraged to practise the language presented in the book in a variety of speaking and writing activities. The themes and texts in Units 1–9 provide an introduction to some important aspects of the English legal system – these materials present the language of different areas of the law in their natural context. The final section of the book contains International Law materials.

### Who the book is for

*English for Law* is intended for everybody who has a special interest in law and needs to use the English of the law for their studies or work. In particular it is for law students and academic lawyers at universities and law schools all over the world, but I hope that it will also be of use and interest to the practising lawyer. The book is for intermediate to advanced students of English: you will be able to use it if you have already studied general English probably for two or three years, you know some basic English vocabulary and structures and can understand what you read at this level, even if you find it more difficult to speak, listen or write. The book is designed for use as a class coursebook on courses in English for law, or for self-study for readers studying without a teacher alone or in groups.

### The structure of the book

The book contains an Introductory Unit which teaches some basic vocabulary and skills and introduces you to the style and method of the course. This is followed by 12 main Units. After each group of three Units there is a Revision and Consolidation Unit which provides a chance to check and practise what you have learnt from the book (Units 4, 8 and 12). Each of the other Units is based on a theme (e.g. Criminal Law, State and Government) and is divided into two or three sections.

At the beginning of the book there is a full list of Contents which gives the materials and themes in each section of each Unit and explains the skills and language presented and practised in the Unit.

The *Key* at the back of the book gives the answers to all the exercises marked with the symbol ●. This includes all the reading, vocabulary and writing exercises based on the text and some other exercises and oral activities.

The *Glossary* at the end of the book contains about 400 law terms which appear in the book. It shows pronunciation and gives a short definition of each term in simple English.

A complete *List of References* is given on pages xv–xvi for readers who are interested in studying a subject further.

## Use of the book

The book contains clear instructions for each exercise so that you can use it in class with a teacher, or as a self-study course alone or in groups. Sometimes there are different instructions for readers working alone and readers working in classes or groups. If you are working alone, follow the instructions marked with the symbol ■. If you are working with other people follow the instructions marked ▲. Activities marked with the symbol ▲ are done in pairs or groups – this gives everyone a chance to speak and practise the language and also gives you the opportunity to think of your ideas and gain confidence before comparing your work with the rest of the class.

Before you start each Unit, you may like to read the Contents page for that Unit to see what you will learn; you can also refer to it at any time during a Unit or at the end.

Follow the instructions for each exercise in the Unit, which are in clear, simple English; they tell you what to do and often explain what language skills you are learning and why. Each Section generally begins with questions for you to think about and discuss – this is to introduce the subject, and may also bring in some useful vocabulary. It is not a test of your knowledge, so don't worry if you don't know the answers – try giving your own ideas and don't be afraid to guess!

After this comes a variety of exercises based on an authentic legal text – these include reading comprehension, language, vocabulary, writing and speaking activities (see *Skills* below for more details). Each Section generally ends with a discussion on a subject related to the theme, or the presentation of an imaginary case in court; often you are invited to compare aspects of your own legal system with what you have learnt about the English legal system.

### Use of the Key
As you work through the exercises in each Unit, refer to the Key when you see the symbol ● (not before or after). Always try to understand *why* your answers are right or wrong. For many exercises the Key will help you to do this, for others the Key gives line references in the text which you can refer to, in order to correct wrong answers. In some cases there is no single correct answer to an exercise and the answer given in the Key is only an example; in other cases the Key is a model which you can use to compare with your own work: in both cases this is always specified in the Key.

### Use of the Glossary
The Glossary is a permanent reference section of the law terms which appear in the book. You can use it as you read the texts and do the exercises in the book in the following ways: to check the meaning of words which you have already studied in the book, but which you have forgotten; to find or check the meaning of terms such as 'judge' and 'court' which are not explained in the book because they are very common; when the instructions in the book tell you to do so; at the end of a Section or Unit for personal vocabulary study and consolidation. You can also use it for general reference when you meet words you have studied in the book in the course of your work or studies). Apart from the above, do *not* use the Glossary to find the meaning of new words as you study the book. This would stop you from learning and practising

the vocabulary skills taught in the book, and these important skills will eventually help you to read legal texts and learn new terms independently.

*Use of a dictionary*
For the same reasons, only use a dictionary (for non-law terms) in the same way as the Glossary when studying the book. Using a dictionary correctly is itself an important vocabulary skill which is taught and practised in the book.

*Revision and Consolidation Units*
The purpose of Units 4, 8 and 12 is to check and practise what you have learnt in previous Units. If possible you should complete each Revision and Consolidation Unit in a single session of about 1½–2 hours. Do not refer to your previous work or a dictionary or the Glossary as you work, except where this is specified in the exercises. The exercises include reading and vocabulary skills, law and law terms and a structure exercise. There is a maximum total of 100 marks: about ⅓ of the marks are for reading comprehension, ⅓ are for vocabulary, and ⅓ are for law and structure. These Units are designed to be marked independently by the reader, and clear instructions are given. If at the end of the Unit, you are not satisfied with your result, go back to the parts of the book which you need to study again. If your problem is remembering vocabulary, refer to Unit 5 for ideas.

## Choosing which units to study

The book is designed for study as a continuous course. However, you may find that a particular Unit is especially difficult for you, or does not interest you much. If so, stop and go on to the next Unit.

If you are a specialised or academic lawyer you may only be interested in studying some Units in the book. This is certainly possible, but it may be more difficult for you to follow some of the instructions and complete some of the exercises, because reading and vocabulary skills are developed gradually in the book and activities are explained fully the first time they appear. You will probably need to use a dictionary and the Glossary more than other readers, and refer to the Contents page to find the part of the book which contains a full explanation of any language activities you don't understand.

## Skills and language

*Reading skills*
The reading skills developed in this book include: the ability to choose texts of personal interest to the reader and quickly find the sections of a text you want to study in detail; learning to think about what you already know about a subject and using all the information which is available before you read to help you understand a text; learning to use different styles of reading for different reading purposes (e.g. reading to understand the general themes, organisation and development of ideas in a text; intensive reading for very detailed understanding); learning to focus on the main points of a text, noting other points of personal interest, and reformulating the information in a text in another form such as a summary, chart or diagram for easy future reference; understanding the author's attitude to information in a text. You will also learn to use a complete reading strategy for the independent, personal study of texts of your own choice in your work or studies.

*Vocabulary skills*
The vocabulary skills developed in this book include: learning to focus only on the

words which are important to your understanding of a text; using other languages and the English you know to understand the meaning of new words (e.g. using related words, the grammatical form of a word, etc.); using the context to understand new words and phrases; fast and accurate dictionary use; how to study, store and remember English vocabulary; translating law terms.

*Language and structure*
This book does not teach basic English grammar. It explains the form and function of some structures which are typical of legal English. This will help you to understand legal texts which contain these structures and in some cases there are exercises which will teach you to use them yourself.
*Note:* for a complete list of the skills and language taught in the book, please read the Contents pages.

## Is *English for Law* too difficult for you?

All the materials used in *English for Law* are authentic legal texts. They are difficult, even for a native speaker of English, perhaps very difficult for your language level: they contain a lot of unusual vocabulary and specialised terms, and the language is complex.

Do not expect to understand every word of the texts. At first you may understand very little. Do not try to translate the texts into your own language as you read. The exercises in the book are designed to teach you gradually a wide variety of reading, vocabulary and language skills, and a good basic legal vocabulary which will help you to understand and use the English of the law. If you complete most of the exercises, by the end of the book you will be able to read and understand authentic legal texts of your own choice independently and can continue to build up your own vocabulary of law terms. If you make a lot of mistakes, but can use the Key to understand why and correct yourself, don't worry – this means that you are learning. If, on the other hand, you find that you cannot do most of the exercises, or most of your answers are wrong, you probably need to do a general English course before coming back to this book.

I hope you enjoy using *English for Law*. Please write to me at the following address to tell me about your experience using the book, and to give me your comments, criticisms and ideas: c/o ELT Department, International Division, Macmillan Publishers Ltd, Houndmills, Basingstoke RG21 2XS, Hampshire, UK.

Alison Riley

# Introduction to the Teacher

Please read the Introduction to the Reader for information about the purpose, intended readership, structure and use of the book and details of language and skills work.

This book is suitable as the coursebook on an ESP course in English for law, or as a specialised supplementary text on a general English course. It may be used at any stage of a degree course or similar course of studies (from undergraduate to postgraduate), or for researchers, lecturers or practising lawyers. The more highly-trained the readers, the more they will gain from the legal content of the text and the more they will be able to contribute in terms of legal knowledge and understanding to discussion work and comparative legal work.

Although the book is intended principally for intermediate to advanced students of English, you may find that with greater guidance, highly-motivated readers will be able to follow and learn from the book even if they have only a low intermediate, passive knowledge of English.

The course contains a minimum of about 60 hours of class work, considerably more if greater space is given to developing the oral activities, which range from controlled practice to free discussion and moots (the presentation of imaginary cases in court).

You will find that the instructions in the text explaining how to complete the activities in the book are very detailed. This is necessary for readers using the course as self-study material, but naturally you should feel free to modify and adapt the course as you think best and teach it in your own way.

## Legal knowledge
No legal knowledge is required to teach the course. If you are not familiar with the law or the language of the law, use the Key and Glossary when preparing lessons to find definitions of law terms and other information about various aspects of the law, legal texts and language. The book itself provides all the legal knowledge necessary to complete the exercises and full answers are given in the Key, so that if you wish, your job can remain purely that of a language teacher.

The questions for discussion which introduce each section of a Unit (to which there is no Key) are simply brief warm-up activities to introduce the subject. General legal questions are often included. These may refer to facts already presented in previous Units. If not, it is perfectly acceptable for you (and your students) to say that you don't know the answers, and give personal ideas and opinions which you are not sure of. You will generally find the answers during the course of the Unit and may like to return to these questions later for confirmation.

Some activities encourage students to compare aspects of their own legal systems with aspects of the English legal system presented in the text. These will generally lead to a lot of lively oral work; expect your students to provide all the foreign legal input, while you can check their understanding of English law (so far as it is explained in the text) and help with language.

If you would like to know more about the English legal system, a useful general introduction, which includes a summary of the main branches of English law and requires no previous knowledge of the law or legal terminology, is *Introduction to English Law* by Philip S. James, 11th edition, 1985 (London: Butterworth).

I hope you enjoy teaching the course. I would be delighted to hear from any teachers who would like to write to me with comments, criticisms or ideas for improvements at the following address: c/o ELT Department, International Division, Macmillan Publishers Ltd, Houndmills, Basingstoke RG21 2XS, Hampshire, UK.

Alison Riley

# INTRODUCTORY UNIT
# The Study and Classification of Law

## A  Understanding the Branches of English Law

*1*  Are you a student? If so, where are you studying law?
   If not, have you studied law at college or university? Where?
   Do you know the names of any English universities?

   i)  At an English university Law is divided into different subjects or *'branches'* for
       study. On page 2 is a list of subjects students study in the Law Faculty at Cambridge
       University. Can you work out the names of some of these subjects in your own
       language from their English names? First study the examples in Table 1.1.

**Table 1.1**   Group I subjects

| *Language* | *Paper 1* | *Paper 2* | *Paper 3* | *Paper 4* |
|---|---|---|---|---|
| English | *Roman Law* | *Constitutional* Law | *Criminal* Law | Law of *Tort* |
| French | droit *romain* | droit *constitutionnel* | droit *criminel* | (*tort*) |
| German | *röm*isches Recht | (*Konstitution*) | (*Kriminal*) | – |
| | | Verfassungsrecht | Strafrecht | |
| Italian | diritto *romano* | diritto *costituzionale* | (*crimine, criminale*) | (*torto*) |
| | | | diritto penale | |
| Polish | prawo *rzymskie* | prawo *konstytucyjne* | (*kryminalista, kryminalna*) | – |
| | | | prawo karne | |
| Spanish | derecho *romano* | derecho *constitucional* | (*crimen, criminal*) | (tuerto) |
| | | | derecho penale | |
| Swedish | *Romansk lag* | (*Konstitutionell*) | (*kriminal*) | – |
| | | Regeringsrätt | Straffrätt | |
| *Words you may know* | Rome Roman | constitution | crime criminal | – |

From the examples in Table 1.1 you can see that if you speak French, German, Italian,
or another language which is related to English, you can use that language to
understand many of the English subjects. This is true even if the name is not exactly the
same in the two languages (e.g. Roman Law/römisches Recht), or if the name is
completely different (e.g. Criminal Law/Straffrätt) but related words exist to help you
(e.g. kriminal).

   If you speak a Romance language, such as French or Spanish, you may also have
some idea about the meaning of the subject called *Law of Tort*.

   If you don't speak a language related to English, you can still use other English words
you know to help you understand some of the subjects.

   Now study the other subjects in Groups II, III and IV of the list on page 2 in the same
way.

Where possible, decide:
●  the name of the subject in your language
●  if law students study that subject at your university or in your country.

To help you decide, use words in your own language, or a language related to English which you know, and English words you already know. Don't be afraid to guess when you're not sure!

ii) How many of the 25 subjects studied at Cambridge University (see the list below) do you think you understand?

▲ If you are studying this book in a class or group, compare your ideas with someone else.

---

UNIVERSITY OF CAMBRIDGE

FACULTY OF LAW

CHOICE OF SUBJECTS

The papers for the Law Tripos, which are divided into Groups I–IV, are as follows:

GROUP I

| Paper 1 | Roman Law I |
| Paper 2 | Constitutional Law |
| Paper 3 | Criminal Law |
| Paper 4 | Law of Tort |

GROUP II

| Paper 10 | Law of Contract |
| Paper 11 | Land Law |
| Paper 12 | International Law |
| Paper 13 | Roman Law II |

GROUP III

| Paper 20 | Administrative Law |
| Paper 21 | Family Law |
| Paper 22 | Legal History |
| Paper 23 | Criminology |
| Paper 24 | Criminal Procedure and Criminal Evidence |
| Paper 25 | Equity |

GROUP IV

| Paper 40 | Commercial Law |
| Paper 41 | Labour Law |
| Paper 42 | Principles of Conveyancing Law |
| Paper 43 | Company Law |
| Paper 44 | Contract and Tort II |
| Paper 45 | Conflict of Laws |
| Paper 46 | E.E.C. Law |
| Paper 47 | French Law |
| Paper 48 | Jurisprudence |
| Paper 49 | Prescribed subjects (Half-papers) |

---

## 2 Check your answers

### i) True cognates

a) In the examples on page 1, *Roman* and *romano* are similar in both English and Italian and they have the same meaning. They are *true cognates*. *Romano* is the Italian cognate of *Roman*, *Roman* is the English cognate of *romano*. Is *Roman* a cognate in your language, too?

b) *Criminal* is the English cognate of *criminal* (Spanish) and *Kriminal* (German). These words have the same meaning, but they are not always used in the same context in the different languages. So the words *criminal* (Spanish) and *Kriminal* (German) exist, but 'derecho penale' and 'Strafrecht' are used instead for this branch of the law. In English the word '*penal*' (cognate of Spanish *penale*) also exists, but Criminal Law is the name of this subject. The important thing is that we can still use the cognates to understand the meaning of these terms in the other language.

c) *Tort* (English) and *tort* (French) don't have exactly the same meaning. But it is still possible for a French speaker to use the similarity to understand something about the English word. In French, *tort* means a wrong, error, harm or injury. The meaning of *tort* in English is related to this. Which branch of the law do you think the Law of Tort could be?

- Which other words in the list are cognates and help you to decide the name of the subject in your language?

### ii) False friends

BUT . . . sometimes a word that looks like a true cognate has a completely different meaning in the two languages. Look at these examples from the list:

a) Does *jurisprudence* look like a cognate in your language?
In English *jurisprudence* is another name for the philosophy of law.
Is it a true cognate or a false friend?

b) Does *evidence* look like a cognate in your language?
In English *evidence* means the signs or proof of something; in criminal law the evidence includes everything (objects, statements, documents, etc.) which helps to show how a crime happened. Is it a true cognate or a false friend?

c) Does *Equity* look like a cognate in your language?
In general English, *equity* means fairness, justice. In this sense, is it a true cognate or a false friend?
In English law *Equity* is a special area of law which was first created by the Lord Chancellor and then developed by a special court – the Court of Chancery. It consists of principles of justice which add to or supplement the ordinary law when this is necessary for justice in a particular case.
In this special legal sense is *Equity* a cognate?
Is Equity studied as a subject in your country?

d) Is *international* a cognate in your language?
*International Law* is the law which regulates or governs relations between States.
Is it a true cognate in your language in this context?

- Are there any other false friends in the list?
How many true cognates and how many false friends have you found altogether?
What do you notice?

### iii) Some other subjects

a) Land Law: you may know the word *land*. If not, look it up in your dictionary. Refer to the glossary to check the legal definition of *land*. Does it have the same meaning in general English and in legal English?
*Land* is the most important form of _____. What do you think *Land Law* could be?

b) Labour Law: perhaps you know the word *labour*. It means work. What do you suppose Labour Law could be?

c) Principles of Conveyancing Law: in the legal sense *to convey* means *to transfer*. *Conveyancing Law* is closely related to Land Law. Have you any idea what it could be?
Is this subject studied separately in your country?

d) Conflict of Laws: do you know the word *conflict*? It is used for a difference, or about things which don't agree. In what area of law could there be conflict *of laws*?

e) EEC Law: do you know what the letters EEC stand for?
It is the European _____. Is your country a member of the EEC?
What is EEC Law? *Note*: the wider terms EC and EC Law are also now in general use.

f) Prescribed subjects: this is a list of other subjects offered by the University each year.

- Check all your answers by referring to each subject in the glossary.

| B | Practice Activities |

## 1 Pronunciation practice

Listen to the tape and practise saying the list of law subjects, or use the glossary to help you pronounce the words. Notice how the pronunciation of cognates is sometimes very different in the two languages.

*Example:* *procedure* (English) is pronounced \prə'sı:dʒə\
*procedura* (Italian cognate) is pronounced \protʃe'duræ\

What is the importance of this if you speak a cognate language?

## 2 Oral practice

■ If you are studying this book alone:
Which law subjects are you studying now? Which ones have you studied in the past?

▲ If you are studying this book in a class or group:
Work in pairs. Find out which law subjects your partner is studying now and which subjects s/he has studied in the past.

## 3 Test your memory

From memory write a list in English of all the subjects on your *curriculum* (the complete course of studies that you personally are following or have followed at university, college, etc.). First write the subjects you already know in English.

■ To find the names of any other subjects in English, use a dictionary or the glossary (look for cognates).

▲ To find the names of any other subjects in English, ask other members of the class or your teacher, or use a dictionary or the glossary (look for cognates).

| C | Reading about a Law Course: Before you Read |

1 Can you answer the questions below, and fill in the blanks? Use a dictionary to help you if necessary.

   i) a) A student who completes his or her course at university gets a _ _ _ _ _ _ from the university.
       b) S/he is then called a _ _ _ _ _ _ _ _.

   ii) a) In some countries graduates can use a title, like 'doctor', in front of their names.
       Does this happen in your country? If so, give an example.
       b) How can you identify an English graduate?
●        c) And an English law graduate?

   iii) In English universities there are several different kinds of degree, depending on the level of specialisation.
       Most students studying at university for the first time take a normal degree, called a *first degree*.
       Some students continue to study or return to university some years later to take a second more specialised degree called a *Master's degree*.

Which of these two kinds of students do you think is called an *undergraduate* and which is a *postgraduate*?

iv) Look again at the list of subjects studied at Cambridge University on page 2. Can you find the special word which means a course or examination at Cambridge University?

● v) Do you know the name of the exams English schoolchildren can take at the age of 18? They must pass these exams if they want to go to university.

## D First Reading: Understanding the General Content of the Text

**1** Below is a description of the Law course at Cambridge University, published by the University for people interested in following the course. Before you look at the description, decide what kind of information you think it might contain.

**2** The first time you read the description, you only want to know what information it gives in general. Check that you understand the following instructions.
The text has four paragraphs marked A, B, C and D. Read the text quickly and decide which paragraph:
(1) gives information about the subjects students can study on a first degree course
(2) explains the general purpose and method of the course
(3) gives information about Master's degree courses
(4) says what most law students do before and after they go to university.

For this activity do *not* try to understand the text in detail. Do *not* stop when you come to words or sections of the text you don't understand, if you can complete this activity.

---

## Law

A   The Law course at Cambridge is intended to give a thorough grounding in the principles of law viewed from an academic rather than a vocational perspective. There are opportunities
5   to study the history of law and to consider the subject in its wider social context. The emphasis is on principle and technique. Skills of interpretation and logical reasoning are developed, and students are encouraged to
10  consider broader questions such as ethical judgement, political liberty and social control.

B   Although many undergraduates who read law do so with the intention of practising, many do not, preferring instead to go into
15  administration, industrial management or accountancy. Candidates intending to read law need not have studied any particular subject at school. It is as common for undergraduates to have a scientific or
20  mathematical background at A-level as it is for them to have studied history or languages.

C   Undergraduates reading law for three years take Part IA of the Tripos at the end of the first year. This comprises four papers: Criminal
25  Law, Constitutional Law, the Law of Tort and Roman Law. In the second year five subjects are studied for Part IB of the Law Tripos which is taken at the end of the year. The range of subjects on offer is wide – from
30  Family Law to International Law – though in practice most undergraduates take Contract and Land Law as two of their papers. In the third year, five subjects are studied for Part II of the Tripos. The range of options is even
35  wider than in Part IB. According to preference an undergraduate may develop his or her interest in property law (including trusts and conveyancing law), commercial law, public law (including Administrative Law and EEC
40  Law), or in more academic and sociological aspects of law, such as Jurisprudence, Legal History, Labour Law and Criminology. Candidates may also participate in the seminar course, submitting a dissertation in
45  place of one paper.

D   Candidates for the postgraduate LL.M. take any four papers selected from a wide range of options in English Law, Legal History, Civil Law, Public Law, International Law, and
50  Comparative Law and Legal Philosophy.

**3** Quickly find out:
   a) how many years a first degree course lasts.
● b) how many subjects undergraduates study.

---

## E   Second Reading: Reading for Detail

You now know what each section of the text is about in general. To understand it in more detail, complete the exercises below.

### 1   Word study

Find words or phrases in the text which mean the following:

#### i)   In paragraph A

*Example 1:* basic education
*Answer:* grounding (line 2)

Example 2: relating to a profession or occupation
*Answer:* vocational (line 4)

   a)   abilities
   b)   the process of logical thinking
   c)   relating to moral principles

#### ii)   In paragraph B

   a)   follow a course (such as Law or Medicine) at university
   b)   working in a profession
   c)   to work in

#### iii) In paragraph C

   a)   examinations
   b)   things you can choose
   c)   a long piece of academic written work

#### iv) In paragraph D

● a)   If LL.B. means Bachelor of Laws, what do you suppose *LL.M.* means?

### 2   Reading for detail

First check that you understand the questions below, then read the text carefully to find the answers.
   a)   Does the course (1) give an academic legal education or (2) teach students to become lawyers?
   b)   What intellectual abilities does the course develop?
   c)   Does the course only include strict (pure) law?
   d)   Do most Cambridge Law graduates become lawyers?
   e)   Should people who want to read Law study (1) science subjects or (2) humanities (history, languages, etc.) at school?

f) Can students choose the subjects they study in the first and second years of the law course?

g) Do students have the same options in the second year and in the third year?

h) What is the relationship between the four groups of subjects (I, II, III and IV) listed on page 2 and each year of study on a first-degree course?

i) Must students take an exam in all the subjects they study?

j) How many exams do postgraduates take?

## F    Practice Activities

### 1    Oral practice

■    If you are studying this book alone, answer the questions below. If you want to practise speaking English, say your answers out loud or record them on tape, then listen to your recording. If you prefer, write your answers down.
  - What sort of school education did you have?
  - What do you do now?
  - If you are a student, what subjects are you studying now?
  - If you are a graduate, what subjects did you study before?
  - If you were a student at Cambridge University, which subjects would you choose to study?
  - What area of law interests you most?
  - What are your plans for the future?

▲    If you are studying this book in a class or group:
  work in pairs. Interview your partner and find out:
  - about his or her school education
  - about what s/he does now
  - if s/he is a student, about the subjects s/he is studying now
  - if s/he is a graduate, about the subjects s/he studied before
  - if s/he was a student at Cambridge University, which subjects would s/he choose to study?
  - about what area of law interests him or her most
  - about his or her plans for the future
  When you are ready, introduce your partner to the rest of the class.

### 2    Discussion points

Choose one of the topics below. First, think about the topic for a few moments.

◆    *The contents of a law course*  Look again at the list of subjects studied at Cambridge University on page 2 and the personal curriculum you wrote in activity B3. Is your curriculum typical of a law course in your country?
Compare the subjects studied at Cambridge and your university. Note any particular similarities or differences.

◆    *The purpose and style of a law course*  Read paragraph A of the text on page 5 again. What are the methods and purpose of *your* law course? Is this typical of a law course in your country?
Are the method and style of study at Cambridge and at your university basically similar or are there important differences?

◆ *The students on a law course*  Read paragraph B of the text on page 5 again.
What sort of school education did most law students *you* know have?
What do most law graduates from your university do? Is this typical of your country?
Note any particular differences or similarities between law students at your university, college, etc., and Cambridge.

■ To practise speaking, say your ideas out loud or record them on tape, then listen to your recording. If you prefer, write your ideas down.

▲ Discuss your ideas in pairs or small groups. If you like, prepare one or two questions to ask your teacher about the English university system.
When you have finished, exchange your ideas with the rest of the class.

## G  Development

### 1  Public and private law

i)  What do you understand by *private law*?
And *public law*?

ii) Can you give an example of a branch of private law and one of public law?
Refer again to the list of subjects studied at Cambridge University to find more examples.

iii) Is the distinction between private law and public law clear in your legal system?
Is the distinction important?

iv) Do you think the distinction between public and private law is important in English law? Check this by reading the passage below from Kenneth R. Simmonds, *International Encyclopaedia of Comparative Law, National Report, the U.K.*

> The absence of a code has the effect that there is no scientific classification and no 'authoritative arrangement' of English law. The distinction, fundamental in the Romano-Germanic system, between public and private law does not exist as such; no distinction between public and private law jurisdictions has existed since the Court of Star Chamber was abolished in 1641. Similarly a clear-cut distinction between civil and commercial law does not exist. . . .

Is your answer to iii) still the same?

v)  Read the text again and note all the law terms you can find:

> The absence of a code  has the effect that there is no scientific classification and no 'authoritative arrangement' of English law. . . .

Where possible, decide what you think each term means. Then check your ideas, using a dictionary or the glossary to this book.

vi) Read the text carefully and answer the questions below.
   a) Is there a single, fixed classification of English law? What reason does the writer give?
   b) Is the distinction between public and private law important in the Romano-Germanic legal system?
   c) Are there separate jurisdictions for public and private law in the English legal system?

d) Are civil and commercial law clearly separate in the English system?

e) Can you name some countries which have a Romano-Germanic legal system today?

f) Why do you think English law is generally divided into branches, as in the Cambridge University list of subjects? Is law divided into branches in your country?

■● Check your answers in the key.

▲● Compare your answers in small groups before checking in the key.

▲ vii) Work together in small groups.

■▲ a) Are there separate jurisdictions for public and private law in your legal system?

b) Are civil and commercial law clearly separate in your system?

c) Compare the distinction between public and private law in the English legal system and in your legal system.

## 2 *Personal study activity: the contents of a single Law course*

Complete the following activity in your own time.

i) Which subjects offered by Cambridge University interest you most?
Choose one of the following courses: Conflict of Laws, Constitutional Law, Law of Contract, EC Law, Family Law, International Law, Jurisprudence, Roman Law or Tort.

▲ See if any other students in the class are interested in the same course.

ii) Working together or alone, decide what you *think* the Cambridge course you have chosen will include. Think of some subjects or topics you think it will contain.

*Example:* the Law of Contract will probably include: the formation of a contract, the conditions of a contract, the form of a contract, who can make a contract, what happens if a contract is broken and how a contract comes to an end.

iii) Do you know the names in English for the things you have thought of?

■ Use a dictionary to find some of them in English.

▲ Ask your teacher or use a dictionary to find some of them in English.
Write a list in English of the topics you thought of in ii) above.

iv) Find the section in the Cambridge Schedule of Subjects on pages 10–12 which gives details about the course you are interested in.
If you can, compare the actual contents of the course with the list of topics you wrote in iii) above. Think about the following points:
  • what are the main topics on the course?
  • are all the topics you thought of included?
  • are there any extra topics you didn't think of?
  • which part of the course interests you most?
  • is the course basically similar to a course in the same subject at your university or college?
  • what differences are there?
For this activity, do not expect to understand everything you read. Try to form a general idea of the main topics on the course.
There are probably a lot of words you don't understand. Don't worry! Choose about five words you would like to understand, and find out what they mean. If you understand absolutely nothing, go back to step i) above and choose another subject!

    v) Prepare to describe the course you have chosen.

      You should:

- say what the main topics on the course are
- if possible, say how the Cambridge course is different from or similar to a course in the same subject at your university
- say which part of the course you would find most interesting and use and explain some of the most important vocabulary you have learnt.

▲   Describe your course to the other members of the class. Discuss any points of interest.

■   Write your description down, or if you prefer to practise speaking, say it out loud or record it on tape, then listen to your recording.

---

Paper 1.   Roman Law I.

(a) Sources of law. Written law and unwritten law; legal development through the grant of new remedies; praetor and iudex under the formulary system; judge and jury under the writ system. Equity; the role of praetor and Chancellor, especially in the grant of remedies other than damages. The role of legal experts; jurists in Roman law and their analogues in English law.

(b) Persons. The legal position of the family and of its paterfamilias in Roman law; an outline of marriage and of personality in Roman and English law.

(c) Property. Categories of things in Roman and English law; Roman dominium, bonitary ownership, possession; delivery, usucapion, occupation, accession. Feudal property; tenures, estates, life interests, leases; relativity of title, trusts, and equitable ownership. Rights in another's property; servitudes and easements; usufructs; real security.

(d) Obligations. Contracts, quasi-contracts, and delicts in Roman Law, with general comparisons with English law.

(e) Succession. Intestate and testamentary succession in Roman law and English law; Roman inheritance and heirship; personal representatives; freedom of testation in both systems.

Paper 2.   Constitutional Law.

1. INTRODUCTION

    Nature and Sources of Constitutional Law; principal organs of government (including the judiciary); structure of the United Kingdom.

2. PARLIAMENT

  (a) Composition and elections; process of legislation.

  (b) Parliamentary Sovereignty (incl. EEC).

3. THE EXECUTIVE

  (a) The Crown and Constitutional Monarchy; the Prime Minister and the Cabinet; the Civil Service and Departments of State; the powers of the Executive.

  (b) Control and Accountability:
    i   Ministerial Accountability (collective and individual)
    ii   Parliamentary Questions, Select Committees, and the Ombudsman
    iii   Scrutiny of Subordinate Legislation.

  (c) Judicial Control of the Executive:
    i   Scope and Remedies
    ii   Subordinate Legislation
    iii   Discretionary powers (including the prerogative).

  (d) Crown Proceedings (incl. public interest immunity and Act of State).

4. THE STATE AND THE INDIVIDUAL

  (a) Introduction (including the European Convention on Human Rights).

  (b) British Citizenship.

  (c) Freedom of Expression: official secrets and contempt of court.

  (d) Freedom of Assembly and Public Order.

  (e) Freedom of the Person (including Habeas Corpus).

  (f) Deportation and Extradition.

  (g) Police Powers; search, arrest and detention.

  (h) Accountability of the Police.

Paper 4.   Law of Tort.

A paper covering the substantive law of tort, as follows:

(a) Negligence, including occupier's liability;

---

statutory liabilities; trespass to the person, land and chattels; nuisance and *Rylands v. Fletcher*; animals; defamation, falsehood and misrepresentation; abuse of legal process.

(b) Causation and remoteness of damage.

(c) Death in relation to tort.

(d) Vicarious liability and non-delegable duties.

(e) Joint and several liability, and contribution.

(f) General defences.

(g) Remedies, especially damages.

(h) Foundations of tortious liability.

(i) Aims and adequacy of the law of tort.

Paper 10.   Law of Contract.

(a) Formation of contract: offer and acceptance; consideration; intention to create legal relations; privity.

(b) Contents of contract: express and implied terms; exemption clauses; principles of construction and interpretation.

(c) Discharge of contracts: performance; agreement; breach; frustration.

(d) Remedies for breach of contract.

(e) Vitiating factors: non-disclosure; misrepresentation; mistake; duress and undue influence; illegality.

Paper 12.   International Law.

(a) The place of law in international relations.

(b) Sources of international law; international law and municipal law; personality; recognition; succession.

(c) Territory including airspace; the law of the sea; outer space.

(d) Jurisdiction.

(e) State responsibility; the individual; nationality; human rights; extradition.

(f) Treaties.

(g) Settlement of disputes; the International Court of Justice.

(h) The problems of force; international institutions; the United Nations: the role of.

Paper 21.   Family Law.

(a) Marriage: capacity and formal requirements; proof of marriage; void and voidable marriages; nullity.

(b) Husband and Wife: doctrine of unity; consortium; confidentiality; evidentiary privilege; occupation of the home; remedies for violence; separation and maintenance agreements; property rights, including gifts, ascertainment of ownership, trusts for sale, and effects on a will of marriage or divorce; domestic court orders; judicial separation.

(c) Termination of marriage: intestate succession; family provision orders on death; presumption of death; divorce; 'special procedure'; orders for financial relief.

(d) Unmarried couples: the extent of legal recognition.

(e) Parent and child: legitimacy and illegitimacy; parental powers and duties, and resolution of disputes; orders for custody, access, custodianship, and financial support; step-parenthood; guardianship; wardship; adoption; children in care of local authorities.

(f) General: the courts, past, present and future, which administer family law; historical background, especially of marriage; reconciliation and conciliation of spouses; proposals for reform of the law.

Paper 45.   Conflict of Laws.

(a) Preliminary topics; definitions, theories; characterization; application of foreign law; connecting factors; renvoi; proof of foreign law.

(b) Domicile; Corporations.

(c) Husband and wife; marriage and matrimonial causes.

(d) Children; legitimacy, legitimation, and adoption.

(e) Jurisdiction of the English Courts.

(f) Recognition and enforcement of foreign judgments.

(g) Obligations; contract; tort; quasi-contract.

(h) Property relations *inter vivos* (excluding negotiable instruments and bankruptcy); movables and immovables.

(i) Administration of estates and succession (excluding the exercise of powers of appointment and the doctrine of election).

(j) Substance and procedure.

(k) Exclusion of foreign law; public policy.

Paper 46.   E.E.C. Law.

(a) The historical and political background to European integration.

(b) The constitutional structure and functioning of the Communities, their international status, and their relationship to the national legal systems.

(c) The law and functioning of the customs union and the international trade relations of the E.C.

(d) The law relating to the movement of persons within the Community, their employment and common social security arrangements.

(e) The law relating to the trans-national establishment of companies and provision of professional services.

(f) The structure and operation of the Common Agricultural Policy.

(g) The law relating to trans-national monopolies and restrictive practices (Community competition law).

(h) The jurisdiction and procedures of the European Court of Justice.

Paper 48.   Jurisprudence.

(a) Outline of the structure of society.

(b) The concept of law and the identification of its subject-matter.

(c) Theories as to the nature and function of law.

(d) The main schools of jurisprudence.

(e) The sources from which the law is developed.

(f) The judicial process.

(g) The structure and analysis of legal rules.

(h) Legal concepts. Personality, ownership, property and their changing functions.

Candidates will be required to answer not more than four questions out of a larger number.

# UNIT 1

# English Law

Reading a Law Textbook

## A   Before you read

Even in your own language you will generally understand a text better if you already know something about the subject. In a foreign language it is especially useful to think about the subject of the text for a few moments before you start to read. This will help you to know what you expect to read about and some of the language you may find.

i)   Before reading about the sources of English law, think about the subject in general:
   • Where do laws come from in your legal system? Which kinds of rules and principles have the authority and force of law? In other words, what are the *sources of law*?
   • What other sources of law do you know? For example, do you know any sources of International Law?
   • Do you know the English names for the sources you have thought of?

■   To find the terms in English, use a dictionary or the glossary (look for cognates).
▲   To find the terms in English, use a dictionary or the glossary (look for cognates) or ask other members of the class or your teacher, then compare your ideas with the rest of the class.

ii)   Write a list of about five other law terms you think you may find in a text on this subject. Find the words in English.

iii)   Were any of the words below in your list? Check that you understand their meaning. Refer to a dictionary or the glossary if necessary.

| | |
|---|---|
| the courts | rights |
| a law | the constitution |
| legislation | a judge |
| judicial precedent | custom |
| parliament | a code |

## B   Reasons for reading: reading to understand the general content of a text

### *Reasons for reading*

There are different reasons for reading.
   • Sometimes we read because we want to know about a subject in detail (*reading for detail*)

13

● Sometimes we want to find or check a particular piece of information (*reading for specific information*)
● Sometimes we want to know what a text is about in general (*reading for gist*)
The way we read depends on our reason for reading.

## 1 Reading for gist

When you read for gist you only want to know *what the text is about in general*, so you do *not* need to read or understand every word. This style of reading is called *skimming*. It is often a good idea to read a text for gist *before* you try to understand it in detail. To practise skimming, complete the activity below. Do *not* try to read or understand the whole text for this activity.

*As quickly as you can*, skim the text on pages 14–17 to decide which heading (title) at the top of the text (e.g. (1) THE SUBSIDIARY SOURCES, (2) The sources of English law) goes with which section of the text. Choose one heading for each space marked * (letters A–G). Make a note of the correct headings in the right order in your notebook.
● Suggested time: 3 minutes.

---

(1) THE SUBSIDIARY SOURCES

(2) The sources of English law

(3) CUSTOM

(4) JUDICIAL PRECEDENT

(5) LEGISLATION

(6) THE PRINCIPAL SOURCES

(7) BOOKS OF AUTHORITY

---

Example:
**A** ＊ The sources of English law
Answer A2

1 The courts are the interpreters and declarers of the law, the 'sources' of law are therefore the sources to which the courts turn in order to determine what it is. Considered from the
5 aspect of their sources, laws are traditionally divided into two main categories according to the solemnity of the form in which they are made. They may either be *written* or *unwritten*. These traditional terms are misleading, because
10 the expression 'written' law signifies any law that is formally *enacted*, whether reduced to writing or not, and the expression 'unwritten' law signifies all *unenacted* law. For example, as will appear, judicial decisions are often reduced
15 to writing in the form of law reports, but because they are not formal enactments they are 'unwritten' law.
    Since the fashion was set by the *Code Napoléon* many continental countries have
20 codified much of their law, public and private; on the Continent, therefore, the volume of written law tends to preponderate over the volume of unwritten. But in England unwritten law is predominant, for more of our law derives

25 from judicial precedents than from legislative enactment. This does not, of course, mean that none of our law is codified, for many parts of it are; such as the law relating to the sale of goods (Sale of Goods Act 1979) and the law relating to
30 partnership (Partnership Act 1890). All that is meant is that, as yet at least, although Parliament casts increasing multitudes of statutes upon us, we have not adopted the system of wholesale codification which prevails
35 in many continental countries.
    Two principal and two subsidiary sources of English law must be mentioned. These principal sources are Legislation, and Judicial Precedent; the subsidiary sources are Custom and Books of
40 Authority.

**B** ＊

**C** ＊

Legislation is enacted law. In England the ultimate legislator is Parliament, for in our *traditional* constitutional theory Parliament is sovereign . . . here we are only concerned to explain the significance of the doctrine of *'parliamentary sovereignty'*. It means first, that all legislative power within the realm is vested in Parliament, or is derived from the authority of Parliament – Parliament thus has no rival within the legislative sphere – and it means secondly that there is no legal limit to the power of Parliament. Parliament may therefore, and constantly does, by Act delegate legislative powers to other bodies and even to individuals but it may also, by Act, remove these powers as simply as it has conferred them. By Act, moreover, Parliament may make any laws it pleases however perverse or 'wrong' and the courts are bound to apply them. The enactments of Parliament are not subject to question, for our constitution knows no entrenched rights similar to the fundamental liberties guaranteed by the Constitution of the United States and safeguarded by the Supreme Court. It will have been noted that we have referred to the 'traditional' theory. This is intended to serve as a warning that when constitutional law falls to be discussed the effects of 'Common Market' membership upon that theory will have to be considered.

In the legislative sphere Parliament is thus legally 'sovereign' and master, but this does not mean that the courts have no influence upon the development of enacted law; for, in order to be applied, every enactment, however it be promulgated, has to be interpreted (or *construed*), and the courts are the recognized interpreters of the law. The meaning of words is seldom self-evident; they will often bear two, or even more, possible interpretations and hence the courts must always exercise a considerable degree of control over the practical application of statutes (enactments of Parliament). The difficulty of interpretation may be illustrated by a simple example. Suppose that Old King Cole, who is an absolute despot, commands that all 'dogs' in his kingdom are to be killed. Suppose that Jack Sprat, one of his subjects, who has an alsatian wolfhound, applies to the courts for a decree that it shall be spared, alleging that it is a 'hound' and that the royal command is only concerned with 'dogs'. The court will have to decide whether the word 'dogs' is to be taken to embrace 'hounds': whichever way it decides, it will influence the practical application of the King's command.

**D** ✳

In all countries, at all times, the decisions of courts are treated with respect, and they tend to be regarded as 'precedents' which subsequent courts will follow when they are called upon to determine issues of a similar kind.

This reliance upon precedent has been both the hallmark and the strength of the common law. Its rules have been evolved *inductively*

from decision to decision involving similar facts, so that they are firmly grounded upon the actualities of litigation and the reality of human conduct. And new cases lead onwards to reach forward to new rules. Its principles are, to employ a popular phrase 'open ended'; they are not firm and inflexible decrees. This characteristic of the common law contrasts, again, with the European civil law. There, harking back to the tradition of the *Corpus Juris*, law is characteristically derived from a code; that is, from an enacted body of rules either (as in the case of Justinian's or of Napoleon's legislation) embodying the whole of, or some considerable part of, the law, or embracing some special aspect of it. Thus the task of the courts is *deductive*: to subsume the present case under the mantle of the generalized and codified rule. The word 'codification' was an invention of the ingenious Jeremy Bentham (1743–1832). In principle this method carries the danger that the encoded rule may, being the work of a theorist divorced from reality, be out of touch with actual needs; and certainly, as noted above, in course of time it may become so, and thus may require judicial adaptation to meet changed conditions. But in practice many codes are really restatements of rules previously embodied in the opinions of jurists (as was the *Digest* which formed the most important part of the *Corpus Juris*) or from case law (like the English Sale of Goods Act 1979) or from custom or from some other tried and tested source. So that although the approach to legal decision is on the one hand inductive at common law and on the other hand deductive in the civil law, in reality (apart from interpretive method) the two systems are not quite so divergent as might appear. One thing, however, which is distinctive of the English system is that because the English judge has, through precedent, power to make new law his position in the legal system is central.

Another salient feature of the English system is the doctrine of the *binding* case. By this doctrine the authority of the courts is hierarchical; a court which is inferior in authority to another court is obliged to follow ('bound by') a court of superior authority if called upon to decide upon facts similar to facts already tried by the superior court.

The precedents formed by decided cases are, <u>thus</u>, as Bacon wrote of the Reports of Sir Edward Coke, the 'anchors of the laws'. A practitioner who is asked to consider a legal matter will <u>therefore</u> look to the reported decisions of the courts; and he will do this even though the point in issue is regulated by a statute, <u>for</u>, as has been explained, statutes are interpreted by the courts, and a decision which is concerned with the interpretation of the statute is just as binding as any other decision. When this much has been said, it must not, <u>however</u>, be imagined that the law is always

discoverable by the simple process of looking
170 up, and finding, the right precedent. For facts
are infinitely various and by no means all cases
are exactly covered by previous authority.
Quite the reverse, the facts in issue often
resemble two or more divergent authorities. In
175 these circumstances the courts therefore have
freedom of choice in deciding which of the
divergent authorities or streams of authority to
'follow', and much of the ingenuity of counsel is
directed to 'distinguishing' the facts of
180 precedents which appear to bind the court to
decide against him. Further, even today cases of
'first impression' sometimes arise; cases arising
upon facts which bear no resemblance to the
facts of any previous case. When the judge rules
185 in such a case he legislates, because future
courts must usually 'follow' him. A remark
which leads to the comment that in
'distinguishing' between previous decisions and
'following' one rather than another the judge,
190 though appearing only to apply existing law, in
fact exercises a quasi-legislative discretion: a
fact which the system of 'binding' precedent
serves to conceal.

The administration of justice is not therefore
195 a slot-machine process of matching precedents.
The judges have a field of choice in making their
decisions. But they do not exercise their
discretion in an arbitrary way; they rest their
judgments upon the general *principles*
200 enshrined in case-law as a whole. Case-law does
not consist of a blind series of decisions, 'A will
succeed', or 'B will fail', but of reasoned
judgments based upon rational principles.
These principles have been evolved by the
205 courts through the centuries: and, building
precedent upon precedent, they have framed
them with two ends in view. First, they have
sought so to formulate them that their
application may be capable of effecting
210 substantial justice in particular cases; second,
they have sought to make them sufficiently
general in scope to serve as guides to lawyers
faced with the task of giving advice in future
legal disputes. Thus in a sense the history of the
215 common law (as opposed to statute law – for
statutes are sometimes arbitrary and they have
often wrought injustice) is the story of the
evolution of the judges' conception of justice (a
kind of natural law – see above) realized in the
220 form of rules of law intended to be general in
their application and as easily ascertainable as
possible. The task of attempting to dispense
*justice*, while satisfying the essential need for
*certainty*, has not been an easy one; in fact the
225 attempt can never achieve more than a
compromise; but, on the whole, it has been well
performed and the common law of England is
no mean rival to the romanistic systems.

E  *

F  *

Customs are social habits, patterns of
230 behaviour, which all societies seem to evolve
without express formulation or conscious
creation. In a sense custom should be accorded
pride of place as one of the principal sources of
law for much, if not most, law was originally
235 based upon it. Moreover custom is not solely
important as a source of *law*, for even today
some customary rules are observed in their own
right and they command almost as much
obedience as rules of law proper; they only
240 differ from rules of law in that their observance
is not *enforced* by the organs of the State. Thus,
it will be seen . . . that many of the fundamental
rules governing the Constitution are
'conventional' (i.e. customary), rather than
245 legal, rules.

But in modern times most general customs
(i.e. customs universally observed throughout
the realm) have either fallen into desuetude or
become absorbed in rules of law. For example
250 many of the early rules of the common law were
general customs which the courts adopted, and
by this very act of adoption made into law. So
too, much of the modern mercantile law owes
its origin to the general customs of merchants
255 which the courts assimilated during the course
of the seventeenth and eighteenth centuries
and, indeed, they are still assimilating
international banking practice. So also many of
the rules of the law relating to the sale of goods
260 originated as customs, were adopted by the
courts, and eventually moulded into a statutory
code by the Sale of Goods Act 1893. General
custom has therefore now ceased to operate as
an important source of law. For law, whether
265 enacted or judicially declared, has in most fields
superseded custom.

On the other hand customs, prevailing among
particular groups of people living in particular
localities, are sometimes still recognized by the
270 courts as capable of creating a special 'law' for
the locality in question at variance with the
general law of the land. For instance in a well-
known case the fishermen of Walmer were held
entitled, by reason of a local custom, to a
275 special right to dry their nets upon a particular
beach. But recognition of such variants upon
the general law will only be accorded if certain
conditions are satisfied. The following are
among the more important of those
280 conditions:– The custom sought to be
established must (1) not be unreasonable, (2) be
'certain', that is to say the right which is claimed
must be asserted by or on behalf of a defined
group of people, (3) must have existed since
285 'time immemorial'. Literally this means that it
must go back to 1189 (by historical accident the
terminal date of 'legal memory') . . . . But in

practice the burden upon a plaintiff to establish such a custom – for example a customary duty in
290 his neighbour to fence against a common upon which he has grazing rights – is not so formidable. For if he can prove that such a usage has in fact existed in the locality for a reasonable time a lawful origin for the usage
295 will be *presumed*, provided, of course, that such an origin was possible; and custom itself is such a lawful origin.

G *

On the Continent the writings of legal authors form an important source of law. In England, in
300 accordance with our tradition that the law is to be sought in *judicial decisions*, their writings have in the past been treated with comparatively little respect. They have been cited in court, if cited at all, rather by way of
305 evidence of what the law is than as independent sources from which it may be derived.
   This general rule has, however, always been subject to certain recognized exceptions; for there are certain 'books of authority', written by
310 authors of outstanding eminence, which may not only be cited as independent sources in themselves for the law of their times but which also carry a weight of authority almost equal to that of precedents. Among the most important
315 of these works are Bracton's *De Legibus et Consuetudinibus Angliae* (thirteenth century), Coke's *Institutes* (1628–1641) and Blackstone's *Commentaries* (1765).
   When this much has been explained, it must
320 nevertheless be admitted that in modern times the established tradition appears to have been breaking down, because many textbooks are now in practice constantly cited in the courts, though only the best of them are likely to
325 command attention. The reason for this departure from the established tradition is probably that in comparatively recent years a large increase in the popularity of the study of English law in all our major universities has
330 done much to improve the quality of legal writing and to increase the volume of legal literature. Thus, today Salmond's *Law of Torts* is commonly referred to in court and even works of living authors, such as Smith and
335 Hogan's *Criminal Law*, are now often cited, though by a rule of etiquette, counsel who refers to works of the latter category should not cite them directly as authorities, but should request the leave of the court to 'adopt' the
340 arguments which they contain as part of his own submissions. In practice, however, even this latter etiquette is now not always observed.

Philip S. James, *Introduction to English Law*

## 2 Reading for general understanding

Check that you understand the questions below. Do *not* try to answer the questions yet.

a) What are the two main types of sources of law?
b) Is most English law written in a code?
c) Who makes legislation in England?
d) Can the English courts influence the effect of legislation?
e) Has English law developed (1) from fixed general rules? or (2) through decisions in individual cases?
f) Is the development of judicial precedent based on general principles of justice?
g) Is custom important as a source of law (1) in the history of the law? (2) in England today?
h) Are books of authority more important as a source of law in England or on the Continent?

These questions are about some of the main points in the text. Which sections of the text do you think will contain the answers?
Read the relevant sections of the text *quickly* to find the answers. Do *not* stop and spend time on words or parts of the text you don't understand if you can answer the questions.

You now know what each section of the text is about and you understand some of the main points. You are going to study the principal sources of English law in detail in short sections.

## C Reading for detail and language study: Introductory Section – lines 1–40

### 1 Understanding new vocabulary

i) Read lines 1–40 quickly. Note all the words or phrases which you don't know or are not sure of clearly and their line number.

ii) How many words or phrases have you noted?
You can see that you already know *most* of the language. The language you don't know is *limited*. And you were probably able to understand the main points of the text – that there are written and unwritten sources of law, and that English law is not written in a code – questions B 2a) and b) above – without understanding every word.

iii) Check that you understand the detailed questions below. Do *not* try to answer the questions yet.
a) Is all law which is written defined as '*written law*'?
b) Is any '*unwritten law*' in fact written?
c) Are codes of law popular in Continental countries?
d) Is most Continental law generally written or unwritten?
e) Is most English law found in the form of legislation or judicial precedent?
f) What is the law relating to the sale of goods?
g) What is the Partnership Act?

iv) Refer to the text and decide which of the 20 words and phrases below you need to understand to answer the questions in iii) above. Do *not* try to answer the questions yet.

a) declarers (line 1)
b) aspect (5)
c) solemnity (7)
d) misleading (9)
e) enacted (11)
f) whether reduced to writing or not (11–12)
g) unenacted (13)
h) law reports (15)
i) formal enactments (16)
j) set (18)
k) codified (20)
l) preponderate over (22)
m) predominant (24)
n) legislative enactment (25–6)
o) codified (27)
p) sale of goods (28)
q) partnership (30)
r) casts (32)
s) statutes (33)
t) wholesale codification (34)

▲ Compare your ideas with other members of the class.

v) This exercise will show you that you can often use words you know, information in the text and logical reasoning, as well as cognates, to find the meaning of new words that you need to understand in a text. Complete the exercise, where possible using cognates to confirm your ideas. As you work, you will see when to answer the questions from iii) above.
(1) A law which is passed (made) by the UK Parliament is called an *ACT of Parliament*. What do you think *enACTed* (line 11) means?
(2) In simple English *reduced to writing* (lines 11–12) means _____.
Whether . . . or not (lines 11–12) is used when there are two alternatives – one positive and one negative.
(3) If *UNwritten law* is the opposite of *written law*, what is UNenacted law (13)?
(4) An *enactment* is a single law.
Now answer questions iii a) and b).
What do answers a) and b) tell you about the meaning of words in legal English?
(5) You know the word *code* (noun). What do you think the verb *codified* (20) means?
To check: you know that countries have done this since the Code Napoléon,

which created a fashion (18–19). What have they *probably* done?
Answer question iii c).

(6) You know that many countries have codified their law, therefore . . . (21). *Therefore* introduces a consequence. In countries where law is codified, will the volume of written law therefore (as a consequence) probably be larger or smaller than the volume of unwritten law? Therefore, what does *preponderate over* (22) mean?
Answer question iii d).

(7) You know the words *legislation* and *enactment*. What do you think *legislative enactment* (25–6) is? Answer question iii e).

(8) The text refers to '*the law relating* to the sale of goods . . .' (28). *Sale of goods* must be an area of law. Do you know the noun *sale*? It is related to the verb *to sell*. What sort of things could be the object of a sale? What branch of law do you think sale of goods is part of?
Answer question iii f)

(9) '. . . *and the law relating to* partnership' (29–30). Like sale of goods, *partnership* must be an area of law. You know the word partner – a person who takes part in some activity with another or others. In the context of the law, partners have a special kind of business relationship.
*Partnership* is a related noun. What branch of law could include partnership?
Answer question iii g).

vi) Go back to the list of words in iv) above. Which ones did you in fact use to answer the questions in iii)? You can see that to answer the questions you only need to understand *some* of the words. Which words those are, depends on your reading purpose.

## 2 Check your knowledge

Complete the following passage to check that you have understood the text so far and can use the new vocabulary. For each blank space choose the correct word from the list below. Use each word *once* only.

*The Importance of Legislation as a Source in English and Continental Law*
In many (1) __ *continental* __ countries much of the law is (2) _____.
For this reason there is more written, or (3) _____ law than
(4) _____ law. In contrast, there is no general code of
(5) _____ law. Still, (6) _____ is common, and many areas of
law, e.g. (7) _____ are codified, but (8) _____ is the main
source of the law.

*Choose from:*

| | | | |
|---|---|---|---|
| a) partnership | b) enacted | c) Continental | d) unwritten |
| e) English | f) judicial precedent | g) legislation | h) codified |

## 3 Comparing legal systems

i) Work in pairs or alone. Think about your legal system.
   • Is the law codified in your country?
   • Are there written and unwritten sources of law?
   • Is most of the law written or unwritten?

ii) In these phrases from the text the author compares English law and Continental law:

'*On the Continent*, . . . the volume of written law tends to preponderate . . .'
'*But in England* unwritten law is predominant . . .' (lines 21–4)

We could also say:

On the Continent the volume of written law tends to preponderate, | but / while / whereas / however | in England unwritten law is predominant.

Use your own knowledge and information from the text to compare the following:
- codification of law on the Continent and in England
- codification of law in your country and in England
- written sources of law on the Continent and in your country
- written sources of law in your country and in England
- unwritten sources of law in England and in your country

*Examples*
'Many continental countries have codified their law, whereas this has not happened in England. In fact, only some areas of English law, such as the sale of goods, are codified.'
'In England most of the law is unwritten and the same is true in my country. In fact the principal sources of law in the legal system in my country are . . .'

■ Write your comparisons down, or if you prefer to practise speaking, say them out loud or record them on tape, then listen to your recording.

▲ Work in pairs. In turns, compare the different legal systems. Do you agree with your partner's comparisons?

## D  Reading for detail and language study: Legislation – lines 41–96

### 1  Identifying law terms

i) Study this passage from the text. All the law terms are marked. Choose the correct alternatives:
a) words and phrases connected with legislation and the courts are underlined/circled
b) other law terms are underlined/circled

> Legislation is enacted law. In England the ultimate legislator is Parliament, for in our *traditional* constitutional theory Parliament is sovereign . . . here we are only concerned to explain the significance of the doctrine of '*parliamentary sovereignty*'. It means first, that all legislative power within the realm is vested in Parliament, or is derived from the authority of Parliament – Parliament thus has no rival within the legislative sphere – and it means secondly that there is no legal limit to the power of Parliament. Parliament may therefore, and constantly does, by Act delegate legislative powers to other bodies and even to individuals, but it may also, by Act, remove these powers as simply as it has conferred them.

ii) Try to find all the law terms in lines 41–96 of the text and list them as you think best.

iii) Transfer the marked words and phrases in lines 41–56 to two separate lists. There is not necessarily *one* correct position for each word – the choice is personal.

Example:

| A   *Legislation and the courts* | B   *Other law terms* |
|---|---|
| legislation | constitutional (theory) |
| enacted law | sovereign (adjective) |
| legislator | doctrine |
| Parliament | parliamentary sovereignty |

▲ iv) Compare your lists with someone else. Have you chosen the same words and phrases? Have you put them in the same lists?

v) Choose list A or B. Try to decide what you think each word or phrase means. Use cognates, other words you know, the context and logical reasoning to form your ideas. Sometimes you may have to guess! When you have finished, check your ideas by referring to the glossary and your dictionary.

▲ If you prefer, work together with someone else who has chosen the same list.

■ vi) If you have time, repeat step iv) above with the other list. If not, refer directly to the glossary and your dictionary to check the meaning of the other words and phrases.

▲ Work in pairs or small groups with someone who has not studied the same list as you have. In turns, explain the meaning of the law terms in your list to your partner.


## 2   *Comprehension check*

Read lines 41–96 of the text carefully and use information in the text and your own knowledge to answer the following questions.

a) Are you familiar with the legal concept of *sovereignty*?
   *Sovereignty* is supreme power in a State. Who exercises sovereignty in your legal system? Is it an individual person or a body (an organised group)?
   Does *parliamentary sovereignty* in Britain mean that (1) only Parliament can legislate? or (2) Parliament has unlimited power to legislate?
b) Is delegated legislation possible in your country? Is it common?
   Compare the situation in Britain.
c) If Parliament makes a law which is not just, must the English courts apply it?
d) What do you suppose some of the 'fundamental liberties' guaranteed by the US Constitution are?
e) Are basic rights entrenched in the English constitution? What does this tell you about parliamentary sovereignty in Britain?
f) In your opinion, what effect could international obligations such as membership of the Common Market (European Community) have on parliamentary sovereignty? Is this a problem in your country, too?  ·
g) *Self-evident* (line 79) means *obvious, clear*.
   Use the context to decide if seldom (line 79) means *often* or *rarely*.
   Do you agree with the statement?
h) Why does the author describe the case of Old King Cole and Jack Sprat?
i) Did this case actually happen? Which phrase tells you this?
j) What command did Old King Cole give?

k) The example is full of pronouns: words like *who, it, that, which*, etc., which refer to other nouns mentioned in the text. To understand a text in detail, you need to know exactly *who* or *what* each pronoun refers to – it is not always the word next to it in the text. Study lines 85–96 and decide what the pronouns on the left below refer to, answering the questions on the right to check your understanding.

*Example: his* (line 88)   Is Jack Sprat a national of Old King Cole's kingdom?
*Answer: his* refers to Old King Cole. Yes, Jack Sprat is a national of Old King Cole's kingdom.

(1) who (line 88)   Does the alsatian belong to Jack Sprat or Old King Cole?
(2) it (line 90, first)   What does Jack Sprat want to save ('spare')?
                          Does he ask the King to save it?
(3) it (line 90, second)   Does Jack Sprat say the decree or the alsatian is a 'hound'? What word must the courts interpret?
(4) it (line 94, second)   What will influence the King's command?
(5) What legal point does the example illustrate?
    What is the importance of this point in the context of sources of law?
(6) Do law textbooks in your country contain imaginary examples like this?
● Look at the language of the English example. What forms do you notice?

## 3  Transfer

The classic definition of murder in English law is:

'the unlawful killing of a reasonable creature . . . with malice aforethought . . . the death following within one year and a day'.

*Lawful* is an adjective. What do you think it means? (Compare *beautiful, helpful,* etc.)
And *unlawful*? (Compare *unwritten, unenacted,* etc.)
*With malice aforethought* means with the intention to kill or seriously hurt.

i) Invent a simple example like the one in the text to show how the interpretation of words can influence the effect of the law. Remember to introduce the facts with 'Suppose that . . .' and use the simple present tense as in the example in the text.

■ ii) Is your example probable in real life, or do you know of a case where this has happened?
▲ When you are ready, work together in groups of three. In turns, explain your examples. Which one is most probable in real life?

## 4  Law terms: legislation

How many different terms do you now know referring to *legislation*?
Can you complete the box? The number of letters in each word or phrase is given in brackets e.g. (7) = 7 letters. Make a note of your answers and refer to the text to check
● your answers.

## E Reading for detail and language study: Judicial precedent – lines 97–228

### 1 Reading for detail: lines 97–155

i) Before you read the next section of the text, decide where you think some of the following pieces of information belong in the table:

A civil law/common law

B central importance of enacted law/central importance of precedent

C inductive/decisions reached by reasoning from general rules to particular cases/reasoning in individual cases leads to general rules/deductive

D principles are flexible/principles are based on real facts/in time fixed principles may not correspond to changing circumstances/principles develop in individual cases/general enacted principles are applied to individual cases.

E original source of principles may be case-law, custom, etc./inferior courts must follow decisions of superior courts/central position of judges

|   |                              | *English law* | *Continental law* |
|---|------------------------------|---------------|-------------------|
| A | Type of legal system         |               |                   |
| B | Basic characteristic of system |             |                   |
| C | Style of legal reasoning     |               |                   |
| D | Legal principles             |               |                   |
| E | Other characteristics        |               |                   |

ii) Read lines 97–155 of the text carefully to check your ideas. Copy and complete the table.

### 2 Word study: lines 97–155

Match each word or phrase on the left to the correct definition on the right for groups i) to iv) below. Check that your ideas make sense in the context of the text.

*Example: issues* (line 101) are *questions* or *matters*
*Answer: group i: a/2*

i) *words or phrases from lines 97–110*
a) issues (line 101)
b) grounded (line 106)
c) actualities (107)
d) litigation (107)
e) cases (108)

*definitions*
(1) legal actions or sets of legal circumstances
(2) questions, matters
(3) legal action
(4) real conditions or facts
(5) based

ii) *words or phrases from lines 111–131*
a) code (line 116)
b) codification (124)
c) encoded (126)
d) theorist (127)
e) judicial adaptation (130–31)

*definitions*
(1) put into a code (adjective)
(2) a person who forms theories
(3) a written set or collection of laws
(4) modification by judges for a particular purpose
(5) the act of making into a code

iii) *words and phrases from lines 131–43*     *definitions*
a) restatements (132)     (1) different from each other
b) jurists (134)     (2) law based on judicial precedent
c) case-law (135–6)     (3) declarations or statements in a new form
d) approach to (138)     (4) experts in law, especially legal writers
e) divergent (143)     (5) method of dealing with

iv) *words and phrases from lines 143–55*     *definitions*
a) salient feature (148)     (1) reach the same decision as
b) binding case (149)     (2) striking or especially important
c) hierarchical (151)     characteristic
d) follow (152)     (3) case containing principles which a court
e) tried (155)     must apply to similar facts in a later case
  (4) heard, judged (in a court of law)
  (5) classified into higher and lower grades or
  levels

● 

## 3 Discussion point

i) At lines 142–3 the writer says that the common-law and civil-law systems 'are not quite so divergent as might appear'. Use lines 97–155 of the text and the table in exercise E1 to decide:

◆ in what ways the systems are divergent
◆ why they are not in practice 'quite so divergent as might appear'.

Remind yourself of the language of contrast you practised in exercise C3.

ii) When you are ready:

■ ● To practise speaking, say your answers out loud or record them on tape, then listen to your recording. If you prefer, write your answers down. Check your ideas in the key.

▲ ● Discuss your answers in small groups before checking in the key.

## 4 Reading for general understanding: lines 156–228

The 'doctrine of the binding case' (line 149) is usually called the *doctrine of binding precedent*.

Read lines 156–228 of the text quickly and answer the following questions. Do *not* try to understand everything you read for this activity.

a) Given the doctrine of binding precedent, is the work of the English courts relatively simple?

b) In what way is the position of the judge central to the common-law system?

## 5 Word study: lines 156–228

Study the sections of the text containing the words and phrases on the left and use the context to decide if the definitions on the right are *true* or *false*.

*Example:* a practitioner (line 159)     *Definition:* a practising lawyer

a) reported decisions of the courts (160–61)     the law reports

b) in issue (162)     in publication

c) authority (172)     person(s) with power to act or judge
  authorities (174, 177)

| | |
|---|---|
| d) counsel (178) | the lawyer who conducts the case in court |
| e) distinguishing (179, 188) | pointing to differences between the present case and a past precedent |
| f) cases of first impression (181–2) | first session of cases in court |
| g) rules (184) | gives a decision |
| h) discretion (191, 198) | difference |
| i) arbitrary (198) | based on individual opinion, not on reason |
| j) judgments (199, 203) | judges in lower courts |
| k) substantial justice (210) | real, effective justice |
| l) disputes (214) | agreements |

## 6 Language study: connectors – lines 156–228

Connectors are words like *and, so, but, because*, which are used to join, or connect different pieces of language together. They show the relation between what the speaker or writer said before and what they will say next.

In the formal language typical of the law (particularly in written texts) you will find many connectors which are not common in everyday language. Learning to understand these words will help you to follow the arguments in legal texts.

i) Study the sections of the text containing underlined words (e.g. <u>thus</u>, lines 157, 214). Copy and complete the table below, showing the meaning and use of each one.

*Connectors*: (1) thus (2) therefore (3) for (4) however (5) further

| | Connector | Meaning | Use |
|---|---|---|---|
| a) | *Therefore* | for that reason, consequently | to give a logical consequence |
| b) | | because, since | to give a reason |
| c) | | more, in addition | to state another fact |
| d) | | so, in this way, consequently | to give a logical consequence |
| e) | | by contrast, on the other hand | to show a contrast with something that was said before |

ii) Choose the best connector from the table above to complete the following passage.

*Judicial precedent*

Judicial precedent is of fundamental importance in the English legal system, (1) _____ the principles of the common law, which have developed gradually through case-law over the centuries, are the main source of English law.

The English courts are bound to follow decisions of higher courts in the judicial hierarchy; (2) _____ in many cases they must also follow their own decisions. Decisions of inferior courts, (3) _____, do not have binding force. Decisions concerning the interpretation of statutes are also binding, (4) _____ English lawyers must always refer to case-law even if the facts of the case they are preparing are covered by statute-law and not common-law rules. The law reports are (5) _____ basic works of reference for members of the English legal profession.

## 7 Reading for detail: lines 156–228

Read lines 156–228 of the text carefully and decide which of statements a), b) and c) in the exercise below corresponds exactly to the meaning of the text and best completes each statement.

i) To decide a question of law, a practising lawyer
   a) only refers to judicial precedent if the case concerns statute law
   b) refers to judicial precedent in all cases
   c) only refers to judicial precedent if the case does not concern statute law.

ii) If the facts of a case are similar to two different precedents, the courts
   a) can choose which of the previous cases to follow
   b) are not bound by the previous authorities
   c) can use their discretion to legislate and create a new precedent.

iii) In the case-law system
   a) judges do not exercise discretion, they simply match precedents
   b) judges can reach any decision they consider right in cases where they have a choice
   c) judges follow general principles developed by the common law when they exercise their discretion.

iv) In developing legal principles, the English courts have had two aims:
   a) (1) to give real justice in individual cases and
       (2) to form general principles for lawyers to use in the future so that the law is certain
   b) (1) to give a lot of justice in individual cases and
       (2) to help lawyers involved in future cases.
   c) (1) to give justice in particular cases and
       (2) to form general rules which the courts can apply in future cases

*Note:* A detailed study of the hierarchy of the English courts and the operation of the doctrine of binding precedent is made in Unit 6.

## F  Development

## 1  Vocabulary revision: law terms

You have learnt a lot of law terms in this Section. This activity will help you to remember many of them.

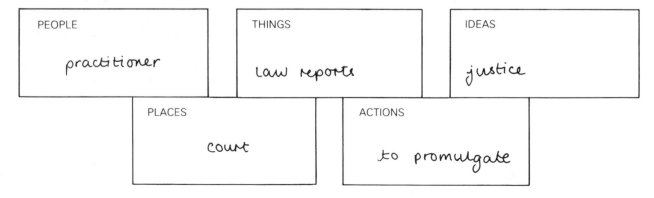

| PEOPLE | THINGS | IDEAS |
|--------|--------|-------|
| practitioner | law reports | justice |

| PLACES | ACTIONS |
|--------|---------|
| court | to promulgate |

i) Try to think of about three words or phrases to write in each of the boxes on page 26. There is not always one 'correct' position for a particular word!

ii) Scan the text and exercises in Sections A–E above to find at least three more terms for each of your boxes. Check that you can remember what all the terms mean!

▲ Compare your completed boxes with someone else.

## 2 Comparing sources of law

i) In your notebooks complete this chart showing the main sources of English law.

| | Source of law | Note any points of particular interest or contrast |
|---|---|---|
| PRINCIPAL | | |
| | | |
| SECONDARY | | |
| | AUTHORITATIVE WRITINGS | More important as a source in continental systems than in England |

ii) Draw a similar chart of your own showing the main sources of law in your legal system. Note any particular points of interest or contrast.

iii) Use the two charts from i) and ii) above and facts and language you have learnt from the text to compare the sources of law in the English legal system and in your legal system.

■ To practise speaking, say your ideas out loud. If you prefer, write some of your ideas down.

▲ Work together in pairs and discuss the information in your charts.

## 3 Case-law or codes?

What are the relative advantages and disadvantages of a legal system based on case-law and a legal system based on codes?

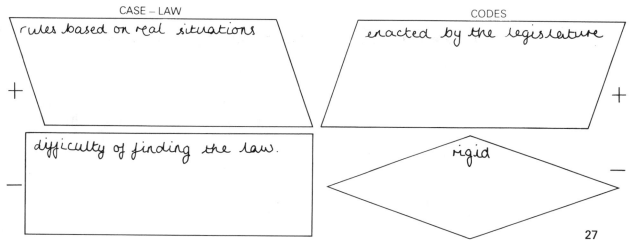

CASE – LAW

rules based on real situations

+

difficulty of finding the law.

−

CODES

enacted by the legislature

+

rigid

−

You will find some points in the text, especially in the section on Judicial decision. Think of some ideas of your own, too and write notes for the boxes at the foot of page 27.

▲ Compare and discuss your ideas with someone else. Do you agree with each other? When you are ready, exchange your opinions with the rest of the class.

■● Compare your ideas with the ones in the key – you may not agree with them all!

## 4 Personal study

If you are especially interested in the sources of law, you may like to continue studying this topic in detail on your own. Choose either custom (lines 249–97) or books of authority (lines 298–342). Read carefully the section of the text you have chosen and try to understand the main points. Use some of the techniques you have learnt in this Unit to understand new vocabulary where necessary. How important are custom or books of authority as sources of English law?

## Section Two:  Common Law

### Reading extracts from law dictionaries and works of reference

## A  Before you read

### 1  Think about the subject

Before you read about common law, think about the following:
◆ What do you understand by *common law*? If necessary, refer to Section One of this Unit (page 13) to check your ideas.
◆ Does a common-law legal system operate in your country?
◆ Does a term like 'common law' exist in your own language? If so, what does it mean?
▲ Discuss your ideas with other members of the class.

## B  Reading for specific information and general understanding

### Reading for specific information

*1* i) Look quickly at one or two of the dictionary extracts on pages 29–30, giving definitions of common law. Do *not* try to read them in detail. What do you notice
● about the term 'common law'?

ii) In Section One of this Unit you learned that the common-law legal system contrasts strongly with the civil-law legal systems of Continental countries. Quickly find the definition which corresponds to this meaning of common law in texts A, B, C and D on pages 29–30. Do *not* try to read the whole text for this
● activity. Suggested time: 2 minutes.

**TEXT A: Gavin McFarlane, *The Layman's Dictionary of English Law***

1 **common law**

Strictly, the general law contained in decided cases, as opposed to Acts of Parliament. But also used to include law in
5 Acts of Parliament and decided cases as a contrast with EQUITY (q.v.) A third use is to distinguish the English (common-law) legal system from a foreign (codified) system of law.

**TEXT B: Roger Bird, *Osborne's Concise Law Dictionary*, Seventh Edition**

1 **common law.** That part of the law of England formulated, developed and administered by the old common law courts, based originally on the common customs of the country, and unwritten. It is
5 opposed to equity (the body of rules administered by the Court of Chancery); to statute law (the law laid down in Acts of Parliament); to special law (the law administered in special courts such as ecclesiastical law, and the law merchant); and to the civil
10 law (the law of Rome).

It is 'the commonsense of the community, crystallised and formulated by our forefathers'. It is not local law, nor the result of legislation.

**TEXT C: *The Encyclopaedia Britannica***

1 **common law,** also called ANGLO-AMERICAN LAW, the body of customary law, based upon judicial decisions and embodied in reports of decided cases, which has been administered by the common-law courts of England since the Middle Ages. From this has evolved the type of legal system now found also in the United States and in most of the member states of the Common-
5 wealth of Nations. Common law stands in contrast to the rules developed by the separate courts of equity (*q.v.*), to statute law (*i.e.*, the acts of legislative bodies), and to the legal system derived from civil law (*q.v.*) now widespread in western Europe and elsewhere.

**TEXT D: David M. Walker, *The Oxford Companion to Law***

1 **Common law.** A term used in various distinct senses. (1) It was originally used by the canonists (q.v.) jus commune, as denoting the general law of the Church, as distinct from divergent local customs which in
5 particular areas modified the common law of Christendom;

(2) As the powerful centralized system of justice of the English kings developed in the twelfth and later centuries, the royal justices increasingly
10 developed and administered general rules common to the whole of England, the common law of England, as distinct from local customs, peculiarities, and variations, such as gavelkind (q.v.);
15 (3) The common law accordingly came to mean the whole law of England, including ecclesiastical law and maritime and mercantile law, as administered in England, as distinct from that of other countries, particularly those based on the Roman law;
20 (4) Hence, in the context of comparative law, a common law system is one based fundamentally on English common law, as distinct from a civil law system based on the civil law of Rome;

(5) With the development of equity (q.v.) and
25 equitable rights and remedies, common law and equitable courts, procedure, rights, remedies, etc., are frequently contrasted, and in this sense common law is distinguished from equity; thus at common law a person aggrieved by a breach of contract could
30 claim damages only, but in equity he could claim specific performance (q.v.);

(6) Common law was similarly distinguished from ecclesiastical law;

(7) Common law rights, powers, remedies,
35 crimes, etc., are frequently distinguished from statutory rights, powers, remedies, crimes, etc., according to the formal source of the particular right, etc., in principles of common law or in the prescriptions of statute.
40 In French and German law common law (droit commun, Gemeinrecht) mean law common to the whole area of the State as distinct from local or regional customs or peculiarities.

---

TEXT E: *Black's Law Dictionary*, Fifth Edition

1   **Common law.** As distinguished from law created by the enactment of legislatures, the common law comprises the body of those principles and rules of action, relating to the government and security of persons and property, which
5   derive their authority solely from usages and customs of immemorial antiquity, or from the judgments and decrees of the courts recognizing, affirming, and enforcing such usages and customs; and in this sense, particularly the ancient unwritten law of England. The 'common law' is all
10   the statutory and case law background of England and the American colonies before the American revolution. People v. Rehman, 253 C.A. 2d 119, 61 Cal.Rptr. 65, 85. 'Common law' consists of those principles, usage and rules of action applicable to government and security of
15   persons and property which do not rest for their authority upon any express and positive declaration of the will of the legislature. Bishop v. U.S., D.C.Tex., 334 F. Supp. 415, 418.

  As distinguished from ecclesiastical law, it is the system
20   of jurisprudence administered by the purely secular tribunals.
  Calif. Civil Code, Section 22.2, provides that the 'common law of England, so far as it is not repugnant to or inconsistent with the Constitution of the United States,
25   or the Constitution or laws of this State, is the rule of decision in all the courts of this State.'
  In a broad sense 'common law' may designate all that part of the positive law, juristic theory, and ancient custom of any state or nation which is of general and
30   universal application, thus marking off special or local rules or customs.
  For 'Federal common law', see that title.
  As a compound adjective 'common-law' is understood as contrasted with or opposed to 'statutory' and
35   sometimes also to 'equitable' or to 'criminal'.

---

*2*   Sometimes when we read we are only interested in a specific piece of information, or a single section of a book, article, etc. Learning to find the information or section of the text we want quickly is an important reading skill because it helps us to save time and concentrate only on the parts of a text that interest us.

    This style of reading (which you used to complete Activity 1 ii) above) is called *scanning*. To practise this skill, *scan* the texts on pages 29–30 to find the following information as quickly as you can. Do *not* try to read or understand the whole text for this activity.

a)   Which extract gives the greatest number of different definitions of common law?
b)   Which extract is from an American law dictionary?
c)   Which extract does not come from a law dictionary?
d)   How many distinct meanings of common law does *The Layman's Dictionary of English Law* give?
e)   What is the name of the court which administered Equity?
f)   What was the original source of common-law principles?
g)   What other countries apart from England have a common-law legal system?
h)   Find the name for the study and comparison of legal systems, used in text D.
i)   Does 'common law' have the same meaning in both French and German law?
j)   What force does 'the common law of England' have in the American state of California?
k)   Find the name of two cases in US law.

## 3   *Reading for general understanding*

  Skim through the texts to understand their general meaning, answering the questions below. Do not worry about words or sections of the text that you don't understand if you can complete this activity.

a)   What three basic definitions of common law are given in all the British dictionary extracts?
b)   Find the extra meaning that 'common law' has in the US.
c)   Which definition of common law do you think gave it its name?
d)   Which definitions in the American law dictionary correspond to Text D, definitions 6 and 7?

## C  Language study and law

### 1  Sentence structure

    a)  Study these examples from the text:
       (1) 'That part of the law of England formulated, developed and administered by the old common-law courts' (Text B, lines 1–2).
       (2) 'Strictly, the general law contained in decided cases.' (Text A, line 1)

    b)  We could also say:
       (1) That part of the law of England *which was* formulated, developed and administered by the old common-law courts.
       (2) Strictly, the general law *which is* contained in decided cases.

    c)  Notice how in these passive phrases the relative pronoun (*which*) and the auxiliary verb (*was/is*) can be left out, to make a shorter, more compact phrase with the same meaning. Notice that the phrase may either be past (example 1: which *was* formulated) or present (example 2: which *is* contained) in meaning. The correct tense should be clear from the context.

    d)  Scan Texts B and C and find more examples of this compact form. To check your understanding, can you 'translate' each example into its full form, as in b) above?

    ●  e)  Does a similar compact form exist in your own language?

### 2  Equity

    i)  You can see that one definition of common law contrasts the body of law developed by the common-law courts and statute law, with *Equity* – the body of law originally formulated and developed by the Lord Chancellor and the Court of Chancery. The purpose of Equity was to add to or supplement common-law rules in cases where these were too rigid to give justice. These two parallel systems of justice exist side by side in English law and since 1873 they have been administered by the same courts.

    The following example will show the different effect of common law and Equity in an actual case:

       Suppose that Smith and Jones form a contract in which Smith agrees to sell Jones a certain piece of land. Smith later changes his mind and breaks the contract. At common law the court will order Smith to pay Jones money as compensation for the land he has lost. In Equity the court has discretion to order Smith to perform his part of the contract (to transfer the piece of land to Jones) if this is fair in the circumstances.

    a)  What is the difference between the result given by Equity and common law in the example?
    b)  Note the phrase 'if this is *fair* in the circumstances'. Equity always looks to justice.

    ii)  Find the exact names for the following in the section of Text D which contrasts common law with Equity.

    *Example:* rights granted (given) by Equity
    *Answer:* equitable rights (Text D, line 25)

    a) breaking a contract
    b) compensation in the form of money
    c) an order to perform the obligations in a contract (in this case to transfer the land to Jones)
    d) b and c above are two different _____. c is a common-law _____ and d is an equitable _____.

iii) What remedy would Jones have for a similar breach of contract in your legal system?

Equity is a complex area of English law, mainly concerned with the law of property.

If you wish to know more about it, refer to the following for a short introduction:
David M. Walker, *The Oxford Companion to Law* (Oxford University Press, 1980) pp. 424–7.
Philip S. James, *Introduction to English Law*, 11th edition (Butterworth 1985), pp. 29–32, 34 and see Chapter 13.

For Equity in American law see:
*Black's Law Dictionary*, 5th edition (West Publishing Company, 1979), pp. 484–5.

## 3  *Discussion points*

Think about the following points for a few moments:

◆ Does your legal system contain rules of equity?
◆ If so, what is the role of equity – is it a separate system of rules, as in English law, or is it an integral part of the ordinary law?
◆ Is it possible to compare equity in your system, if it exists, with Equity in English law?
◆ You have seen that in England, Equity and common law are two separate bodies of legal principles which are now administered by the same courts – what is your opinion of this system?

■ To practise speaking, say your answers out loud; if possible record them on tape, then listen to your recording. Or if you prefer, write your answers down.
▲ Discuss and compare your answers in small groups.

## D  Development

## 1  *Remembering vocabulary: expressions with 'law'*

i) Using the box, write in your notebook all the expressions containing the word 'law' which you can remember.

> Source of law – civil law – law reports – comparative law

ii) Scan the texts in Sections One and Two of this Unit to continue your box.

iii) Which of the phrases did you know before and which have you learnt studying this book?

## 2 Connections

Which word in BOX A below do you think is most closely connected with which word in BOX B? What is the connection between each pair of words?

*Example: 15/a) CONNECTION: parliamentary sovereignty* is a basic doctrine of British *constitutional law*

You must find a partner for every word, but there is not necessarily only one correct solution!

Box A

```
 1 statute
 2 case-law
 3 justice
 4 however
 5 damages
 6 Court of Chancery
 7 common law
 8 thus
 9 custom
10 Parliament
11 jurist
12 to construe
13 legal action
14 to promulgate
15 parliamentary sovereignty
```

Box B

```
a) constitutional law
b) to enact
c) to interpret
d) books of authority
e) usage
f) specific performance
g) equity
h) on the other hand
i) litigation
j) enactment
k) civil law
l) therefore
m) legislator
n) Equity
o) law reports
```

■   Compare your answers with the solution suggested in the key. Can you give a good
●   reason for any pairs which are different? Has every word got a partner?
▲   Work in pairs. Explain your solution to your partner. S/he will decide whether to
●   accept the connections you give. If you can't agree about all the pairs, refer to the key.

# UNIT 2 State and Government

Reading a Descriptive Legal Report

## Section One: The State — Composition and Formation of the UK

## A Before you read

In this Unit you are going to read a report on the UK system of government. It describes the relationship between some of the main state organs: the legislature, executive and monarchy. What are their relative powers and functions? And what is the role of the monarchy in the twentieth century?

But first, what and where exactly is the UK? Where exactly does the English legal system operate? The text in Section One gives some brief geographical and historical facts.

Before you read, test your general knowledge in the quiz below. There are nine true statements. Then read the first paragraph *only* of the text on page 36 to check your answers.

TEST YOUR KNOWLEDGE QUIZ

■ i) Which of the following are parts of the UK?
a) England
b) Eire (Southern Ireland)
c) Scotland
d) Northern Ireland (Ulster)
e) Wales

■ ii) Which of the following is/are not part of the UK?
a) The Isle of Man
b) The Channel Isles

■ iii) Which of the following is a completely independent republic?
a) Eire
b) Scotland
c) Ulster

■ iv) The UK is
a) a federation of states
b) a unitary state.

■   v)  The UK is
   a)  an absolute monarchy
   b)  a constitutional monarchy.

●   vi)  The full name of the UK is: The United K_____ of _____
        _____ and _____ _____.

## B   First reading: understanding the contents and organisation of the text

*1*   We could give paragraph 1 on page 36 the heading 'Composition of the UK' or
     'Geographical and Political Division of the British Isles'. Quickly skim paragraphs 2
     and 3 and give each one a heading of your own. This quick first reading will help you
     to identify the general contents and organisation of the text and will make it easier for
     you to read it in detail later. *Do not* try to read or understand every word at this stage,
     just skim quickly to get an idea of the general content.

# United Kingdom

*Para.1* 1 The United Kingdom of Great Britain and Northern Ireland is a constitutional monarchy and a unitary state which is made up of the island of Great Britain (including

5 England, Scotland and Wales) and of Northern Ireland (which consists of the County Boroughs of Belfast and Londonderry, and the counties of Antrim, Armagh, Down, Fermanagh, Londonderry

10 and Tyrone – being part of the ancient Irish province of Ulster). The common language is English; Welsh and Gaelic are spoken regionally. The British Islands are not constitutionally part of the United Kingdom;

15 these islands, comprising the Channel Islands (of which the principal islands are Jersey, Guernsey, Alderney and Sark) and the Isle of Man are separate dependencies of the British Crown.

*Para.2* 20 The independent Kingdoms of England and Scotland were first linked by personal union of the Crowns of both countries when *James VI* of Scotland succeeded to the throne of England (as *King James I*) in 1603. The

25 political unification of the two countries was only effected more than 100 years later through the Treaty of Union of 1707 (6 Anne, c. 11). The treaty and the subsequent Acts of Union abolished the

30 separate parliaments and established one parliament for Great Britain which was situated in London. Great Britain was united with Ireland by the Act of Union of 1800 (39 & 40 Geo. 3, c. 67) which came into effect

35 in the following year. By this Act provision was made for Irish representation in the Parliament at Westminster, as provision had been made for Scottish representation in the Act of 1707. The United Kingdom of Great

40 Britain and Ireland existed from 1801 until 1922, at which time, in consequence of the partition of Northern and Southern Ireland, the title was changed to the present one of The United Kingdom of Great Britain and

45 Northern Ireland. The Irish Treaty of 6 Dec. 1921 gave Dominion Status to 26 Irish counties under the name of the Irish Free

State (*Saorstat Eireann*); in 1937 the Irish Free State assumed a republican form of

50 government but the new state continued in association with the British Commonwealth until 18 April 1949. Under the Government of Ireland Act, 1920 (10 & 11 Geo. 5, c. 67), as amended by the Irish Free State

55 (Consequential Provisions) Act, 1922 (12 & 13 Geo. 5, c. 4), a separate parliament and government, each with limited powers, were established for Northern Ireland. The Northern Ireland Assembly Act, 1973 (c. 17)

60 and the Northern Ireland Constitution Act, 1973 (c. 36) established a new constitutional framework to replace that provided by the Government of Ireland Act, 1920. The Northern Ireland Parliament was replaced by

65 an elected Assembly and the government by an executive, the composition of which was to be agreed by the Assembly. The Northern Ireland Act, 1974 (c. 28) dissolved the Assembly, and provided that a Constitutional

70 Convention should be held on the future of Northern Ireland. The Convention has since collapsed, and rule at present is direct from Westminster.

*Para.3* English law and Scots law are very

75 different from each other in form and substance. The separate evolution of the two legal systems, both before and after Union, has resulted in different principles, institutions and traditions. Although in

80 modern times Scots law has been greatly influenced by English law, it is still based upon principles of Roman or Civil law and upon rules of Canon, feudal or customary law origin. In spite of the existence of a common

85 Parliament for England and Scotland for over 250 years there has been no assimilation of the legal systems of the two countries. A fusion of law has, however, taken place between England and Wales, as a

90 consequence of the subjugation of the latter country in the middle ages. The law of Northern Ireland, although administered as a separate system, is similar in many essentials to English law.

Kenneth R. Simmonds, *International Encyclopaedia of Comparative Law: National Report – the U.K.*

▲ Compare your headings with other members of the class. Are all the headings
● possible?
■ Try to think of an alternative heading for some of the paragraphs. Are different
● headings possible?

## C  Reading for detail and language study: paragraph 2

### 1  Reading for detail

i) Paragraph 2 describes the most important events in the history of Britain and Ireland. A *summary* (a brief description of the main points in different words) of each event is given in note form in the chart below. First, check that you understand the notes in the chart, then copy it into your notebook.

ii) Read paragraph 2 carefully and put each event in the correct historical order by giving it a number from 1 to 10. To do this you will need to match the summary of each event to the corresponding part of the text.

*Example:* The phrase 'Union of Crowns of Scotland and England' (f) is a summary of the first five lines of paragraph 2. It happened in 1603 and so was the first historic event.

This activity will help you to think carefully about the meaning of the text as you read it. It is also a first step towards reformulating a text – that is, expressing the information contained in the text in a different form such as a summary, chart or table.

| | Event | Date | Order |
|---|---|---|---|
| a) | Northern Ireland Assembly constituted | | |
| b) | Political unification of Scotland and England | | |
| c) | Republican government adopted in Irish Free State | | |
| d) | Northern Ireland Assembly dissolved | | |
| e) | Single parliament established for Great Britain | | |
| f) | Union of Crowns of Scotland and England | 1603 | 1 |
| g) | The Republic of Ireland left the British Commonwealth | | |
| h) | Union of Great Britain and Ireland | | |
| i) | Southern Ireland became a dominion – the Irish Free State | | |
| j) | Northern Ireland given separate parliament and government | | |

### 2  Vocabulary study: understanding new words

As you saw in Unit One, it is often possible to understand the meaning of a new word from the context. Read carefully the section of the text containing each word listed in the first column at the top of page 38, then choose its meaning in the context from definitions (1) and (2) on the right. Try to decide which information in the text helps you to choose.

*Example:* Crown (lines 19, 22) (1) monarch, monarchy (2) object the monarch wears on her/his head, symbol of sovereignty.
*Answer:* (1)
*Note:* this word can have both meanings, depending on the context. *Clues:* in this case it would not make sense for the Isle of Man etc. to have a particular relationship with the object the monarch wears on his head (lines 18–19), or talk about the 'personal union' of two physical crowns (21–2). Also, when *Crown* means monarch/monarchy it is normally written with a capital 'C' as in the text.

a)  linked (line 21)                (1) joined, connected      (2) divided, separated
b)  abolished (29)                  (1) created, set up        (2) took away, eliminated
c)  established (30)                (1) created, set up        (2) took away, eliminated
d)  *framework* (62) refers to      (1) work and jobs          (2) a structure or system
e)  rule (72)                       (1) a law or norm          (2) government

● f)  Which verb in lines 58–64 means *to substitute, to take the place of*?

## 3  Vocabulary theme: legislation

i)  In paragraph 2 several expressions are used to describe the *effect* or *content* of a law. You will find the first three phrases in the box below. Scan the text to find the other expressions and write them in your notebook.

●

> The Acts of Union *abolished* the separate parliaments . . . .
> The Acts of Union *established* one parliament . . . .
> Great Britain was united with Ireland *by the Act of Union* . . . .

52  ii) a)  Which phrase denotes a *change* in a previous law?
    b)  Can you distinguish between *abolished / established / gave / dissolved*?
    c)  The verbs in b) all refer to a specific type of action, e.g. the creation of something (to establish), the abolition of something (to abolish).

    The expressions below are more general and are commonly used to describe the effect or content of any law.

> The . . . . . Act provides that . . . . .
> Under the . . . . . Act . . . . .
> By the . . . . . Act . . . . .

*Examples:*
● Under the Road Traffic Act 1972 it is illegal to drive under the influence of alcohol.
● By s.57 of the Offences Against the Person Act 1861 anyone who 'marries' any other person when s/he is still lawfully married to someone else commits the crime of bigamy.
● The Parliament Act 1911 provides that a parliament shall not last for more than five years.

iii) Practise the expressions from i) and ii) above by completing the sentences below with a suitable word or phrase. To do this you may need to refer to the text to check some information.

*Example:* ___*Under*___ the Parliament Act 1911 a parliament cannot last for more than five years.

a)  The Road Traffic Act 1972 _____ it is an offence (crime) to drive when drunk.
b)  (1) _____ the Northern Ireland Assembly Act 1973 (2) _____ an elected Assembly for Northern Ireland.
c)  The Government of Ireland Act 1920 was _____ by the Irish Free State Act 1922.
d)  These two Acts (see c) (1) _____ the Northern Ireland Parliament and
●   (2) _____ an elected Assembly in its place.

## 4 Language study: the passive

i) Study this sentence from the text:

Great Britain *was united* with Ireland by the Act of Union of 1800 (lines 32–3).

It is in the passive. Compare the active form:

The Act of Union of 1800 *united* Great Britain with Ireland.
   (subject)          (verb)   (object)

ACTIVE:  The Act of Union united Great Britain with Ireland ...
PASSIVE:  Great Britain was united with Ireland by the Act of Union ...
ACTIVE:  English law has greatly influenced Scots law ....
PASSIVE:  Scots law has been greatly influenced by English law ....

To form the passive, use the verb *to be* in the same tense as the active verb followed by the *past participle* of the main verb:

| ACTIVE (main verb) | PASSIVE (to be + past participle of main verb) |
|---|---|
| united (simple past) | was (simple past)        + united |
| has influenced (present perfect) | has been (present perfect) + influenced |

Use *by* if you want to say who or what did the action (... *by* the Act of Union/... *by* English law). This is called the *agent*.
We often prefer the passive form when the action (*united/influenced*) or the object (*Great Britain/Scots law*) is the most important element in the sentence, or when we do not know who did the action (e.g. her bag was stolen). It is important that you recognise and understand the passive form because it is extremely common in legal English.

ii) Scan paragraph 2 to find more examples of passive phrases. Check that you understand them.

iii) Transform the following active sentences into the passive form and decide whether it is necessary to specify who did the action (the agent): first find the object of the active sentence.

*Example:*   Special courts administer ecclesiastical law.
*Answer:*   Ecclesiastical law is administered by special courts.

a) The English courts interpret Acts of Parliament according to fixed rules of precedent.
    *Answer:* Acts of Parliament .....

b) It is possible that Parliament will eventually codify much English law.
c) Roman law has influenced many modern European legal systems.
d) The Treaty and Acts of Union of 1706 and 1707 established one parliament for Great Britain.
e) A person who marries a second husband or wife while still legally married to the first one commits bigamy.

## 5 Oral practice

i) Use the information in the chart from Exercise C1 above to describe the history of the UK, using some of the new vocabulary you have learnt and the passive where you think this is the best form.

*Start like this:*

> 'The Crowns of England and Scotland were united in 1603, but the political unification of the two countries did not take place until ...'.

▲ Work in pairs: take turns to describe some of the main events in the history of the UK.

■ Speak aloud. If possible record your description on tape, then listen to your recording.

ii) Describe the formation and historical development of your own country in the same way. Use some of the new language you have learnt where possible.

▲ Work in pairs or small groups.

## 6  Discussion point

a) Do you know anything about the 'Troubles', or situation of tension in Northern Ireland?

b) Read this very simple summary to check your ideas:
The people of Ulster are divided into two groups – the Catholic minority, who want to join the Republic of Ireland, and the Protestant majority, who want to remain in the UK. The British government have sent the army to Ulster to control the violence between the two groups, but both sides hate this interference and many soldiers have been killed. The government say that Ulster is part of the UK and they therefore have a duty to keep the peace there. And how can they cede (give) Ulster to Eire when the majority of its people are against this?

c) You have read about the historical relationship between Britain and Ireland. From a legal point of view, what is your opinion on the matter? Can you see a solution to the problem?

▲ Discuss your ideas with other members of the class.

## D  Study in detail: paragraph 3

## 1  Reformulating a text: taking notes step by step

In this exercise you will learn to focus on the main points of a text and transfer this information to a simple chart in note form. This will involve understanding the main points of the text and will help you to remember them. A chart, table or summary is also useful for quick and easy reference in the future.

i) Quickly read paragraph 3 of the text on page 36 and divide it into three sections describing the relationship between the legal systems of:

● 1) England and Scotland, 2) England and Wales, 3) England and Northern Ireland. Using the line numbers, list the divisions in your notebook.

ii) Read each section carefully and make a note of the parts of the text which:
   a)  compare the two legal systems
   b)  give reasons for the differences or similarities between them.

iii) Transfer this information in note form to the following chart in your notebook. Use your own words where possible, e.g. 'The law of Northern Ireland is similar in many essentials to English law' (lines 91–4). In other words: the law of Northern Ireland is basically similar to English law. In note form in the table: 'basically similar'.

| Legal system | Relationship with English law | Reasons for differences/similarities |
|---|---|---|
| Scotland | | |
| Wales | | |
| Northern Ireland | *basically similar* | |

iv) Choose the legal system of Northern Ireland, Scotland or Wales. Use the information in your chart to describe the relationship between the system you have chosen and English law.

▲ ● Work in small groups. Decide together if your information is correct and complete, before checking in the key to make sure.

■ ● Speak aloud. If possible record your description on tape, then listen to your recording. If you prefer, use your notes to write a brief description. Then check your information in the key.

## 2 Discussion points

Consider each of the following points, then do some personal research to check your ideas. For example, for the first point, you will find some information in the text from *The Encyclopaedia Britannica* on page 29.

▲ Work in pairs.

◆ What other legal systems are based on the English common law?
◆ What are the historical reasons for this?
◆ Has your legal system been influenced by English law or another legal system in any way? Can you give reasons for this?
◆ Has your legal system influenced other legal systems? Can you explain the reasons for this?

▲ Discuss your ideas and findings in small groups.

## 3 Scanning for expressions with 'law'

Scan the whole text and find other expressions with 'law' to add to your box from page 32, Unit One (e.g. feudal law – line 83).

## E Development

## 1 Personal vocabulary research: state systems

The text refers to several different types of State or State systems (e.g. constitutional monarchy, unitary State).

i) Quickly scan Paragraphs 1 and 2 to find more examples and write them in column 1 of the following table in your notebook. Do you know the meaning of each term?

| Type of State | UK | Eire | Your country | Another example |
|---|---|---|---|---|
| constitutional monarchy | √ | × | | Sweden |
| unitary State | √ | √ | | France |
| | | | | |
| | | | | |
| | | | | |

ii) Use a dictionary to find some other terms in English (at least five) to add to the list, e.g. presidential republic, dictatorship.

iii) Complete the other four columns of the table, giving a different example State for each system.

▲   Compare your list with someone else and discuss your examples together.

iv) To practise the vocabulary in your table, describe the State system in the countries from your table that you know something about.

> *Example:*   'Eire is a *unitary State*, which is now a *republic*. It was part of the UK until 1922. It became a *dominion*, and later a completely *independent republic* about 50 years ago.'

▲   Work in pairs.


## 2   States of the world

Each group of countries on the right has the same State system. Can you find it from the list on the left?

*Example:*   Burma, China, Ethiopia and Mozambique are all PEOPLE'S REPUBLICS.
*Answer:*      1 / f

| | |
|---|---|
| 1. PEOPLE'S REPUBLIC<br>2. COLONY<br>3. CONSTITUTIONAL MONARCHY<br>4. FEDERAL REPUBLIC<br>5. REPUBLIC<br>6. MONARCHY | a) Bahrain, Brunei, Oman, Saudi Arabia<br>b) Bermuda, the Falkland Islands, Gibraltar, Hong Kong (until 1997)<br>c) Brazil, India, Mexico, the United States of America<br>d) Egypt, France, Indonesia, Peru<br>e) Belgium, Denmark, Japan, the Netherlands<br>f) Burma, China, Ethiopia, Mozambique |

●   When you have finished, check your answers in the key. Do any of the groups or answers surprise you?


## 3   Discussion point

Choose one state system from Exercise 2 above and any country or countries you know well to use as an example of that system. Describe the state system in the country or countries you have chosen in outline and consider any points of interest and comparison.

▲ Work in small groups.

■ Speak aloud. If possible record your description on tape, then listen to the recording. If you prefer, write a short description for written practice.

## Section Two:   The UK System of Government

### A   Before you read

i) Write down all the words and expressions you can think of on the topic of STATE AND GOVERNMENT.
You have 3 minutes!

ii) Can you continue your list by including other related words? For example, if you have written *politics*, you could include *political* and *politician*.

▲ When you have finished, compare your list with those of other members of the class.

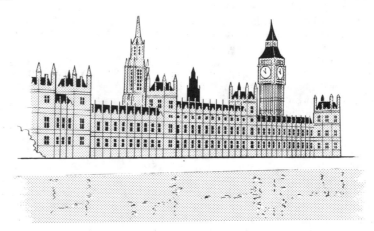

### B   Reading for confirmation

The three main topics in the text on pages 44–6 are:
a)  The monarchy
b)  The legislature
c)  The executive.

i)  Do *not* read the text yet.
▲   Work in pairs. Choose topic a, b or c.
■   Work on topics a, b and c.
▲■  Write three lists in note form containing the following information about your topic(s):

A.  Facts you know      B.  Facts you're not sure of      C.  Facts you want to know

### 3. State Organs

1 The constitutional principles, rules and practices of the United Kingdom have never been codified; they derive from statute law, from common law, and from conventions of the constitution, which
5 are not laws at all, but political practices which have become considered as indispensable to the smooth working of the machinery of government. The monarchy, followed by the legislative, executive and judicial organs of government will
10 be discussed in turn.

a. The *monarchy* is the most ancient secular institution in the United Kingdom, with a continuous history stretching back over a thousand years. The monarchy is hereditary and
15 the present title to the Crown derives from provisions of the Act of Settlement of 1701 (12 & 13 Will 3, c. 2) which secured the Protestant succession. This succession cannot now be altered, under a provision of the Statute of Westminster,
20 1931 (22 & 23 Geo. 5, c. 4), except by common consensus of the member states of the Commonwealth which owe allegiance to the Crown.
*Queen Elizabeth II*, who succeeded to the
25 throne in 1952, is, in addition to being an integral part of the legislature, the head of the judiciary, the commander-in-chief of the armed forces of the Crown and the temporal head of the established Church of England.
30 The monarchy in the United Kingdom has evolved over the centuries from absolute personal authority to the present constitutional form by which the Queen reigns but does not rule. Her Majesty's government governs in the name of the
35 Queen who must act on the advice of her ministers. The Queen summons, prorogues (dismisses at the end of a session) and dissolves Parliament; she usually opens new sessions of Parliament with a speech from the throne in which
40 the major governmental policies are outlined. These acts form part of the Royal Prerogative, defined by *Dicey* as 'the residue of discretionary or arbitrary authority, which at any given time is left in the hands of the Crown'. Prerogative rights are
45 of legislative, executive and judicial character. The Monarch must give the Royal Assent before a Bill which has passed all its stages in both Houses of Parliament can become a legal enactment (Act of Parliament). The Monarch's consent and
50 approval is required before a Cabinet (see *infra*, c) can be formed or a minister take up office. As Head of State the Monarch has the power to sign international agreements, to cede or receive territory, and to declare war or make peace. The
55 Monarch confers honours and makes appointments to all important offices of state, including judges, officers in the armed services, diplomats and the leading positions in the Established Church. As the 'fountain of justice', it
60 is only the Monarch who is able to remit all or part of the penalties imposed upon persons convicted of crimes through the exercise of the prerogative of mercy on the advice of the appropriate minister.

At the present time the Monarch, although
65 exercising residual authority by consent of Parliament and according to the advice of the government of the day, is regularly informed and consulted on many aspects of public affairs. The Privy Council is the body on whose advice and
70 through which the Monarch exercises most statutory and many prerogative powers. There are about 330 members of the Privy Council, which, however, only meets as a full body on the death of the Monarch. It conducts much of its business in
75 committees at which the Monarch may not constitutionally be present. All Cabinet ministers are members; other members are appointed by the Monarch on the recommendation of the Prime Minister.

80 b. *Legislature.* – Parliament is the legislative organ and is constitutionally composed of the Monarch, the House of Lords, and the House of Commons. The Queen in Parliament represents the supreme authority within the United
85 Kingdom.
(1) The *Parliament at Westminster* legislates for the United Kingdom, for any one of the constituent countries, or for any combination of them. It may legislate on certain 'excepted' and
90 'reserved' matters for Northern Ireland (see *infra* (2)), subject to the provisions of the Northern Ireland Constitution Act, 1973 (c. 36). It may also legislate for the Channel Islands and the Isle of Man, under certain conditions, although these
95 islands possess their own ancient legislatures. The Parliament Act, 1911 (1 & 2 Geo. 5, c. 13) s. 7 provides that the life of one Parliament may not exceed five years.
Parliament consists of two Houses: the House
100 of Lords and the House of Commons.
The *House of Lords* is for the most part still a hereditary body. It consists of the Lords Temporal and the Lords Spiritual. The Lords Temporal include hereditary peers and peeresses who have
105 not disclaimed their peerages under the Peerages Act, 1963 (c. 48); life peers and peeresses created by the Crown under the Life Peerages Act, 1958 (6 & 7 Eliz. 2, c. 21) in recognition of public service; and the Lords of Appeal in Ordinary. The
110 House of Lords is presided over by the Lord Chancellor who is *ex officio* chairman of the House. The Lords Spiritual include the Archbishops of Canterbury and York, the Bishops of London, Durham and Winchester, and the 21
115 most senior diocesan bishops of the Church of England.
The *House of Commons* is an elected and representative body; members (at present 650) are elected by almost universal adult suffrage to
120 represent constituencies in England (523),

Scotland (72), Wales (38) and Northern Ireland (17). The law relating to Parliamentary elections is contained in substance in the Representation of the People Act, 1949, as amended. Any British
125 subject aged 21 or over, not otherwise disqualified (as for example, members of the House of Lords, certain clergy, undischarged bankrupts, civil servants, holders of judicial office, members of the regular armed services and the police forces) may
130 be elected a Member of Parliament (M.P.). Members are paid a salary and an allowance for secretarial and office expenses; after a Parliament is dissolved all seats are subject to a General Election. By-elections take place when a vacancy
135 occurs during the life of a Parliament, as when a member dies, is elevated to the House of Lords or accepts an 'office of profit' under the Crown.

The *Speaker of the House of Commons* is elected by the members from the members to
140 preside over the House immediately after each new Parliament is formed. He is an impartial arbiter over Parliamentary procedure and the traditional guardian of the rights and privileges of the House of Commons.
145 The *supremacy*, or *sovereignty*, of the United Kingdom Parliament is probably the most basic principle of British constitutional law. Parliament has of its own will settled the duration of the life of a Parliament, acts in such a way as not to bind its
150 successors in the manner or form of their legislation, and, in the Parliament Acts of 1911 and 1949 has provided that in certain circumstances a Bill may become law without the concurrence of all the component parts of
155 Parliament. These two Acts have clarified the supremacy of the House of Commons over the House of Lords, which can only delay the passage of Public Bills for a maximum period of one year and cannot delay at all the passage of Money Bills
160 (financial measures).

The European Communities Act, 1972 (c. 68), which made legislative changes in order to enable the United Kingdom to comply with the obligations entailed by membership of the
165 European Coal and Steel Community, the European Economic Community, and the European Atomic Energy Community, from 1 Jan. 1973, gives the force of law in the United Kingdom to existing and future Community law
170 which under the Community treaties is directly enforceable in member states, and provides for subordinate legislation in connection with the implementation of obligations or the exercise of rights derived from the Community Treaties.
175 (2) The *Parliament of Northern Ireland* established by the Government of Ireland Act, 1920, was abolished and replaced by the Assembly elected under the provisions of the Northern Ireland Assembly Act, 1973 (*supra* Introduction
180 preceding I). The first Northern Ireland Executive agreed upon by this Assembly took office in November 1973, but collapsed in May 1974. Direct rule by the Parliament at Westminster has

185 been reimposed, under the provisions of the Northern Ireland Constitution Act, 1973, in consequence.

c. *Executive*. – The government consists of the ministers appointed by the Crown on the recommendation of the Prime Minister, who is
190 appointed directly by the Crown and is the leader of the political party which for the time being has a majority of seats in the House of Commons. The office of Prime Minister dates from the eighteenth century and is the subject of a number of
195 constitutional conventions. The Prime Minister is the head of the government and presides over meetings of the Cabinet; by convention he is always a Member of the House of Commons. He consults and advises the Monarch on government
200 business, supervises and to some extent co-ordinates the work of the various ministries and departments and is the principal spokesman for the government in the House of Commons. He also makes recommendations to the Monarch on
205 many important public appointments, including the Lord Chief Justice, Lords of Appeal in Ordinary, and Lords Justices of Appeal.

The Cabinet is the nucleus of government; its members consist of a small group of the most
210 important ministers who are selected by the Prime Minister. The size of the Cabinet is today about 23 and its principal function, much of the work being carried out in Committee, is to determine, control and integrate the policies of the government for
215 submission to Parliament. The Cabinet meets in private and its deliberations are secret; no vote is taken, and, by the principle of 'Cabinet unanimity', collective responsibility is assumed for all decisions taken.
220 The central government ministries and departments give effect to government policies and have powers and duties conferred on them by legislation, and, sometimes, under the Royal Prerogative. Each is headed by a minister who is
225 in most cases a member of either the House of Lords or the House of Commons. There are over 100 ministers of the Crown at the present time; they include departmental ministers (e.g., the Secretary of State for Foreign and Commonwealth
230 Affairs; Chancellor of the Exchequer (Treasury); Secretary of State for Social Services); non-departmental ministers (e.g., Lord President of the (Privy) Council, Paymaster-General, Ministers without Portfolio); ministers of state
235 (additional ministers in departments whose work is heavy); and junior ministers (usually known as Parliamentary Secretary or Parliamentary Under-Secretary) in all ministries and departments.

The Lord Chancellor and the Law Officers of
240 the Crown deserve special mention at this point. The Lord High Chancellor of Great Britain presides over the House of Lords both in its legislative capacity (*supra* b (1)) and as a final court of appeal; he is a member of the Cabinet and
245 also has departmental responsibilities in

250 connection with the appointment of certain
judges. He advises on, and frequently initiates,
law reform programmes with the aid of the Law
Commissions, the Law Reform Committee and *ad
hoc* committees. The four Law Officers of the
Crown include, for England and Wales, the
Attorney-General and the Solicitor-General; for
Scotland, the Lord Advocate and the Solicitor-
General for Scotland. The English Law Officers
255 are usually members of the House of Commons
and the Scottish Law Officers may be. They
represent the Crown in civil litigation, prosecute
in certain exceptionally important criminal cases,
and advise government on points of law. They
260 may appear in proceedings before the
International Court of Justice, the European
Commission of Human Rights and Court of
Human Rights. They may also intervene generally
in litigation in the United Kingdom as
265 representatives of the public interest.
    The United Kingdom has no Ministry of Justice.
Responsibility for the administration of the
judicial system in England and Wales is divided
between the courts themselves, the Lord
270 Chancellor, and the Home Secretary. The Lord
Chancellor is concerned with the composition of
the courts, with civil law, parts of criminal
procedure and law reform in general; the Home
Secretary is concerned with the prevention of
275 criminal offences, the apprehension, trial and
treatment of offenders, and with the prison
service.

Kenneth R. Simmonds, *International Encyclopaedia of Comparative Law: National Report – the U.K.*

ii) Read the relevant section(s) of the text to confirm or check your facts and find some answers. Do not worry about words or phrases you don't understand if you can complete this activity.

iii) Was most of the information in list A correct? And list B? Did you find the answers to your questions in list C?

▲ iv) Form groups of three people who have each read a different section. Exchange the information you have learnt and discuss any points of particular interest.

v) Think about this method of reading. Did you find it easier to read the text after thinking about the topic, and with personal information to check and find?
You can use this method with any text of your choice. Even if you don't know much about the subject, it can still be helpful to think of some ideas and questions *before you read*.

## C    Reformulating text information

You are going to study the text in detail one section at a time, and transfer the most important information to your chart from page 47, showing the main components of the system of government in the UK today.

### *Identifying relevant information*

*1*  First you need to identify the most important points to include in the chart. The choice is personal, but remember that the completed chart should illustrate *the modern position of each state organ (monarchy, legislature and executive) from the legal point of view, and give the main facts about its composition, powers and functions today*. Choose your information carefully and don't try to include everything from the text!
To practise the skill of identifying and selecting relevant information, decide which five of the following 10 points from the beginning of the text on the monarchy you would choose to include:
a)  most ancient secular (non-religious) institution in UK

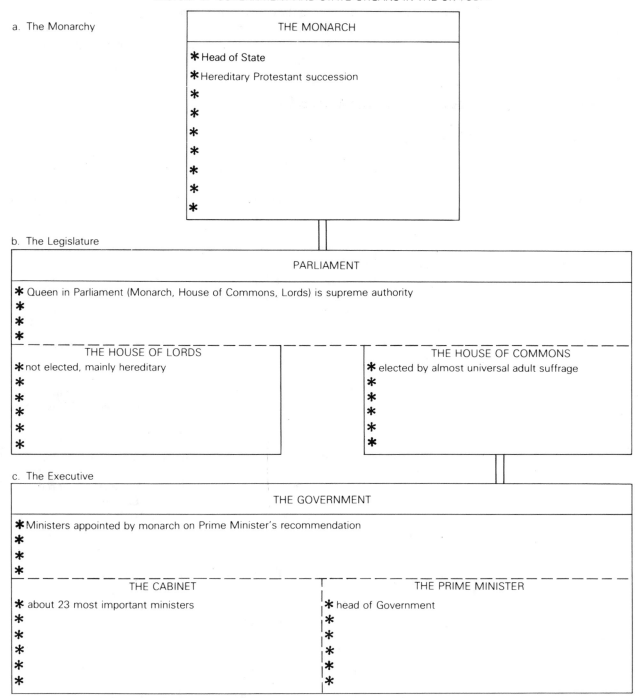

SYSTEM OF GOVERNMENT AND STATE ORGANS IN THE UK TODAY

a. The Monarchy

**THE MONARCH**

* Head of State
* Hereditary Protestant succession
*
*
*
*
*
*
*

b. The Legislature

**PARLIAMENT**

* Queen in Parliament (Monarch, House of Commons, Lords) is supreme authority
*
*
*

**THE HOUSE OF LORDS**

* not elected, mainly hereditary
*
*
*
*
*

**THE HOUSE OF COMMONS**

* elected by almost universal adult suffrage
*
*
*
*
*

c. The Executive

**THE GOVERNMENT**

* Ministers appointed by monarch on Prime Minister's recommendation
*
*
*

**THE CABINET**

* about 23 most important ministers
*
*
*
*
*

**THE PRIME MINISTER**

* head of Government
*
*
*
*
*

b) continuous history of over 1000 years
c) hereditary succession (monarchy passes from one member of family to another)
d) Queen Elizabeth II became queen in 1952
e) integral part of legislature
f) head of judiciary
g) head of armed forces
h) temporal head of Church of England
i) constitutional position has changed from absolute power to no real power
● j) remaining rights and duties are part of the 'Royal Prerogative'

**2** i) Read section a of the text carefully (lines 11–79: the monarchy) and identify the points you wish to include on the chart from page 47. List these points in your notebooks. Do *not* transfer them to your chart yet. Do not worry about individual words or phrases you don't understand, just try to follow the main arguments so that you can complete this activity.

## D Study in detail: the monarchy

### 1 Word study

i) a) Which phrase in lines 11–29 of the text means *became queen?*
   b) Which word in lines 11–23 means *a legal condition in an enactment?*
   c) What is the difference in meaning between the two verbs in the phrase 'the Queen *reigns* but does not *rule*' (line 33)? Why is the difference vital to the British constitution?
   d) What do you understand by *advice* (line 35)? Is the word normally used in exactly this sense?
   e) What do you suppose *outlined* (line 40) means?
   f) Use the context to decide what a Bill (line 47) is.
   g) What role does the monarch have in legislating?
   h) Notice the use of *can* with the passive in lines 49–51.
   i) *Remit* (line 60) means *reduce.* What do you think *the prerogative of mercy* (lines 62–3) is?

ii) Study lines 36–40. Using this box, match the letters on the left with the numbers on the right to form three true statements about some of the Queen's duties. Don't be afraid to guess!

| | |
|---|---|
| A  Parliament is prorogued by the Queen | 1.  before a new legislature can be elected |
| B  Parliament is summoned by the Queen | 2.  when the Prime Minister requests a General Election |
| C  Parliament is dissolved by the Queen | 3.  at the end of the year's session. |

Who summons, prorogues and dissolves parliament in your country? When?

### 2 Language study: power and obligation

i) Look at this phrase from the text:
   The Queen summons, prorogues and dissolves Parliament (lines 36–8)

It simply tells us that the Queen does these actions. Now look at phrases a) to e) below, taken from the text. They do not simply tell us what the Queen does: they also give an extra idea of obligation (e.g. *must*) or capacity (e.g. *is able to*). Obviously the language of the law often includes concepts like these. Decide which phrases express obligation, and which express capacity, and put a tick (√) in the corresponding box on the right.

|  | Obligation | Capacity |
|---|---|---|
| a) | √ | |

a) The Queen *must* act on the advice of her ministers   a)

|  | Obligation | Capacity |
|---|---|---|
| b) |  | ✓ |
| c) |  |  |
| d) |  |  |
| e) |  |  |

    b)  The monarch *is able to* remit penalties      b)

    c)  The monarch's consent *is required* before a Cabinet   c)
        can be formed

    d)  The monarch *has the power* to sign international   d)
        agreements

    e)  The monarch *may not* be present at Privy Council   e)
        meetings.

   ii)  Think of some other words or phrases which express power and obligation, and make an example sentence with each one. For instance, the Queen *is obliged to* act on her ministers' advice.

## 3  *Comprehension check*

Read the text carefully to answer the following questions.
    a)  Could Prince Charles, the Queen's eldest son and heir, succeed to the throne if he became a Catholic?
    b)  How has the role of the monarchy changed over the centuries?
    c)  What do you understand by the *Royal Prerogative*?
    d)  Does the monarch still have real power? Which sections of the text tell you this?

## 4  *Reformulation*

Now that you understand this section of the text fully, transfer the main points (your list from C2 above) to the first section of your chart from page 47. Write brief notes and use your own words where possible as you learnt to do in Section One of this Unit (Exercise D1).
▲  When you have finished, compare your chart with other members of the class. Have you chosen the same information?
■  When you have finished, compare your chart with the version in the key. Have you
●  chosen the same information?

## 5  *Oral practice*

Use the information in your chart from page 47, and the language and vocabulary you have learnt in the exercises above, to describe the British monarchy. Who is Head of State in your country? Is their role at all similar to that of the British monarch?

*Start like this:* 'Succession to the British monarchy is hereditary. The monarch, who must be a Protestant, is part of the legislature and head of . . .'.

■  Speak aloud. If possible record your description on tape, then listen to the recording.
▲  Work in pairs. Take turns to describe some aspects of the British monarchy.

## E   Study in detail: the legislature

### 1   Identifying relevant information

Repeat exercise C2 above for section b of the text (lines 80–186: the Legislature).

### 2   Word study

i)   a)   Use the context to help you decide what the following words probably mean:
    a)   peer/peeress (lines 104, 106)    b)   suffrage (line 119)
    c)   constituencies (line 120)    d)   by-election (134)

ii)   People who work in government departments cannot become Members of Parliament. What are they called?

iii)   Find words or phrases in the text that mean the following:
    a)   to place under legal obligation (lines 145–55)
    b)   agreement, accord (145–55)
    c)   to cause something to wait (155–60)
    d)   written legal agreements between states (161–74)

### 3   Language study: understanding complex sentences

i)   Study these phrases from the text:

A   *Queen Elizabeth II,* who succeeded to the throne in 1952, *is*, in addition to being an integral part of the legislature, *the head of the judiciary* ......

B   *The monarch must give the Royal Assent before a Bill* which has passed all its stages in both Houses of Parliament *can become a legal enactment.*

Read the italic part of each sentence. This is the basic part. The boxed phrases beginning WHO and WHICH give us extra information: they are *relative clauses*. The first gives us more information about the subject (A – Queen Elizabeth II became Queen in 1952); the second defines the subject (B – which kind of Bill is referred to? One which has passed all its stages in both Houses of Parliament).

The use of relative clauses can make it more difficult to understand a sentence because it interrupts the basic subject–verb–object sequence. This is especially true in the long, complex sentences typical of legal English.

If you have difficulty understanding a phrase containing a relative, read it twice. If you still have difficulty, take out the relative clause and study the basic part of the sentence first. Then consider the meaning of the phrase *with* the relative clause. What does the relative pronoun (who, that, which, whom, whose) refer to? What extra information does it give you, or how does it define the word it refers to?

ii)   Practise these skills by studying the sentences containing relative clauses in sections a and b of the text. Decide *what* or *who* each of the following pronouns refers to and check that you understand each complete sentence by answering the questions:

*Example:*   which (line 39): on what occasion does the Queen present the main government policies?
*Answer:*   *which* refers to the Queen's speech from the throne. The Queen presents the main Government policies in her speech when she opens Parliament.

a) which (line 43): is the Royal Prerogative the same today as it was many years ago?
b) who (60): can the monarch reduce criminal penalties?
c) whose (69): what important function does the Privy Council perform?
d) which (73): what unusual event happens when the monarch dies?
e) which (157): which House of Parliament can delay Bills for a year?

iii) Study lines 161–74 of the text.
a) In this complex sentence, can you find the subject, main verbs and objects?
b) What are the two basic points of the sentence?
c) What do the relative pronouns *which* (162) and *which* (170) refer to?
d) What extra information do the relative clauses give?

## 4  Vocabulary skills: word families

i) Study these phrases from the text:
(1) Parliament is the *legislative* organ (lines 80–81)
(2) The Parliament at Westminster *legislates* for the UK (lines 86–7)
(3) The Channel Isles and the Isle of Man possess their own ancient *legislatures* (lines 94–5)
(4) The European Communities Act 1972 (...) provides for subordinate *legislation* (lines 171–2)
The four words in italics clearly share the same origin and belong to the same *family*: they all have the same ROOT (basic part of the word) and their meaning is related. What is the exact difference in their meaning and grammatical function?

*Example:* (1) *legislative* is an adjective. It describes *organ*. A *legislative organ* is an organ which has power to make law (legislate).

ii) Many words belong to families like this. Learning to recognise root words and understand the relationship between different members of a family is one of the best ways to improve your vocabulary and understanding of new words. If you know just one word in a family, you will be able to work out the function and meaning of many other members of that family.

Quickly scan the whole text to find one other word which is related to each of the following (the words appear in the same order in the text):
a) succeed     b) constitution     c) represent     d) qualify     e) hold
f) judiciary   g) guard            h) supreme          i) member    j) impose
If you do not already know it, work out the meaning of each related word. Use the grammatical form and the context to help you. Can you think of other words in each family?

## 5  Comprehension check

Read the text carefully to answer the following questions.
a) Is the UK legislature composed only of the House of Lords and the House of Commons?
b) Are all UK laws national in their effect?
c) Is Parliament a democratically elected body?
d) Which of the three categories of Lords Temporal do you think are called 'The Law Lords'?
e) Can a judge become a Member of Parliament?

f) Can Parliament pass any law it chooses, or are there constitutional limits on its power?

g) From what you have read, can you see any external limit to Parliamentary
● sovereignty?

## 6 Reformulation

Now that you understand this section of the text fully, transfer the main points (the information you have listed from E1 above) to the second section of your chart from page 47. Write brief notes and use your own words where possible.

▲ When you have finished, compare your chart with other members of the class. Have you chosen the same information?

■ When you have finished, compare your chart with the version in the key. Have you
● chosen the same information?

## 7 Oral practice

Use the information in your chart from page 47, and the language and vocabulary you have learnt in the exercises above, to describe the UK legislature.
How is the legislature composed in your country? Is it democratically elected?

*Start like this:* 'The UK legislature is also called the Queen in Parliament. It is composed of the Monarch, the House of Lords and the House of Commons. One Parliament cannot last for more than ...'.

■ Speak aloud. If possible record your description on tape, then listen to the recording.
▲ Work in pairs. Take turns to describe some aspects of the UK legislature.

## F Study in detail: the executive

### 1 Identifying relevant information

Repeat exercise C2 above for section c of the text (lines 187–277: the Executive).

### 2 Word study

a) *Spokesman* (line 202) is a noun formed from more than one word: it is a *compound noun*. What two basic words is it formed from? Use their individual meaning and the context to decide what *spokesman* probably means.

b) The Prime Minister is described as 'the *head* of the government' (line 196). In line 224 the same word is used as a verb – what does it mean?

c) 'The Prime Minister *presides* over meetings of the Cabinet' (lines 196–7). What noun, common in the context of state and government, is related to the verb *preside*? What do you think the verb means? Who presides over the House of Commons, and the House of Lords (see section b of the text)?

d) What is a *Committee* (line 213)? If necessary, use your dictionary to find out. Is government work ever done in Committee in your country?
What advantages does the system have?

e) Which adjective in lines 220–34 is closely related to *department*? What does it mean?
Find the word with the opposite meaning.

f)  Which phrase repeated in lines 247–77 means the process of changing and revising the law to make it better?

g)  The Law Officers advise the government on *points of law* (line 259). What do you think these are?

● h)  What important area of law is distinguished in this section from criminal law?


## 3   *Vocabulary skills: choosing the right meaning*

In Section One of this Unit you saw that some words, e.g. *crown*, *rule*, have more than one meaning, depending on the context. The ability to choose the correct meaning of a word in a particular context is an important vocabulary skill which will help you to understand and use correctly words you already know, and also to use a dictionary effectively.

Below are some simple dictionary definitions of the word TITLE:

(1)  name of a book, poem, picture, etc.
(2)  name used to show a person's position, status or occupation
(3)  right to the possession of a position or property

Which of these three meanings do you think TITLE will usually have in the context of the law?

● Will this always be true? Does it have this meaning in line 15 of the text?

Find and study the sentences in the text containing the words in capitals in the next exercise. First decide from the context what you think the word could mean, then choose the appropriate dictionary definition.

---

E.g. THRONE (lines 25, 39)
1)  ceremonial chair or seat of a monarch, bishop, etc.
2)  royal authority, the sovereign

*Answer:* line 25 – definition 2
        line 39 – definition 1

---

a)  OFFICE (lines 51, 193)
   1)  room used as a place of business
   2)  buildings of a government department
   3)  public position of authority

b)  EXERCISE (line 62)
   1)  use or practice of powers, duties or rights
   2)  activity for physical, mental or spiritual training

c)  BODY (lines 69, 118)
   1)  the whole physical structure of a person or animal
   2)  an organised group of people working as a unit

d)  SUBJECT (line 125)
   1)  any member of a State except the supreme ruler
   2)  a topic or argument which is talked, written about, or studied

e)  SEAT (lines 133, 192)
   1)  something for sitting on, e.g. a chair
   2)  a place where something is, or is located or based
   3)  a parliamentary constituency
   4)  membership in a legislative body

f)  PASSAGE (line 157)
   1)  passing of a Bill so that it becomes law
   2)  passing, act of going through or past
   3)  voyage, journey
   4)  short extract from a speech or piece of writing

g)  BUSINESS (line 200)
   1)  buying, selling, commerce, trade
   2)  affairs, matters
   3)  shop, commercial or industrial enterprise

h) APPOINTMENT (line 205)
   1) arrangement to meet somebody
   2) position or office
i) SUBMISSION (line 215)
   1) act of accepting the power or
      authority of another

2) legal theory, opinion presented
   to a judge or jury
3) the act of presenting something,
   e.g. a plan or document, for
   consideration

*Note:* The last two paragraphs of the text (lines 239–77) contain a lot of new vocabulary relating to the administration of justice. You will learn this area of language later in the book, but if you are interested now, use a dictionary to find out what some of these terms mean. Choose about five words or phrases. First decide from the context what you think each word might mean, then look it up to find out.

## 4 Comprehension check

Read the text carefully to answer the following questions.
a) How is the Prime Minister selected in the UK?
b) What is the relationship between the Prime Minister and the monarch?
c) What is the relationship between the Cabinet and Parliament?
d) What is the vital difference between the role of the Cabinet and the role of government ministries or departments?
e) The Lord Chancellor is the most important legal figure in the UK. What do you notice about his role and functions?
f) Who is the UK Minister of Justice?

## 5 Reformulation

Now that you understand this section of the text fully, transfer the main points (the information you have listed from F1 above) to the third section of your chart from page 47. Write brief notes and use your own words where possible.
▲ When you have finished, compare your chart with other members of the class. Have you chosen the same information?
■ When you have finished, compare your chart with the version in the key. Have you chosen the same information?

## 6 Oral practice

Use the information in your chart from page 47, and the language and vocabulary you have learnt in the exercises above, to describe the UK executive.
Who is the leader of the executive in your country? Is there a body like the Cabinet, which plans and decides government policy?

*Start like this:* 'The UK Government consists of a body of Ministers called the Cabinet, who are appointed by the Crown. The head of the Cabinet is the Prime Minister, who is the leader of . . .'.

■ Speak aloud. If possible record your description on tape, then listen to the recording.
▲ Work in pairs. Take turns to describe some aspects of the UK executive.

## G Development

### 1 Remembering vocabulary: word categories

You have met a lot of new vocabulary in this Unit. One way to fix words in your mind is to put them into groups or categories of related words. The act of choosing and classifying the words will help you to remember them and so will other words in the group that you know.

i) Copy the following table into your notebooks. Write as many words and expressions as you can think of to complete it.
There is not necessarily a 'correct' position for a particular word. The choice is personal.

| Parliament | Monarchy | Government | Legislation | Other |
|---|---|---|---|---|
| House of Lords | the Queen *reigns* but does not *rule* | | Bill as amended by | suffrage European Community |

ii) Scan the whole text for other words and phrases that you want to remember and write them in the table. If you like, create more columns for other topics.

### 2 Translation focus: national institutions

i) Study the following words and phrases from the text, relating to UK institutions:
Bill    the judiciary    Cabinet    MP    Lord Chancellor    constituency
by-election    Community law    Prime Minister    peer    Act of Parliament
Do similar institutions, etc. exist in your system, with comparable characteristics and functions?

▲   Discuss your ideas with other members of the class.

ii) Which English terms do you think it is possible to translate directly into your own language? In your opinion, what does this depend on?
When a direct translation is not possible, how can you refer to the English terms when speaking your own language?

▲   Work in pairs. When you have finished, exchange your ideas with other members of the class.

iii) What does this activity teach you about translating law terms, and in particular
●   terms describing the national institutions of a State?

iv) Choose five institutional terms from your own system and decide how you would refer to them when speaking English.

▲ Compare your ideas with other members of the class.


## 3 Describing a system of government: your country

i) Prepare to describe the system of government in your own country. Use the elements of the UK system of government as a guide and make brief notes if you like.

*Include the following points:*
THE HEAD OF STATE: appointment, functions and powers, relationship with other state organs
THE LEGISLATURE: composition, functions and powers, relationship with other state organs
THE EXECUTIVE: composition, functions and powers, relationship with other state organs.

■ ii) Speak aloud. If possible record your description on tape, then listen to the recording.

▲ Work in small groups. Take turns to describe different aspects of the system of government in your own country.


## 4 Vocabulary theme: law and laws

LAWS are separate, individual rules. A LAW is one individual rule, or one Act of Parliament.
LAW or THE LAW is a whole system.
Each rule, which we call A LAW, is part of the whole system, which we call LAW or THE LAW.

i) Study each of the four sentences in the text containing the word *law* (lines 3, 122, 147, 168). Which two refer to individual laws, and which two refer to law as a whole system?

ii) All the words in the box are used in the text to refer to law and laws. Look at each word in context and try to decide its exact use or uses.
Which terms are similar or equivalent?
Which words are quite different from all the others?

```
LAW  (5, 122, 147, 168)
CONVENTION  (4, 195, 197)
RULE  (1)
PRACTICE  (1, 5)
PROVISION  (16, 19)
BILL  (47, 153)
ACT OF PARLIAMENT  (48–9, 155)
LEGAL ENACTMENT  (48)
STATUTE LAW  (3)
LEGISLATION  (151, 172)
```

iii) Complete the passage below by choosing the best word from the box for each
blank space. Do *not* use any word more than once. Choose the singular or plural
form and the article *a* or *an* as appropriate.

*English laws*
A proposal of law, or (1) _____ only becomes a/an (2) _____
called a/an (3) _____ when all its (4) _____ have been
approved by the Queen in Parliament. Many (5) _____ of English
constitutional (6) _____ do not derive (come) from (7) _____ or
common law, but are political (8) _____ called (9) _____,
which have the force of law.

## 5 *Comparing systems of government*

▲  Work alone or in pairs.

■ ▲  Think about the following points for a few minutes. Take time to refer back to the
text and the activities you have completed in this Unit and write short notes if you
like.
Refer to Unit One (page 20) for some expressions of contrast and comparison which
you can use to introduce your ideas when you speak about them.

◆  What are the most striking differences between the UK system of government and
your own?
◆  Are there significant similarities between the two systems?
◆  Compare one or more aspects of government that particularly interest you.

▲  When you are ready, compare and discuss the different systems of government in
small groups. Then exchange your most interesting ideas with the rest of the class.

■  When you are ready, compare the different systems of government. Speak aloud. If
possible record your ideas on tape, then listen to the recording. If you prefer, write
some of your ideas down.

## UNIT 3    The Constitution

Reading a Critical Analysis

---

### Section One:    Parliamentary Sovereignty

---

**A    Using prediction and understanding the general themes of the text**

### 1    Making predictions

All the words and phrases in the box below come from the text you are going to read in this Section.

■    i) Check that you understand their meaning, using your own ideas and a dictionary or the glossary to help you if necessary.

▲    Work in small groups. Discuss the meaning of the words and phrases using your own ideas and your teacher, a dictionary and the glossary to help you if necessary.

| |
|---|
| House of Commons      hundred years      the British constitution |
| the electoral system      sovereign      representative government |
| dictatorship      the party machine      control      customs |

ii) Use the words and phrases in the box to predict what you think the text may be about. What sort of topics and ideas do you think it will contain?

▲    When you have finished, compare your ideas with other groups in the class.

### 2    Checking predictions

i) Skim the text on page 59 to check your predictions from Exercise 1 above and find out what the text is about in general. Do *not* read the text in detail for this activity.

ii) Which of your ideas from 1 were right? Were any of your predictions completely wrong?

▲    Compare and discuss your answers with the other members of the group you worked with in 1.

### 3    Understanding the general themes of a text

i) Without looking at the text again, decide which of the following you think are *main* themes.

58

# Elective Dictatorship

1

The extent to which the perception of the British constitution has changed over the last hundred years is well illustrated by quotations from Dicey's *Law of the Constitution* (1885) and Lord Hailsham's lecture 'Elective
5 Dictatorship' (1976). First, Dicey on sovereignty: 'The essential property of representative government is to produce coincidence between the wishes of the sovereign and the wishes of the subject . . . This, which is true in its nature of all real representative government, applies with special truth to the English House of Commons' (p. 84). On conventions, Dicey said: 'The
10 conventions of the constitution now consist of customs which (whatever their historical origin) are at the present day maintained for the sake of ensuring the supremacy of the House of Commons, and ultimately, through the elective House of Commons, of the nation' (pp. 430–1). Contrast these quotations with Lord Hailsham, 'So the sovereignty of Parliament has
15 increasingly become, in practice, the sovereignty of the Commons, and the sovereignty of the Commons has increasingly become the sovereignty of the government, which in addition to its influence in Parliament, controls the party whips, the party machine and the civil service. This means that what has always been an elective dictatorship in theory, but one in which the
20 component parts operated, in practice, to control one another, has become a machine in which one of those parts has come to exercise a predominant influence over the rest' (p. 497). And more succinctly: 'The government controls Parliament and not Parliament the government' (p. 496). So the nub of the indictment is that the elected part of Parliament, namely the
25 House of Commons, having achieved supremacy over the unelected parts, namely the Queen and the House of Lords, has surrendered its sovereignty to the government which controls it through the party machine.

Which of these snapshots represents a more accurate picture of the constitution as it exists today? If the aim of representative government is 'to
30 produce coincidence between the wishes of the sovereign and the wishes of the subjects' the representative body must reflect the wishes of the electorate and exercise control over the government. The crucial issues, therefore, are the electoral system and the relationship between the government and Parliament.

Gabriele Ganz, *Understanding Public Law*

Choose three only.
   a) The changing balance of power between state organs in Britain
   b) The role of the monarch in the British constitution
   c) An analysis of the UK electoral system
   d) The role of the House of Commons in the British constitution 100 years ago
   e) The relationship between Parliament and the government in modern Britain
   f) The role of political parties in modern Britain.

ii) Refer quickly to the text to check your answers to i) above, but do *not* spend time reading in detail for this activity.

| B Reading for detail and language study |
|---|

## 1 Reading for detail; selecting vocabulary for study

i) Check that you understand the following questions. Do *not* try to answer the questions yet.

a) One of the two famous authorities mentioned in the text (Dicey and Lord Hailsham) was made Lord Chancellor in 1970. Which one?

b) According to Dicey, did the English House of Commons provide representative government for the people?

c) Constitutional conventions are a source of British constitutional law. Which other source of law are they closely related to?

d) In Dicey's opinion, what was the purpose of constitutional conventions?

e) How has the balance of power changed in Lord Hailsham's view?

f) Why does the government have so much influence today?

g) What danger does Lord Hailsham see in the present situation?

h) Complete this phrase: according to Lord Hailsham the government controls Parliament; Parliament _____ the government.

i) Are Dicey's and Lord Hailsham's views of the British constitution very different?

j) According to the author, which of the two views (see question i) is more accurate today?

ii) Read the text carefully to answer the questions from i) above. As you read, note the words and phrases you don't know or understand in the text. You can use a dictionary to find the meaning of two words only. Decide carefully which two unknown words or phrases you need to understand to answer the questions.

iii) Which unknown words did you select for study? Could you answer the questions without understanding *all* the vocabulary in the text?

■● Check your answers in the key.

▲ Discuss your answers with other members of the class and compare the words you

● selected for study before checking your answers in the key.

## 2 Word families: the suffix -ship

The nouns below can all be used to form another noun which has a related, but slightly different meaning by adding the suffix -ship. Complete the sentences which follow by choosing a suitable noun in -ship from the list below as in the example. Decide what meanings -ship can give to the main noun.

*Choose from*: (1) member (2) scholar (3) citizen (4) relation (5) leader
(6) friend (7) partner (8) owner (9) dictator (10) author

*Example:* Some people thought that Britain was becoming a/an _ *dictatorship* _ under Margaret Thatcher's iron rule.
*Answer:* (9)

a) British _____ can be gained by birth, adoption, registration or naturalisation.

b) Anita Mason was extremely pleased when Smith and Jones, the owners of the company she had directed for five years, asked her to form a _____ with them.

c) 'This country needs a strong _____ to tell people what to do and get things working again!'

d) 'This is an exclusive club. May I see your _____ card, please, sir?'

e) Home _____ is growing in Britain as more and more people are able to buy their own house.

## 3 Word study

a) Does the noun *sovereign* in line 7 refer to the British monarch?

b) Have you any idea what a *party whip* (line 18) is?

c) What do you understand by the *party machine* (18, 27)?

d) Study lines 18–22 of the text and decide:
   (1) has the British constitution always been an elective dictatorship in theory?
   (2) and in practice?
   (3) what has happened to change the situation?

*Language note:* In lines 19–22 the subject of the main verb is the phrase 'what has always been an elective dictatorship in theory'. *'What'* refers to *'a system which'*.
(*what has always been an elective dictatorship in theory*) . . . (*has become*) (*a machine* . . .).
          **main subject**                    **main verb**

Notice that in this sentence the subject and verb are separated by the comment 'but one in which the component parts operated, in practice, to control one another'
Now check your answers to questions (1), (2) and (3) above.

e) You know the verb *to elect* and the noun *election*. What do you suppose the *electoral system* (line 33) is?

## 4 Reformulation: completing a diagram

Without looking at the text again, complete the two diagrams below by choosing a suitable word or phrase from the list provided. When you have finished, check your diagrams by referring carefully to the text.

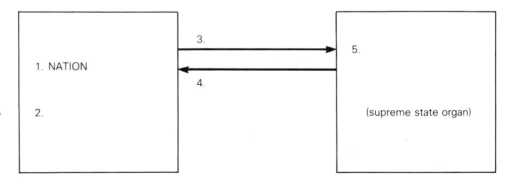

Figure 3.1 Dicey's view of the British Constitution in 1885: representative government

*Choose from:* a) represents    b) exercises sovereignty through the House of Commons
                c) NATION    d) HOUSE OF COMMONS    e) elects

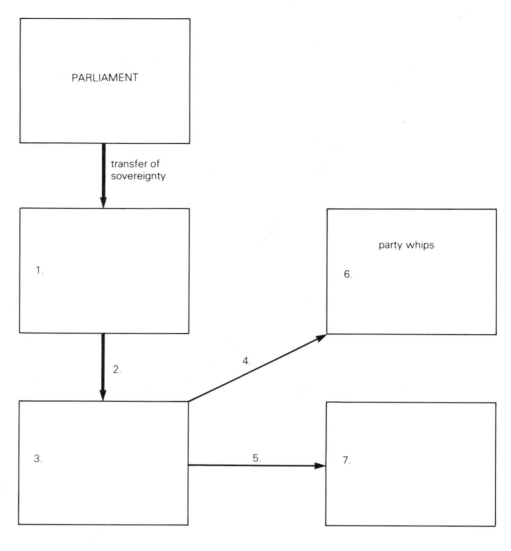

Figure 3.2 Lord Hailsham's view of the British constitution in 1976: elective dictatorship

*Choose from:* a) party machine    b) GOVERNMENT    c) civil service
d) controls    e) controls
f) HOUSE OF COMMONS      g) transfer of sovereignty

## 5 *Oral practice*

Use your completed diagrams from 4 above to describe:
(1) sovereignty in Britain according to Dicey in 1885;
(2) sovereignty in Britain according to Lord Hailsham in 1976.
Why do you think Lord Hailsham describes the system as an 'elective dictatorship'?
Start like this:
(1) 'According to Dicey, writing in 1885, the House of Commons is the supreme state organ in Britain. It is elected by the nation and . . .'.
(2) 'Lord Hailsham, on the other hand, writing nearly 100 years later, finds a very different situation. In his view, the sovereignty of Parliament has been transferred first to the House of Commons and then to . . .'.

■ Speak aloud. If possible, record your description on tape, then listen to the recording. If you prefer, write your description down.

▲ Work in pairs. Take turns to describe some of the information in each of the diagrams.

## C  Development

### 1  Understanding the author's attitude

    a) Do you think Lord Hailsham is in favour of the developments he describes in the British constitution, or is he against them?
Which words or phrases in the text help you to decide?

    b) At the end of the text, the author asks which view of the British constitution is more accurate today: Dicey's or Lord Hailsham's. Does he express his own opinion about this?

▲ ● Discuss your answers with other members of the class before referring to the key.

### 2  Prediction

    a) How do you think this text will continue?
What is your prediction based on?

▲     Compare your prediction with other members of the class.

    b) To check your prediction from a), look at the title of the next part of the text, reproduced on pages 64–5. Do *not* read the text yet!

### 3  Discussion points

Think about the following points for a few minutes.

◆ Could the constitutional system in your country develop into an elective dictatorship? Give reasons for your answer.

◆ Do party whips exist in your country's political system?

◆ Must elected representatives in your country (like MPs in Britain) always 'follow the party line' in Parliament, or are they free to vote independently of their political party? What advantages and disadvantages can you see in each case?

◆ Do you think a strong 'party machine' and the 'whipping system' encourage representative government?

■ Talk about your ideas. If possible record them on tape, then listen to your recording.

▲ Compare and discuss your ideas in small groups.

# Section Two:  The UK Electoral System

## A  Before you read

### 1  Think about the subject

Before you read about the UK electoral system, consider the following points.

  ● What sort of electoral system does your country have?

  ● What do you know about different electoral systems in other countries?

  ● Do you know anything about the UK electoral system?

  ● Do you know anything about Britain's political parties?

▲ Discuss your ideas in small groups.

2 Which of the following political parties do you think have members in the UK
   Parliament?

| | |
|---|---|
| The Republican Party | The Social Democratic Party |
| The Labour Party | The Liberal Party |
| The Royalist Party | The Socialist Party |
| The Communist Party | The Conservative Party |
| The Social and Liberal Democrats | The Green Party |

## B  Reading for rapid information; reading for general understanding

### 1  Reading for rapid information

● Scan the text on pages 64 and 65 to find the names of Britain's political parties at the
  time of writing and check your ideas from Exercise 2. You have 30 seconds!

### 1  ELECTORAL SYSTEM

Every British citizen aged eighteen years or over
who is not serving a sentence of imprisonment and
is not a peer is eligible to be placed on the electoral
5 register in a constituency (Representation of the
People Act 1983). Normally this involves residence
in the constituency on a certain day (10 October)
but members of the armed forces and now British
citizens who live abroad but have been registered
10 within the previous five years can be entered on
the register (Representation of the People Act
1985). At the moment there are 650 constituencies,
the boundaries being drawn by impartial
Boundary Commissions whose recommendations
15 need the approval of both Houses of Parliament
(Parliamentary Constituencies Act 1986). Their
impartiality has not prevented their
recommendations being highly controversial as
the way the boundaries are drawn can profoundly
20 affect the electoral prospects of a particular party.
The parties draw their support from different
sections of the electorate and the exclusion or
inclusion of a particular area can turn a safe seat
into a marginal one and vice versa. In 1969 the
25 Labour government refused to implement the
Boundary Commission's recommendations and
in 1983 unsuccessfully challenged them in court
(*R v. Boundary Commission for England ex parte
Foot*, 1983).
30   Not only the delimitation of boundaries but the
choice of candidates by the parties profoundly
affects the extent to which the voters' wishes are
reflected in the House of Commons because the
voter can only choose between rival candidates.
35 Unlike the USA where in some states voters
through primaries have a voice in choosing
between the parties' candidates, each party here
has its own method for choosing candidates. The
Labour Party in 1980 insisted that all Labour
40 MPs must undergo a reselection process if they
wished to be candidates at the next General
Election. Anyone can form a political party, as
happened in 1981 when the Social Democratic
Party (SDP) was launched. Though election law

45 puts strict limits on expenditure during an
election campaign, to prevent bribery and
corruption, it is very expensive to fight an
election, particularly as national propaganda
does not count towards election expenses. The
50 Labour and Conservative parties draw their
financial support mainly from the trade unions
and industry respectively. The other parties have
no such firm financial base and to that extent
suffer a considerable electoral disadvantage.
55   Their main disadvantage is, however, the
British electoral system. Electors vote in their
constituency and whichever candidate obtains
most votes is elected an MP, even if he or she
obtains only one vote more than his or her nearest
60 rival and only a small percentage of the total vote.
This system works best when there are only two
parties, though even then it is possible for a party
to obtain more votes over the country as a whole
but have fewer seats in the House of Commons
65 because its support may be unevenly distributed,
so that it obtains big majorities in some seats and
loses narrowly in others. This result is
accentuated when there are three or more
parties. A third party like the Liberals or now the
70 Social Democratic and Liberal Alliance, whose
support is spread fairly evenly throughout the
country, is likely to win few seats but come second
in many. Thus in the General Election of 1983,
the Alliance obtained 25 per cent of the vote but
75 only 4 per cent of the seats. Small parties like the
Scottish National Party, whose support is
concentrated in a particular part of the country,
are more likely to win seats.
  It is this lack of correlation between votes and
80 seats which has given a strong impetus to the call
for a different electoral system which would allow
voters to express preferences between candidates
so that if their first-choice candidate is not elected
or has not received sufficient votes to be elected,
85 his second-preference votes can help to elect that
candidate. Thus these votes are not completely
wasted and a candidate may be elected because

more voters have put him as their second choice. This system of voting can be used for one MP, i.e. in single-member constituencies (the alternative vote), or for several MPs, i.e. in multi-member constituencies (the single transferable vote). These systems give more chance to a third party such as the Alliance to win seats, because its candidates can be elected by being the voters' second choice. If this system were adopted in this country it would be very unlikely that either of the two main parties would win an overall majority of seats (i.e. more seats than all other parties combined) and this would have a profound effect on who would form the government.

Gabriele Ganz, *Understanding Public Law*

## 2 Reading for general understanding

● Read the text quickly to decide if the author thinks the UK electoral system is generally fair or unfair. Find at least three reasons for your answer. Do *not* try to understand the text in detail for this activity.

## C Reading for detail and language study

## 1 Word families

In Unit Two you learnt that words are not just separate units – they often belong to groups called word families, which have the same basic root and are closely related in form and meaning.

i) Use your own knowledge and scan the texts in Sections One and Two of this Unit to complete the table overleaf showing the relationship between the adjective, noun and verb forms in 12 different word families. You need one word for each of the spaces numbered 1–20.

As you work, check that you understand the meaning of all the words in each family. Use the grammatical part of speech (verb, noun, etc.) and relationships with other words in the family to understand unknown words.

ii) *Looking for regular patterns*
   a) Which part of speech usually corresponds to the root word in each family?
   b) Which typical noun endings do you notice in the second column? For example, -ship (dictatorship)
   c) Which typical noun endings refer to persons?
   d) Some adjectives and nouns have exactly the same form, e.g. election (adj.)/ election (noun). What other typical adjectival forms do you notice?

iii) In some families there is more than one noun in the second column. Use your own knowledge and the text to decide the difference in meaning between the following nouns, then check your answers in your dictionary.
   a) an *election* (line 42) and the *electorate* (22)
   b) the *sovereign* (Section One text, line 7) and *sovereignty* (Section One text, 5, 14, 15, 16 (twice), 26)
   c) a *prison* and *imprisonment* (line 3)
   d) a *register* (lines 5, 11) and *registration*
   e) *expenses* (line 49) and *expenditure* (45)

iv) Choose a suitable adjective from the list below to complete each of the following sentences.
   *Example:* The UK Parliament exercises __*sovereign*__ power. *Answer:* (2)
   *Choose from:* (1) resident   (2) sovereign   (3) voting   (4) electoral   (5) prison
      (6) residence   (7) election

**Table 3.1**
The Electoral System

| Verb | Noun (thing or concept) | Noun (person) | Adjective |
|---|---|---|---|
| dictate | 1. *dictatorship* | dictator | – |
| reign | a) sovereign<br>2. b) | 3. | sovereign |
| imprison | a) prison<br>4. b) | 5. | prison |
| elect | a) election<br>6. b) | elector | 7. a)<br>6. b) election<br>c) elective<br>d) elected |
| 8. | 9. a)<br>b) registration | registrar | registered |
| represent | 10. | representative | 11. |
| reside | 12. | resident | 13. a)<br>b) residence |
| recommend | 14. | – | recommended |
| approve | 15. | – | approved |
| 16. | vote | 17. | voting |
| spend | a) expenses<br>18. b) | spender | 19. |
| 20. | preference | – | preferred |

a) On first arriving in Britain she applied for a/an _____ permit for one year.
b) The register of electors is also known as the _____ roll.
c) He worked for 20 years as a/an _____ officer in the top security wing.
d) How long have you been _____ in the UK?
e) TV plays an important part in modern _____ campaigns.
f) Voters must show which candidate they choose at an election by putting a cross on their 'ballot paper' or '_____ paper'.

v) In the sentences below, fill each blank space with a suitable word from the word family given in CAPITALS on the right.
*Example:* The president was ___*elected*___ by a large majority          (ELECT)
a) Members of the lower house of the American Congress are called
_____.                                                            (REPRESENT)
b) Nearly all British citizens over the age of 18 are members of the _____.
                                                                        (ELECT)
c) The district (1) _____ is the official who (2) _____ births,
marriages and deaths in a certain area.          (REGISTER)
d) In the British constitution the Queen in Parliament is the legislative
_____.                                       (SOVEREIGN)
e) Many British (1) _____ are in favour of changing the (2) _____
system.                                          ((1) VOTE)
                                                 ((2) ELECT)

f) Sums of money which are (1) _____ to pay fees to lawyers are called legal (2) _____.  (SPEND)

g) Dangerous criminals are always sent to a/an _____ where there is very strict security.  (PRISON)

h) For the purposes of tax, a person is _____ in the UK if s/he stays there for more than six months of the year.  (RESIDE)

i) Parliament (1) _____ the (2) _____ of the special Commission last week.  ((1) APPROVE)
((2) RECOMMEND)

j) Direct _____ to the European Parliament are held every five years.  (ELECT)

## 2  Word study

i) Study the following words and phrases in their context in the text and match each one to the correct definition from the list below.
*Example:* a *constituency* (b) is an electoral area in the UK which is represented by a Member of Parliament (5). *Answer:* b/5
a) eligible (line 4)  b) constituency (5)  c) boundary (14, 19)
d) impartial (13)  e) safe seat (23)  f) marginal seat (24)

*Choose from:*
(1) electoral area in which an MP is elected by only a small majority
(2) suitable, with the right qualifications
(3) electoral area in which it is certain that the candidate of one particular party, e.g. Labour, will win
(4) dividing line that marks the limit between two areas
(5) electoral area in the UK which is represented by a Member of Parliament
(6) fair, not favouring one more than another.

ii) What do you suppose *a reselection process* (line 40) is? What does the prefix re- often indicate?
Work out the meaning of the following words, then choose the correct form of one of them to complete the sentences which follow.
(1) reconsideration  (2) reorganisation  (3) to re-state  (4) to rewrite
(5) to rearrange  (6) to remarry

*Example:* to rewrite (4) means to write something again. *Answer:* a/4
a) There are three spelling mistakes in this letter, will you __*rewrite*__ it, please?
b) He _____ soon after his divorce from his first wife.
c) She is ill, so her appointments will have to be _____.
d) After careful _____ of the facts, the Committee changed their original decision.
e) At the protest meeting last Monday the council representative _____ the official arguments in favour of the new road.

iii) a) Which word in lines 16–20 means *because*?
b) *R v. Boundary Commission for England and Wales ex parte Foot*, 1983 (lines 28–9) is the name of a case in which the Crown (R = *Regina* or *Rex*, Latin for Queen or King) represents the State against the Boundary Commission. *Ex parte Foot* shows that in this case the application to the court was made by an individual – Michael Foot, leader of the Labour Party 1980–83.

   c) What do you understand by the following phrase from the text?
'*whichever candidate* obtains most votes is elected an MP.' (57–8)

   d) What do you understand by 'a lack of *correlation* between votes and seats' (line 79)?

iv) *The prefix un-*

Read the parts of the text which contain the answers to the following questions carefully. In each case find a word beginning with un- in the text which helps you to answer, and decide exactly what that word means.

   a) Did the Crown win the case against the Boundary Commission in 1983?

   b) Do voters help to choose electoral candidates (1) in some USA states? (2) in the UK?

   c) If there are two parties in Britain, when can the one which gains more than 50 per cent of the votes obtain less than 50 per cent of the seats in the House of Commons?

   d) If the system of the alternative vote were adopted in Britain, would one of the two main parties probably win more than 50 per cent of the seats in the House of Commons?

## 3  Language study

i) *though*

Study the following sentences from the text:
'*Though* election law puts strict limits on expenditure // it is very expensive to fight an election' (lines 44–8)

'This system works best when there are only two parties // *though* even then it is possible for a party to obtain more votes over the country as a whole, but have fewer seats in the House of Commons' (lines 61–4)

In each example, *though* shows the relation between the first and second parts of the sentence. Which of the following could be used in place of *though* without changing the meaning of each sentence in the full context of the text? Choose one alternative only.

   a) because (introduces a reason or cause)    b) if (introduces a condition)
   c) even if (shows contrast between facts)    d) when (indicates a time)

ii) *whose*

Study this phrase from the text:
'the boundaries [of the 650 constituencies in the UK are] drawn by impartial Boundary Commissions *whose* recommendations need the approval of both Houses of Parliament' (13–15)

   a) *Question:* who makes the recommendations which Parliament must approve?
*Answer:* _____.
Notice the use of the relative pronoun *whose* to indicate *of which* or *of whom*. It refers to a noun which comes before it: '*the Boundary Commission* whose recommendations . . .'.

   b) Complete this phrase: Parliament must approve the (1) _____ of the (2) _____.
Read lines 55–78 of the text carefully and decide:

   c) what kind of party will not win many seats at an election even if it has quite a lot of support in the country?

   d) Why is the Scottish National Party more likely to win seats in Parliament than a party like the Liberals?

iii) Read lines 77–101 of the text carefully and decide:
    a)   which expression means *in such a way that*?
    b)   which word means *in this way* or *so*?
    c)   which form means *that is (to say)*?
    d)   in this paragraph the author describes an alternative electoral system – does he think the system will probably be adopted in the UK?

## 4  Reading for detail

Read the whole text on pages 64 and 65 carefully and for each of the following choose *one* correct answer from the four alternatives.

*Example:* Which of the following people was eligible to be registered on the electoral roll and vote in the Basingstoke constituency in the June 1987 General Elections?
(1)  Alan Tweedy, a yuppy who went to live in the constituency on 10 November 1986;
(2)  Maggie Tatter, a Basingstoke woman who has been serving a 10-year prison sentence for armed robbery since 1983;
(3)  Jane McGee, a constituent who lives in Spain and was last registered in Basingstoke in October 1984;
(4)  Lord Mole, last of a noble family who have lived in Basingstoke since the Norman Conquest.
*Answer:* not (1) – he was not yet resident in Basingstoke on 10 October (line 7)
not (2) – she was serving a sentence of imprisonment (line 3)
*correct answer* (3) – she lives abroad, but has been registered within the last five years (lines 9–12)
not (4) – he is a peer (line 4)

a)  The Boundary Commissions
    (1)  decide the exact boundaries of constituencies;
    (2)  draw their support from different sections of the electorate;
    (3)  make recommendations about constituency boundaries which people do not always agree with;
    (4)  make recommendations which favour the Conservative Party.

b)  Party candidates
    (1)  are chosen by voters;
    (2)  are chosen differently in each party;
    (3)  reflect voters' wishes in the Commons;
    (4)  must be reselected if they want to be candidates in more than one General Election.

c)  Expenditure during an election campaign
    (1)  officially includes national propaganda;
    (2)  encourages corruption;
    (3)  does not include election expenses;
    (4)  is strictly limited by law.

d)  The money needed by political parties in Britain comes from
    (1)  different sources;
    (2)  national propaganda;
    (3)  industry;
    (4)  the trade unions.

e)  The election results for a UK constituency in which 100 000 people voted were as follows:

| Candidate | Number of votes | Approximate % of total votes |
|-----------|-----------------|------------------------------|
| Conservative | 29 999 | 30 |
| Democrat | 29 998 | 30 |
| Green Party | 4 500 | 4.5 |
| Independent | 9 046 | 9 |
| Labour | 25 503 | 25.5 |
| votes not valid | 954 | 1 |

Who was elected?
(1) no one – no candidate obtained a majority of total votes;
(2) the Conservative and Democrat candidates;
(3) the Democrat candidate;
(4) the Conservative candidate.

f) In Britain,
(1) to be elected, a candidate must have more than a small percentage of total votes in a constituency;
(2) it is always a disadvantage for a party to have unevenly distributed support in the country;
(3) the Social Democratic and Liberal Alliance became the second party in 1983;
(4) it is possible for a party to obtain a large percentage of total votes, but only a small percentage of seats in the House of Commons.

g) Many British people are in favour of changing the electoral system because they want
(1) a system which would give a single party an overall majority in the Commons;
(2) to elect the Alliance;
(3) a system in which the number of seats a party obtains corresponds to the number of votes they win;
(4) to elect second-choice candidates.

## 5   Oral practice: describing electoral systems

i) Using the text, and language and information from the completed exercises above, prepare to talk about the UK electoral system. Include the following points.
- THE ELECTORATE: who can vote?
- PARLIAMENTARY CONSTITUENCIES: number of constituencies/role of the Boundary Commissions/political effects of drawing boundaries
- PARLIAMENTARY CANDIDATES: who chooses candidates?/how?
- FINANCING POLITICAL PARTIES: expenditure during election campaigns/who finances parties?
- THE ELECTORAL SYSTEM: which candidates are elected?/the importance of the distribution of political support in the country
- ELECTORAL REFORM: reason for changing the system/possible alternative systems/possible effects of electoral reform on UK constitution

ii) Talk about the UK electoral system, by describing each of the points listed above. If possible, record your description on tape, then listen to the recording.
Work in pairs. In turns, talk about different aspects of the UK electoral system by describing each of the points listed above.
*Start like this*
'Nearly all British citizens who are 18 years old or over are members of the electorate. They are eligible to be registered on the electoral roll in a constituency if they are resident there on . . .'

iii) Describe the electoral system in your own country. Use some of the points listed in capitals in i) above as a basis for your description and include any other information which you think is important.

▲ ● Work in pairs or small groups.

## D Development

### 1 Completing a ballot paper

The procedure in the UK for elections to the European Parliament (an institution of the European Communities) is the same as for elections to the UK Parliament. Members, called MEPs – Members of the European Parliament – are elected under the European Assembly Act 1978 for constituencies comprising two or more UK constituencies. Below is a ballot paper for the:

Election for the
Leeds European Parliamentary Constituency
15th day of June 1989

Use information you have learnt in the text and the instructions given below to decide if the vote is valid.

| | | |
|---|---|---|
| | **VOTE FOR ONE CANDIDATE ONLY** | |
| 1 | **EWENS**<br>Joan (known as Penny) Ewens<br>3 Holmwood Drive, Leeds LS6 4NF<br>Social and Liberal Democrat | |
| 2 | **LORD**<br>Clive Richard Lord<br>44 Upper Batley Low Lane, Batley<br>West Yorkshire WF17 0AP<br>Green Party U.K. | ✕ |
| 3 | **McGOWAN**<br>Michael McGowen<br>3 Grosvenor Terrace, Otley<br>West Yorkshire LS21 1HJ<br>The Labour Party Candidate | |
| 4 | **TWEDDLE**<br>John Wilfred Tweddle<br>9 Barrowby Avenue, Austhorpe<br>Leeds LS15 8QD<br>The Conservative Party Candidate | |

INSTRUCTIONS TO THE VOTER

Vote for one candidate only. Put no other mark on the ballot paper or your vote may not be counted.

Mark a cross(X) in the box on the right hand side of the ballot paper opposite the name of the candidate you are voting for.

●

## 2  Understanding the author's attitude

i) Which of the following do you think best describes the author's attitude in the text to the UK electoral system?
   a) He is strongly in favour of the system     b) He is in favour of the system
   c) He expresses no particular opinion for or against the system
   d) He is against the system                   e) He is strongly against the system

ii) Which parts or aspects of the text help you to answer i) above? Think about the facts and arguments the author chooses, his choice of vocabulary and style of writing.

iii) From what you have read in Section Two of this Unit, do you suppose that the author believes that Dicey's or Lord Hailsham's view of the British constitution (see Section One) is more accurate today?

▲● Compare your answers with other members of the class before referring to the key.
■● Refer to the key to check your answers.

## 3  Vocabulary consolidation

i) The text contains many words and phrases which are directly related to elections and electoral systems (e.g. the electorate, to be elected, safe seat, multi-member constituency).
   It contains many other words and phrases which you can use to talk about either electoral law, or other areas of the law (e.g. eligible, boundary, citizen).
   Scan the text to find all the vocabulary relating to electoral systems and other terms which you think are useful. Copy these words and phrases on to a separate piece of paper.

ii) Design a vocabulary table (similar to the one which you completed from page 55, Unit Two) and put the words and phrases from i) above in groups and categories of your own choice. Your table will be a personal record which will help you to remember some of the vocabulary you have learnt in this Unit. Remember there is no one 'correct' way to design and complete your table!

▲ When you have finished, compare your completed table with other members of the class and discuss your choice of categories and vocabulary.

## 4  Discussion points

▲ Work in pairs.
■▲ Choose one of A, B or C below and follow the instructions in steps i) and ii).
   If necessary, refer to page 20, Unit One, to revise the language of comparison.
   A  Compare the UK electoral system with another electoral system that you know well. What are the main similarities and differences? What are the best and worst aspects of each system in your opinion?
   B  Plan a model electoral system which you think would be completely fair and democratic. How is it different from the UK system and the system in your country?
   C  What are the main disadvantages of the UK electoral system and the electoral system in your country? What advantages does each system have? Suggest one change you would make to each system.
   i) Take time to think about your ideas. If you wish, make brief notes.
■ ii) Explain your ideas aloud. If possible, record them on tape, then listen to your recording. If you wish, write some of your ideas down.
▲    Form larger groups. Explain and compare your ideas and discuss any points of interest.

# UNIT 4

# Revision and Consolidation, Units 1–3

Reading a Work of Legal Reference

## A Reading and vocabulary skills: language and structure

In Units 1–3 you have learnt that there are different reasons for reading, and you have practised using different styles of reading depending on your reading purpose.

You have learnt that it is *not* usually necessary to understand every word in a text, and that you can often use words in your own language, other English words you know and the context to understand new vocabulary which is necessary to your reading purpose.

Follow the instructions for each exercise in Part A to see how well you have learnt to use some of the skills practised so far in this book:

READING SKILLS
- reading for gist: understanding what a text is about in general
- reading for specific information: scanning a text to find specific pieces of information
- reformulation: identifying the main points of a text and taking notes in chart form.

VOCABULARY SKILLS
- using the general context to work out the probable meaning of new words in a text
- recognising root words and using word families to work out the meaning of new words in a text.

## 1 Before you read: think about the subject

You are going to read a text about *constitutional conventions*, a subject which has already been mentioned in Units Two and Three. Before you read, think about what you already know on this subject for a few minutes, as you have learnt to do in the first three Units. Try to decide in general:
- what are constitutional conventions?
- what is their role in British constitutional law?
- do you know anything else about them?

You may want to refer to pages 44–6 and 59 to check your ideas.

## 2 Reading for gist: understanding what a text is about in general (8 points; suggested time: 3 minutes)

Quickly skim the text on pages 74 and 75 to decide what each of paragraphs 817–820 is about in general and put the following headings into the correct numbered positions (1–4) as quickly as you can. Do not try to read the text in detail for this activity.

*Choose from:*

A   Principal conventions
B   The nature of conventions
C   Cabinet control of legislative and executive functions
D   Legislature and executive coordinated by conventions.

## 3   Reading for specific information (5 points; suggested time: 3 minutes)

Quickly scan the text to find the following information.
a)   Three names which refer to the monarch.
b)   Three names which refer to one or both parts of the UK Parliament.
c)   Four names which refer to persons or bodies which are part of the executive.

---

1   **PARAGRAPH 817**

1)   At all periods in English history it has been necessary for the legislature and the executive to act in harmony if the government is to be carried on efficiently. It is in order to effect this object that constitutional conventions, which have varied from age to age, have been devised. Today, as in the past, much of the practical working of the
5   constitution depends less upon substantive law enforced by the courts than upon conventional usages founded partly upon the precedents afforded by history and partly upon the needs of the time, which may be said for practical purposes of government to have acquired the force of customary law.

The rules and principles embodied in these conventional usages have been found from experience to be essential to the cooperation of the three parties in whom the legislative and executive functions of government are
10   vested, namely the Crown, the Lords, and the Commons. They are now mainly directed towards ensuring that the government of the country is controlled by a ministry and Cabinet chosen by the electorate, which, while remaining responsible to the electorate and so acting in conformity with public opinion, are not unnecessarily hampered in their action either by lack of funds or by inability to procure the legislation they require. Where the party or combination of parties to which the Cabinet belongs does not control a majority in the House of Commons,
15   this object is not completely attained. In any event, in case of a serious disagreement between the Cabinet and the House of Commons, steps must immediately be taken to restore harmony between the executive and legislature, either by a resignation of the government or by a dissolution of Parliament.

On the other hand the electorate must have the means of choosing a ministry, and for that purpose there must be an Opposition ready to take over the government at a moment's notice. The Opposition must not be hampered
20   in its task of criticising the ministry's conduct and of persuading the electorate that it is better qualified to govern in its stead.

**PARAGRAPH 818**

2)   In general it may be said that conventions differ from rules of law in that they are not enforceable by judicial process, but are sanctioned by settled practice and political convenience. The existence of some conventions is
25   certain and they can be defined accurately. The nature and even the existence of others are subject to varying degrees of doubt. Although the existence and contents of some, such as the standing orders of the Houses of Parliament, are quite certain, whether they are mere conventions or genuine rules of law is entirely a matter of definition. Conventions may or may not be more flexible than rules of law.

To be a genuine convention, a rule or principle must be regarded as binding; but here again there may be
30   doubt, not only whether it is not a mere convenient practice, but also when a rule of practice turns into a binding convention.

There can therefore be no authoritative source to which reference can be made to ascertain whether a convention exists or what it is. One can only refer to works on constitutional law or on constitutional or political history or the biographies of public figures, more especially where they deal with crises of one kind or another.

35 **PARAGRAPH 819**

3)    The paramount convention is that the Sovereign must act on the advice tendered to her by her ministers, in particular the Prime Minister. She must appoint as Prime Minister that member of the House of Commons who can acquire the confidence of the House, and must appoint such persons to be members of the ministry and Cabinet as he recommends. She must, in ordinary circumstances, accept any recommendation he may submit that Parliament
40 be dissolved. The Sovereign must assent to any bill that has passed both Houses of Parliament (or the House of Commons alone under the Parliament Acts 1911 and 1949). If the ministry has not or loses the confidence of the House of Commons the Prime Minister must either recommend a dissolution of Parliament or tender the resignation of himself and the ministry.

Since the Sovereign must always act upon ministerial advice, ministers are always politically responsible to the
45 House of Commons for their acts, even if done in her name. Their responsibility is both personal and collective. Civil servants are not responsible to the House, since they must carry out the policy for which the departmental minister is responsible and must obey any instructions he may give. They must be politically neutral, in the sense that they must cooperate loyally with whatever government is for the time being in power. Accordingly they are not to be dismissed upon a change of ministry but are removable only for misconduct or inefficiency.

50 The independence of the superior judges is fortified by the conventional rule that the conduct of a judge cannot be called in question in the House of Commons except on a motion specifically criticising him or supporting an address for his removal; and in general a matter cannot be raised in Parliament if it is sub judice. The separation of the judicial from the legislative functions of the House of Lords is protected by the rule that lay peers shall not take part in the hearing of an appeal. For the purpose of maintaining the impartiality of the administration of criminal
55 justice, the Attorney General is required to act upon his own independent judgment in such matters as deciding whether to institute or approve a prosecution or to take or defend or intervene in civil proceedings on behalf of the Crown.

Certain conventions govern the conduct of the Houses of Parliament. Thus it is a convention that all money bills must originate in the House of Commons. The Speaker of the House of Commons must control debate impartially
60 and must do his best to see that all parties have fair opportunities to take part. Although he is normally elected from among members of the party then in power, he can expect to retain office even though that party ceases to hold office. The membership of committees is conventionally arranged so as to afford a proper party representation. Moreover, although each House can change its standing orders at will, there is a convention that some of them shall not be abolished or substantially altered. Such are the standing orders that require that every amendment or
65 motion to authorise central government expenditure, or to increase or impose a tax, must have the Queen's recommendation, and those that lay down an elaborate quasi-judicial procedure for legislation by private bill.

Certain conventions regulate the relations between members of the Commonwealth. Some practices of fairly long standing may or may not have become conventions. Such are the rule that the Public Accounts Committee of the House of Commons is not to consider policy questions, and that its chairman shall be a member of the
70 Opposition; that the choice of topics for debate on the twenty-nine supply days in a session shall be made by the Opposition; and that members of a ministry should relinquish company directorships the holding of which might affect their conduct in office. Many understandings operative in local administration have the same ambiguous character.

**PARAGRAPH 820**

75 4)    As a result of these conventions the most marked feature of the modern English system of government is the concentration of the control of both legislative and executive functions in a small body of men, presided over by the Prime Minister, who are agreed on fundamentals and decide the most important questions of policy secretly in the Cabinet.[1] The most important check on their power is the existence of a powerful and organised parliamentary Opposition, and the possibility that measures proposed or carried by the government may subject them to popular
80 disapproval and enable the Opposition to defeat them at the next general election and supplant them in their control of the executive.

1.    The relation of the Prime Minister to the Cabinet is necessarily ill-defined and obscure, and depends to a great extent on personal characteristics and the current political environment and atmosphere. The Prime Minister is certainly not a mere chairman, a 'first among equals'. He is entrusted by the Sovereign with the choice of ministers and the formation of a Cabinet,
85 the membership of which he controls from time to time; he settles the agenda for Cabinet meetings; as Minister for the Civil Service he is in a peculiar relationship to the administration; and he has a small group of experts to help him by providing and co-ordinating information in the formulation of high policy. The special position thus enjoyed has led some good authorities to conclude that Cabinet government has given way to prime-ministerial government, whereas others emphasise the Prime Minister's dependence on, and need to keep in line with him, powerful members of his party who have their own marked personalities and opinion. See de Smith, *Constitutional and Administrative Law* (2nd Edn) 154–62.
90

Lord Hailsham, *Halsbury's Laws of England*

## 4 Prediction

i) You now know what the text is about in general and some of the main themes. Use your answers to exercises 2 and 3 above to predict what the text is about in more detail. What sort of information do you think each of paragraphs 817–20 will contain?

ii) Read the text to check your predictions from i). Do not try to understand the text in detail for this activity. Which of your ideas were right? Were any of your predictions completely wrong?

## 5 Vocabulary skills: word families (8 points)

i) Use your knowledge of root words and word families to decide what the following words probably mean. For each word, look for the root word and other component parts and use the grammatical part of speech to help you decide. Give a simple definition, then check that your ideas make sense in the text.
*Example:* originate (verb, line 59)
*Answer:*     root word = origin.   -ate is a common verb suffix, e.g. to indic*ate*
*Probable meaning:* to have origin, to begin. Does this make sense in the context?

a) dissolution (noun, 17, 42)      b) removal (noun, 52)
c) impartially (adverb, 59)      d) directorships (noun, 71)
e) fundamentals (noun, 77)      f) disapproval (noun, 80)
g) ill-defined (adjective, 82)      h) prime-ministerial (adjective, 88)

ii) To show that you understand the words in i), choose the best word to complete the following sentences. Use each word once only, and make any necessary changes (e.g. plural forms).
*Example:* The case _ *originated* _ in a disagreement between the two men.

a) He held the _____ of the company for seven years.
b) A General Election was called after the _____ of Parliament.
c) The Commission must hear the arguments for both sides to the dispute and reach its decision _____.
d) In the UK, _____ powers are defined and regulated by constitutional conventions, not by statute law.
e) When boundaries between States are _____, there is usually trouble.
f) The _____ of civil servants from office for political reasons is not possible in the UK.
g) By convention the Sovereign cannot refuse to give the Royal Assent to a Bill even in the case of strong personal _____.
h) The independence of the judiciary and the separation of powers are _____ of many modern constitutional systems.

## 6 Vocabulary skills: contextual deduction (9 points)

Use the context and logical reasoning to work out the probable meaning of the following words and phrases in the text. Your answers should be similar in meaning to the ones in the key, but will not be identical. They may be in English or in your own language.

*Example:*   in conformity with (line 12)
*Answer:*     The Cabinet should remain responsible to the electorate and in this way act *in conformity with* public opinion (lines 10–13). *Public* opinion is the

opinion of the *electorate*. Therefore, to be responsible to the electorate, the Cabinet should act in agreement with public opinion, not against it.
*Probable meaning:* in agreement with.

a) hampered (lines 13, 19)   b) (the) Opposition (19, 79, 80)   c) in its stead (20–21)
d) ascertain (32)                   e) tendered, tender (36, 42)        f) afford (62)
g) standing orders (63, 64)   h) relinquish (71)                      i) supplant (80)

## 7 Language and structure: understanding the use of pronouns (10 points)

Study the parts of the text which contain the pronouns given on the left below. Decide *what* or *who* in the text each pronoun refers to and answer the questions on the right to check your understanding.
*Example:*   which (line 6)   What kind of rules have the force of customary law?
*Answer:*    *which* refers to *conventional usages* (line 5). Conventional usages have the force of customary law.

a) They (line 10)   Who or what makes sure that the government of the country is controlled by 'a ministry . . . chosen by the electorate'?
b) which      (11)   Who or what remains responsible to the electorate?
c) which      (14)   Do Cabinet members always belong to one political party?
d) it          (20) ⎫ The Opposition should persuade the electorate to vote for
e) its         (21) ⎭ (1) _____ in place of (2) _____.
f) who         (37)   Can *any* member of the House of Commons be appointed Prime Minister?
g) he          (39)   Who can recommend the dissolution of Parliament?
h) that        (40)   In what circumstances must the Sovereign assent to a Bill?
i) her         (45)   Why are ministers always politically responsible for their acts?
j) those       (66)   Which rules define the procedure for legislation by private bill?

## 8 Reading for detail (10 points)

Read paragraphs 817, 818 and 820 carefully and decide if the following statements are *true* or *false*.
a) The basic purpose of constitutional conventions is to make it possible for the legislature and the executive to work well together.
b) Conventions have not always been an important source of British constitutional law.
c) If the political party to which the Cabinet belongs does not have a majority in the House of Commons, it may not be possible to pass the laws which the Cabinet wants.
d) The role of the Opposition is to criticise the ministry and offer the electorate the choice of a different Government.
e) The distinction between a convention and a rule of law is always certain.
f) Conventions are always binding.
g) Only constitutional law books by authoritative writers explain whether a convention exists and what it is.
h) In the UK system of government the Prime Minister exercises control over both legislative and executive functions.
i) The power of the Cabinet is limited because if the electorate disapproves of Cabinet policies it may elect the Opposition to govern in their place at the next General Election.
j) The Prime Minister is the head of the Cabinet and has greater powers than the other ministers.

## 9 Reformulation: completing a chart (10 points)

i) Quickly read paragraph 819 and find the sections of the text which describe the constitutional conventions relating to:
   a) the Sovereign     b) the executive     c) the legislature.
ii) Check your answer to i) above:
   a) lines 36–43 describe conventions relating to the Sovereign
   b) lines 44–9 describe conventions relating to the executive
   c) lines 58–66 describe conventions relating to the legislature.
iii) Read each section of the text from ii) above carefully and identify the main conventions relating to:
   a) *the Sovereign*     b) *the Executive*     c) *the Legislature*
   As you work, make a note of the main conventions.
iv) Transfer the information from iii) above to the following chart in your notebook. Write in note form and use your own words where possible, as in the example. The completed chart should show *the main constitutional conventions relating to the Sovereign, Executive and Legislature in the UK today.* You will gain 1 point for each correct convention up to a maximum of 10 points.

| | *Main constitutional conventions* |
|---|---|
| *The Sovereign* | • Must act on advice of ministers, especially Prime Minister<br>• Must appoint member of Commons who can gain confidence of House as Prime Minister |
| *The Executive* | • P.M. must recommend dissolution of Parliament or resign if ministry loses confidence of Commons |
| *The Legislature* | • All money Bills must originate in Commons |

## B Law and law terms

The exercises in Part B will test your knowledge of English law and law terms that you have learnt in the Introductory Unit and Units 1–3.

## 1 Law terms I (10 points)

Choose the correct alternative and complete each of the sentences below.

*Example:*   The __*Cabinet*__ met urgently at 10 Downing Street to decide
Government policy on the new economic crisis.
(1) civil service    (2) Privy Council    (3) Cabinet    (4) ministries
*Answer:*   (3)

a)  The Road Traffic Act 1972 _____ that it is illegal to drive under the
influence of drugs.
(1) legislates    (2) amends    (3) requires    (4) provides
b)  The exact effect of legislation is influenced by judicial _____.
(1) interpretation    (2) custom    (3) sovereignty    (4) codification
c)  Parliament is a _____ body.
(1) legislation    (2) legislature    (3) legislative    (4) legislate
d)  _____, codes and delegated legislation are all sources of written law.
(1) Law reports    (2) Statutes    (3) Rules of law    (4) Litigation
e)  A court must follow _____ rules of precedent.
(1) binding    (2) arbitrary    (3) entrenched    (4) absolute
f)  In general, a Bill becomes an Act of Parliament when it has received the
_____ of both Houses of Parliament and the Sovereign.
(1) consent    (2) ratification    (3) enactment    (4) assent
g)  Everybody was surprised when the Green candidate for Westhampton was
elected, as it was considered a/an _____ for the Conservatives.
(1) marginal seat    (2) single-member constituency    (3) safe seat
(4) eligible seat
h)  The Chancellor of the Exchequer asked Parliament to _____ the existing
tax on alcoholic drinks and replace it with a tax on all drinks except water.
(1) establish    (2) abolish    (3) dissolve    (4) enact
i)  The Minister presented the new Housing _____ to the House of Commons
for reading and debate.
(1) Act    (2) Code    (3) Law    (4) Bill
j)  The Government lost the confidence of the House of Commons, Parliament was
dissolved and a/an _____ was called.
(1) General Election    (2) electoral roll    (3) by-election
(4) election campaign

## 2  Law terms II (8 points)

In the exercise which follows, substitute a suitable word or phrase for the part of each
sentence in italics.
*Example:*   There are 650 *elected representatives with the right to sit in the House of
Commons* in the UK.
*Answer:*   MPs or Members of Parliament.
a)  In contrast to civil-law legal systems, which are based on codes, common-law legal
systems are based on *decisions of judges in previous cases.*
b)  *The system of rights and remedies developed by the Lord Chancellor and the Court of
Chancery* is now administered by the ordinary English courts, side by side with the
common law.
c)  The UK is a *State in which a single person called King or Queen holds the office of
Head of State for life, but does not have power to govern the country.*
d)  At English universities *the branch of law which deals with rights and duties relating to
property* and Conveyancing Law are generally studied separately.
e)  *The supreme power of Parliament to pass any law it wants* is probably the most
fundamental rule of British constitutional law.
f)  In the UK the monarch is head of *all judges.*

g) It may be difficult to find time in Parliament for *revising and changing the law to make it better* when there is no urgent political reason which makes this necessary.

h) The Queen opens new sessions of Parliament with a speech from the throne. This act is part of the *remaining rights and powers of the Crown.*


## 3   Law and law terms (10 points)

Use your knowledge of English law and law terms to decide which word or phrase in each group of five does not belong and why.

*Example:* (1) Bill   (2) case   (3) enactment   (4) statute   (5) provision
*Answer:*   (2) – it is the only word which is *not* connected with legislation.

a) (1) Crown   (2) monarchy   (3) Royal Assent   (4) MP
   (5) heir to the throne

b) (1) recommend   (2) pass   (3) abolish   (4) enact   (5) amend

c) (1) subject   (2) British Nationality Act   (3) citizenship   (4) treaty
   (5) naturalisation

d) (1) the Labour Party   (2) the Social Democratic Party
   (3) the Conservative Party   (4) the Social and Liberal Democrats
   (5) the Republican Party

e) (1) constitutional convention   (2) code   (3) custom   (4) legislation
   (5) judicial precedent

f) (1) constituency   (2) electorate   (3) hereditary peer   ·(4) suffrage
   (5) ballot paper

g) (1) Criminal Law   (2) case-law   (3) Land Law   (4) Jurisprudence
   (5) Law of Tort

h) (1) Opposition   (2) majority party   (3) Cabinet   (4) Prime Minister
   (5) Home Secretary

i) (1) binding precedent   (2) judicial decision   (3) parliamentary sovereignty
   (4) common law   (5) authority

j) (1) life peerage   (2) delaying power   (3) Lord Chancellor
   (4) House of Commons   (5) Lords Spiritual


## 4   The law (12 points)

Use your knowledge of English law to answer the following questions. Give brief, simple answers.


### i)   Unit One – sources of English law and common law

a) What is the basic difference between the main source of law in a civil-law and a common-law country?

b) In the case-law system, how is the power of judges to decide cases as they want limited?

c) The term *common law* has several different meanings, depending on the context. For instance, as a source of law it means the law contained in decided cases, and is contrasted with *legislation*. Give two other definitions of 'common law'.

d) Why did Equity develop?


### ii)   Unit Two – state and government

a) Is Ulster (Northern Ireland) or Eire (Southern Ireland) part of the United Kingdom?

b) Which UK country has a completely separate legal system based on Roman law?
c) What is the significance of the fact that the Sovereign 'reigns but does not rule' for British constitutional law?
d) What is the House of Lords?

### iii) Unit Three – parliamentary sovereignty and the electoral system

a) According to Lord Hailsham, how has the balance of power in the British constitution changed in modern times?
b) Why does Lord Hailsham describe the present system as an 'elective dictatorship'?
c) Do all British citizens aged 18 or over have the right to vote in the UK?
d) Which candidates are elected at UK parliamentary elections?

*Now check all your answers in the key.*

## C  Word games

### *A crossword puzzle*

Can you complete the puzzle on page 82 by solving the clues below, and finding the word or phrase that fits in each space?

CLUES ACROSS

1 An English law graduate is a Bachelor of Laws and can put these letters after his or her name (abbreviation) (3)
5 The plan of action of a government or political party (6)
6 A member of the European Parliament (abbreviation) (3)
9 Without the Royal Assent it will never become an Act (4)
10 Legal action in a court of law . . . or everything that happens in Parliament or the Cabinet, for example (11)
11 The Queen or King in her or his official capacity . . . and the precious gold object s/he wears at ceremonies, symbol of royal power (5)
12 It may not be safe for a 7 *down* to sit on (4) (see CLUES DOWN – 7)
14 The government is elected to do this (6)
15 A formal discussion: in parliament. for example (6)
16 Queen Elizabeth II has been _ _ _ _ _ _ _ _ _ of the UK since 1952 (9)
18 A general term for a person who has studied law and can act for people on legal business (6)
21 Fair or right, what every law should be (4)
23 An independent nation under a sovereign government (5)
24 The _ _ _ _ _ to the throne hopes to become *16 across* one day (4) (see CLUES ACROSS – 16)

25 This branch of private law deals with civil wrongs (4)
26 A member of the electorate (7)
27 A highly specialised legal expert, who may write works of authority (6)
28 To make into a law by a legislative act (5)
29 Their job is to interpret and apply the law (6)
30 A government department headed by a minister, or the body of ministers of the government (8)

CLUES DOWN

2 Election to Parliament held by itself and not during a General Election, for example because of the death of a member during a legislature (2,8)
3 In 1979 Her Majesty the Queen _ _ _ _ _ _ _ _ _ Margaret Thatcher Prime Minister for the first time (9)
4 He works in the State administration . . . and sounds very polite! (5,7)
5 It may be hereditary or for life, and it gives the holder the right to sit in the House of Lords (7)
7 This representative is a member of the House of Commons (abbreviation) (2)
8 This dividing line separates one constituency from another . . . and may help a party to win or lose a 12 across! (8)
13 _ _ _ _ _ _ _ _ rights are rights recognised by Equity (9)

17 Constitutional conventions are part of
_____ law, and in fact the common law
has the same original source (9)
19 This member of the Commons must make sure
that all his party's MPs follow the party line and
vote as they should (4)
20 In *R v. Smith __ parte Jones*, we know that

Jones has applied to the court to try the case
against Smith (2)
22 The main _____ of English law are judicial
precedent and legislation (7)
24 The two chambers of the UK Parliament –
Commons and Lords – are called the _____ of
Parliament (6)

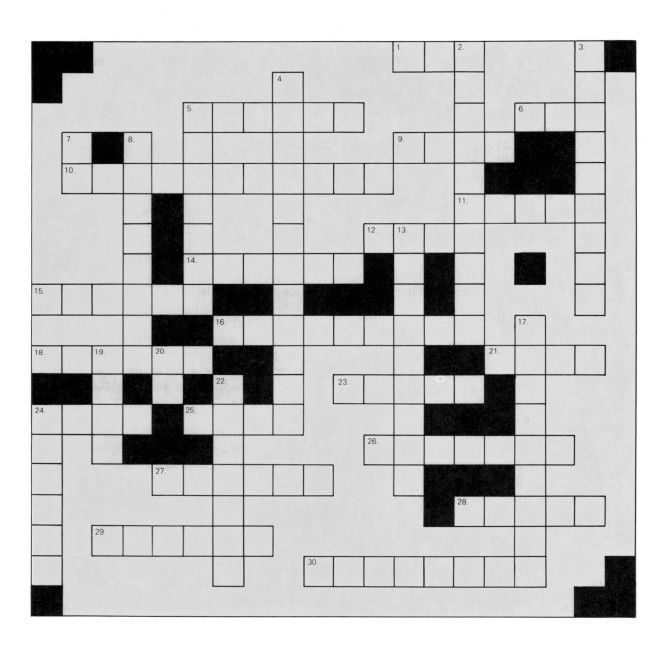

# UNIT 5 Statutory Interpretation and EC Law

---

## Section One: Statutory Interpretation

Reading a Law Textbook

### A  Before you read

#### 1  *Think about the subject*

Work alone or in pairs. Consider the following points:
- Who interprets and applies legislation in your legal system?
  Is it the same in the English legal system? (If you can't remember, refer again to Unit One, page 15).
- How are statutes interpreted in your legal system? (For example, by looking only at the words of the statute, by looking at the statute in its historical context, etc.)
- Can you think of any other possible methods of interpretation?
- Do you know of any legal orders (including International Law and EC Law – the law of the European Communities (see glossary), for instance) where a different method of interpretation is used?

▲ Discuss your ideas with other members of the class.

#### 2  *Vocabulary revision*

In this Unit you will use again some of the vocabulary that you learnt at the beginning of this book – but how good is your memory? To find out, complete the exercise below.

To help you *recall* the words (that is, bring them back to your memory) they are arranged in three general groups. Before you do each group of exercises, think of some words and phrases you know which belong to that group. This will help you to recall specific words more easily.

#### i)  GROUP 1: National law and European Community law

a) The international agreement setting up the EEC (3,6)
b) Another (unofficial) name for the EEC (6,6)
c) The courts of an individual country, as opposed to an international court (8,6)
d) A short name for the law of the European Communities (9,3)
e) This type of EC law can be applied directly in individual Member States without national legislation (adverb + adjective) (8,10)

ii) **GROUP 2: Parliament and legislation**

a) A single enacted law; a statute (9)
b) A person or body with power to make law (10)
c) To make a law in parliament (infinitive) (2,4,1,3)
d) The _____ are the individual rules or conditions in a statute (10)
e) *By* (or _____) the Equal Pay Act 1970 men and women have the right to equal pay for equal work (5)
f) Relating to parliament (adjective) (13)
g) The executive power in England, Scotland, Wales and Northern Ireland (1,1,10)

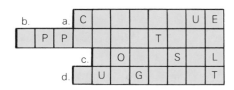

iii) **GROUP 3: Litigation and the courts**

a) The courts must _____ the words of a statute before they can apply it (8)
b) A request to a court or administrative body (11)
c) The lawyer or lawyers (called 'barristers') who conduct a case in court (7)
d) The legal decision of a court (8)

---

## B    Reading skills: prediction

*1*    The main rules of interpretation of UK legislation are given in the text on page 85.
   i)  Before you read, look quickly at the text.
       Why do you suppose the author has divided it into sections?
   ii) Look at the four *headings* only (e.g. i) The literal rule ii) The golden rule)
       What do the headings tell you?
       You know that this text is about statutory interpretation: what information do you think each section of the text will contain?
   iii) Use the headings to form a few questions of your own about each section of the text.
       This will give you a personal purpose for reading and will help you to read with more attention and understanding.

   *Examples: Section i)* has been done for you. If you like add other questions of your own.
   *The literal rule*
   a) What is the literal rule?
   b) Does it mean that the words in the statute have their literal meaning?
   c) When is the literal rule applied?
   d) Are there any exceptions to the literal rule?

Complete the following questions for *Section ii*. If you like add other questions of your own.

*The golden rule*

a) What is the _____ rule?

b) When _____?

c) Are there any exceptions to _____?

Write your own questions for *Section iii* and *Section iv*.

iv) Read the text to find the answers to your questions.

v) Did the text answer all your questions? What other main points does the text include?

▲● vi) Compare your work with other members of the class before referring to the key.

■● Check your work in the key.

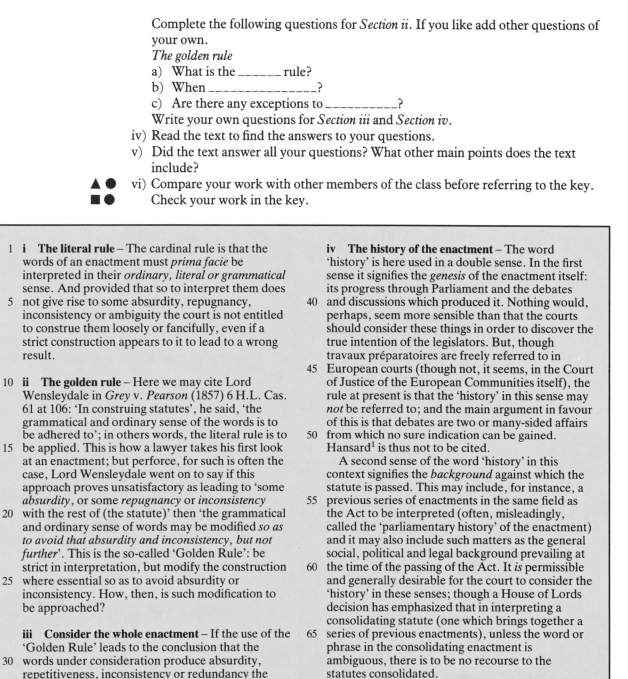

1 **i   The literal rule** – The cardinal rule is that the words of an enactment must *prima facie* be interpreted in their *ordinary, literal or grammatical* sense. And provided that so to interpret them does
5 not give rise to some absurdity, repugnancy, inconsistency or ambiguity the court is not entitled to construe them loosely or fancifully, even if a strict construction appears to it to lead to a wrong result.

10 **ii   The golden rule** – Here we may cite Lord Wensleydale in *Grey* v. *Pearson* (1857) 6 H.L. Cas. 61 at 106: 'In construing statutes', he said, 'the grammatical and ordinary sense of the words is to be adhered to'; in others words, the literal rule is to
15 be applied. This is how a lawyer takes his first look at an enactment; but perforce, for such is often the case, Lord Wensleydale went on to say if this approach proves unsatisfactory as leading to 'some *absurdity*, or some *repugnancy* or *inconsistency*
20 with the rest of (the statute)' then 'the grammatical and ordinary sense of words may be modified *so as to avoid that absurdity and inconsistency, but not further*'. This is the so-called 'Golden Rule': be strict in interpretation, but modify the construction
25 where essential so as to avoid absurdity or inconsistency. How, then, is such modification to be approached?

**iii   Consider the whole enactment** – If the use of the 'Golden Rule' leads to the conclusion that the
30 words under consideration produce absurdity, repetitiveness, inconsistency or redundancy the next thing the lawyer must do is to look at the whole of the enactment in question. For what seems absurd or redundant as it stands may take on
35 meaning in the light of the whole context.

**iv   The history of the enactment** – The word 'history' is here used in a double sense. In the first sense it signifies the *genesis* of the enactment itself: its progress through Parliament and the debates
40 and discussions which produced it. Nothing would, perhaps, seem more sensible than that the courts should consider these things in order to discover the true intention of the legislators. But, though travaux préparatoires are freely referred to in
45 European courts (though not, it seems, in the Court of Justice of the European Communities itself), the rule at present is that the 'history' in this sense may *not* be referred to; and the main argument in favour of this is that debates are two or many-sided affairs
50 from which no sure indication can be gained. Hansard[1] is thus not to be cited.

A second sense of the word 'history' in this context signifies the *background* against which the statute is passed. This may include, for instance, a
55 previous series of enactments in the same field as the Act to be interpreted (often, misleadingly, called the 'parliamentary history' of the enactment) and it may also include such matters as the general social, political and legal background prevailing at
60 the time of the passing of the Act. It *is* permissible and generally desirable for the court to consider the 'history' in these senses; though a House of Lords decision has emphasized that in interpreting a consolidating statute (one which brings together a
65 series of previous enactments), unless the word or phrase in the consolidating enactment is ambiguous, there is to be no recourse to the statutes consolidated.

1. *Hansard* is the name of the official report of debates in the UK Parliament.

Philip S. James, *Introduction to English Law*

## C   Reading for detail and language study

### 1   *Sentence structure: expressing purpose*

a) Study this phrase from lines 20–22 of the text:

[When the application of the literal rule leads to absurdity . . .] 'the grammatical and ordinary sense of words may be modified *so as to avoid that absurdity*'
Can the grammatical and ordinary sense of words be modified? In what circumstances? For what *reason* or *purpose*?

b) The phrase 'so as to avoid absurdity' expresses the *purpose* of the first action – that is the reason for doing that action. It is called a 'purpose clause'.

| so as + infinitive with 'to' |

Find another example of this type of purpose clause in Section ii of the text.
Find an example of a different type of purpose clause in Section iv of the text.
In each case decide: what is the main action? What is the purpose of the action?
Apart from the form '*so as to*', what other type of purpose clause did you find?
Do you know any other ways of expressing purpose?
● If so, give an example using information from the text.

## 2  *Obligation and possibility: further study*

The text describes in detail what the courts *must* and *can* do when interpreting legislation, e.g. the courts must first apply the literal rule of interpretation.

i) What other expressions do you know with the same meaning as 'must' and 'can'? To recall some of the language of obligation and possibility, refer again to your table from Unit Two, pages 48–9.

ii) What different forms are used in the text on page 85 to say what the courts *must* and *must not* or *can* and *cannot* do? Scan the text and note all the examples you can find.

● iii) Add any new forms to your table from pages 48–9.

## 3  *Contextual deduction*

In these statements from the text, the *phrases in italics* (called 'context clues') can help you to understand the meaning of the words in CAPITALS. Use the context clues in italics to decide what the words in capitals probably mean.

*Example:*  Here we may CITE *Lord Wensleydale in Grey v. Pearson*: 'In construing statutes', *he said*

*Answer:*  The words Lord Wensleydale spoke in a case are given here. We may CITE Lord Wensleydale = we may *give Lord Wensleydale's words*.

*Probable meaning:* CITE = to give someone's exact words.

a) The word '*history*' . . . signifies *the genesis of the enactment* itself: *its progress through Parliament* and *the debates and discussions which produced it* . . . But, though TRAVAUX PREPARATOIRES *are freely referred to in European courts* . . . the rule at present [*in the UK*] is that the '*history*' in this sense may not be referred to. . . .

b) . . . in interpreting a CONSOLIDATING STATUTE (*one which brings together a*
● *series of enactments*), there is to be no recourse to the statutes consolidated.

## 4  *Word Study: Section One*

a) What do you suppose 'the *cardinal* rule' (line 1) means?
b) Do you suppose 'prima facie' (line 2) means *always* or *first*?
c) Find the word which means '*in this way*'.
d) Things are *consistent* when they have a regular form or pattern and do not contradict.
Which related noun in this section means '*contradiction*' or '*irregular pattern*'?

Does a similar word exist in your language? If so, is it a true cognate or a false friend?

e) Which noun is closely related to the verb '*to construe*'? What does it mean?

f) A *strict construction* (line 8) means an exact literal interpretation.

● Which phrase in Section i means the opposite?


## 5  Reading for detail

Read the text carefully and answer the following questions.

a) Must the courts always first construe the words of a statute in their ordinary, literal and grammatical meaning?

b) Can the courts construe the words differently if their literal interpretation leads to a wrong result?

c) What can the courts do if the literal interpretation of the words is absurd or ambiguous?

d) What is the 'golden rule' of interpretation?

e) Can the court consider the words of one section of a statute in the context of the whole statute?

f) Can the UK courts use parliamentary discussion (from debates when the Act was passed) to help them construe a statute?

g) Can the Court of Justice of the European Communities do this (see f)?

h) Can European courts in general do this (see f)?

i) Can the UK courts consider the political background to the Act they must interpret?

j) Can the UK courts consider previous enactments on the same subject when
● interpreting a later Act of Parliament?


## 6  Oral practice

You have read some of the main rules of statutory interpretation in English law.

▲ Form pairs. Each choose two different rules of statutory interpretation from page 85.

■ ▲ Use the text and your answers to exercises B1 and C5 to decide:

◆ What exactly do the rules consist of?

◆ When are the rules applied?

◆ Are there any exceptions to the rules?

■ When you are ready, describe the main rules of English statutory interpretation. To practise speaking, say your answers out loud, or record them on tape, then listen to your recording. If you prefer, write your answers down.

▲ When you are ready, work with your partner and in turns describe the main rules of English statutory interpretation.


## D  Development

## 1  Interpreting the words of a statute

To help and guide the courts, modern statutes often include an interpretation section with definitions of words and expressions used in the statute. The courts must use the definitions in the interpretation section to construe those words when applying the statute. The Public Order Act 1986 is an example. Part of the Act is reproduced on page 88. Complete the following activities.

i) The Public Order Act was passed in order to abolish some old common-law and statutory offences and to create new offences. From its name, what kind of situations do you think the Act deals with?

ii) Scan the extracts from the Act below to find seven words and phrases whose meaning is defined in the interpretation sections of the Act. Do not read the definitions yet. Write the seven words on a separate piece of paper.

iii) Do any of the seven words and phrases confirm or change your ideas from i) above?

iv) In fact, the purpose of the Act is to prevent and control all situations of public violence, including racial violence and violence at sporting events such as football matches.

*Without* reading the definitions of the seven words given in the Act, decide what you think their literal meaning is. Where necessary, use a dictionary to help you.

*Example:* you may think a 'public assembly' is an assembly of people in a public place, or an assembly which the public can go to.

▲ Compare your ideas with two or three other members of the class.

v) Read the definitions in Sections 16, 17 and 29 of the Act below. Which of your definitions are similar? Are any completely different? In general, what do you notice about the definitions in the Act?

▲ Discuss your findings in small groups.

vi) Read the Act carefully and decide:
   a) Is a political meeting of 200 people in the town square a 'public assembly'?
   b) And if the same meeting is held in an old theatre?
   c) Is a road a 'public place'?
   d) Is a football stadium a 'public place' when a match is played?
   e) Is hatred of the Welsh (people from Wales) 'racial hatred'?
   f) And hatred of a group of French visitors on holiday in Britain?
   g) If three people live in a tent, is it a 'dwelling'?
   h) Is a garage for the car, attached to the family home, a 'dwelling'?
   i) How must the courts construe the word 'recording'?
   j) Is a poster 'written material'?

---

## ELIZABETH II

## PUBLIC ORDER ACT 1986

1986 CHAPTER 64

BE IT ENACTED by the Queen's most Excellent Majesty, by and with the advice and consent of the
5 Lords Spiritual and Temporal, and Commons, in this present Parliament assembled, and by the authority of the same, as follows:–

PART II INTERPRETATION.

16. In this Part–
10 'public assembly' means an assembly of 20 or more persons in a public place which is wholly or partly open to the air;

'public place' means–
   (*a*) any highway, or in Scotland any road
15 within the meaning of the Roads (Scotland) Act 1984, and
   (*b*) any place to which at the material time the public or any section of the public has access, on payment or otherwise, as of right or by virtue of
20 express or implied permission;

'public procession' means a procession in a public place.

PART III MEANING OF 'RACIAL HATRED'.
17. In this Part 'racial hatred' means hatred against
25 a group of persons in Great Britain defined by reference to colour, race, nationality (including citizenship) or ethnic or national origins.

29. In this Part–
'dwelling' means any structure or part of a structure
30 occupied as a person's home or other living accommodation (whether the occupation is separate or shared with others) but does not include any part not so occupied, and for this purpose 'structure' includes a tent, caravan, vehicle, ves-
35 sel or other temporary or movable structure;

'recording' has the meaning given by section 21(2), and 'play' and 'show', and related expressions, in relation to a recording, shall be construed in accordance with that provision;

40 'written material' includes any sign or other visible representation.

## 2   Discuss and compare

*On the Continent:* statutes contain general principles of law rather than very small detail.

To construe legislation, courts look at the general intent or purpose of the legislator, and the spirit of the statute, rather than only the literal sense of the words used.

▲ ■     i)   Choose A, and B or C.

▲            Work in pairs. Choose either A, B or C.

| A | Statutory interpretation in the English legal system |
| B | Statutory interpretation in your legal system |
| C | Statutory interpretation in Continental legal systems |

Think about each of the following discussion points for the legal system(s) you have chosen. Use information from this book and your own knowledge and ideas. Prepare to explain and discuss your ideas, taking notes if you like.

◆     What is the basic style of interpretation in the legal system(s) you have chosen?

◆     What are some of the main rules of interpretation?

◆     How do you think this style of interpretation influences relationships within the legal system (e.g. between judge-made law and statute law, between the judiciary and legislature)?

◆     What advantages do you think this method of interpretation has?

◆     Can you see any disadvantages?

▲     ii)   Form groups of 3–6 in which the different members have prepared at least two of A, B and C.

▲ ■     Explain your answers to the questions in i) above, comparing statutory interpretation in the different legal systems. Which method of statutory interpretation do you prefer?

▲          Discuss your ideas in the group, then compare your decision with the rest of the class.

■          For oral practice, say your answers out loud, or record them on tape, then listen to your recording. Alternatively, you may wish to write your ideas down.

## 3   Techniques for storing vocabulary

i)   What do you do when you meet new English words that you want to remember? Do you write them in a special place? What other information do you write? (For instance, a translation, an example?) Do you mark the words on the text you are reading?

Does your system work – do you find that you can in fact remember most of the words after a few days, weeks, months or years?

▲          Compare your vocabulary habits with other members of the class.

ii)   Here is one idea for storing vocabulary.

You need a small piece of paper or card for each word or phrase.

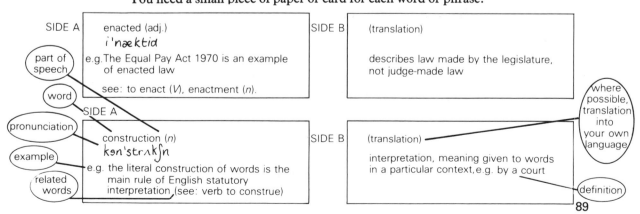

*Instructions*

(1) If possible, make your cards at the end of a lesson or period of study or during the next 24 hours.

(2) Choose words and expressions you have just studied that you personally want to remember.

(3) Use a dictionary, the glossary, text and exercises in this book to find the information you need to make your cards.

(4) Use the cards to test and exercise your memory in two ways:
     look at side A, remember side B / look at side B, remember side A.

(5) Mix the cards so that your memory does not depend on the order of the words. Repeat step (4). As you work, take out the cards you already know, continue with the ones you still find it difficult to remember, until you know all the words by heart.

(6) Repeat step (5) at regular intervals, so that you will remember the words permanently.

Suggested intervals are:
the next day
a week later
a month later
6 months later

> You can carry the cards in your bag or pocket and do this anywhere in just a few minutes. Your collection of cards and vocabulary will grow rapidly!

iii) Make some cards now, choosing words from Section One of this Unit. Do the same after each period you spend studying Section Two. At the end of Section Two you will learn more ways to use the cards to consolidate your vocabulary. *Then* decide if you like the system. At the end of this Unit, you may decide that you prefer your own personal system of storing vocabulary. In any case, here are some points to note:

● Be methodical – any system which works is good

● Always write vocabulary in a special, separate place

● Give full information about each word, including at least one example

● Spend time memorising the words – if not, you will quickly forget most of them

● Revise them at regular intervals (e.g. 24 hours, a week, a month, six months) – if not you will forget most of them before long

● Read as much as you can in English – this is the best way to learn and consolidate vocabulary.

## Section Two: EC Law

### Reading a Case

### A Before you read

*Think about the subject*

■ i) Think about each of points A, B and C below. Make notes of your ideas if you like.

▲ In pairs, choose one of points A, B and C below. Think about your ideas alone, then discuss them with your partner.

A In Section One of this Unit you learnt about the English style of statutory interpretation, and compared this with Continental legal systems and your legal system. See Exercise D 2, page 89.

● What is the basic difference between statutory interpretation in the UK and most European legal systems?

- In two situations the UK courts must use the Continental style of interpretation:
  in construing European Conventions adopted by the UK;
  in construing the EC Treaties and secondary legislation enacted by EC bodies.
  Do you think the UK courts might find this difficult? Give reasons.

B  The purpose of Articles 30–37 EEC is to allow completely free trade between Member States. In the case of *Henn v. Darby* [1978] 2 C.M.L.R. 688, the English Court of Appeal found that the phrase 'quantitative restrictions' in Article 30 EEC did not refer to the *total* exclusion of products, but only to their exclusion *in part*. This interpretation was wrong.

- Why do you suppose the Court of Appeal construed 'quantitative restrictions' in this way? To help you answer, use a dictionary, and think about the English style of interpretation.
- Why do you suppose the construction was wrong? Think about the European style of interpretation.
- What does the example illustrate?

C  What happens when provisions of EC law conflict with national law?
  Under the EC Treaties, Community law is supreme, but under the English doctrine of parliamentary sovereignty, the UK Parliament is supreme and has absolute power to pass any law it wants. In Unit Two you learnt that it cannot pass a law which binds future Parliaments, and in fact a later law is always supreme over an earlier one.

- What exactly is the problem? Can you see a solution?
- Does your country belong to the EC, or another similar international organisation?
- If so, does the same problem exist? How has it been solved?

ii) Compare your ideas with the ones in the key.

Form groups in which the different members have studied each of points A, B and C above.

In turns, explain the problem you have studied to other members of the group and discuss your answers. Then compare your ideas with the ones in the key.

## B  Reading for rapid information and understanding the organisation of themes in a text

You are going to read part of the judgment of an English court case. The judgment is the process of reasoning by which the court arrives at a decision in a particular case and the decision itself.

## 1  Reading for rapid information (suggested time: 2–3 minutes)

Scan the whole text on pages 92–3 to find the following information about the case as quickly as you can. Do not try to read the whole text for this activity.

a) The name of the case
b) Two different courts which heard the case
c) The names of the judges who heard the case in the English court
d) If the case involved a man or a woman
e) The UK Acts of Parliament referred to

f) The Article of the EEC Treaty referred to in the case
g) If all the English judges agreed on the decision
h) The exact date of the final judgment

1
# Macarthys Ltd v Smith
## (Case 129/79)

COURT OF JUSTICE OF THE EUROPEAN COMMUNITIES
JUDGES KUTSCHER (PRESIDENT), O'KEEFFE, TOUFFAIT (PRESIDENTS OF CHAMBERS), MERTENS DE WILMARS,
5  PESCATORE, LORD MACKENZIE STUART, BOSCO, KOOPMANS, DUE
30th JANUARY, 28th FEBRUARY, 27th MARCH 1980

COURT OF APPEAL, CIVIL DIVISION
LORD DENNING MR, LAWTON AND CUMMING-BRUCE LJJ
17th APRIL 1980

10  *Employment – Equality of treatment of men and women – Like work – Comparison of woman's work with duties of former male employee – Substantial interval between respective employments – Whether comparison restricted to comparing woman's work with that of man in contemporaneous employment – Equal Pay Act 1970 (as amended by the Sex Discrimination Act 1975), s 1(2)(a)(i) – EEC Treaty, art 119.*

*Costs – Order for costs – Action concerned with construction of legislation – United Kingdom law inconsistent
15  with EEC law – Litigant arguing case on basis of meaning of United Kingdom law – Whether litigant required to have regard to EEC law – Whether litigant required to pay costs of action when United Kingdom law on which he relied is struck down as being inconsistent with EEC law.*

**LORD DENNING MR.** Although this application is only about costs, I will say a word about it; because it is of public importance.
20    The applicant, Mrs Wendy Smith, was employed by wholesale dealers in pharmaceutical products. She was paid a salary of £50 a week. She discovered that a man (who had left) had previously been performing her task. He had been paid £60 a week. She took proceedings under our English statute, the Equal Pay Act 1970 (as amended by the Sex Discrimination Act 1975). She claimed that her pay should be equal to his. An objection was taken that her application was bad in point of law, because our English statute did not apply in the the case of
25  successive employment, and it only applied when the man and the woman were employed together at the same time contemporaneously.
    That point was argued before this court. The majority of the court held that the objection was well founded. They interpreted it as meaning that the equal pay provisions only applied when the man and the woman were employed at the same time contemporaneously. But then the point arose: what was the position under
30  Community law? We were referred to art 119 of the EEC Treaty. The Court of Justice of the European Communities sitting at Luxembourg had decided that art 119 of the Treaty was directly applicable in the national courts of each country. It was submitted that under art 119 there was no requirement that the man and the woman should be employed contemporaneously at the same time, and that, under that article, the woman was entitled to equal pay even though the man had left before she joined and the woman had taken his job
35  afterwards.
    The majority of this court felt that art 119 was uncertain. So this court referred the problem to the European Court at Luxembourg. We have now been provided with the decision of that court. It is important now to declare, and it must be made plain, that the provisions of art 119 of the EEC Treaty take priority over anything in our English statute on equal pay which is inconsistent with art 119. That priority is given by our own law. It is
40  given by the European Communities Act 1972 itself. Community law is now part of our law; and, whenever there is any inconsistency, Community law has priority. It is not supplanting English law. It is part of our law which overrides any other part which is inconsistent with it. I turn therefore to the decision given by the European Court. The answer they gave was that the man and the woman need not be employed at the same time. The woman is entitled to equal pay for equal work, even when the woman is employed after the man has left.
45  That interpretation must now be given by all the courts in England. It will apply in this case and in any such case hereafter.
    Applying it in this case, the applicant was right. Although she was employed subsequently to the man, she was entitled to be paid the same as the man. She was entitled to be paid not £50, but £60. That is the result of the Community law as applied to our present law. So that must be the decision.
50    The appeal that the employers brought to this court must therefore be dismissed.
    The argument before us today was as to costs. It was argued before us that at the hearing before the tribunals, and indeed before this court, the employers were entitled to look solely to our English statute on equal pay. It was said that, in that statute, our parliamentary draftsmen thought they were carrying out, and intended to carry

55 out, the provisions of the EEC Treaty. So much so that, before the European Court at Luxembourg, the United Kingdom government argued that, in order for the woman to be entitled to equal pay, her employment had to be contemporaneous. Accordingly the employers said that they were entitled to go by the English statute, and not the EEC Treaty, and so the costs should not fall on them of the appeal to this court.

The answer is this: the employers had no right to look at our English statute alone. They ought throughout to have looked at the EEC Treaty as well. Community law is part of our law by our own statute, the European
60 Communities Act 1972. In applying it, we should regard it in the same way as if we found an inconsistency between two English Acts of Parliament; and the court had to decide which had to be given priority. In such a case the party who loses has to pay the costs. So it seems to me that the employers should pay all the costs of the appeal to this court.

**LAWTON LJ.** I agree.

65 **CUMMING-BRUCE LJ.** I agree. I would only add a word in view of that fact that counsel for the applicant has drawn the attention of this court to the existence of a note by Professor Hood Phillips in the Law Quarterly Review ((1980) 96 LQR 31) which apparently expressed the view that the decision of this court has created a doubt about the constitutional position arising from a conflict between an English statute and European law. In my view there is no real room for doubt, and, if anything that I said in my judgment has given rise to doubt
70 which is based on misunderstanding, I repeat what I said on the last occasion, that 'If the terms of the Treaty are adjudged in Luxembourg to be inconsistent with the provisions of the Equal Pay Act 1970, European law will prevail over that municipal legislation'. I went on to say this: 'But such a judgment in Luxembourg cannot affect the meaning of the English statute' (see [1979] 3 All ER 325 at 335–336).

Perhaps I expressed myself a little too widely there. The majority in this court took the view that there was no
75 ambiguity about the words of the Equal Pay Act 1970 which we had to construe; and, as there was no ambiguity, the majority took the view that it was not appropriate, according to English canons of construction, to look outside the statute at art 119 as an aid to construction. In my view that was clearly right, but I would make it clear that had I been of the view that there was an ambiguity in the English statute, I would have taken the view that it was appropriate to look at art 119 in order to assist in resolving the ambiguity.
80 I only add those words because of the doubt which has arisen in the article in the Law Quarterly Review.

*Appeal dismissed.*

Solicitors: *Baileys, Shaw & Gillett* (for the employers); *John L Williams* (for the applicant).

Sumra Green    Barrister.

Case 129/79 *Macarthys Ltd v. Smith* [1981] 1 All ER 111

## 2    Understanding the organisation of themes in the text

Do not read the case in detail. Quickly skim the text to find the following sections and make a note of them, using line numbers:
*Example:* the summary in note form of the issues involved in the case
*Answer:* lines 10–17.
a)    the summary of the facts of the case
b)    two sections of the text which discuss what happens when UK and EC law conflict
c)    two sections of the text which give Lord Denning's decision in this case
d)    the section in which Cumming-Bruce LJ discusses the interpretation of English statutes

## 3    Read the relevant sections of the text to find the two main practical issues in the case.
● What do you think is the most interesting legal issue?

**4** From exercises 1,2, and 3, how much do you know now about *Macarthys Ltd v. Smith?*

## 5 Abbreviations

In the title of the case *Macarthys Ltd v. Smith, v.* is an abbreviation for *versus.*
What do you think it means? This word is often used in a completely different context
from the law – do you know which one?
Find the abbreviations in the text used for:
a) Limited (a type of company)
b) Master of the Rolls (the President of the Civil Division of the Court of Appeal – the
   most important civil judge in England outside the House of Lords)
c) Lord Justice [of Appeal] (the title given to an ordinary Court of Appeal judge)
d) Lords Justices [of Appeal] (plural form of c)
e) All England Law Reports (one of the main collections of law reports of English cases
   – like all the law reports it is a private publication – there is no official edition).

## C  Language study and reading for detail

### 1 Word-building

Study the words from the text in the column on the left below. Write all the words in the
same family, prefixes and suffixes you know in the your notebook, and use this
information to decide what you think each word might mean. Then check your ideas by
looking at the word in context in the text, before referring to the key.

| | Word from the text | Related words, prefixes, suffixes | Possible meaning |
|---|---|---|---|
| a) | uncertain (adj) 36 | *un- certain* | *not certain, not sure* |
| b) | applicant (n) 20,47,65 | *to apply, application, -ant* | |
| c) | requirement (n) 32 | | |
| d) | inconsistent (adj) 39,42 | | |
| e) | whenever (adv) 40 | | |
| f) | overrides (v) 42 | | |
| g) | hereafter (adv) 46 | | |
| h) | costs (n) 57,62 | | |
| i) | parliamentary draftsmen (n) 53 | | |
| j) | misunderstanding (n) 70 | | |

### 2 Contextual deduction

i) Study the words and phrases below in their context in the text and decide what
   you think each one probably means. Which information in the text helps you to
   decide?

   a) she took proceedings (line 22)      f) dismissed (50, 81)
   b) she claimed (23)                    g) as to (51)
   c) successive employment (25)          h) hearing (51)
   d) held (27)                           i) party (62)
   e) was entitled to (33–4, 47–8, 48)    j) will prevail over (71–2)
      is entitled to (44)                 k) solicitors (82)

ii) Choose the correct form of one of the words or phrases from i) to complete the following sentences. Use each word or phrase *once* only.

*Example:* In cases of conflict, EC law _prevails over_ national law.

a) Poor people in England _____ free legal advice and help called 'Legal Aid'.
b) Mrs Adams _____ against the man who broke her car windows.
c) The _____ is at Winchester Crown Court on Tuesday March 23rd.
d) The two _____ to the case have not spoken to each other since the incident.
● e) The applicant _____ that his employer had broken the law.

## 3  Reading for detail

Read the parts of the text containing the answers to the following questions carefully:

a) Why did Mrs Smith take proceedings against her employers?
b) What was the position under English law?
c) Why did the English court refer the case to the European Court of Justice?
d) What was the decision of the European Court on the interpretation of Article 119?
e) In what way did national law and EEC law conflict?
f) Did the Court of Appeal apply European law (Article 119 EEC) or national law (Equal Pay Act 1970)? Why?
g) What secondary issue of the case did the court decide on 17 April 1980?
h) Why did the losing party claim that they should *not* pay costs?
● i) What was the Court's decision on this issue?

## 4  The passive: further study

i) In Unit Two you studied the passive form, e.g. Mrs Smith *was employed* by Macarthy's Ltd. If necessary, refer again to Unit Two, page 39, to see how the passive is formed.

Study these phrases from the text:

(1) 'the man and woman *need not be employed* at the same time' (line 43)
(2) 'that interpretation *must now be given* by all the courts in England' (line 45)

How are these two examples different in form from the one above (Mrs Smith *was employed*)?

In these passive phrases the modal verbs *need* and *must* express the extra ideas of *necessity* and *obligation*. When a modal verb (NEED, MUST, CAN, MIGHT, SHOULD, etc.) is used in the passive form, the construction is:

| *Modal verb* | + *be* (infinitive) | + *Main verb* (past participle) |
| --- | --- | --- |
| must | be | given |
| need (not) | be | employed |
| ought to | be | done |

Use *by* if you want to say who did the action, e.g. by all the courts in England (example (2) above).

ii) Scan the text to find three more examples of modal passives. Check that you understand them.

iii) First identify the modal verbs in the sentences below. What is the object of the active phrase? Then transform each active phrase into the passive:

*Example:* In applying [Community law] we should regard it in the same way as if

we found an inconsistency between two English Acts of Parliament. (lines 60–61)
*Answer:* In applying Community law it should be regarded in the same way as if we found an inconsistency between two English Acts of Parliament.
  a)  In such a case the party who loses has to pay the costs. (61–2)
  b)  The employers should pay all the costs of the appeal to this court. (62–3)
  c)  But such a judgment in Luxembourg cannot affect the meaning of the English statute. (72–3)
  d)  The majority in this court took the view that there was no ambiguity about the words of the Equal Pay Act 1970 which we had to construe. (74–5)

## 5  Adjectives: positive and negative forms

i)  Complete the table by giving the missing positive or negative form of each adjective. You will find some of the missing words in the text. What different negative prefixes do you notice (e.g. *un*certain)?
    Can you think of other examples of each type of negative?
    When you have finished, complete the phrase in ii) by choosing the best *negative* adjective from your table.

| Positive adjective | Negative adjective |
|---|---|
| applicable | *inapplicable* |
| *certain* | uncertain |
|  | inconsistent |
| appropriate |  |
|  | illegal |
| lawful |  |
|  | invalid |
| ambiguous |  |
| relevant |  |
|  | unsatisfactory |

ii)  *Example:* When the meaning of EC law is __*uncertain*__ national courts can ask the European Court of Justice for help in interpretation.
  a)  The man accused the police officer of _____ arrest.
  b)  If the words of a statute are _____, the court must construe them literally.
  c)  Don't forget it's _____ to park your car on double yellow lines in England.
  d)  When a UK statute is _____ with EC law, EC law prevails.
  e)  The Equal Pay Act is _____ when a woman is paid less than another woman in the same job.

## 6  Oral practice

i)  Use these cues to describe the facts and decision in *Macarthys*:
    *Facts:*    applicant worked for Macarthys Ltd / £50 a week / man before / £60 a week
    *UK law:*   Equal Pay Act 1970/ Sex Discrimination Act 1975/ not employed at same time
    *EEC law:* Art. 119 EC / directly applicable / interpretation uncertain / referred to European Court of Justice / EC and UK law inconsistent

*Decision:* EC law prevails / applicant right / £60 a week / employers pay costs.

Start like this: 'In the case of *Macarthys Ltd v. Smith* the applicant, Mrs Smith, worked for Macarthys Ltd for £50 a week. She found out that . . .'.

ii) Choose A or B:

A  Ms Jones is paid £120 a week. Mr Adams is paid £150 a week.
Both work for Industrial Holdings Ltd now and do the same work.

B  Ms Felps was paid £160 a week. Mr Wilson is paid £145 a week.
Ms Felps left her job at Brain and Co. a month ago.
Mr Wilson is now employed to do the same job there.

iii) Imagine the facts and decision of the case you have chosen in detail, and write simple cues as in i) above, of the *Facts, UK law, EEC law* and *Decision*. You will find all the legal information you need in the text and in your answers to the comprehension exercises.

■  iv) Use your cues from iii) to describe the facts and decision in the case you have
●      chosen, then refer to the key to check your decision and legal reasoning.
▲      Work in pairs with someone who has not prepared the same case as you. In turns, use your cues to describe the facts and decision in each case. Do you agree with your partner's legal reasoning? When you have finished, check your decisions in
●      the key.

## D  Development

*1*  If you have not already done so, finish making vocabulary cards for all the law terms in Section Two of this Unit which you want to remember, following the instructions on page 90.

## *2  Storing vocabulary*

i)  Divide all the vocabulary cards you have made during this Unit into three general groups:
- words and phrases related to *Legal action, The courts*, etc.
- words and phrases related to *UK and EC law, Parliament, Legislation*, etc.
- other words and phrases.

ii)  One useful way to store vocabulary which will also help you to remember words better is to arrange them in logical categories or groups. You can use your vocabulary cards (or vocabulary lists) to create categories of words in this way and consolidate your knowledge of vocabulary on a particular subject which interests you.

You may prefer to:
- sort and store your vocabulary cards in groups of related words;
- copy groups of related words from your vocabulary cards or lists on to simple lists and tables of your own like the ones on page 89 of this book;
- create vocabulary networks like the ones in iii) which show a group of words on a particular subject and the relationship between them.

iii)  Study and complete vocabulary networks (1) and (2) on page 98. This activity will help you to store and remember words you have learnt in this Unit. There is no *one* correct solution to the networks.

▲      When you have finished, compare and discuss your networks with other members of the class.

■●      When you have finished, compare your networks with the ones in the key.
NETWORK (1) Choose a suitable word or phrase from the list overleaf for each space:

1. Appeal   2. The court held that . . .   3. Party   4. Tribunals   5. He was entitled to . . . 6. Counsel   7. Judge   8. European Court of Justice   9. Versus (*Macarthys Ltd v. Smith*)   10. Litigant   11. She took proceedings against . . .

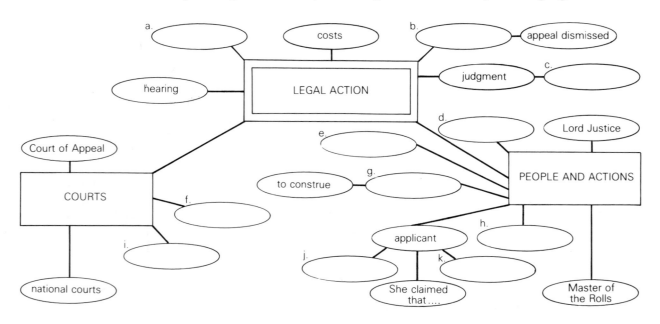

NETWORK (2)  Use your vocabulary cards or lists or the texts from this Unit to complete the network by putting a suitable word or phrase at the end of each line as in the example.

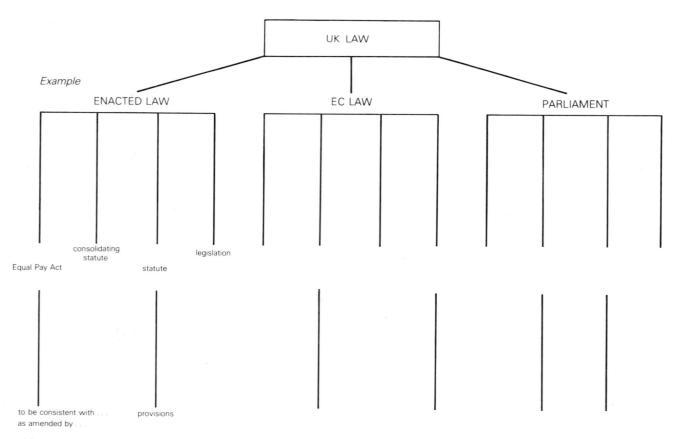

### 3   Discussion points

Use the text of *Macarthys Ltd v. Smith* and your own knowledge to decide the following.

◆ For what reason did Lord Denning hold that EC law prevails over UK law?

◆ Is his decision consistent with the doctrine of parliamentary sovereignty?

◆ Did Lord Justice Cumming-Bruce agree with Lord Denning about the supremacy of EC law?

◆ The Court of Appeal had two alternatives:
   ● to use the EEC Treaty to help interpret the English Equal Pay Act
   ● to look at the meaning of the Equal Pay Act and the EEC Treaty quite separately.
   Which alternative did they choose? In your opinion, why?

■ For practice in speaking, say your answers out loud. If you prefer, write your ideas down.

▲ Discuss your answers in small groups before exchanging your ideas with the rest of the class.

■ ▲ ● Confirm your ideas in the key.

# The Judicial System

## Section One: The Courts

Reading Works of Legal Reference

### A Before you read

*1* Before you read about the English courts, think about your own judicial system:
- How is the administration of justice organised in your country?
- Are there separate jurisdictions for different areas of law (e.g. public and private)?
- What is the relationship between the different courts?
- What is the role and position of judges and other lawyers in your country?

▲ Discuss your ideas with other members of the class.

*2* You have already learnt many words in this book relating to the judicial system.
i) Use the glossary to check that you remember the meaning of all the words in the vocabulary network below. Then put the following headings in the correct spaces marked A–E.

● (1) Criminal law   (2) The judiciary   (3) The courts   (4) Civil law   (5) The case

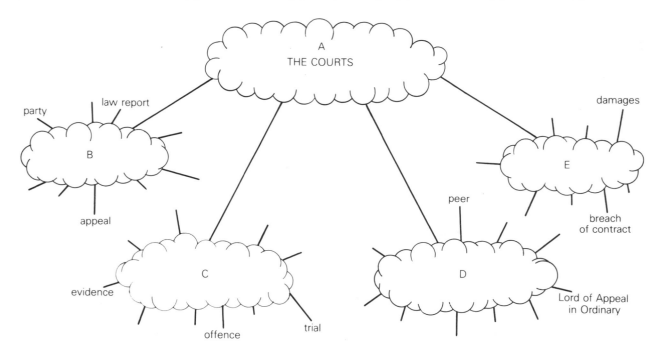

ii) Continue the network yourself with other words and phrases that you know on this subject. You may wish to refer to Units One, Two and Five for some ideas.

▲    Compare your work with other members of the class.

## B    First reading: understanding the general content of the text

*1*    The text on pages 101–2 describes judicial organisation in England and Wales. Quickly skim the text and give each paragraph (A, B, C, etc.) a suitable heading. Suggested time: 3 minutes.
*Example*: suitable headings for paragraph A are:
'Jurisdiction of the House of Lords' or 'The House of Lords'.
Look for key words and phrases to help you decide the main subject of each paragraph, but do *not* try to read every word or understand the whole text for this
●    activity.

## *2    Reformulating information in the text: completing a diagram*

Read the text in more detail and complete the diagram on page 102, which shows the hierarchy and jurisdiction of the Courts in England and Wales, in your notebooks. Write the name of each court in the correct box as in the example and indicate which are inferior and superior courts. Do *not* worry about words and phrases you don't
●    know or understand if you can complete this activity.

*3*    Which words from the vocabulary network on page 100 did you find in the text?

---

1         *Judicial organization*
A    *Superior courts*. The highest court is the House of
     Lords, which exercises the judicial function of
     Parliament. In theory appeal to the House of
5    Lords is an appeal to the whole House but in
     practice, particularly since the Appellate
     Jurisdiction Act, 1876, created a group of salaried
     life peers, the Lords of Appeal in Ordinary, or
     'law lords', there is an established convention
10   dating from 1844 that lay peers do not
     participate in judicial sittings of the House.
     Appeals are referred to an Appellate Committee
     of the House. By that Act an appeal must be
     heard by at least three of the Lord Chancellor,
15   the Lords of Appeal in Ordinary, and such peers
     as hold or have held high judicial office. The
     House has almost entirely appellate jurisdiction
     only, in civil and criminal cases from the Courts
     of Appeal in England and in Northern Ireland
20   and in civil cases only from the Court of Session
     in Scotland.
B        The Court of Appeal sits in both civil and
     criminal divisions. The Civil division hears
     appeals from the High Court, county courts, the
25   Restrictive Practices court, certain special courts,
     and certain tribunals, such as the Lands Tribunal.
     The Criminal division hears appeals by persons
     convicted on indictment in the Crown Courts.
C        The High Court in its civil jurisdiction is
30   divided into three Divisions (Queen's Bench,

     Chancery, and Family (formerly Probate,
     Divorce and Admiralty)) to each of which certain
     kinds of cases are assigned. Divisional courts
     (q.v.) of each of the divisions, consisting of two
35   or more judges, have limited appellate
     jurisdiction in certain cases. The main civil
     jurisdiction is exercised by single judges hearing
     cases of the kind appropriate to the divisions to
     which the judges belong.
D 40     The criminal jurisdiction of the High Court is
     exercised exclusively by the Queen's Bench
     Division. A divisional court of two or three
     judges of that Division deals with appeals from a
     Crown Court and magistrates' courts, and also
45   exercises the supervisory jurisdiction of the court,
     issuing the prerogative writ of habeas corpus and
     to ensure that magistrates' courts and inferior
     tribunals exercise their power properly, by
     granting orders of mandamus, prohibition and
50   *certiorari*.
E        The Crown Court, created in 1972, replaces the
     former assizes and quarter sessions. It exercises
     criminal jurisdiction and sittings are held
     regularly at major towns throughout England and
55   Wales. It comprises judges of the Queen's Bench
     Division of the High Court, circuit judges and
     Recorders (part-time judges). They sit singly with
     juries trying persons charged on indictment with
     crimes. A judge of the Crown Court sits with two
60   to four justices of the peace to hear appeals

---

from magistrates' courts and proceedings on committal by magistrates to the Crown Court for sentence.

**F** The Central Criminal Court, known as the Old
65 Bailey, is a sitting of the Crown Court, having criminal jurisdiction only, over indictable offences committed in Greater London or on the high seas. The court consists of *ex officio* judges and in practice consists of judges of the Queen's
70 Bench Division, the Recorder of London, the Common Serjeant, and certain additional judges of the Central Criminal Court.

**G** *Inferior courts.* County courts have exclusively civil jurisdiction, which is limited in extent and in
75 area, and which is entirely statutory. The judges are persons who also hold office as Circuit judges of the Crown Court.

**H** Magistrates' courts consist of a stipendiary magistrate or of from two to seven (usually two
80 or three) lay justices of the peace; a single lay justice has a very limited jurisdiction. Magistrates' courts have civil jurisdiction in relation to certain debts, licences, and domestic proceedings. In the exercise of criminal
85 jurisdiction one or more justices may sit as examining magistrates to conduct a preliminary investigation into an indictable offence. A magistrates' court may try summarily many minor statutory offences, and also certain
90 offences if the prosecutor applies for the case to be heard summarily, the court agrees it is a suitable mode of trial and the defendant does not elect jury trial. Cases may be appealed to the Crown Court or defendants remitted for
95 sentence to the Crown Court.

David M. Walker, *The Oxford Companion to Law*

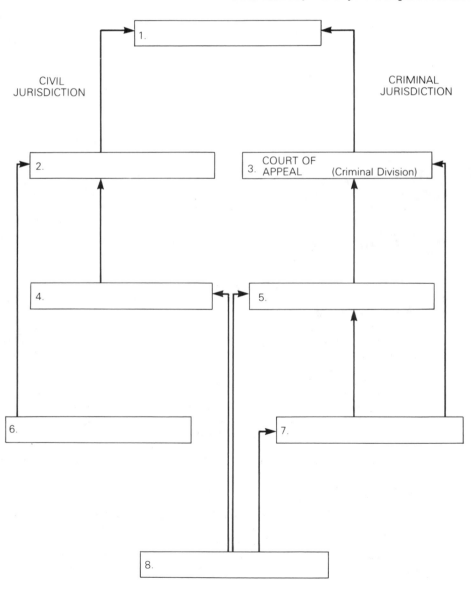

1.

CIVIL JURISDICTION        CRIMINAL JURISDICTION

2.        3. COURT OF APPEAL        (Criminal Division)

4.        5.

6.        7.

8.

Courts of England
and Wales

## 4   Reading for general understanding

Use your completed diagram to answer these questions:
a)   What are the two main areas of jurisdiction of English courts?
b)   Which courts exercise jurisdiction in both areas?
c)   Which are the superior courts in England and Wales?
d)   Which is the final court of appeal?
e)   Which Division of the High Court has criminal jurisdiction?
f)   What is the maximum number of appeals in a civil case?
g)   And in a criminal case?
h)   Do the county courts hear all civil cases?

## C   Language study and reading for detail

### 1   Dictionary use – choosing the right word

i)   Do you use a dictionary to help you study English?
What kind of dictionary do you use? Is it monolingual (all in English) or bilingual (with translations into another language)?
What do you use it for (to find the meaning of a word, to check the meaning of a word, to check spelling or grammar)?
Do you like using the dictionary? How useful do you find it?
Do you have any problems using it, or find any disadvantages?
Compare your dictionary habits with other members of the class.

ii)   You know that some words, like *body*, *office* and *authority* have several different meanings depending on the context. Other words, like *cost* and *judge*, have more than one grammatical function (they are both verbs and nouns). When you look a word up in the dictionary you will find a list of all its different meanings and functions. Learning to choose the correct definition from the list is therefore an important vocabulary skill.
Look at the boxed words in the text on pages 101–2. If possible decide what you think each word means here: use cognates, word-families, logical reasoning and the context to help you decide. Even if you have no idea what the word means, decide if it is a verb, adjective, noun, etc. This will make it easier for you to choose the correct dictionary definition for each word later.

iii)   Choose the correct definition for each word from the following extracts from *The Oxford Advanced Learner's Dictionary*. First choose the correct definition for *sittings* (lines 11, 53, 65), then compare your answer with the example below.

*Example:* sittings (11, 53) has the meaning given in definition 1 (time during which a court of law is sitting continuously). But note that sitting (65) does not have any of the meanings given in this dictionary. What do you think it means? What does this teach you about using a dictionary?

---

**hear** /hɪə(r)/ *v* (*pt, pp* **heard** /hɜːd/) **1** [I, Tn, Tng, Tnɪ] perceive (sounds) with the ears: *She doesn't/ can't hear very well*, ie is rather deaf. ○ *We listened but could hear nothing.* ○ *Have you ever heard that song sung in Italian?* ○ *I heard someone laughing.* ○ *Did you hear him go out?* ○ *He was heard to groan.* **2** [Tn, Tw] listen or pay attention to (sb/sth): *You're not to go — do you hear me!* ○ *We'd better hear what they have to say.* ⇨Usage at FEEL¹. **3** [Tn] listen to and try (a case) in a lawcourt: *The court heard the evidence.* ○ *Which judge will hear the case?* **4** [I, Tn, Tf] be told or informed about (sth): *You sing very well, I hear.* ○ *Have you heard the news?* ○ *I heard (that) he was ill.* ○ *I've heard (say) that it's a good film.* **5** [Tn] grant (a prayer). **6** (idm) **,hear!** '**hear!** (used to express agreement and approval). **hear/see the last of sb/sth** ⇨

LAST¹. **hear a 'pin drop** hear the slightest noise: *The audience was so quiet you could have heard a pin drop.* **hear tell of sth** hear people talking about sth: *I've often heard tell of such things.* **listen to/hear reason** ⇨ REASON. **make one's voice heard** ⇨ VOICE. **not/never hear the end of sth** not be finished with sth as the subject of discussion or matter that affects one: *If we don't give her what she wants we'll never hear the end of it.* **7** (phr v) **hear about sth** be given information about sth: *I've only just heard about his dismissal.* ○ *You will hear about this* (ie will receive a formal rebuke about it) *later.* **hear from sb** receive a letter, telephone call, etc from sb: *How often do you hear from your sister?* **hear of sb/sth** be told about or have knowledge of sb/sth: *I've never heard of the place.* ○ *She disappeared and was never heard of*

*again.* **not hear of sth** (usu with *will* or *would*) refuse to allow sth: *He wouldn't hear of my walking home alone.* ○ *I can't let you pay my debts — I won't hear of such a thing.* **hear sb out** listen until sb has finished saying what he wants to say: *I know you don't believe me but please hear me out!*
▷ **hearer** /ˈhɪərə(r)/ *n* person who hears sth, esp a member of an audience.

**in·dict** /ɪnˈdaɪt/ *v* [Tn, Tn·pr] ~ **sb** (**for sth**) (*law*) accuse sb officially (of sth); charge sb: *He was indicted for murder/on three counts of murder.*
▷ **in·dict·able** *adj* for which one may be indicted: *indictable offences*, ie that may be tried by a jury.
**in·dict·ment** *n* **1** [C] (**a**) ~ (**against sb**) written statement that indicts sb: *bring in an indictment against sb.* (**b**) ~ **of sb/sth** (*fig*) reason for

---

condemning sb/sth: *The rise in delinquency is an indictment of our society and its values.* **2** [U] indicting or being indicted.

**jury** /ˈdʒʊərɪ/ *n* [CGp] **1** group of people in a lawcourt who have been chosen to listen to the facts in a case and to decide whether the accused person is guilty or not guilty: *Seven men and five women sat on* (ie were members of) *the jury.* ○ *The jury returned a verdict of* (ie reached a decision that the accused was) *not guilty.* ○ *The jury is/are still out,* ie Members of the jury are still thinking about their decision. ○ *trial by jury.* **2** group of people chosen to decide the winner or winners in a competition: *The jury is/are about to announce the winners.*

□ **ˈjury-box** *n* enclosure where a jury sits in a court.

**juryman** /ˈdʒʊərɪmən/ *n* (*fem* **jurywoman** /ˈdʒʊərɪwʊmən/) member of a jury.

**just·ice** /ˈdʒʌstɪs/ *n* **1** [U] (a) right and fair behaviour or treatment: *laws based on the principles of justice* ○ *efforts to achieve complete social justice.* (b) quality of being reasonable or fair: *He demanded, with some justice, that he should be given an opportunity to express his views.* **2** [U] the law and its administration: *a court of justice* ○ *a miscarriage of justice,* ie a wrong legal decision. **3 Justice** [C] (used as a title of a High Court Judge): *Mr Justice Smith.* **4** [C] (*US*) judge of a lawcourt. **5** (idm) **bring sb to ˈjustice** arrest, try and sentence (a criminal). **ˌdo oneself ˈjustice** behave in a way that is worthy of one's abilities: *He didn't do himself justice in the exams,* ie did not perform as well as he was capable of doing. **do justice to sb/sth** (a) recognize the true value of sb/sth; treat sb/sth fairly: *To do her justice, we must admit that she did deserve to win.* ○ *The photograph does not do full justice to* (ie does not truly reproduce) *the rich colours of the gardens.* (b) deal with sb/sth adequately: *Since we'd already eaten, we couldn't do justice to her cooking,* ie could not eat all the food she had cooked.

□ **ˌJustice of the ˈPeace** (*abbr* **JP**) person who judges less serious cases in a local lawcourt; magistrate.

**lay¹** /leɪ/ *v* (*pt, pp* **laid** /leɪd/)

► PLACING SOMETHING IN A CERTAIN POSITION OR ON A SURFACE **1** (a) [Tn·pr, Tn·p, Cn·a] put (sth/sb) in a certain position or on a surface: *lay the book on the table* ○ *lay the blanket over the sleeping child* ○ *lay oneself down to sleep* ○ *He laid his hand on my shoulder.* ○ *The horse laid back its ears.* ○ *The storm laid the crops flat.* (b) [Tn, Tn·pr] put (sth) in the correct position for a particular purpose: *lay a carpet, cable, pipe* ○ *lay the foundations of a house* ○ *lay the table,* ie put plates, cutlery, etc on it for a meal ○ *A bricklayer lays bricks to make a wall.* ○ *They are laying new sewers along the road.* **2** [Tn, Tn·pr] ~ A (on/over B); ~ B with A spread sth (on sth); cover or coat sth with sth: *lay the paint evenly* ○ *lay straw everywhere* ○ *lay carpeting on the floor/lay the floor with carpeting.* ⇨Usage at LIE².

► CAUSING SOMEBODY OR SOMETHING TO BE IN A CERTAIN STATE **3** [Tn·pr] (*fml*) cause (sb/sth) to be in a certain state or situation: *lay sb under an obligation* (ie oblige sb) *to do sth* ○ *lay new laws before parliament.* **4** [Tn] cause (sth) to settle: *sprinkle water to lay the dust.* **5** [Tn] make (sth) smooth or flat: *using hair cream to lay the hair sticking up at the back.* **6** [Tn] (*fml*) cause (sth) to be less strong; allay: *lay sb's fears, doubts, suspicions, etc.*

► OTHER MEANINGS **7** [Tn, Tn·pr, Dn·n, Dn·f no passive] ~ **sth (on sth)** bet (money) on sth; place (a bet): *gamblers laying their stakes in roulette* ○ *How much did you lay on that race?* ○ *I'll lay you £5 that she won't come.* **8** [Tn esp passive] (⚠ *sl*) (of a man) have sexual intercourse with (a woman): *get laid.* **9** [I, Tn] (of birds, insects, etc) produce (eggs): *The hens are not laying well* (ie not producing many eggs) *at the moment.* ○ *The cuckoo lays its eggs in other birds' nests.* ○ *new-laid eggs at 90p a dozen.* **10** (in some combinations of *lay* + *n* + *prep*/infinitive, having the same meaning as a *v* related in form to the *n*, eg *lay the emphasis on certain points* = *emphasize certain points*): *lay stress on neatness,* ie stress it ○ *Who should we lay the blame on?* ie Who should we blame? ○ *lay (one's) plans* (ie plan) *to do sth* ○ *lay a trap for* (ie prepare to trap) *sb.* **11** (idm) **lay it ˈon (ˈthick/ with a ˈtrowel)** (*infml*) use exaggerated praise, flattery, etc: *To call him a genius is laying it on a bit (too thick)!* (For other idioms containing **lay**, see entries for *ns, adjs,* etc, eg **lay one's hands on sb/sth** ⇨ HAND¹; **lay sth bare** ⇨ BARE¹.)

**12** (phr v) **lay aˈbout one (with sth)** hit out in all directions: *As we approached her, she laid about her with a stick.* **lay about sb/sth (with sth)** attack sb/sth with words or blows: *She laid about him, calling him a liar and a cheat.*

**lay sth aside** (*fml*) (a) put sth aside: *I laid my book aside, turned off the light and went to sleep.* (b) abandon sth; give sth up: *lay aside one's studies, one's responsibilities.* (c) (also **lay sth by**) keep sth for future use; save sth: *lay some money aside for one's old age.*

**lay sth away** (*US*) pay a deposit on sth to reserve it until full payment is made.

**lay sth down** (a) store (wine) in a cellar, etc: *lay down claret.* (b) (begin to) build sth: *lay down a new ship, railway track.* (c) (*fml*) cease to perform sth; give sth up: *lay down one's office, duties.* **lay sth down; lay it ˈdown that...** give sth as a rule, principle, etc; establish: *You can't lay down hard and fast rules.* ○ *It is laid down that all applicants must sit a written exam.*

**lay sth in** provide oneself with a stock of sth: *lay in food, coal, supplies, etc.*

**lay into sb/sth** (*infml*) attack sb/sth violently, with words or blows: *He really laid into her, saying she was arrogant and unfeeling.*

**lay ˈoff (sb)** (*infml*) stop doing sth that irritates, annoys, etc: *Lay off! You're messing up my hair!* ○ *Lay off him! Can't you see he's badly hurt?* **lay ˈoff (sth)** (*infml*) stop doing or using sth harmful, etc: *I've smoked cigarettes for years, but now I'm going to lay off (them).* ○ *You must lay off alcohol for a while.* **lay sb ˈoff** dismiss (workers), usu for a short time: *They were laid off because of the lack of new orders.*

**lay sth ˈon** (a) supply (gas, water, etc) for a house, etc: *We can't move in until the electricity has been laid on.* (b) (*infml*) provide sth; arrange sth: *lay on a party, show, trip* ○ *lay on food and drink* ○ *Sightseeing tours are laid on for visitors.*

**lay sb ˈout** knock sb unconscious: *The boxer was laid out in the fifth round.* **lay sth ˈout** (a) spread sth out ready for use or to be seen easily: *beautiful jewellery laid out in the shop window* ○ *Please lay out all the clothes you want to take on holiday.* (b) (often passive) arrange sth in a planned way: *lay out a town, garden* ○ *a well laid out magazine.* (c) (*infml*) spend (money): *I had to lay out a fortune on that car.* (d) prepare (a corpse) for burial.

**lay ˈover** (*US*) stop at a place on a journey: *We laid over in Arizona on the way to California.* Cf STOP OVER (STOP¹).

**lay sb ˈup** (usu passive) cause sb to stay in bed, not be able to work, etc: *She's laid up with a broken leg.* ○ *I've been laid up with flu for a week.* **lay sth up** (a) save sth; store sth: *lay up supplies, fuel, etc.* (b) put (a vehicle, ship, etc) out of use: *lay a ship up for repairs* ○ *My car's laid up at the moment.* **lay sth up (for oneself)** ensure by what one does or fails to do that one will have trouble in the future: *You're only laying up trouble (for yourself) by not mending that roof now.*

▷ **lay** *n* (⚠ *sl esp sexist*) partner in sexual intercourse (esp a woman): *an easy lay,* ie a person who is ready and willing to have sexual intercourse.

□ **ˈlayaway** *n* [U] (*US*) system of reserving goods by putting a deposit on them until full payment is made: *She buys her Xmas presents on layaway.*

**ˈlay-off** *n* (a) dismissal of a worker, usu for a short time: *many lay-offs among factory workers.* (b) period of this: *a long lay-off over the winter.*

**ˈlayout** *n* way in which the parts of sth are arranged according to a plan: *the layout of rooms in a building* ○ *a magazine's attractive new page layout.*

**ˈlay-over** *n* (*US*) short stop on a journey. Cf STOPOVER (STOP¹).

**lay²** /leɪ/ *adj* [attrib] **1** not belonging to the clergy: *a lay preacher.* **2** (a) not having expert knowledge of a subject: *lay opinion* ○ *speaking as a lay person.* (b) not professionally qualified, esp in law or medicine.

□ **ˈlayman** /-mən/ *n* (*pl* **-men** /-mən/) **1** person who does not have an expert knowledge of a subject: *a book written for professionals and laymen alike.* **2** Church member who is not a clergyman or priest.

**lay³** /leɪ/ *n* (*arch*) poem that was written to be sung; ballad.

**lay⁴** *pt* of LIE².

**ma·gis·trate** /ˈmædʒɪstreɪt/ *n* official who acts as a judge in the lowest courts; Justice of the Peace: *The Magistrates' Courts* ○ *come up before the magistrate.*

▷ **ma·gis·tracy** /ˈmædʒɪstrəsɪ/ *n* **1** [C] position of a magistrate. **2 the magistracy** [Gp] magistrates as a group: *He's been elected to the magistracy.*

**pro·ceed** /prəˈsiːd, prəʊ-/ *v* **1** (a) [I, Ipr, It] ~ **(to sth)** go to a further or the next stage; go on: *Work is proceeding slowly.* ○ *What is the best way of proceeding?* ○ *Let us proceed (to the next item on the agenda).* ○ *Having said how much she liked it, she then proceeded to criticize the way I'd done it.* (b) [Ipr] (*fml*) make one's way; go: *I was proceeding along the High Street in a northerly direction when....* (c) [I, Ipr] ~ **(with sth)** begin or continue (sth): *Please proceed with your report.* ○ *Shall we proceed with the planned investment?* **2** [Ipr] ~ **against sb** (*law*) take legal action against sb; start a lawsuit against sb. **3** [Ipr] ~ **from sth** (*fml*) arise or originate from sth: *the evils that proceed from war.* **4** [Ipr] ~ **to sth** (*fml*) go on to obtain a higher university degree after obtaining a first degree: *He was allowed to proceed to an MA.*

**pro·ceed·ings** /prəˈsiːdɪŋz/ *n* [pl] **1** ~ **(against sb/for sth)** lawsuit: *start proceedings (against sb) for divorce* ○ *institute divorce proceedings.* **2** what takes place, esp at a meeting, ceremony, etc: *The proceedings will begin with a speech to welcome the guests.* ○ *The proceedings were interrupted by the fire alarm.* **3** ~ **(of sth)** (published) report or record of a discussion, meeting, conference, etc; minutes: *His paper was published in the proceedings of the Kent Archaeological Society.*

**sen·tence** /ˈsentəns/ *n* **1** [C] (*grammar*) largest unit of grammar, usu containing a subject, a verb, an object, etc and expressing a statement, question or command. **2** [C, U] (*law*) (statement of the) punishment given by a lawcourt: *The judge passed/pronounced sentence (on the prisoner),* ie said what his punishment would be. ○ *She has served her sentence, and will now be released.* ○ *under sentence of death,* ie to be officially killed as a punishment ○ *a sentence of ten years' imprisonment.*

▷ **sen·tence** *v* [Tn, Tn·pr, Dn·t] ~ **sb (to sth)** state that sb is to have a certain punishment: *sentence a thief to six months' imprisonment* ○ *He has been sentenced to pay a fine of £1000.* ○ (*fig*) *a crippling disease which sentenced him to a lifetime in a wheel-chair.*

**sit** /sɪt/ *v* (-tt-; *pt, pp* **sat** /sæt/) **1** (a) [I, Ipr, Ip] be in a position in which the body is upright and resting on the buttocks, either on a seat or on the ground: *Never stand when you can sit.* ○ *Are you sitting comfortably?* ○ *sit on a chair, on the floor, in an armchair, etc* ○ *sit at (a) table to eat* ○ *sit on a horse.* (b) [I, Ip, Tn, Tn·p] ~ **(sb) (down)**; ~ **oneself down** (cause sb to) take up such a position; place (sb) in a sitting position: *She sat (down) on the chair and took her shoes off.* ○ *He lifted the child and sat* (ie seated) *her on the wall.* ○ *Sit yourself down and tell us what happened.* ○ (*fig*) *We must sit down together and settle our differences.* **2** [I, Ipr] ~ **(for sb)** pose for a portrait: *I sat every day for a week until the painting was finished.* ○ *sit for a famous painter.* **3** [I] (of a parliament, lawcourt, committee, etc) hold a meeting: *The House of Commons was still sitting at 3 am.* **4** [I, Ipr] (a) (of birds) perch: *a sparrow sitting on a branch.* (b) (of certain animals, esp dogs) rest with the hind legs bent and the rear end on the ground: *'Sit!' she told the dog.* **5** [I] (of birds) stay on the nest to hatch eggs: *The hen sits for most of the day.* **6** [I, Ipr] ~ **(on sb)** (usu followed by an *adv*) (of clothes) fit the body well: *a dress that sits well, loosely, etc on sb* ○ *The coat sits badly across the shoulders.* ○ (*fig*) *His new-found prosperity sits well on him,* ie suits him well. **7** [Ipr] be in a certain position; lie: *The book's still sitting on my shelf,* ie I haven't read it. ○ *The farm sits on top of the hill.* **8** [Ipr, Tn] ~ **(for) sth** be a candidate for (an examination): *sit (for) an exam/a test* ○ *sit for a scholarship.* **9** (idm) **sit at**

sb's 'feet be sb's pupil or follower: *She sat at the feet of Freud himself.* **sit in 'judgement (on/over sb)** judge sb, esp when one has no right to do so: *How dare you sit in judgement on me?* **sit on the 'fence** hesitate or fail to decide between two opposite courses of action, sets of beliefs, etc. **sit on one's 'hands** do nothing: *Are you going to sit on your hands while she does all the work?* **a ,sitting 'duck** person or thing that is an easy target, or is easy to attack: *Without my gun, I'm a sitting duck for any terrorist.* **,sitting 'pretty** (*infml*) in a fortunate situation, esp when others are unlucky: *I was properly insured so I'm sitting pretty.* **,sit 'tight (a)** remain where one is: *All the others ran away, but I sat tight.* **(b)** refuse to take action, yield, etc: *She threatened us with dismissal if we didn't agree, but we all sat tight.* **sit 'up (and take notice)** (*infml*) suddenly start paying attention to what is happening, being said, etc: *I called her a damned hypocrite and that made her sit up.* ○ *This news made us all sit up and take notice.*

**10** (phr v) **sit around** spend one's time sitting down, unwilling or unable to do anything: *I've been sitting around waiting for the phone to ring all day.* **sit back (a)** settle oneself comfortably back, eg in a chair: *I sat back and enjoyed a cup of tea.* **(b)** relax after working; do nothing: *I like to sit back and rest in the evenings.* ○ *Are you going to sit back and let me do everything?*

**sit down under sth** (*fml*) suffer (insults, etc) without protest or complaint: *He should not sit down under these accusations.*

**sit for sth** (no passive) (*Brit*) be the Member of Parliament for (a constituency): *I sit for Bristol West.*

**sit in** occupy (part of) a building as a protest: *The workers are sitting in against the factory closures.* **sit in on sth** attend (a discussion, etc) as an observer, not as a participant: *The teachers allowed a pupil to sit in on their meeting.*

**sit on sth (a)** (no passive) be a member of (a committee, jury, etc): *How many people sit on the commission?* **(b)** (*infml*) fail to deal with sth: *They have been sitting on my application for a month.* **sit on sb** stop sb's bad or awkward behaviour: *I have to sit on the class when they get too rowdy.* ○ *She thinks she knows everything, and needs sitting on.* **sit out** sit outdoors: *The garden's so lovely, I think I'll sit out.* **sit sth out (a)** stay to the end of (a performance, etc): *sit out a boring play.* **(b)** not take part in (a particular dance): *I think I'll sit out the rumba.*

**sit through sth** remain in a theatre, etc from the beginning to the end of (a performance, etc): *I can't sit through six hours of Wagner!*

**sit up (for sb)** not go to bed until later than the usual time, esp because one is waiting for sb: *I shall get back late, so don't sit up (for me).* ○ *The nurse sat up with the patient all night.* ○ *We sat up late watching a film on TV.* **sit (sb) up** (cause sb to) move to an upright position after lying flat, slouching, etc: *The patient is well enough to sit up*

in bed now. ○ *We sat the baby up to feed her.* ○ *Sit up straight!* Cf SIT UP (AND TAKE NOTICE).

☐ **'sit-down** *n* **1** (also **,sit-down 'strike**) strike in which workers occupy a factory, etc until their demands are considered or met. **2** [attrib] (of a meal) served to people sitting down: *a sit-down lunch.*

**'sit-in** *n* protest made by sitting in: *a sit-in at the city council offices.*

**,sitting 'member** (*Brit*) candidate at a general election who holds the seat until the next election is called.

**'sitting-room** *n* (*esp Brit*) = LIVING-ROOM (LIVING²).

**,sitting 'tenant** tenant who is actually occupying a flat, house, etc: *It's difficult to sell a house with a sitting tenant.*

[▷ **sum·mary** *adj* [usu attrib] **1** (*sometimes derog*) done or given immediately, without attention to details or formal procedure: *summary justice, punishment, methods* ○ *Such an offence will lead to a summary fine.* **2** giving the main points only; brief: *a summary account of a long debate.* **sum·mar·ily** /'sʌmərəlɪ; *US* sə'merəlɪ/ *adv*: *summarily dismissed.*

**sum·mar·ize, -ise** /'sʌməraɪz/ *v* [I, Tn] be or make a summary of (sth): *a talk summarizing recent trends in philosophy.*

## 2   Word study

i)   Which nouns that you already know are related to the adjectives on the left and what do the phrases on the right mean?
*Example:*   judicial       (1) judicial function (line 3)
*Answer:*    *judicial* is related to *judge.* The judicial function is the function of a person or body acting as a judge. In the text it refers to the function of the House of Lords as a court, not as a legislative body.

   a)  appellate     (1) Appellate Committee (line 12)
                     (2) appellate jurisdiction (17)
   b)  divisional    (1) divisional court (33, 42)
   c)  statutory     (1) statutory jurisdiction (74–5)
                     (2) statutory offences (89)

ii)  The adjective *domestic* refers to the home and family. What do you suppose domestic proceedings (lines 83–4) are?

iii) Answer the questions below, then use your dictionary to check.
   a)  The person who starts criminal proceedings (usually in the name of the Crown) is called the *prosecutor* (line 90). Find the name for *the person accused of a crime* used in lines 87–95 of the text.
   b)  In line 93 of the text do you think the verb *elect* has its usual meaning – *to choose by vote*?
   c)  Does the verb *to try* have its usual meaning in lines 58 and 88?
       Find the related noun in paragraph H. What do you think it means?

iv)  A special part of the work of the Queen's Bench Division of the High Court is the judicial review of administrative action – the court has the power to make sure that the acts and decisions of inferior courts, tribunals and administrative bodies are legal and valid.
   a)  Which lines of the text describe this part of the court's jurisdiction?
   b)  Find the names of four special orders the court can make as part of this jurisdiction. Use your dictionary if necessary.

## 3 Reading for detail

Read the text carefully and decide if the following statements are *true* or *false:*

*Example:* When the House of Lords sits as a court, it only hears appeals.

*Answer:* False. (The House of Lords has 'almost entirely' appellate jurisdiction (line 17), *not* entirely.)

a) When the House of Lords sits as a court (not a legislative body) only peers who are senior members of the judiciary can take part in the proceedings.

b) The House of Lords is the final court of appeal for civil and criminal cases in the UK.

c) The three Divisions of the High Court each hear different kinds of cases.

d) The Queen's Bench Division of the High Court is responsible for judicial review of administrative action.

e) A jury is always present at Crown Court hearings.

f) The Old Bailey is the name of the Crown Court for the London area.

g) The county courts only hear cases concerning statute law.

h) All English judges and magistrates are professional lawyers.

i) The magistrates' courts hear certain categories of less important cases.

j) The magistrates' courts investigate some cases which are later tried by jury in the Crown Court.

● k) The magistrates' courts can choose to hear cases with or without a jury.

## 4 Taking Notes

i) Read the text again and pick out the most important points about each court as in the example. As you work, look up any new words which interest you in your own dictionary – remember to decide *first* what you think the word means and if it is a verb, noun, etc.

ii) Transfer the words you have chosen to your diagram on page 102. Write notes, using your own words where possible, as in the example.

1        *Judicial organization*

A   *Superior courts.* The highest court is the House of Lords, which exercises the judicial function of Parliament. In theory appeal to the House of
5   Lords is an appeal to the whole House but in practice, particularly since the Appellate Jurisdiction Act, 1876, created a group of salaried life peers, the Lords of Appeal in Ordinary, or 'law lords', there is an established convention
10   dating from 1844 that lay peers do not participate in judicial sittings of the House. Appeals are referred to an Appellate Committee of the House. By that Act an appeal must be heard by at least three of the Lord Chancellor,
15   the Lords of Appeal in Ordinary, and such peers as hold or have held high judicial office. The House has almost entirely appellate jurisdiction only, in civil and criminal cases from the Courts of Appeal in England and in Northern Ireland
20   and in civil cases only from the Court of Session in Scotland.

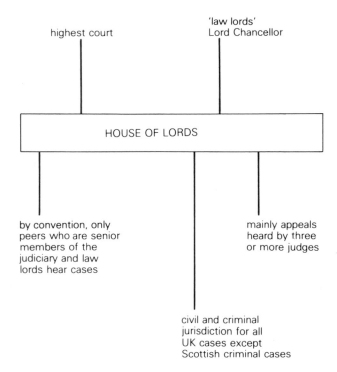

## 5   Oral practice

Use your completed diagram to describe the organisation of the courts and judiciary in England and Wales. Include the following points:
- Courts of civil and criminal jurisdiction
- The hierarchy of courts
- the role and jurisdiction of each court

▲   Work together in pairs or small groups.

## D   Development

*1*   Study the table below giving information about the judiciary in England and Wales. Each number from 1 to 10 corresponds to a piece of missing information given in the list below.
  i)   Can you complete the table by putting the missing information in the correct spaces? Number 1 has been done for you.
       *Example:*   1 / d    law lord

JUDGES

| Called | Court | Referred to as | Title | Addressed In Court | Retiring age | Salary |
|---|---|---|---|---|---|---|
| Lord of Appeal in Ordinary or *1. law lord* | House of Lords | Lord Wise | 5.<br>6. | My Lord | 75 | £69 000 |
| 2.<br><br>(appeal court judge) | 3. | Lord Justice Wise | Knighthood –<br>7. | My Lord | 75 | 9. |
| High Court Judge | High Court | Mr (or Mrs) Justice Wise | Knighthood –<br>Sir John (or Dame Jean) Wise | My Lord<br><br>My Lady | 75 | 10. |
| Circuit Judge | Crown Court or 4. | His (or Her) Honour Judge Wise QC (if a QC) | 8. | Your honour* | 72 | £40 000 |
| Recorder | Crown Court | Mr (or Mrs) Recorder Wise | None | Your honour | 72 | £191 per day |

*Judges of the Old Bailey, although strictly ordinary circuit judges, are addressed as 'My Lord'. Marcel Berlins and Clare Dyer, *The Law Machine*.

   *Missing information:*   a) Court of Appeal      b) None      c) £66 000
   d) law lord      e) County Court      f) peerage      g) Lord Justice of Appeal
   h) Lord Wise      i) £60 000      j) Sir John Wise
  ii)   What does the table tell you about the economic and social position of English judges?

*2*   If you have not already done so, make vocabulary cards for the words from this Section that you want to remember, or add them to your own personal vocabulary lists. Then complete the vocabulary network from page 100 with some of the words you have chosen.

### 3 *Discussion points*

Compare the organisation of the courts and judiciary in England and Wales, and in your own country. Choose at least two of the following points which interest you and prepare to talk about your ideas:

◆ Areas of jurisdiction of the courts
◆ Hierarchy of the courts and system of appeals
◆ Use of lay magistrates to decide less important civil and criminal cases
◆ Judicial and legislative functions of the House of Lords
◆ Social and economic position of judges
◆ Use of the jury, composed of 12 ordinary men and women, to try serious crimes (the jury decides questions of fact, the judge decides questions of law).

▲ Discuss your ideas in small groups, then exchange opinions with the whole class.

■ For practice in speaking, say your answers out loud. If possible, record them on tape, then listen to your recording. If you prefer, write some of your ideas down.

## Section Two: Judicial Precedent

### Reading a House of Lords Statement; reading works of legal reference

### A Before you read

*1* How much have you learnt about judicial precedent so far in this book?
Can you answer the following questions? If necessary, refer again to Units One and Five.

● What do you understand by the doctrine of *judicial precedent*?
● Why is judicial precedent central to the English legal system?
● What is a *binding* decision?
● In the context of case-law, what is an *authority*?

▲● Discuss your answers with other members of the class before checking in the key.
■● Check your answers in the key.

*2* In 1966 the House of Lords made a statement in which they changed the rules of precedent.
Before you read the statement, think of one or two advantages of the system of binding precedent. Can you think of any disadvantages? Copy and complete the table in your notebooks.

| *Binding precedent* | |
|---|---|
| *Advantages* | *Disadvantages* |
|  |  |

▲ Discuss and compare your tables in small groups.

## B Reading a House of Lords statement

### 1 Skimming and scanning activities

    i)  Quickly skim the statement below to find the section of the text which:
        *Example:* describes the advantages of precedent    *Answer:* lines 12–18
        a)  describes the disadvantages of precedent
        b)  explains in note form what the statement is about
        c)  gives the new rule of precedent.
    ii)  Quickly scan the statement to find out:
        a)  who read it     b)  on what date
        c)  If the statement was made by the House of Lords acting as a *judicial* or as a *legislative* body
        d)  the name of the work of legal reference which describes the binding effect of House of Lords decisions.

---

1                                *NOTE.*

*Judgment – Judicial decision as authority – Stare decisis – House of Lords – Freedom of House of Lords to depart from their previous*
5 *decisions where right to do so – Doctrine of precedent nevertheless an indispensable foundation of decisions of law.*

Before judgments were given in the House of Lords on July 26, 1966, LORD GARDINER, L.C.,
10 made the following statement on behalf of himself and the Lords of Appeal in Ordinary:

Their lordships regard the use of precedent (1) as an indispensable foundation upon which to decide what is the law and its application to
15 individual cases. It provides at least some degree of certainty upon which individuals can rely in the conduct of their affairs, as well as a basis for orderly development of legal rules.

Their lordships nevertheless recognise that
20 too rigid adherence to precedent may lead to injustice in a particular case and also unduly restrict the proper development of the law. They propose therefore to modify their present practice and, while treating former decisions of this
25 House as normally binding, to depart from a previous decision when it appears right to do so.

In this connexion they will bear in mind the danger of disturbing retrospectively the basis on which contracts, settlements of property and
30 fiscal arrangements have been entered into and also the especial need for certainty as to the criminal law.

This announcement is not intended to affect the use of precedent elsewhere than in this
35 House.

(1) As regards the binding effect of decisions of the House of Lords, see 22 HALSBURY'S LAWS (3rd Edn.) 798, 799, para. 1686; and for cases on the subject, see 30 DIGEST (Repl.) 219-221, *624-646.*

---

    *2*    Use information from the text to complete the table in activity A 2, opposite.
    ●    Were any of your own ideas the same as those in the text?

    *3*    Read the statement carefully to answer the following questions:
        Before 1966 all House of Lords decisions were binding on lower courts (the Court of Appeal and below) and on the House of Lords itself.
        a)  What is the new rule?
        b)  How does the 1966 statement change the rules of precedent (1) in the House of Lords? (2) in lower courts?
        c)  The statement says that the House of Lords will 'depart from a previous decision when it appears right to do so' (lines 25–6). Do you think this means that in future
            (1)  the House of Lords can choose not to follow a precedent in a particular case, but the previous decision remains the precedent for all other cases? *or*
            (2)  the House of Lords can choose not to follow a precedent in a particular case, and the new decision becomes the precedent for future cases?
    ●    d)  In what branches of law can the new rule create problems? Why?

## 4  Word study

a) Do you know Latin? Even today, many principles of English law are expressed in Latin. Find the Latin phrase in lines 2–7 of the text. Do you know what it means? Lawyers pronounce Latin in a special traditional way, e.g. the phrase in the text is pronounced /staːreɪ deˈsiːsɪs/.

b) In 1966 Lord Gardiner held the most important legal office in the English legal system and presided over the House of Lords. The abbreviation for the position he held is LC (line 9). What was he?

c) Which expression in the text refers to the peers who made the statement?

d) From the context decide if 'nevertheless' (lines 6, 19) means *never*, *however*, or *therefore*.

## C  Reading a work of legal reference

### 1  The binding part of a decision

i) In the extracts which follow, quickly find the Latin terms which are pronounced:
   a) /ˈdɪktə/   b) /ˈɒbɪtə ˈdɪktə/   c) /ˌreɪʃɪəʊ desɪˈdendɪ/

ii) Read the extracts and find the difference between the *ratio decidendi* and *dicta*. Which constitutes binding precedent?

iii) a)  Do *dicta* bind judges in later cases?

   b)  Which will have more influence: *obiter dicta* or judicial *dicta*?

---

1  **573. Ratio decidendi.**  The enunciation of the reason or principle upon which a question before a court has been decided is alone binding as a precedent. This underlying principle is called the ratio
5  decidendi, namely the general reasons given for the decision or the general grounds upon which it is based, detached or abstracted from the specific peculiarities of the particular case which gives rise to the decision. What constitutes binding precedent is the
10  ratio decidendi.

**574. Dicta.**  Statements which are not necessary to the decision, which go beyond the occasion and lay down a rule that it is unnecessary for the purpose in hand are generally termed 'dicta'. They have no
15  binding authority on another court, although they may have some persuasive efficacy. Mere passing remarks of a judge are known as 'obiter dicta', whilst considered enunciations of the judge's opinion on a point not arising for decision, and so not part of the
20  ratio decidendi, have been termed 'judicial dicta'.

---

Lord Hailsham, *Halsbury's Laws of England*

### 2  First reading: personal reading comprehension

The extracts on this page and the next are from *Halsbury's Laws of England*, the work of reference referred to in the 1966 House of Lords statement. The text on pages 110–11 explains in detail how the system of binding precedent operates in the English courts.

i) First read the paragraph headings *only* (e.g. paragraph **577 House of Lords decisions**) to see exactly what the text on pages 110–11 is about. Do *not* read the text yet. Which paragraph refers to High Court decisions?

---

1  **JUDICIAL DECISIONS AS AUTHORITIES**

**577. House of Lords decisions.** The decisions of the House of Lords upon questions of law are normally considered by the House to be binding upon itself,
5  but because too rigid adherence to precedent may

lead to injustice in a particular case and unduly restrict the proper development of the law the House will depart from a previous decision when it appears right to do so, although it bears in mind the danger of

---

10 disturbing retrospectively the basis upon which contracts, property settlements and fiscal arrangements
have been entered into and the especial need for
certainty as to the criminal law. When a broad principle has been clearly decided by the House, the
15 decision should not be weakened or frittered away by
fine distinctions, and an erroneous decision of the
House upon a question of law can be set right only by
Act of Parliament. A decision of the House of Lords
occasioned by members of the House being equally
20 divided is as binding on the House and on all inferior
tribunals as if it had been unanimous. Decisions of
the House of Lords are binding on every court
inferior to it.

**578. Court of Appeal decisions.** The decisions of the
25 Court of Appeal upon questions of law must be followed by Divisional Courts and courts of first
instance, and, as a general rule, are binding on the
Court of Appeal until a contrary determination has
been arrived at by the House of Lords. There are,
30 however, three, and only three, exceptions to this
rule; thus (1) the Court of Appeal is entitled and
bound to decide which of two conflicting decisions of
its own it will follow; (2) it is bound to refuse to
follow a decision of its own which, although not
35 expressly overruled, cannot, in its opinion, stand
with a decision of the House of Lords; and (3) the
Court of Appeal is not bound to follow a decision of
its own if given per incuriam. Unlike the House of
Lords, the Court of Appeal does not have liberty to
40 review its own earlier decisions.

A decision is given per incuriam when the court
has acted in ignorance of a previous decision of its
own or of a court of co-ordinate jurisdiction which
covered the case before it, in which case it must
45 decide which case to follow; or when it has acted in
ignorance of a House of Lords decision, in which
case it must follow that decision; or when the
decision is given in ignorance of the terms of a statute
or rule having statutory force.

50 In its criminal jurisdiction the Court of Appeal
applies the same principles as on the civil side, but
recognises that there are exceptions (a) where the
applicant is in prison and in the full court's opinion
wrongly so; (b) where the court thinks that the law
55 was misunderstood or misapplied; and (c) where the
full court is carrying out its duty to lay down principles and guidelines in relation to sentencing.

**579. Divisional Court decisions.** A Divisional Court
is bound by its own previous decisions, regardless of
60 how many judges are sitting, with limited exceptions
in criminal cases, subject always to the per incuriam
rule. Faced with conflicting earlier decisions the
court is free to decide which to follow. Divisional
Court decisions bind judges of first instance, even of
65 a different division, but not the Employment Appeal
Tribunal.

**585. Scottish and Irish decisions.** Decisions of the
Scottish and Irish courts are not binding upon English courts, although entitled to the highest respect.
70 On questions of principle it is desirable that the laws
of England and Scotland should be uniform and that
a decision of the House of Lords, when founded on
principle and not on authority, should be regarded as
applicable to both countries, unless the House itself
75 says otherwise. There is a well-settled practice that in
revenue and taxation matters courts of first instance
in England endeavour to keep in line with the courts
of Scotland. Further, an English court ought to follow the unanimous judgment of the higher Scottish
80 and Irish courts, where the question is one which
turns upon the construction of a statute which
extends to those countries as well as to England,
leaving it to be reviewed, if thought fit, by the appeal
court, as it is desirable that interpretations should be
85 avoided which result in one meaning in one country
and one in another.

**586. Overseas decisions.** A decision of an overseas
court in a common law country is not of course
binding on an English court, but may be useful as a
90 guide to the court to which it is cited as to what its
decision ought to be. Thus, for example, great
respect is paid to the views of eminent judges of the
United States Supreme Court and to decisions of the
highest tribunal of the State of New York. English
95 courts should be in keeping with United States courts
on carriage by sea and carriage by air, although if
English law proved to be different, effect would have
to be given to the difference, whatever the inconvenience.
100 It is desirable that the great common law jurisdictions should not differ lightly, particularly on so
universal a matter as commercial law, or the measure
of damages, or remoteness of damage, or interpretation, or privilege, or patent law.

Lord Hailsham, *Halsbury's Laws of England*

ii) You now know what the text is about in general. Before you read, write down a
few questions you hope the text will answer. This will give you a personal purpose
for reading, and will help you to read with more understanding and focus on the
points of interest to you.

iii) Read the text to find the answers to your questions from ii). Do not worry about
parts of the text you don't understand if you can complete this activity.

iv) Did you find the answers to all your questions? What other important points does
the text contain?

▲ Compare your work with other members of the class.

## 3 Language study

i) Study the following sentences from the text and decide which of the forms given in the list below means exactly the same as each phrase in italics in a) to e):
*Choose from:*
(1) need not (2) need not be followed by (3) must
(4) must be followed by (5) must follow.
*Example:* a) the Court of Appeal *is bound to* decide which of two conflicting decisions of its own it will follow (lines 31–3)
*Answer:* a / 3 must
b) the Court of Appeal *is not bound to* follow a decision of its own if given per incuriam (37–8)
c) A divisional court *is bound by* its own previous decisions (58–9)
d) Divisional Court decisions *bind* judges of first instance (63–4)
e) A decision of an overseas court *is not binding on* an English court (87–9)

ii) Notice the construction of the different types of phrase with *bind*, *binding* and *bound*:

| | | |
|---|---|---|
| to be bound TO | + infinitive | Lower courts are bound to follow House of Lords decisions |
| to be bound BY | + noun | Lower courts are bound by House of Lords decisions |
| to be binding ON | + noun | House of Lords decisions are binding on lower courts |
| to bind | + noun | House of Lords decisions bind lower courts |

● Which two pairs of sentences have exactly the same meaning and emphasis?

iii) Complete the following sentences correctly using a phrase with *bind*, *bound*, or *binding*.
Refer to **paragraph 578** of the text for the legal information you need.
a) Divisional Courts _____ by Court of Appeal decisions on questions of law.
b) In general the Court of Appeal _____ follow its own decisions.
c) A Court of Appeal decision given per incuriam _____ on the Court of Appeal in a later case.
● d) Court of Appeal decisions _____ the House of Lords.

iv) Study these phrases from the text:
An English court *ought to follow* the unanimous judgment of the higher Scottish courts (78–80)
The laws of England and Scotland *should be* uniform (70–71)
a) Are judgments of higher Scottish courts binding on an English court?
b) Must the laws of England and Scotland be uniform?
c) Scan **paragraphs 585** and **586** of the text to find some more phrases containing *should* and *ought to*.
d) Study the phrases from c) above. In what way is the meaning of the modal verbs *should* and *ought to* different from *must*, *to be bound to* and similar
● expressions of obligation?

## 4 Word study

i) Study lines 41–9 of the text. The word 'case' is repeated four times.
For each example, decide if *case* is used with its special legal meaning of a legal action or set of legal circumstances. What do you think the expression 'in which case' means?

ii) *Word families:* use your knowledge of word families to work out the probable meaning of the following words from the text. Make sure that your ideas are possible in the context before checking in the key.

    a) 'weakened' (line 15): think of the adjective *weak*; what do you suppose the related verb *to weaken* means?

    b) 'overruled' (35): when the judge *rules* in a case, s/he decides what the law is and gives judgment. What do you suppose the judge does when s/he *overrules* a previous decision?

    c) if the law is 'misunderstood' or 'misapplied' (55) do you think it is:
      (1) not understood or not applied    (2) understood or applied correctly
      (3) understood or applied wrongly
      What does the prefix *mis-* mean? Do you know any other words beginning with *mis-*?

    ● d) What do you suppose 'guidelines' (57) are?

## 5   *Reformulating a text: designing a diagram*

In Section One of this Unit, you read a text and completed a diagram showing the main points of the text in visual form. Like taking notes, reformulating a text in this way both helps you to understand and shows understanding of the text.

i) Read the text on pages 110–11 again and make a note of the main points.

ii) Using information from the text, design your own diagram to show how the doctrine of binding precedent operates in the English judicial system. Concentrate on the main points of the text only. Your diagram should include the operation of precedent in the House of Lords, the Court of Appeal, the High Court and lower courts, and the effect of Scottish, Irish and overseas decisions on the courts of England and Wales.

▲ When you have finished, compare your work with other members of the class.

■● When you have finished, compare your diagram with the one in the key.

## 6   *Cognates and false friends*

i) Study the sections of the text containing the words in italics in the exercise below and decide which of the two definitions which follow is correct in the context.
In each case, does a similar word exist in your language? If so, decide whether it is a true cognate or a false friend in this context.
*Example:* The court has acted in *ignorance* of a previous decision (lines 41–2)
(1) the court didn't know about a previous decision
(2) the court knew about a previous decision, but chose not to follow it.
    *Answer:* definition (1) is correct.
    Is *ignorance* similar to a word in your language? If so, does it have the same meaning?

a) the *proper* development of the law (line 7)
    (1) the typical, characteristic development of the law
    (2) the correct, appropriate development of the law.

b) fiscal *arrangements* (11)
    (1) agreements, accords relating to tax payments
    (2) plans, preparations relating to tax payments.

c) an *erroneous* decision (16)
    (1) a wrong decision
    (2) a decision which is not precise or exact

    d) a contrary *determination* (28)
      (1) a contrary decision
      (2) a contrary definition
    e) *sentencing* (57)
      (1) deciding the punishment for a crime, e.g. a sum of money, a certain period in prison
      (2) giving judgment in a case: deciding if the defendant is right or wrong and why.
    f) *patent* law (105)
      (1) the law relating to licences and permits
●       (2) the law relating to the exclusive right to make and sell an invention

  ii) Which verbs are closely related to the italicised nouns in b), d), e) and f) above?
    E.g.  b) *arrangements* (noun)    Answer: *to arrange* (verb)

 iii) Complete the following sentences with a suitable word from exercises i) or ii) above:
    *Example:* _*Ignorance*_ of the law is no defence.
    a) The designer immediately applied for a _____ for the new model he had created.
    b) The court _____ that the defendant was in breach of his obligations.
    c) The _____ remedy for breach of contract is often an order of specific performance.
●     d) The judge _____ the murderer to life imprisonment.

## 7  *Oral practice*

Use your diagram to describe how the doctrine of binding precedent operates in the English judicial system. Include the following points:
- Decisions of the English superior courts
- Decisions of Scottish and Irish courts
- Overseas decisions.

▲ Work together in pairs or small groups, and in turns describe precedent in each court.

## D   Development

### 1  *Applying the doctrine of binding precedent*

Use your diagram and the text to solve the following practical problems:
a) If the House of Lords follows its own precedent in the present case (concerning the law of property) the result will not be just. Is it bound to follow the precedent or not?
b) The House of Lords has reached a wrong decision on a question of law. Can it overrule the decision in a later case?
c) The House of Lords has reached a decision which the Court of Appeal does not consider just. Is the Court of Appeal bound by the House of Lords authority in a later case?
d) There are two previous authorities for the present case before the Civil Division of the Court of Appeal – a Court of Appeal precedent and a conflicting House of Lords precedent. Which authority binds the court?
e) Two previous, but conflicting Court of Appeal decisions exist. In the present case, the Civil Division of the Court of Appeal would prefer to follow the earlier decision. Can it do so?
f) The Court of Appeal decides that if it follows a precedent of its own, the result in the present case will be unjust. Can it depart from its previous decision?

g) The members of the Court of Appeal agree that they did not apply the law correctly in a previous case. Must they follow the precedent in the present case?

h) The first hearing of a civil case takes place at the County Court. Must the court follow a precedent of the Family Division of the High Court?

i) The first hearing of a criminal case takes place at the Crown Court. Is the court bound by a Court of Appeal precedent?

j) In a previous case, a Scottish superior court has interpreted a statute which is applicable in all the UK. Is the English High Court bound to construe the statute in the same way?

● k) Is the English Court of Appeal bound to follow a decision of the US Supreme Court concerning patent law?


*2* Design and complete your own vocabulary network on the subject of the judicial system. Use vocabulary from the whole of this Unit and include other words and phrases you knew before, too. See the networks on pages 100 and 102 for some ideas about design.


*3* *Discussion points*

Think about the following points for a few minutes and prepare to talk about them:

◆ In your legal system, do some judicial decisions bind or influence courts in future cases? If so, in what circumstances? How important is precedent in your judicial system?

◆ Compare the use of judicial precedent in the English judicial system and in your country.

■ To practise speaking, talk about your ideas. If possible, record them on tape. If you prefer to practise writing, write some of your ideas down.

▲ Compare and discuss your ideas with other members of the class.

# Private Law – Contract

Reading the Judgment of an English Court Case

## Section One: The facts of the Case; the Defence

### A  Before you read

*1*  You are going to read part of the judgment of an English court case which created an important precedent in the law of contract. Judgments of superior courts which contain decisions or 'rulings' on important questions of law, like *Carlill v. Carbolic Smoke Ball Co.*, are published in the law reports. It is because decisions are recorded in this way that the English case-law system, based on the doctrine of binding precedent, can operate.

  i)  Before you read, write a list of some vocabulary (about 10 words or phrases) that you think you might find in a text of this type.

■    If necessary, use a dictionary to find the terms that you need in English.

▲    If necessary use other members of the class, your teacher or a dictionary to find the terms you need in English, then compare your list with the rest of the class.

  ii) Use your knowledge of word families to continue your list: e.g. if you have written the noun *appeal*, you could add the verb *to appeal*, and the related noun *appellant*.

*2*  Did your list include any of these words, which appear in the text? Try to match each word to the correct definition.

|   |   |   |   |
|---|---|---|---|
| 1 | plaintiff | a. | the first hearing of a case, not an appeal |
| 2 | defendant | b. | money given as legal compensation |
| 3 | to hold | c | to reject, or not accept an appeal |
| 4 | to be entitled | d | a person who brings [i.e. starts] an action in civil law |
| 5 | to dismiss an appeal | e | to have a right to something |
| 6 | to sue | f | to decide in legal proceedings |
| 7 | case of first instance | g | a person who defends a civil or criminal action |
| 8 | to deliver judgment | h | to take legal action against someone in a civil case |
| 9 | damages | i | to give a judicial decision |

### 3  Abbreviations

a)  Look at the title of the case. Do you understand the abbreviations: v. and Co.?

b)  [1893] 1 Q.B. 256 is the reference number of this case in the law reports: it is reported in volume 1 of the Q.B. law reports for the year 1893 at page 256. Q.B. refers to the series of law reports (the Queen's Bench law reports) in which the case was reported, NOT the court in which it was heard. It was heard in the Court of Appeal.

●   c)   What information does the title of the case give you *without* looking *at* the case?

## B   First reading: understanding the contents and organisation of the text

*1*   The first part of the case, which is reproduced on pages 117–18, contains five main elements:
   i)   legal principles decided in the case
   ii)   the facts of the case
   iii)   decision in the case of first instance
   iv)   first judge's decision in the appeal
   v)   second judge's decision and judgment in the appeal: arguments for the defendant.
   Skim the text and divide it clearly into these five sections, so that you can see exactly how the material is organised. *Do not* try to read the text in detail or
●   understand everything you read for this activity.

*2*   Look at the development of the text. Why do you think the case *starts* by stating the
●   legal principles decided in the case?

*3*   Scan the text to find four other abbreviations: what do they mean?

---

### Carlill v. Carbolic Smoke Ball Co.
### [1893] 1 Q.B. 256

An offer, to be capable of acceptance, must involve a definite promise by the offeror that he
5   will bind himself if the exact terms specified by him are accepted.

An offer may be made either to a particular person or to the public at large.

If an offer takes the form of a promise in
10   return for an act, the performance of that act is in itself an adequate indication of assent.

APPEAL from a decision of Hawkins, J.

The defendants, who were the proprietors and vendors of a medical preparation called
15   "The Carbolic Smoke Ball," inserted in the *Pall Mall Gazette* of November 13, 1891, and in other newspapers, the following advertisement:

"100*l*. reward will be paid by the Carbolic Smoke Ball Company to any person who contracts
20   the increasing epidemic influenza, colds, or any disease caused by taking cold, after having used the ball three times daily for two weeks according to the printed directions supplied with each ball. 1000*l*. is deposited with the Alliance Bank,
25   Regent Street, shewing our sincerity in the matter. During the last epidemic of influenza many thousand carbolic smoke balls were sold as preventives against this disease, and in no ascertained case was the disease contracted by
30   those using the carbolic smoke ball. One carbolic smoke ball will last a family several months,

making it the cheapest remedy in the world at the price, 10*s*. post free. The ball can be refilled at a cost of 5*s*. Address, Carbolic Smoke Ball
35   Company, 27, Princes Street, Hanover Square, London."

The plaintiff, a lady, on the faith of this advertisement, bought one of the balls at a chemist's, and used it as directed, three times a
40   day, from November 20, 1891, to January 17, 1892, when she was attacked by influenza.

HAWKINS, J., held that she was entitled to recover the 100*l*. The defendants appealed.

LINDLEY, L.J., delivered judgment
45   dismissing the appeal.

BOWEN, L.J. I am of the same opinion. We were asked to say that this document was a contract too vague to be enforced.

The first observation which arises is that the
50   document itself is not a contract at all, it is only an offer made to the public. The defendants contend next, that it is an offer the terms of which are too vague to be treated as a definite offer, inasmuch as there is no limit of time fixed
55   for the catching of the influenza, and it cannot be supposed that the advertisers seriously meant to promise to pay money to every person who

---

catches the influenza at any time after the inhaling of the smoke ball. It was urged also,

60  that if you look at this document you will find much vagueness as to the persons with whom the contract was intended to be made—that, in the first place, its terms are wide enough to include persons who may have used the smoke

65  ball before the advertisement was issued; at all events, that it is an offer to the world in general, and, also, that it is unreasonable to suppose it to

be a definite offer, because nobody in their senses would contract themselves out of the

70  opportunity of checking the experiment which was going to be made at their own expense. It is also contended that the advertisement is rather in the nature of a puff or a proclamation than a promise or offer intended to mature into a

75  contract when accepted. But the main point seems to be that the vagueness of the document shews that no contract whatever was intended.

## C  Reading for detail and language study: the facts of the case

**1**  Scan the text to find the following facts:
   a) Who was the plaintiff in the case of first instance?
   b) Who were the defendants?
   c) Who won the case of first instance?
   ● d) Who appealed against that decision?

## 2  Vocabulary: using context clues (1)

In previous units you have seen that it is often possible to use the context to understand the meaning of new words in a text. Sometimes the general context will help you to understand a word, and sometimes specific words or phrases in the text will indicate its meaning. Words or phrases that help you understand unknown words in this way are called 'context clues'.

In the exercise below, try to work out the probable meaning of the words in CAPITALS by using the context clues *in italics*. In Section Two of this Unit you will have to find the context clues yourself.

*Example:*

*100ℓ.* REWARD *will be paid* . . . *to any person who contracts influenza* . . . .

REWARD = money you offer to someone who does a certain thing.
REWARD = money offered for a certain action

a) the increasing epidemic *influenza, colds or any* DISEASE *caused by taking cold* . . .

DISEASE = a general term ('any') which includes colds and 'flu. DISEASE =

118

b) *1000ℓ. is DEPOSITED with the*     DEPOSITED =
*Alliance Bank*

c) many thousand smoke balls were sold     PREVENTIVES =
*as* PREVENTIVES *against this*
*disease* and *in no case was the disease*
*contracted* . . .

d) *Hawkins J. held* that *she* [the plaintiff]     RECOVER =
*was entitled to* RECOVER *the 100ℓ.*
*The defendants appealed.*

▲ Compare your work with other members of the class, then check your answers in the key.

■ ▲ ● Do your definitions correspond exactly to the key? If not, are they similar in meaning?

## 3 *Reading for detail*

Read the text carefully and answer the following questions:

a) What did the Carbolic Smoke Ball Co. sell?

b) What were they for?

c) According to the company, did they work?

d) Were they expensive?

e) Who did the Company offer to pay 100ℓ. to?

f) Why did they deposit 1000ℓ. with the bank?

g) Why did the plaintiff buy the product?

h) Did she follow the instructions?

i) Did it work in her case?

j) Why do you suppose the company made this offer?

k) In your opinion, does it look like a serious offer? Give reasons for your answer.

## 4

Which summary of the facts given below corresponds exactly to the text?

As a preventive against flu the plaintiff bought a carbolic smoke ball from the defendant company because she had read their advertisement. She used it according to the instructions.

i) She later sued the company for damages because she caught flu.

ii) She later sued the company for the 100ℓ. reward they had advertised because she caught flu.

iii) She later sued the company because she caught flu, and then appealed against the decision of the court of first instance.

## 5 *Oral practice*

Use your answers to exercises 3 and 4 to describe the facts of the case briefly.

*Start like this*: 'The defendants, The Carbolic Smoke Ball Company, sold a product called carbolic smoke balls, which they advertised as a very good preventive against influenza. In their advertisement the Company offered to pay . . .'.

▲ Work together in pairs, taking turns to describe some of the facts.

## D   Reading for detail and language study: the defence

## 1   Was the advertisement a contract?

## 2 Understanding complex sentences

The use of long, complex sentences, typical of legal English, may make this section of the text difficult to read. As a general rule, if you have difficulty understanding a sentence, read it twice. If you still have difficulty, try this technique:

- divide the sentence into short phrases
- study each phrase: (1) for *content* – what information does it give? (2) for *function* – what is its relation to the rest of the sentence?
- think about the global meaning of the sentence: (1) what are the main points? (2) what other information is important?

i) When you first use this technique it is helpful to write each stage down. Study the example below. The sentence on the left has been divided into short phrases and the function of each phrase is described in the box on the right. Note any important points in the final column. This activity will help you to understand the relation between the different parts of the sentence and the value of each new piece of information.

| *Example sentence from the text* | *Function of each phrase* | *Notes* |
|---|---|---|
| *It was urged also* | The speaker is REPORTING | *what the defendants said* |
| 1 *that*, if you look at this document | Preliminary CONDITION | |
| you will find much vagueness | ASSERTING | *that the document is vague* |
| as to the persons with whom the contract was intended to be made – | SPECIFYING | |
| 2 *that*, in the first place, its terms are wide enough | ASSERTING | |
| to include persons who may have used the smoke ball before the advertisement was issued; | SPECIFYING | |
| 3 at all events, *that* it is an offer to the world in general, | ASSERTING | |
| 4 and, also, *that* it is unreasonable to suppose it to be a definite offer, | ASSERTING | |
| because nobody in their senses would contract themselves out of the opportunity | EXPLAINING | |
| of checking the experiment which was going to be made at their own expense. | SPECIFYING | |

ii) You can see that the sentence contains four main assertions. The first one is done for you in the following table. What are the other three, in your own words? What other important information is given?

| Main assertions | Other important information |
|---|---|
| The defendants contend that:<br>1. *the document is very vague*<br>2......<br>3......<br>4...... | *regarding the persons involved* |

iii) You can use this technique every time you have difficulty understanding a complex section of text. At first, it may seem slow, but with practice, you will soon be able to mark the divisions directly on the text and analyse the meaning and importance of each short phrase in your head.

Practise the technique now as follows:

(1) Divide the sentence beginning 'The defendants contend next . . .' (lines 51–2) into short, logical phrases.

(2) Compare your division of the sentence to the one on the left below (it should be similar, but need not be exactly the same).

(3) Choose the function of each phrase from the list below the box.

(4) Ask yourself what piece of information each phrase gives and make notes in the space provided.

|  | *Function of each phrase* | *Notes* |
|---|---|---|
| a)  The defendants contend next, | *REPORTING* | |
| b)  that it is an offer | *ASSERTING* | |
| c)  the terms of which are too vague to be treated as a definite offer, | | |
| d)  inasmuch as there is no limit of time fixed for the catching of the influenza | | |
| e)  and it cannot be supposed that the advertisers seriously meant | | |
| f)  to promise to pay money | | |
| g)  to every person | | |
| h)  who catches the influenza at any time after the inhaling of the smoke ball. | | |

*Functions:* (some functions are used more than once)
reporting / specifying / explaining / asserting

(5) Identify the main assertions and decide if there is any other important information.

Copy the box into your notebook.

| Main assertions | Other important information |
|---|---|
| The defendants contend that: | |

●

3  i)  Use the text together with your answers to Exercise 2 to complete part A of the table below, in your notebook, showing the different arguments presented by the defendants in *Carlill*. State the arguments briefly and simply in your own words. You will complete Part B of this table at the end of Section Two of this Unit.

Part A                          Part B

| Defendants' arguments | Bowen LJ's ruling on the point of law |
|---|---|
| The advertisement is only an offer, not a contract. | |

ii)  What are the defendants' basic arguments?

▲●  Compare your work with other members of the class before looking at the key.

## 4  Oral practice

i)  Scan the section of the text containing arguments for the defence: find the phrases used by the judge to introduce the legal arguments presented by the defence. For instance:

| Introductory phrase | Legal argument |
|---|---|
| 'The defendants contend next | (that it is an offer the terms of which are too vague . . .') |

●  Can you think of any other phrases of this type?

ii)  Use Part A of your completed table in Exercise 3 above to present the defendants' arguments in *Carlill*.
Introduce each argument with one of the phrases from i) above.

▲  Work in pairs, taking turns to present the different arguments.

## 5  Prediction

You have seen that Bowen LJ begins his judgment by stating the defendants' arguments. How do you think the judgment will continue?

## E Development

### 1 People in private law

The suffixes -er and -or are often added to nouns or verbs to form related nouns (called 'agent nouns') which refer to the person or thing that does an action.

*Examples:*

| *Noun or verb* | *Agent noun* | *Meaning* |
|---|---|---|
| offer | offeror (line 4) | person who offers |
| advertise | advertiser (56) | person, company, etc. who advertises |
| property | proprietor (13) | person who owns property (also owner) |

Can you think of some more examples of agent nouns ending in -or and -er?

i)  Check that you understand the list of topics in CAPITALS in exercise ii) below (e.g. CIVIL ACTION, LEGAL ADVICE, WILL, etc.). Use your dictionary to find any new terms.

ii) Complete the phrases on the right by choosing the two people related to each topic from the list given on page 124. Where possible, use word families to help you choose.

*Example:*

CIVIL
ACTION   In a civil case, the party who takes legal action against the
__*defendant*__ (for example for a tort, or breach of contract) is called
the __*plaintiff*__

*Answer:* l, h

(1) LEGAL ADVICE  A _____ is a lawyer who gives legal advice to his or her _____ and may sometimes represent them in court.

(2) WILL  The _____ is the person appointed to 'execute' the will, that is to give effect to the wishes expressed in the will by the _____.

(3) TORT  A _____ is a person who commits a civil wrong, called a tort, which causes damage or injury to the _____.

(4) SALE  The _____ sells an article or product to the buyer, or _____, who buys, or 'purchases' it.

(5) TRUST (repeat each word twice)  A _____ is the legal owner of property which s/he holds in trust for the benefit of the _____. Under rules of Equity, the _____ must act in the interests of the _____, according to the terms of the trust.

(6) CONTRACT  In English law a contract is formed when the _____ accepts the offer which the _____ has made.

(7) EMPLOYMENT  A contract of employment creates a special legal relationship in which the two parties have certain rights and duties. For example, the _____ has the duty to make sure that the _____'s place of work is safe.

(8) LEASE OF LAND The _____ is the person who owns land which the _____ uses (e.g. as a dwelling or place of work), and for which s/he pays a sum of money called rent.

*List of people:*

| | | | |
|---|---|---|---|
| a) client | b) injured party | c) offeror | d) executor |
| e) trustee | f) vendor | g) beneficiary | h) plaintiff | i) landlord |
| j) employee | k) solicitor | l) defendant | m) testator | n) offeree |
| o) purchaser | p) employer | q) tortfeasor | r) tenant |

iii) You have seen that the suffixes -er and -or indicate the agent, or person who does the action. What does the suffix -ee indicate in nouns like *employee* and *offeree*?

## 2 Role play

i) Consider for a few moments the facts of *Carlill*.

◆ Would there be a valid contract under your legal system in these circumstances?
◆ Would the defendants be able to present similar arguments?
◆ What arguments would the plaintiff present?
Decide whether you think a contract would or would not exist under your own legal system.

▲ ii) Form groups of three. Each choose one of the following roles:
■ In this activity, you will play the role of three different people:
▲● THE JUDGE    COUNSEL FOR THE DEFENDANT
COUNSEL FOR THE PLAINTIFF
Follow the instructions below, applying principles of contract law from your legal system to the facts of *Carlill*.
Speak aloud, if possible recording yourself on tape, then listen to your recording.

(1) Read the instructions, then spend a few minutes preparing your role(s).
(2) JUDGE: present the facts of the case.
(3) COUNSEL FOR THE PLAINTIFF: present your case. (Introduce your arguments with these phrases, used by English lawyers in court: 'In my submission, the advertisement . . .', 'In my respectful submission . . .', 'It is submitted that . . .'
(4) COUNSEL FOR THE DEFENDANT: present your case. (Introduce your arguments as in (3) above)
(5) JUDGE: comment on counsels' submissions. (Introduce your comments with the phrases you practised in exercise D4) and give judgment in the case.

iii) Do you think the judges in *Carlill* will reach the same decision as you?
▲ Compare your decision with other groups in the class. Do you all agree?

---

# Section Two:   The Decision

## A Understanding the development and organisation of the text: the skill of prediction

*1* In previous units you have practised thinking about a text before you read and predicting what topics and information you think it will contain, to help you read with understanding. The skill of prediction can also be used *while reading* to decide how you think the text will continue or develop. The ability to predict the way the writer has organised ideas in the text, and to follow the developing arguments in a text both helps you to understand better and is a sign of understanding. Most good readers use this technique when reading in their own language, without even thinking about it. *It does not matter if your predictions are wrong.* The important thing is that as you see your predictions confirmed (or not) you will understand how the writer's thoughts develop in the text. As you continue to read Bowen LJ's judgment, answer the questions inserted in the text which follows, to practise the skill of prediction. Read a question and make a prediction, then read the section of the text which follows to see if your prediction was right or wrong. Check your answer, then continue. Always cover the text so that you can't see what follows during this activity. *Do not* try to understand the text in detail. This text is the continuation of the text you read in Section One. Before you start, refer to your answer to Exercise D5 in Section One and decide how you think the text might start, then check this by reading the first extract below.

> 1   It seems to me that in order to arrive at a right conclusion we must read this advertisement in its plain meaning, as the public would understand it. It was intended to be issued to the public and to be read by the public. How would an ordinary person reading this document construe it?

a)   Predict how Bowen LJ will continue. Do you think he will construe the words of the advertisement now?

> 5   It was intended unquestionably to have some effect, and I think the effect which it was intended to have, was to make people use the smoke ball, because the suggestions and allegations which it contains are directed immediately to the use of the smoke ball as distinct from the purchase of it. It did not follow that the smoke ball was to be purchased from the defendants
> 10   directly, or even from agents of theirs directly. The intention was that the circulation of the smoke ball should be promoted, and that the use of it should be increased. The advertisement begins by saying that a reward will be paid by the Carbolic Smoke Ball Company to any person who contracts the increasing epidemic after using the ball.

Was your prediction right? If not, what has the speaker done here?
*Answer:* No, he describes the effect the advertisement was intended to have.

b)   Will he (1) examine this point in detail? or (2) continue to describe the rest of the advertisement?

> 15   It has been said that the words do not apply only to persons who contract the epidemic after the publication of the advertisement, but include persons who had previously contracted the influenza. I cannot so read the advertisement. It is written in colloquial and popular language, and I think that it is equivalent to this:

*Answer:* (1)

c)   Will he explain the meaning of the words in the advertisement?

> 20   "100*l.* will be paid to any person who shall contract the increasing epidemic after having used the carbolic smoke ball three times daily for two weeks." And it seems to me that the way in which the public would read it would be

> this: that if anybody, after the advertisement was published, used three times
> daily for two weeks the carbolic smoke ball, and then caught cold, he would be
> 25   entitled to the reward. Then again it was said: "How long is this protection to
> endure? Is it to go on for ever, or for what limit of time?"

*Answer:* Yes.

d)   What will he do next?

> I think that there are two constructions of this document, each of which is
> good sense, and each of which seems to me to satisfy the exigencies of the
> present action. It may mean that the protection is warranted to last during
> 30   the epidemic, and it was during the epidemic that the plaintiff contracted the
> disease.

*Answer:* He answers the question about the time limit, saying that there are two
possible constructions.

e)   How will the text continue?

> I think, more probably, it means that the smoke ball will be a protection while
> it is in use. That seems to me the way in which an ordinary person would
> understand an advertisement about medicine, and about a specific against
> 35   influenza. It could not be supposed that after you have left off using it you are
> still to be protected for ever, as if there was to be a stamp set upon your
> forehead that you were never to catch influenza because you had once used
> the carbolic smoke ball. I think the immunity is to last during the use of the
> ball. That is the way in which I should naturally read it, and it seems to me
> 40   that the subsequent language of the advertisement supports that
> construction. [ . . . ]
>      Was it intended that the 100*l*. should, if the conditions were fulfilled, be
> paid?

*Answer:* He examines the second possible construction of the document regarding
the time limit.

f)   What method will he use to answer the question?
     Answer the question yourself, then read to check.

> The advertisement says that 1000*l*. is lodged at the bank for the purpose.
> 45   Therefore, it cannot be said that the statement that 100*l*. would be paid was
> intended to be a mere puff. I think it was intended to be understood by the
> public as an offer which was to be acted upon.
>      But it was said there was no check on the part of the persons who issued
> the advertisement, and that it would be an insensate thing to promise 100*l*. to
> 50   a person who used the smoke ball unless you could check or superintend his
> manner of using it.

*Answer:* He examines the words of the advertisement to answer the question.
He thinks it was intended to be a serious offer.

g) How will the text continue?

> The answer to that argument seems to me to be that if a person chooses to
> make extravagant promises of this kind he probably does so because it pays
> him to make them, and, if he has made them, the extravagance of the
> 55 promises is no reason in law why he should not be bound by them.
>    It was also said that the contract is made with all the world – that is, with
> everybody; and that you cannot contract with everybody. It is not a contract
> made with all the world. There is the fallacy of the argument.

*Answer:* He answers the defendants' argument, then goes on to a new point.

h) Will he explain why it is not a contract made with all the world?

> It is an offer made to all the world; and why should not an offer be made to all
> 60 the world which is to ripen into a contract with anybody who comes forward
> and performs the condition? It is an offer to become liable to anyone who,
> before it is retracted, performs the condition, and although the offer is made to
> the world, the contract is made with that limited portion of the public who
> come forward and perform the condition on the faith of the advertisement.
> 65 [ . . . ] Then as to the alleged want of consideration. The definition of
> 'consideration' given in Selwyn's Nisi Prius, 8th edn., p. 47, which is cited and
> adopted by Tindal, C. J., in the case of *Laythoarp* v. *Bryant*, is this:

*Answer:* Yes.

i) How will the text continue?

> "Any act of the plaintiff from which the defendant derives a benefit or
> advantage, or any labour, detriment, or inconvenience sustained by the
> 70 plaintiff, provided such act is performed or such inconvenience suffered by the
> plaintiff, with the consent, either express or implied, of the defendant."

*Answer:* He gives the definition of *consideration* from the work of authority cited.

j) Will he apply these principles to the present case?

> Can it be said here that if the person who reads this advertisement applies
> thrice daily, for such time as may seem to him tolerable, the carbolic smoke
> 75 ball to his nostrils for a whole fortnight, he is doing nothing at all—that it is a
> mere act which is not to count towards consideration to support a promise (for
> the law does not require us to measure the adequacy of the consideration).
> Inconvenience sustained by one party at the request of the other is enough to
> create a consideration. I think, therefore, that it is consideration enough that
> 80 the plaintiff took the trouble of using the smoke ball. But I think also that the
> defendants received a benefit from this user, for the use of the smoke ball was
> contemplated by the defendants as being indirectly a benefit to them, because
> the use of the smoke balls would promote their sale. [ . . . ]
>
> A. L. SMITH, L.J., delivered judgment to the same effect.

*Answer:* Yes.

*2* Use your answers to Exercise 1 above and the main themes of the text to continue this general description of how the judgment develops:

'Bowen LJ begins by defining how the advertisement must be read, and who it was intended for. He goes on to consider the effect the advertisement was intended to have, and then explains who the words of the advertisement apply to and how
● long . . .'.

## B  Language study and reading for detail

*1* Without looking at the text again, decide if you think the following statements are *true* or *false*. Then read the text carefully and check your original answers before looking at the key.

i) *General questions*
- a)  In this section of the text Bowen LJ answers the defendants' arguments.
- b)  He agrees with most of the defendants' arguments.
- c)  He construes the words of the advertisement in detail one section at a time.
- d)  He does not give the words of the advertisement any special legal meaning.

ii) *Detailed questions*
- a)  The words of the advertisement are intended to make people buy the smoke ball.
- b)  It refers to anyone who catches flu before or after the advertisement was published.
- c)  The smoke ball should be used regularly for three weeks.
- d)  In Bowen LJ's opinion the smoke ball should give protection during the period of use.
- e)  The offer of a reward was valid because the company deposited £1000 at the
● bank to prove their sincerity.

Which questions did you get right first time? Which ones did you get right only after referring to the text again? What does this tell you about these two different styles of reading: reading for general understanding (as in exercise A1) and reading for detail?

## *2  Word study*

i) *Dictionary use* First decide what you think the following words might mean in the text on pages 125–7, then use your dictionary to check their exact meaning:
a)  warranted (line 29)     b)  fulfilled (42)     c)  insensate (49)
d)  extravagant (53)     e)  liable (61)

ii) Complete this phrase with information from lines 48–51 of the text, substituting a phrase with *if* for *unless*:
'It would be an insensate thing to promise 100*l.* to a person who used the smoke ball if . . .'.
● What does *unless* mean?

iii) *Vocabulary: context clues (II)*
Find context clues in the text that help you to work out the meaning of the following words and phrases (see Section One, Exercise C2 on page 118 for information about context clues).
*Example:* it pays him (lines 53–4) Context clues: '*if a person chooses to make extravagant promises* of this kind *he probably does so because* IT PAYS HIM to make them . . .' (lines 52–4).
*Meaning:* IT PAYS HIM = refers to a probable reason for making an extravagant promise
IT PAYS HIM = it gives him some advantage.

a) fallacy (line 58)    b) to ripen into (60)    c) retracted (62)
d) benefit (68, 81, 82) e) detriment (69)    f) nostrils (75)

▲ ● Check your ideas with other members of the class before looking at the key.

iv) Complete the sentences below by choosing the correct form of a suitable word from exercises i) and iii) above:

*Example:* a tortfeasor is ___*liable*___ to pay damages to the injured party to compensate for the harm or wrong he has caused.

a) She offered to pay £300 for the painting, but _____ her offer when she learnt that it was not an original.

b) The vendor _____ the high quality of the material.

c) The idea that the law is always just is a _____ – even a good law may sometimes cause injustice in individual cases.

d) In her will the testator created a trust for the _____ of the poor.

e) A contract comes to an end when both parties have _____ all their obligations.

f) Bad working conditions at Smith's Ltd were a serious _____ to the employees' health. In fact, in 1979 a group of workers who fell ill sued their employers for damages.

## 3 Reading in detail

Answer these questions on lines 48–83 of the text, using your own words:

a) Can an extravagant or ridiculous promise be legally binding?

b) Why does Bowen LJ think the company made this extravagant promise?

c) The defendants contend that you can't make a contract with the whole world. Why doesn't Bowen LJ accept this as a defence?

d) When can an offer to the world become a contract?

e) Who does an offer to the world create legal relations with?

f) To create a contract, must the offeree always state that s/he accepts the offer?

g) What happens if the condition is fulfilled after the offeror has retracted the offer?

h) In English law a contract is only valid if it is '*under seal*' (in a special written form) or if there is '*consideration*'. In general terms, what is consideration?

● i) What was the 'double consideration' in this case?

● 4 Was the decision in *Carlill* unanimous?

## 5 The decision

i) Go back to Section One, Exercise D3 on page 122 and complete the table showing the arguments for the defence and the decision, by filling in Bowen LJ's ruling on each point in Part B, in your notebook.

▲ ● Compare your table with other members of the class.

ii) The following phrases are used to introduce the legal principles and decision contained in a judgment:

'*It was held that* an offer may be made to a particular person or to the public in general.'

'*The court held that* the plaintiff was entitled to recover.'

'*It was laid down that* . . .'

'*The court found that* . . .'

Use the information in Part B of your table from page 122 to describe the judgment in *Carlill*. First describe the judgment orally, then write a few sentences giving the decision.

▲   Work in pairs.

## 6   Conclusion

i)   Refer to Part B of your completed table from page 122. Which rulings apply only to the specific facts of *Carlill v. Carbolic Smoke Ball Co.*, and which rulings contain general legal principles?
In your opinion, what is the *ratio decidendi* of *Carlill* – which principles contained in the judgment will be binding on courts in future cases?

ii)   Refer to the legal principles decided in the case, given at the very beginning of the case (page 117) and see which points correspond to your ideas from i) above. (Only the main points are listed in the decision and you have only read part of the judgment, remember.)

iii)   Give an example of *dicta* from Bowen LJ's judgment.

iv)   Use your knowledge of the English judicial system to decide:
    ●   which courts are bound by the decision in *Carlill*?
    ●   how can the binding principles of *Carlill* be changed?

v)   Which sources of law does Bowen LJ use to reach his decision in *Carlill*? (Refer

●   again to the text for your answer.)

## 7   Discussion points

i)   Study the following points for a few moments:

◆   *Consideration*
In the English legal system a promise is legally binding only if it is made under seal or if there is consideration. What is the law in your country? Are all promises legally binding? Is there anything similar to the English doctrine of consideration? If your system is one based on Roman law, compare *causa* and consideration.

◆   *The style of the judgment*
Consider (1) the scope of the judgment (what does it include?) and (2) the style in which Bowen LJ presents his arguments.
Compare the scope and style with the judgment of a superior court in your country.

◆   *The law*
Was the decision of the English High Court the same as the decision you reached in the role play at the end of Section One (Exercise E 2)? Is this part of the law of contract very different from your own system or are there significant similarities?

■   ii)   Choose one or more of the three discussion points in i) which interests you. To practise speaking, talk about your ideas, if possible recording them on tape. Then listen to your recording.
If you prefer, write some of your ideas down in note form.

▲   Choose the discussion point in i) which interests you most.
Work in pairs with someone who has chosen the same point as you. Compare and discuss your ideas, and prepare to present them to other members of the class.
When you are ready, form groups of 3–6 in which the different members have prepared each of the three discussion points. Exchange and discuss your ideas on each topic.

## C  Development

### 1  Summary of the case

Complete the following extract from Philip S. James, *Introduction to English Law* by choosing the correct word or phrase for each blank space from the list below. When you have finished, read the completed extract and consider the importance of *Carlill* in the wider context of the English law of contract.

---

THE INTENTION TO CONTRACT

We have seen that most contracts are _*agreements*_(1). It should now be noted that it is by no means true to say that all agreements are _____(2). Many agreements fall outside the scope of the law of contract, either because they concern matters of moral, rather than of legal, _____(3) or because the _____(4) agree that they are not to be treated as enforceable contracts, or because they are not intended to be such. A familiar example is the _____(5) of a person who drives a friend somewhere in return for payment of the petrol. The _____(6) have, moreover, repeatedly declined jurisdiction over agreements which are expressed in a way which shows an intention to exclude their _____(7). On the other hand, what appears on the face of it to be a business transaction will not lightly be treated as a merely moral obligation, and it should be noted that expressed _____(8) may sometimes have the effect of turning into a _____(9) contract – an agreement which might otherwise have been regarded as _____(10). A famous example of the latter situation was provided by *Carlill v. Carbolic Smoke Ball Co.*, [1893] 1 Q.B. 256. The _____(11) manufactured "carbolic smoke balls" which they advertised as miraculous cures for _____(12). The advertisement stated that £100 _____(13) would be paid to anyone who contracted influenza after having used the ball as prescribed. It was further stated that £1,000 was deposited with a bank to show the sincerity of the _____(14) intention. The _____(15), Mrs. Carlill, used one of these balls, but nevertheless contracted influenza; she _____(16) for the promised reward. _____(17) that she was entitled to _____(18): normally such advertisements are mere "puffs" which are not intended to create _____(19), but in this instance taking into account, amongst other circumstances, the reference to the _____(20) at the bank, the court _____(21) that the Company had intentionally made a binding _____(22) which the plaintiff had _____(23).

---

*Choose from:*

| | | | | |
|---|---|---|---|---|
| a) plaintiff | b) contracts | c) non-contractual | d) accepted | e) *intention* |
| f) defendants | g) parties | h) influenza | i) recover | j) offer |
| k) It was held | l) reward | m) obligation | n) courts | o) deposit |
| p) agreements | q) jurisdiction | r) Company's | s) sued | t) found |
| ● u) case | v) binding | w) legal relations | | |

### 2  A moot

i) A moot is an imaginary case argued by law students for practice in presenting cases in court. Choose case A or case B below. Use the decision in *Carlill* and the information in your table on page 122 to decide the legal position of the plaintiff and the defendant under the English law of contract. Are all the principles of *Carlill* applicable to the case you have chosen, or is it necessary to distinguish some of the facts?

*Case A*
X advertises in the local paper that she will pay a £100 reward to anyone who finds and returns her lost Persian cat, Miaow. Y finds Miaow two months later and takes her back to X, asking for the reward. Meanwhile, X has bought another cat to

replace Miaow. She agrees to take her back, but refuses to pay the reward. Y sues her for the £100 reward.

*Case B*

The Superhair Company produces an expensive new product '*guaranteed to make your hair grow in only 3 weeks or your money back*'. The advertisement specifies that users must follow the instructions on the packet carefully. Z, who is completely bald (he has no hair at all) sees the advertisement and buys the product. He uses it as instructed on the packet, but his hair does not begin to grow again. When Superhair refuse to give Z his money back, he sues them.

▲ ii) For each case, appoint two people to act as counsel for the plaintiff and two people as counsel for the defendant. The other members of the class will act as judges in the case they have chosen.

■ In this activity, you are going to play the roles of counsel for the plaintiff, counsel for the defendant and judge.

▲ ■ Prepare your role(s) carefully. Revise some of the expressions you learnt in Section One, Exercise E 2 if you are acting as counsel and in Section One, Exercise D 4 if you are the judge.

iii) Hold the moot, at which first the plaintiff, then the defendant are represented in turn in court. Deliver judgment, and decide who has won the case.

iv) Issue a short written judgment beginning like this:

'It was held that the plaintiff was/was not entitled to recover on the grounds that [because] . . .'.

● Then check your arguments and decision in the key.

# Revision and Consolidation, Units 5—7

Reading an Offer and the Terms and Conditions of a Contract

## A  Reading and vocabulary skills

You are going to read a text containing an offer and the terms and conditions of a contract. This is a different type of text from the ones you have read so far in this book, but you can use exactly the same reading and vocabulary skills and techniques to understand it.

Follow the instructions for each exercise in Part A to see how well you have learnt to use some of the skills practised so far in this book.

*Reading skills*
- scanning a text to locate information which interests you, quickly
- skimming to understand the main themes and organisation of material in a text
- reading for detailed understanding and using information from the text to solve legal problems.

*Vocabulary skills*
- using the general context and specific context clues to work out the probable meaning of new words in a text
- using a monolingual dictionary to understand the meaning of a word in a given context
- using your knowledge of root words and word families to work out the meaning of new words in a text.

To complete these activities you will not read all the text in detail. If you are interested in studying some of the language and vocabulary in the text in more detail, you can do this independently at the end of the Unit.

Before you read, think of some vocabulary which a text like this might contain. Find out the meaning of *Stock Exchange* and *share* (in the context of the Stock Exchange).

## 1  *Reading for specific information (8 points, suggested time: 3 minutes)*

Quickly scan the text on pages 134 and 135 to find the following information:
a) what is for sale
b) the name of the company
c) how much each one costs in total
d) if the purchaser pays all the money at the same time
e) which company is the vendor
f) when the offer was published
g) what happens on 23 September 1987
h) where you can read the terms of the contract.

## 2 Reading to understand the themes and organisation of material in the text (10 points, suggested time: 5 minutes)

Quickly skim the text to find the sections which give information about the following topics:

*Example:* general information about the sale. *Answer:* lines 1–13.

a) the 'Prospectus'
b) professional advice
c) details of the offer to purchase shares
d) terms of the collateral contract (a secondary contract which depends on the main one)
e) breach of contract.

**THE OBSERVER, SUNDAY 3 MAY 1987**

1

# ROLLS·ROYCE plc

### OFFER FOR SALE

by

5 SAMUEL MONTAGU & CO. LIMITED

on behalf of

## THE SECRETARY OF STATE FOR

## TRADE AND INDUSTRY

of up to 801,470,588

10 Ordinary Shares

of 20p each at 170p per Share

of which 85p is payable on application
and 85p on 23rd September 1987

The information contained in this document has been drawn from, and is to be read
15 together with, that contained in the prospectus dated 28th April 1987 (the "Prospectus")
which comprises listing particulars relating to Rolls·Royce plc (the "Company" or "Rolls·
Royce"). In applying for Ordinary Shares of 20p each in the Company ("Shares"), you will
be treated as applying on the basis of both this document and the Prospectus, which
together govern your rights and obligations. The Prospectus alone contains full details of
20 the history and business of Rolls·Royce and of the Offer. You are therefore advised to read
the Prospectus before completing and returning an application form.

The Council of The Stock Exchange has authorised the issue of this document under section 154(1)(b) of the Financial Services Act 1986, which enables it to do so without approving the contents hereof.

25 If you need advice, you should consult your bank manager, stockbroker, solicitor, accountant or other professional adviser.

 # TERMS AND CONDITIONS OF APPLICATION

1.   Acceptance of applications will be conditional on (i) the admission of the whole of the ordinary share capital of the Company, issued and to be issued, to the Official List of The Stock Exchange becoming
30 effective by not later than 26th May 1987; and (ii) the provisions relating to termination of the Underwriting Agreement referred to in paragraph 8 of "Additional Information" in Part VII of the document dated 28th April 1987, comprising listing particulars for Rolls Royce plc (the "Prospectus"), not being implemented. Application monies will be returned (without interest) if these conditions are not satisfied and, in the meantime, if presented for payment will be kept by the receiving banks appointed in respect of the Offer
35 ("receiving banks") in separate accounts. The right is reserved for the Secretary of State and his agents to present for payment and otherwise process all remittances at any time after receipt thereof. The right is also reserved to treat as valid any application not completed in all respects in accordance with the instructions accompanying the relevant application form. Words and expressions defined in the Prospectus have the same meanings in these terms and conditions and in the application forms, including the Public
40 Application Form, unless the context otherwise requires.

2.   By completing and delivering an application form, you:

(a) offer to purchase from the Secretary of State the number of Shares specified on your application form (or such smaller number for which the application is accepted) and agree that you will accept such Shares as may be allocated to you on the terms of, and subject to the conditions set out in,
45 the Prospectus and subject to the Memorandum and Articles of Association of the Company;

(b) agree, as a collateral contract between you and the Secretary of State which will become binding on posting to, or (in the case of delivery in any other manner) receipt by, a receiving bank of your application and in consideration of the Secretary of State agreeing that he will not, prior to 11th May 1987, offer any of the Shares to any person other than by means of one of the procedures
50 referred to in the Prospectus, that (i) your application cannot be revoked prior to 31st May 1987 and (ii) if you are requested to do so at any time in writing by or on behalf of the Secretary of State or the Company, you will disclose in writing within 21 days of the date of such request, to the person making it, the name(s) and address(es) of any person(s) for whose benefit your application was made or who would, if all the Shares for which your application is accepted had been
55 subscribed, be, to your knowledge, at any time or for any periods prior to such request interested in such Shares for the purposes of section 212 of the Companies Act 1985;

(c) warrant that your remittance will be honoured on first presentation and agree that any letter of allocation and any money returnable may be held pending clearance of your payment;

(d) agree:

60 (i) that time shall be of the essence of the contract constituted by acceptance of your application and that such contract will constitute a separate contract for the purchase of each of the Shares in respect of which your application is accepted and that these terms and conditions shall be construed accordingly;

65 (ii) to pay or procure to be paid by not later than 3.00 p.m. on 23rd September 1987 the second instalment of 85p per Share payable in respect of those Shares for which your application is accepted and that payment of a sum of £10,000 or more will be for value by such time;

(iii) that failure to make such payment by such time (including, in the case of payment of a sum of £10,000 or more, for value by such time) will render the previous payment liable to forfeiture and will constitute a fundamental breach and repudiation of the contract
70 constituted by acceptance of your application, which the Secretary of State will be entitled to accept as bringing the contract to an end and which will render you liable to pay by way of damages full compensation for all loss and damage (including any consequential loss and wasted expenditure) suffered as a result of the breach; and

(iv) that each sale of Shares is conditional on the due prior payment of the second instalment
75 and that neither you nor any renouncee(s) will have any right to vote, or to direct the manner in which the rights attaching to the Shares may be exercised, until such payment is made and until the Shares are registered in the Company's register of members in your name or that of a renouncee;

## 3   Vocabulary skills: dictionary use (6 points)

i)   Study the words and phrases below in context and if possible decide what you think they mean in the text: use cognates, word families, the context and logical reasoning to help you decide.
What is the grammatical function of each word in the text (verb, noun, adjective, etc.)?

a) prior (48, 50, 74)      b) revoked (50)      c) in respect of (62, 65)
d) render (68, 71)      e) liable (68, 71)      f) forfeiture (69)      g) due (73)

ii)   Choose the correct definition for each word or phrase in i) from the following extracts from *The Oxford Advanced Learner's Dictionary of Current English*, 4th edition.

**due¹** /dju:; *US* du:/ *adj* **1** [pred] **(a)** ~ (to sb) owed as a debt or an obligation: *Have they been paid the money due to them?* ○ *I'm still due fifteen days' holiday.* **(b)** ~ **for sth** owed sth; deserving sth: *She's due for promotion soon.* **2** [pred] requiring immediate payment: *fall/become due* ○ *My rent isn't due till Wednesday.* **3** [pred] ~ **(to do sth)** scheduled; arranged; expected: *His book is due to be published in October.* ○ *The train is due (in)* (ie scheduled to arrive) *in five minutes.* **4** [attrib] suitable; right; proper: *after due consideration* ○ *With all due respect, I disagree completely.* **5** ~ **to sth/sb** caused by sb/sth; because of sb/sth: *The team's success was largely due to her efforts.* **6** (idm) **in ,due 'course** at the appropriate time; eventually: *Your request will be dealt with in due course.*

NOTE ON USAGE: **1** Some speakers are careful to use **due to** only after the verb *be*: *His lateness was due to the very heavy traffic on the motorway.* But it is also generally considered acceptable today as a synonym for **owing to**, which is used differently: *He was late owing to/due to the very heavy traffic.* ○ *Due to/Owing to the heavy traffic, he was late.* **2** **Due to** can be used immediately after a noun: *Accidents due to driving at high speed were very common that weekend.*

**due²** /dju:; *US* du:/ *n* **1** [sing] thing that should be given to sb by right: *He received a large reward, which was no more than his due,* ie at least what he deserved. **2** **dues** [pl] charges or fees, eg for membership of a club: *I haven't paid my dues yet.* **3** (idm) **give sb his 'due** (*fml*) be fair to sb: *She's a slow worker but, to give her her due, she does try very hard.* **give the devil his due** ⇨ DEVIL¹.

**due³** /dju:; *US* du:/ *adv* (of points of the compass) exactly: *sail due east* ○ *walk three miles due north.*

**for·feit** /'fɔ:fɪt/ *v* [Tn] (have to) lose or give up (sth) as a consequence of or punishment for having done sth wrong, or in order to achieve sth: *Passengers who cancel their reservations will forfeit their deposit.* ○ *He forfeited the right to represent the people.* ○ *The couple forfeited their independence in order to help those less fortunate.* ▷ **for·feit** *n* **1** [C usu *sing*] thing (to be) paid or given up as a penalty or punishment. **2** (a) **forfeits** [sing *v*] game in which a player gives up various articles if he makes a mistake and can have them back by doing sth ridiculous. **(b)** [C] article given up in this game: *Give me your watch as a forfeit.*
**for·feit** *adj* [pred] ~ **(to sb/sth)** (*fml*) (liable to be) lost, paid or given up as a forfeit: *All goods may be forfeit to the State in time of war.*
**for·feit·ure** /'fɔ:fɪtʃə(r)/ *n* [U] ~ **(of sth)** (act of) forfeiting sth: *(the) forfeiture of one's property.*

**li·ab·il·ity** /ˌlaɪə'bɪlətɪ/ *n* **1** [U] ~ **(for sth)** state of being liable: *liability for military service* ○ *Don't admit liability for the accident.* **2** [C] (*infml*) handicap: *Because of his injury Jones was just a liability to the team.* Cf ASSET. **3** **li·ab·il·it·ies** [pl] debts; financial obligations.
**li·able** /'laɪəbl/ *adj* [pred] **1** ~ **(for sth)** responsible by law: *Is a wife liable for her husband's debts?* ○ *Be careful - if you have an accident I'll be liable.* **2** ~ **to sth** subject to sth: *a road liable to subsidence* ○ *Offenders are liable to fines of up to £100.* **3** ~ **to do sth** likely to do sth: *We're all liable to make mistakes when we're tired.*

**prior¹** /'praɪə(r)/ *adj* [attrib] coming before in time, order or importance: *They have a prior claim to the property,* ie one which invalidates any other claim(s), eg because based on an earlier legal agreement. ○ *My children have a prior claim on my time.* ○ *I shall have to refuse your invitation because of a prior engagement.* ○ *You need no prior knowledge to be able to do this test.* Cf POSTERIOR 1.
**prior²** /'praɪə(r)/ *n* (*fem* **pri·or·ess** /'praɪərɪs, also ˌpraɪə'res/) **(a)** person who is head of a religious order, or of a monastery or convent. **(b)** (in an abbey) person next in rank below an abbot or abbess.
▷ **pri·ory** /'praɪərɪ/ *n* monastery governed by a prior or convent governed by a prioress.

**ren·der** /'rendə(r)/ *v* (*fml*) **1** [Tn, Tn·pr, Dn·n, Dn·pr] ~ **sth (for sth);** ~ **sth (to sb)** give sth in return or exchange, or as sth which is due: *render homage, obedience, allegiance, etc* ○ *a reward for services rendered* ○ *render good for evil* ○ *render insult for insult* ○ *render sb a service/render a service to sb* ○ *render help to disaster victims* ○ *render thanks to God.* **2** [Tn] present or send in (an account) for payment: *account rendered £50.* **3** [Cn·a] cause (sb/sth) to be in a certain condition: *rendered helpless by an accident* ○ *Your action has rendered our contract invalid.* **4** [Tn esp passive] give a performance of (music, a play, a character, etc); give a portrayal of (sb/sth) in painting, etc: *The piano solo was well rendered.* ○ *'Othello' was rendered rather poorly.* ○ *The artist had rendered her gentle smile perfectly.* **5** [Tn, Tn·pr] ~ **sth (into sth)** express sth in another language; translate sth: *How would you render 'bon voyage' (into English)?* ○ *Rendering poetry into other languages is difficult.* **6** [Tn] cover (stone or brick) with a first layer of plaster: *render walls.* **7** (idm) **render an account of oneself, one's behaviour, etc** (*fml*) explain or justify what one has said, done, etc. **8** (phr v) **render sth down** make (eg fat, lard) liquid by heating it; melt sth down. **render sth up** (*fml*) hand over or surrender sth; yield sth: *render up a fort, town, etc to the enemy* ○ (*fig*) *He rendered up his soul to God,* ie died.
▷ **ren·der·ing** /'rendərɪŋ/ *n* **1** [C, U] (instance of) performing a piece of music or a dramatic role: *a moving rendering of a Brahms song* ○ *his rendering of Hamlet.* **2** [C, U] (instance of) translating (sth written): *a Spanish rendering/a rendering in Spanish of the original Arabic.* **3** [C] first layer of plaster (on stone or brick).

**re·spect¹** /rɪ'spekt/ *n* **1** [U] ~ **(for sb/sth)** admiration felt or shown for a person or thing that has good qualities or achievements; regard: *a mark, token, etc of respect* ○ *have a deep, sincere, etc respect for sb* ○ *I have the greatest respect for you/ hold you in the greatest respect.* ○ *The new officer soon won/earned the respect of his men.* **2** [U] ~ **(for sb/sth)** politeness or consideration arising from admiration or regard: *Children should show respect for their teachers.* ○ *Out of respect, he took off his hat.* ○ *have some, little, no, etc respect for sb's feelings* ○ *With (all due) respect, sir, I disagree.* **3** [U] ~ **(for sb/sth)** protection or recognition: *very little respect for human rights.* **4** [C] particular aspect or detail: *in this one respect* ○ *in some/all/many/several/few respects* ○ *In what respect do you think the film is biased?* **5** (idm) **in respect of sth** (*fml or commerce*) as regards sth; with special reference to sth: *The book is*

*admirable in respect of style.* ○ *price rises in respect of gas and water costs.* **with respect to sth** (*fml or commerce*) concerning sth: *This is true with respect to English but not to French.* ○ *With respect to your enquiry, I enclose an explanatory leaflet.*
▷ **re·spects** *n* [pl] (*fml*) **1** polite greetings: *Give/ send/offer him my respects.* **2** (idm) **pay one's respects** ⇨ PAY².

**re·spect²** /rɪ'spekt/ *v* **1** [Tn, Tn·pr] ~ **sb/sth (for sth)** admire or have a high opinion of sb/sth (because of sth): *I respect you for your honesty.* **2** [Tn] show consideration for (sb/sth): *respect sb's wishes, opinions, feelings, etc* ○ *respect the environment,* eg by protecting it ○ *People won't respect my (desire for) privacy.* **3** [Tn, Cn·n/a] ~ **sth (as sth)** avoid interfering with or harming sth; agree to recognize: *respect sb's rights, privileges, etc* ○ *respect a treaty, contract, etc* ○ *respect diplomatic immunity* (eg of foreign embassy staff to British law) *as valid.* **4** [Tn] ~ **oneself** have proper respect for one's own character and behaviour: *If you don't respect yourself, how can you expect others to respect you?*
▷ **re·specter** *n* (idm) **be no/not be any respecter of 'persons** treat everyone in the same way, without being influenced by their importance, wealth, etc: *Death is no respecter of persons.*
**re·spect·ing** *prep* (*fml*) relating to (sth); concerning: *laws respecting property* ○ *information respecting the child's whereabouts.*

**re·spect·able** /rɪ'spektəbl/ *adj* **1** of acceptable social position; decent and proper in appearance or behaviour: *a respectable married couple* ○ *a respectable middle-class background, upbringing, etc* ○ *She looked perfectly respectable in her bathrobe at breakfast.* ○ (*ironic*) *He's a bit too respectable* (ie staid and conventional) *for my tastes.* **2** of a moderately good standard or size, etc; not bringing disgrace or embarrassment: *There was quite a respectable crowd at the match on Saturday.* ○ *£20000 is a very respectable salary.* ○ *Hunt jumped a respectable round although his horse was unfit.*
▷ **re·spect·ably** /-əblɪ/ *adv* in a respectable manner: *respectably dressed, behaved, spoken, etc.*
**re·spect·ab·il·ity** /rɪˌspektə'bɪlətɪ/ *n* [U] quality of being socially respectable; decency.
**re·spect·ful** /rɪ'spektfl/ *adj* ~ **(to/towards sb);** ~ **(of sth)** feeling or showing respect: *listen in respectful silence* ○ *stand at a respectful distance* ○ *respectful of other people's opinions.* ▷ **re·spect·fully** /-fəlɪ/ *adv.* **re·spect·ful·ness** *n* [U].
**re·spect·ive** /rɪ'spektɪv/ *adj* [attrib] of or for or belonging to each as an individual: *They each excel in their respective fields.* ○ *After the party we all went off to our respective rooms.*
▷ **re·spect·ively** *adv* separately or in turn, in the order mentioned: *German and Italian courses are held in Munich and Rome respectively.*

**re·voca·tion** /ˌrevə'keɪʃn/ *n* [C, U] (*fml*) (instance of) revoking or being revoked: *the revocation of laws, contracts, etc.*
**re·voke** /rɪ'vəʊk/ *v* **1** [Tn] (*fml*) withdraw or cancel (a decree, permit, etc): *revoke orders, promises* ○ *His driving licence was revoked after the crash.* **2** [I] (of a player in a card-game) fail to play a card of the same suit as the leading player although able to do so.

*Example:* prior (48, 50, 74)    *Answer:* In lines 48 and 50 'prior' has one of the meanings given in definition 1 – it is a preposition and is used before *to* in formal English to mean *before*.

In line 74 'prior' has a different meaning given in definition 1 – it is an adjective and is used to mean *earlier in time*.

## 4 Vocabulary skills: contextual deduction (6 points)

Use the general context and specific context clues to work out the probable meaning of the following words and phrases in the text. Your answers should be similar in meaning to the ones in the key, but will not be identical. They may be in English or your own language.

*Example:*    Prospectus (15, 18, 19, 21)

> The information contained in this document has been drawn from, and is to be read
> 15 together with, that contained in the prospectus dated 28th April 1987 (the "Prospectus")
> which comprises listing particulars relating to Rolls-Royce plc (the "Company" or "Rolls-
> Royce"). In applying for Ordinary Shares of 20p each in the Company ("Shares"), you will
> be treated as applying on the basis of both this document and the Prospectus, which
> together govern your rights and obligations. The Prospectus alone contains full details of
> 20 the history and business of Rolls-Royce and of the Offer. You are therefore advised to read
> the Prospectus before completing and returning an application form.

*Answer:*    a document containing detailed information about a company (and in this case also about the offer and contract in question)

a) govern (19)          b) on behalf of (6, 51)          c) allocated (44)
d) procedures (49)      e) disclose (52)                 f) instalment (65, 74)

## 5 Reading for detail and using information from the text to solve legal problems (16 points)

Use information from the text on page 135 ('Terms and Conditions of Application') to answer the following questions. Do *not* try to read the whole text for this activity. First find the section of the text which contains the information you need to answer each question, then read that part of the text carefully and use the information to solve the legal problem.

*Example:*    Joe Bloggs posted his application for 500 shares on Monday, 4 May.
             Was he the offeror or the offeree?

*Answer:*    (from lines 41–2 of the text)    He was the offeror.

a) Who was the other party to the contract?
b) Joe was only given 200 shares. Could he sue for breach of contract?
c) He didn't read the Company Prospectus before he made his application. Is he bound by its conditions?
d) On Wednesday 6 May, after talking to his bank manager, Joe decided to cancel his application for shares. He wrote to the Secretary of State the next day. Is the cancellation valid?
e) What is the consideration for the collateral contract?
f) In your opinion, is this valid consideration? Give reasons.
g) Joe received a letter from the Ministry of Trade and Industry asking for the information specified in section 2) b) ii) of the terms and conditions. He replied a month later. Is he in breach of contract?
h) Joe paid the second instalment of 85p per share on 30 September 1987. What can the Secretary of State do?

### 6 Vocabulary skills: word families (6 points)

i) Use your knowledge of root words and word families to decide what the following
words probably mean. Give a simple definition for each word.
*Example:* misinterpretation
*Answer:* (prefix mis- often means wrong, e.g. misunderstanding – wrong or
incorrect interpretation or construction)
(1) juror    (2) incapable    (3) unconditionally    (4) mistrial
(5) requirement    (6) promisee

ii) To show that you understand the words in i), choose the best word to complete the
following sentences. Use each word once only, and make any necessary changes
(e.g. plural forms).
*Example:* If the words of a contract are not clear and precise, there is a danger of
*misinterpretation* by one or both of the parties.
a) The offeree was pleased to accept the excellent offer _____.
b) The 12 _____ were not able to reach a unanimous decision.
c) The hearing was declared a _____ because the court did not have
jurisdiction over the offence.
d) The defendant said that he would give the pony to his cousin for nothing. In
consideration his cousin, the _____, was responsible for the transport of
the pony.
e) Ms Turner's application for shares was not accepted on the grounds that she
did not fulfil the _____ of residence in the UK.
f) A child is considered legally _____ of committing a crime.

## B  Language and structure

### 1 Expressing obligation, possibility, necessity and duty (10 points)

Choose the word or phrase from the list below which best completes each of the
following sentences. The phrase in square brackets [...] will help you to decide.
*Choose from:* (1) shall be    (2) cannot be    (3) ought to    (4) is entitled to
(5) may    (6) are bound to    (7) have to be    (8) need not be
(9) are binding on    (10) may be required    (11) are not entitled to
*Example:* Husbands and wives ___*may*___ now sue each other in contract or tort.
[It is possible]
*Answer:* (5)
a) By the Unfair Contract Terms Act 1977 the parties to a contract _____
always to limit their liability under the contract. [They do not always have the
right]
b) Article 4 of the EEC Treaty provides that the functions of the Community
_____ carried out by the Assembly, the Council, the Commission and the
Court of Justice. [They must be]
c) In English law a valid contract _____ reduced to writing. [It is not
necessary]
d) Under the Police and Criminal Evidence Act 1984 husband and wife _____
give evidence against each other in criminal cases where necessary. [They must
give evidence]
e) The government _____ protect British subjects from criminals. [It has a duty]
f) A woman who stops work in order to have a baby _____ maternity pay for a
period of up to 18 weeks. [She has a right to maternity pay]
g) Under English law transfers of land _____ made by deed. [They must be
made by deed]

h) EC regulations are directly applicable laws which _____ all Member States. [They must be applied and respected]

i) A person who commits murder below the age of 18 years _____ sentenced to life imprisonment. [It is not possible]

j) A breath test _____ when a police officer stops a car and smells alcohol on the driver's breath. [The police officer can demand it]

## C  Law and law terms

The exercises in part C will test your knowledge of English law and law terms you have learnt in this book and particularly in Units 5–7.

### 1  Law terms I (6 points)

In the exercise which follows, substitute a suitable word or phrase for the part of each sentence in italics:

*Example:*  *The lawyer who represented the plaintiff in court* contended that Mr Wilson, the plaintiff, had accepted the defendants' offer by his act.

*Answer:*  Counsel for the plaintiff.

a) By convention, *peers with no professional legal qualifications* do not take part in judicial sittings of the House of Lords.

b) A magistrates' court only hears *cases which are before a court for the first time.*

c) The county court is a *court which does not try criminal cases, but hears actions in the law of contract, tort, family law, etc.*

d) The *international agreement which created the European Community* was first signed by the original Member States – Belgium, France, Holland, Italy, Luxembourg and West Germany – in 1957.

e) By the literal rule of interpretation, English courts must *interpret* the words of a statute in their ordinary, literal and grammatical meaning.

f) English judges are not free to reach any decision they like in a case, they must follow *rules laid down in previous cases which bind the court.*

### 2  Law terms II (10 points)

Choose a suitable word from the list below to complete each of the following sentences. Make any necessary changes (e.g. tense of the verb, plural forms of nouns).

*Choose from:*  (1) to recover  (2) to rule  (3) case-law  (4) trial  (5) case  (6) to cite  (7) beneficiary  (8) to hear  (9) sitting  (10) appellant  (11) to issue

*Example:*  The House of Lords ___*hears*___ both civil and criminal cases.

*Answer:*  (8)

a) The defendant followed his solicitor's advice and elected _____ by jury at the Crown Court.

b) Counsel for the plaintiff _____ *Carlill v. Carbolic Smoke Ball Co.* in his submissions to the court.

c) The judge _____ that the defendants were in breach of contract for failing to pay the plaintiff the sum which they had promised in their offer.

d) The court has the power _____ a writ of habeas corpus if it suspects that a person is held in custody illegally.

e) Since the binding principles of the common law are contained in _____ all English lawyers must often refer to the law reports in their work.

f) The _____ took proceedings against the trustee for breach of trust.

g) Generally, the party who loses the _____ has to pay costs.

h) _____ of the Supreme Court[1] are held during the four periods of the legal year: Michaelmas, Hilary, Easter and Trinity.
[The Supreme Court[1] = the High Court, Court of Appeal and Crown Courts]

i) After losing the case of first instance and the appeal to the High Court, the _____ won her case in the Court of Appeal. However, the decision was reversed by the House of Lords.

j) The general principle of damages for a tort or breach of contract is that the plaintiff is entitled _____ full compensation for his or her loss.

## 3 Law and law terms (10 points)

Use your knowledge of English law and law terms to choose the correct alternative and complete each of the sentences below:

*Example:* The case for the defence was presented to the court by
_counsel for the defendant_
(1) the draftsman    (2) counsel for the defendant    (3) the judge
(4) counsel for the plaintiff

*Answer:* (2)

a) The case was tried _____ in the magistrates' court.
(1) summarily    (2) before a jury    (3) before the Master of the Rolls
(4) on indictment

b) Court of Appeal hearings are reported in _____.
(1) *Hansard*    (2) the Q.B. law reports    (3) the All England law reports    (4) statute law

c) The final appeal was heard in the House of Lords by _____.
(1) three lay peers and the law lords    (2) the justices of the peace
(3) the Lord Chancellor
(4) four Lords of Appeal in Ordinary and the Lord Chancellor

d) The part of a previous authority which binds courts in similar cases is called (the) _____.
(1) *ratio decidendi*    (2) *obiter dicta*    (3) *per incuriam*    (4) *stare decisis*

e) EC law which conflicts with English law _____ the conflicting national law.
(1) is amended by    (2) is consistent with    (3) prevails over
(4) is overruled by

f) To interpret the words of a statute, English courts must first _____.
(1) refer to consolidating statutes
(2) construe the words of the enactment literally
(3) apply the golden rule of interpretation
(4) refer to the history of the enactment

g) The Chancery Division of the English High Court is always bound by previous decisions of _____.
(1) the High Court itself    (2) the Scottish Court of Session
(3) the County Court    (4) the Court of Appeal

h) The High Court issued a writ of *habeas corpus* as part of its _____ jurisdiction.
(1) criminal    (2) civil    (3) supervisory    (4) appellate

i) Domestic proceedings include actions for _____.
(1) divorce    (2) murder    (3) breach of contract    (4) tort

j)  In English law a contract is formed when _____ .
    (1) the offeror makes a binding offer
    (2) the offeree makes a binding offer which is accepted by the offeror
    (3) the offeror and offeree fulfil their contractual obligations
    (4) the offeree accepts an offer made by the offeror before it is retracted.

## 4  The law (12 points)

Use your knowledge of English law to answer the following questions. Give brief, simple answers.

### i)  Unit 5 – Statutory interpretation and EC law

a)  What is the main rule of interpretation of English statutes?
b)  When necessary, which of the following can the English courts refer to in order to construe a statute:
    (1) the legal, social and political background to the enactment?
    (2) discussions and debates in Parliament when the Act was passed?
c)  If an English court has difficulty interpreting Community law, what should it do? (Note: the Court of Appeal did this in *Macarthys Ltd. v. Smith*.)
d)  In *Macarthys Ltd. v. Smith*, it was held that EC law was supreme over national law. What was the legal reason for this?

### ii)  Unit 6 – The judicial system

a)  There are two main areas of jurisdiction in the English judicial system. What are they?
b)  Ordinary lay people play two important roles in the administration of English justice. Name one of these roles.
c)  What is the role of the House of Lords in the English judicial system?
d)  What is the doctrine of binding precedent?

### iii)  Private law – contract

a)  Is the case of *Carlill v. Carbolic Smoke Ball Co.* too old to be a binding precedent today?
b)  In English law, must the offeree say that s/he accepts an offer before a contract is formed? (Note: think about the *ratio decidendi* of *Carlill*.)
c)  Does the decision in *Carlill* mean that extravagant offers made by companies in advertisements are always binding?
d)  Must there always be consideration for a contract to exist in English law?

*Now check all your answers in the key.*

## D  Word games

1  The phrases below form two complete sentences which describe the different hearings and final judgment in an English court case. Can you put them in the correct order to find out who won the case?

i)  *First sentence*
    a) it was held that
    b) In the case of first instance
    c) £500 damages
    d) to recover
    e) before the county court
    f) for breach of contract.
    g) the plaintiff was entitled

ii) *Second sentence*

a) but at the hearing
b) on the grounds that
c) it was held that the appellants
d) The defendants appealed
e) was dismissed.
f) which the offeree had accepted; consequently
g) they had not formed a contract with the plaintiff,
h) before the Court of Appeal
i) had made a binding offer
j) the appeal

*Start like this:*

(i) In the case of first instance . . .
(ii) The defendants appealed . . .

● *Answer:* _ _ _ _ _ _ _ _ _ _ won the case.

## 2 Anagrams

REPE is an anagram of PEER and ATTTEUS is an anagram of STATUTE.
Can you put each group of letters in the anagrams below in the right order, to form a law term connected with the English judicial system?
When you have completed the puzzle, the first letters of each word will spell the name of another important law term.

a) CIRJYAIDU
b) ANOMINUUS
c) TIROA DIDIDCEEN
d) TI SAW LHED
e) CETEENSN
f) GAMSEAD
g) JURIDEN TRYAP
h) TONCRUSE
i) ARLIT
j) ESUIS
k) ROOFREF
l) NINAALOT STUCOR

| | | | | | | | | | | | | | | | |
|---|---|---|---|---|---|---|---|---|---|---|---|---|---|---|---|
| a. | J | U | D | I | C | I | A | R | Y | | | | | | |
| b. | | | | | | | | | | | | | | | |
| c. | | | | | ■ | | | | | | | | | | |
| d. | | ■ | | | ■ | | | | | | | | | | |
| e. | | | | | | | | | | | | | | | |
| f. | | | | | | | | | | | | | | | |
| g. | | | | | | ■ | | | | | | | | | |
| h. | | | | | | | | | | | | | | | |
| i. | | | | | | | | | | | | | | | |
| j. | | | | | | | | | | | | | | | |
| k. | | | | | | | | | | | | | | | |
| l. | | | | | | | ■ | | | | | | | | |

● The first letters of every word spell: _ _ _ _ _ _ _ _ _ _ _ _ _ _

# Public Law — Criminal Law

Reading the Judgment of a European Court of Human Rights case

## Section One: The Facts of the *Tyrer case*; reading a statute

### A Before you read

In Units Nine and Ten you are going to read part of the judgment of a European Court of Human Rights case – the *Tyrer case*. In Unit Nine you will read the facts of the case and the background to the case, involving questions of criminal law and constitutional law. In Unit Ten you will read the decision in the case, involving questions of international human rights law.

*1* Some of the vocabulary in this exercise also appears in the text in Section One. Choose a word or words from the list below to complete the following sentences. Use cognates, word families, and your dictionary to help you decide. Some words are used more than once.

*Choose from:* (1) offender    (2) fine    (3) assault    (4) grievous bodily harm    (5) citizen    (6) guilty    (7) juvenile    (8) punishment    (9) actual bodily harm

*Example:* Under the British Nationality Act 1981 a person may become a British __*citizen*__ by being born in the UK to a parent who is British.

*Answer:* (5)

a) The law can punish criminals in many different ways, but most people would agree that the worst _____ a court can give is the death sentence.

b) A person who commits a criminal offence is called a criminal, or _____.

c) If you attack another person illegally in Britain you will be tried for unlawful _____.

d) If you physically hurt or injure the person you attack, you will be tried for unlawful _____ occasioning [causing] _____.

e) If the injury you cause in the attack is very serious it is called _____.

f) At the beginning of his or her trial the accused person must state whether s/he has committed the offence or not: whether s/he is _____ or not _____.

g) To punish a minor offence the court may order the criminal to pay a sum of money called a _____.

h) Young people who are accused of crimes are tried by a special court called the _____ court.

## 2   Think about the subject

i)   Before you begin to read the *Tyrer case*, think about the following points:
  ● What do you understand by *human rights*?
  ● Can you name some individual human rights?
  ● How is it possible to protect human rights   (1)  in domestic (national) law?
    (2)  in international law?
  ● How are human rights protected in your country?
▲   Compare and discuss your ideas with other members of the class.
ii)  Do you know anything about:
  ● the United Nations Universal Declaration of Human Rights?
  ● the European Court of Human Rights?
iii) Read the following to check your knowledge:

---

The European Court of Human Rights was established by the European Convention for the Protection of Human Rights and Fundamental Freedoms and was set up in Strasbourg in 1959. The Convention, which was drawn up by the Council of Europe in 1950, was inspired by the United Nations Universal Declaration of Human Rights of 1948 and protects many essential rights such as the right to life, freedom from torture and slavery, freedom of thought, conscience and religion, the right to marry and found a family, freedom of peaceable assembly and association, and the right to a fair trial. Only states which are parties to the Convention and the European Commission of Human Rights have the right to bring a case before the Court. Some states have incorporated the Convention into domestic law, but Britain has not, so that it is not directly enforceable as British law. However, British cases have led to some changes in UK domestic law.

---

Based on information from: Ian Brownlie, *Basic Documents in International Law*;
David M. Walker, *The Oxford Companion to Law*

● Which word in the passage means a *treaty*?
  ● Is your country a *signatory* to the European Convention for the Protection of Human Rights?
    In other words has it *signed* the Convention?
  ● Is your country a signatory to the United Nations Universal Declaration of Human Rights?
  ● Which of the individual rights mentioned in the text did you think of during exercise i) above?

## B   First reading: using skimming and scanning to find out about the text

*1*   Do *not* read the text in detail for these activities. Suggested time: 10 minutes.
i)
  a)  Quickly scan the text on pages 145 and 146 for:
    *Headings:* the title and other headings
    *Proper names:* names of people, places, courts and other institutions (look for words beginning with capital letters)
    *Sources:* names of conventions, cases, Acts of Parliament, etc.
    *Numbers:* dates and other numbers
  b)  Use the information from i) to decide the following:
    ● What do you think the text is about?
    ● Who is involved? When?
    ● What do you think the case itself is about?

ii) Quickly find out the main themes of the text by skimming to:
- check your ideas in i) b
- decide in general what the main sections of the text are about.

---

1                 EUROPEAN COURT OF HUMAN RIGHTS
                              25 April 1978

                              **TYRER CASE**
                                JUDGMENT

5   In the Tyrer case,

The European Court of Human Rights sitting, in accordance with Article 43 of the Convention for the Protection of Human Rights and Fundamental Freedoms (hereinafter referred to as 'the Conven-

10 tion') and Rule 21 of the Rules of Court, as a Chamber composed of the following judges:

    Mr. G. Balladore Pallieri, *President*,
    Mr. J. Cremona,
    Mrs. H. Pedersen,

15     Mr. Thor Vilhjálmsson,
    Sir Gerald Fitzmaurice,
    Mr. P.-H. Teitgen,
    Mr. F. Matscher,
    and Mr. H. Petzold, *Deputy Registrar*,

20   Having deliberated in private from 17 to 19 January and on 14 and 15 March 1978,

Delivers the following judgment, which was adopted on the last-mentioned date:

PROCEDURE

25   **1.**   The Tyrer case was referred to the Court by the European Commission of Human Rights (hereinafter referred to as 'the Commission'). The case originated in an application against the United Kingdom of Great Britain and Northern Ireland

30 lodged with the Commission on 21 September 1972 under Article 25 of the Convention by a United Kingdom citizen, Mr Anthony M. Tyrer.

[—————————]

AS TO THE FACTS

**A. The applicant's punishment**

35   **9.**   Mr. Anthony M. Tyrer, a citizen of the United Kingdom born on 21 September 1956, is resident in Castletown, Isle of Man. On 7 March 1972, being then aged 15 and of previous good character, he pleaded guilty before the local

40 juvenile court to unlawful assault occasioning actual bodily harm to a senior pupil at his school. The assault, committed by the applicant in company with three other boys, was apparently motivated by the fact that the victim had reported

45 the boys for taking beer into the school, as a result of which they had been caned. The applicant was sentenced on the same day to three strokes of the birch in accordance with the relevant legislation. See paragraph 11 below.

50   He appealed against sentence to the Staff of Government Division of the High Court of Justice of the Isle of Man. The appeal was heard and dismissed on the afternoon of 28 April 1972; the court considered that an unprovoked assault

55 occasioning actual bodily harm was always very serious and that there were no reasons for interfering with the sentence. The court had ordered the applicant to be medically examined in the morning of the same day and had before it a doctor's report

60 that the applicant was fit to receive the punishment.

  **10.**   After waiting in a police station for a considerable time for a doctor to arrive, Mr. Tyrer was birched late in the afternoon of the same day. His father and a doctor were present. The applicant was

65 made to take down his trousers and underpants and bend over a table; he was held by two policemen whilst a third administered the punishment, pieces of the birch breaking at the first stroke. The applicant's father lost his self-control and after the third

70 stroke 'went for' one of the policemen and had to be restrained.

The birching raised, but did not cut, the applicant's skin and he was sore for about a week and a half afterwards.

75   **11.**   The applicant was sentenced pursuant to section 56 (1) of the Petty Sessions and Summary Jurisdiction Act 1927 (as amended by section 8 of the Summary Jurisdiction Act 1960) whereby:

    'Any person who shall –

80     (a) unlawfully assault or beat any other person;

    (b) make use of provoking language or behaviour tending to a breach of the peace,

85     shall be liable on summary conviction to a fine not exceeding thirty pounds or to be imprisoned for a term not exceeding six months and, in addition to, or instead of, either such punishment, if the offender is a

90     male child or male young person, to be whipped.'

The expressions 'child' and 'young person' mean, respectively, an individual of or over the age 10 and under 14 and an individual of or over the age of 14

95 and under 17.

  **12.**   Execution of the sentence was governed by the following provisions:

(a) *Section 10 of the Summary Jurisdiction Act 1960*

    '(a) the instrument used shall, in the case of a

100     child, be a cane, and in any other case shall be a birch rod;

    (b) the court in its sentence shall specify the number of strokes to be inflicted, being in the case of a child not more than six

105     strokes, and in the case of any other person not more than twelve strokes;

---

110    (c) the whipping shall be inflicted privately as soon as practicable after sentence and in any event shall not take place after the 115 expiration of six months from the passing of the sentence;

(d) the whipping shall be inflicted by a con- stable in the presence of an inspector or other officer of police of higher rank than a constable, and, in the case of a child or young person, also in the presence if he desires to be present, of the parent or guardian of the child or young person.'

Series A, No. 26

iii) Check that you now have the following information about the text:
a) The court:
b) The date:
c) The origin of the case:
d) The parties to the case:
e) The main issue:
f) The main subject of paragraph 9:

                          paragraph 10:

●                           paragraph 11:

## C    Reading for detail: making a summary of the text and language study

### 1    Making a summary of the text I

i) You already know a lot of general information about the text. To find out more about the *Tyrer case* read paragraphs 9 and 10 of the text carefully and identify the main points. Make a note of them. As you do this, you may find several words and phrases which you don't understand. Decide which words you need to understand to follow the main points of the text. Use your vocabulary skills to find the meaning of these words only – use cognates, word families, the context and logical reasoning, and if necessary refer to the glossary or your own dictionary.

ii) For each group of main points in the text write a question.
   *Examples:*

35   **9.** Mr. Anthony M. Tyrer, a citizen of the United Kingdom born on 21 September 1956, is resident in Castletown, Isle of Man. On 7 March 1972, being then aged 15 and of previous good character, he pleaded guilty before the local
40 juvenile court to unlawful assault occasioning actual bodily harm to a senior pupil at his school. The assault, committed by the applicant in company with three other boys, was apparently motivated by the fact that the victim had reported
45 the boys for taking beer into the school, as a result of which they had been caned.

Question (1): Who was the applicant? (lines 35–9)
Question (2): What did he do? (lines 39–46)
When you have finished, compare your questions with the ones in the key to check that you have included all the main points (and the main points only). They should
● be similar, but need not be exactly the same.

iii) For each question, write an answer in note form. Use your own words where possible.
   *Example:* Question (1): Who was the applicant?
   Full answer: The applicant was Mr Anthony M. Tyrer, a UK citizen who was resident on the Isle of Man and aged 15 at the time of the assault.

Notes: applicant – Anthony Tyrer – UK citizen – resident Isle of Man – 15 at time of assault.

Compare the notes and the full answer. Cross out the words in the full answer which are not used in the notes, e.g. ~~The~~ applicant ~~was Mr.~~ Anthony ~~M.~~ Tyrer .... What do you notice?

*Example:* Question (2): What did he do?

Full answer: He committed unlawful assault occasioning actual bodily harm to a pupil at his school together with three other boys. The reason for the assault was that the victim had reported them to the teachers for taking beer into the school and they had been punished for this. He pleaded guilty.

*Write notes on a separate piece of paper.*

● Check your notes for lines 35–46 of the text in the key.
Continue to write the summary of the text yourself by answering your own questions from ii) in note form. Remember to:
  ● include only the main points of the text
  ● use your own words where possible
  ● cut out all words which are not necessary to the meaning

▲ iv) Compare your summary with other members of the class. Have you included the same points?

■ ▲ Compare your summary with the notes in the key. Have you included the same points? The information in your summary should be basically similar, but will not be exactly the same.

● v) Do you know where the Isle of Man is?
Refer to the map of the British Isles on page 35 for the answer.

## 2   Oral practice

Use your answers to Exercise B 1 and your notes from C 1 to describe the facts of the *Tyrer case*.

*Start like this:*

'In 1972 a UK citizen called Anthony Tyrer made an application against the UK to the European Commission of Human Rights. The Commission referred the case to the European Court of Human Rights, which delivered judgment in 1978. The main issue of the case was ...'.

▲ Work together in pairs. Take turns to describe some of the facts.

■ Speak out loud. If possible record the facts on tape, then listen to your recording.

## 3   Word study

a) Use word families and the context to decide the probable meaning of:
   (1) hereinafter (lines 9, 26–7)     (2) whereby (line 78)

b) Find the root word of *imprisoned* (87). Use the context to decide what it means.

c) You have already learnt the terms *breach of contract* and *breach of trust*.
   What do you suppose a *breach of the peace* (83–4) is?
   What kind of language or behaviour do you think could cause a breach of the peace?

d) A *term* is (1) a specialised piece of vocabulary, e.g. 'jurisdiction' is a law term
             (2) a condition in a contract e.g. terms and conditions of application
   Does it have either of these meanings in line 87 of the text?

e) Do you suppose the verb *to exceed* (86, 87) means:
   (1) to be more than, or (2) to be less than?
f) Under the Petty Sessions and Summary Jurisdiction Act 1927:
   (1) is a 13-year-old girl a 'child' or a 'young person'?
   (2) and a 16-year-old boy?
   (3) was Tyrer a 'child' or a 'young person' at the time of the assault?
● g) What does *respectively* (line 93) mean?

**4** Quickly find the following information about the relevant Isle of Man legislation from the text:
a) the name and date of the law which governs sentencing for unlawful assault
b) the different forms of punishment which can be given for unlawful assault
c) if the court can give more than one form of punishment for the same crime
d) if unlawful assault is the only offence for which a person can be whipped
e) if *anyone* can be whipped for unlawful assault
● f) if the way this punishment is inflicted is regulated in detail by the law.

## 5 Tyrer case: procedure, as to the facts

Without looking at the text again, complete as much of the following summary as you can by providing a suitable word or phrase for each blank space. Then refer to the text to complete the summary before checking in the key.

The *Tyrer case* was referred to the (1) *European Court of Human Rights* by the (2) _____ after an application was made by Mr Anthony Tyrer against (3) _____. The Court delivered judgment in April, (4) _____.

At the age of (5) _____, Mr Anthony Tyrer, resident on (6) _____, was convicted of (7) _____ by the local (8) _____. Mr Tyrer had assaulted (9) _____ at (10) _____ together with (11) _____. The reason the boys gave for the (12) _____ was that they had been punished after the (13) _____ had (14) _____. The court sentenced Mr Tyrer under the (15) _____ Act 1927 to (16) _____. His appeal against the (17) _____ to the (18) _____ was (19) _____ on the grounds that the offence committed was (20) _____ and (21) _____. The sentence was carried out according to the provisions of the (22) _____ Act 1960. Mr Tyrer was given a (23) _____ examination in the morning and late that afternoon the (24) _____ was inflicted by (25) _____ in the presence of (26) _____. Mr Tyrer's father was unable to (27)_____ himself during the execution of the punishment and attacked one of the (28) _____.

●

## D    Development

## 1 The criminal process

i) The following events are all connected with the criminal process. Check that you understand their meaning, using a dictionary or the glossary to help you. Note that some of the phrases may have the same meaning as each other!
A  You are charged with an offence.
B  You are sentenced to punishment for an offence.
C  You are suspected of an offence.
D  You are tried for an offence.
E  You are accused of an offence.

F   You are convicted of an offence.
G   You plead guilty or not guilty to an offence.
H   You are arrested for an offence.

ii)  Can you put the different events in i) in the order in which they happen in your country?
     Is there only one possible order of events?

▲         Work in pairs. Discuss your ideas and try to agree on the same order.

■ ▲       Do you think the events happen in the same order in England? Check your ideas
●         in the key.

iii) At what stage or stages of the criminal process is the person involved called:
     (1) the defendant     (2) the offender     (3) the suspect     (4) the convict
●        (5) the criminal      (6) the accused

iv)  Use some of the words and phrases in i) and iii) above to describe what happened
     to Tyrer (take care to use the correct preposition after each of the verbs in i).
     Start like this: 'After attacking another boy at his school Anthony Tyrer was
     accused of unlawful assault occasioning actual bodily harm. He was arrested and
     charged . . .'.

v)   Complete the following report of a crime and criminal case by choosing a suitable
     word or phrase from i) or iii) above for each blank space, making any necessary
     changes.

The police were investigating a series of burglaries in the Westhampton area. A man and a woman
were _suspected_ of the crimes, but there was not enough evidence to (1) _____ them. Then,
one night, during a _burglary_, the victims woke up while the (2) _____ were still in the house.
They found the burglars in the sitting-room stealing the TV and video. The burglars escaped through
the window, leaving behind a black bag containing all their equipment – covered in _fingerprints_!
   The next day Samuel and Felicity Jones were (3) _____ by Westhampton police and (4)
_____ with the offence of _burglary_ with intent. The (5) _____ were tried on indictment in
the Crown Court where they both pleaded not guilty. The jury returned a verdict of guilty. The Joneses
were (6) _____ and (7) _____ to two years' imprisonment.

*Notes*
*Burglary* is the crime of entering a building without the permission of the owner,
with the intention of stealing, causing grievous bodily harm, etc.
*Fingerprints* are marks left by fingers on objects you touch, which the police use to
●        identify criminals.

vi)  Think of a crime story, involving a crime and the trial and conviction of the
     offenders. Use your dictionary to find words you need for the story in English and
     try to use some of the vocabulary you have learnt in this Unit. Write brief notes to
     help you remember the main points of the story.

■         Tell your story. Use your notes to help you describe the crime and criminal case. If
          possible record your crime story, then listen to the recording on tape.

▲         Work in small groups. In turns, use your notes to tell your crime story to the other
          members of the group. At the end, decide which story you enjoyed most.

vii) For written consolidation, use your notes in vi) above to write a detailed report of
     your crime and criminal case, similar to the story in v).

## 2   Punishments

i)   Write a list of the different punishments for crimes which exist in your country.
     Write the names which you do not know in English in your own language.

ii)  Where possible, find the English terms for the different punishments in your list in i) above in the list of punishments for crimes available in the UK given below. Use a dictionary and the glossary to help you.

**Punishments for crimes available in the UK**

capital punishment    life imprisonment    community service order    fine
probation    suspended sentence    corporal punishment    imprisonment

Do the same forms of punishment exist in the criminal justice systems in the UK and in your country?

iii) Put the punishments in ii) in the order you think best on the word ladder below, starting with the least serious and ending with the most serious.
For example, you may think that the least serious punishment is probation, followed by a fine, followed by a community service order, as in the example.
*Example:*

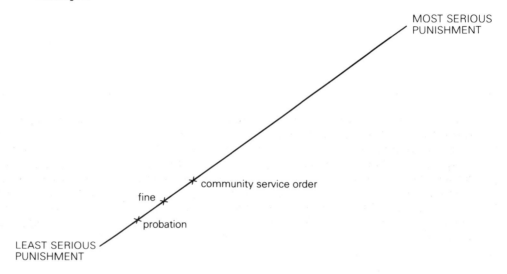

■    Give reasons for the position of each punishment.
▲    Work in small groups. Discuss your reasons for the position of each punishment and try to agree on the same order.
When you have finished, compare your ideas with the rest of the class.

iv) Think of the circumstances of Anthony Tyrer's crime.
◆    Do you think the punishment he received was justified in the circumstances?
◆    Which of the three punishments available for unlawful assault (see the Petty Sessions and Summary Jurisdiction Act – lines 75–91) would *you* have sentenced Tyrer to for his crime?
◆    Of all the punishments in i) and ii) above, which one would you have chosen for Tyrer? Why?
◆    Are there any punishments in the list that you think are *never* justified?
▲    Discuss your ideas with other members of the class.

## 3 Prediction

Now that you know the facts of the *Tyrer case*, why do you think Tyrer applied to the European Commission of Human Rights? Do you personally think he was right to make an application?

## Section Two: The Background to the *Tyrer Case*

### A   Before you read

What do you remember from previous units in this book about the following?
Think about them for a few moments.
- The composition of the UK
- The Royal Assent
- The Home Secretary
- The Privy Council
- Constitutional conventions and their role in British constitutional law

■ Check your ideas by referring again to Units 2 and 4 and the glossary.

▲ Exchange your ideas with other members of the class before checking your information in Units 2 and 4 and the glossary.

### B   Reading to understand the general themes of the text

*1*   Skim the text on pages 151 and 152 and decide which of the three sections marked is about:

A   The application of judicial corporal punishment in the Isle of Man and prospects for the future

B   The constitutional position of the Isle of Man and its relationship with the UK

● C   The legal status of judicial corporal punishment in the UK and Isle of Man

---

1   **B.  General background**

SECTION
1

**13.**   The Isle of Man is not a part of the United Kingdom but a dependency of the Crown with its own government, legislature and courts and its own administrative, fiscal and legal systems. The Crown is ultimately responsible for the good government of the Island and acts in this respect

5   through the Privy Council on the recommendation of Ministers of the United Kingdom Government in their capacity as Privy Counsellors. In that capacity, the Home Secretary is charged with prime responsibility for Isle of Man affairs.

Prior to October 1950, the United Kingdom Government regarded international treaties applicable to the United Kingdom as extending, in the absence of contrary provision, to the Isle of Man.

10   Thereafter, they no longer so regarded such treaties unless there were an express inclusion and they treated the Island as a territory for whose international relations they were responsible. In fact, by letter dated 23 October 1953 addressed to the Secretary-General of the Council of Europe, the Government of the United Kingdom declared, in accordance with Article 63 of the Convention, that the Convention should extend to a number of such territories, including the Isle of Man.

15   The Island's parliament, the Court of Tynwald, is one of the oldest in Europe. It consists of a Lieutenant-Governor appointed by and representing the Crown, an Upper House (the Legislative Council) and a Lower House (the House of Keys). Tynwald legislates in domestic matters, the laws it adopts requiring ratification by the Queen in Council; the Home Secretary is responsible for advising the Privy Council whether or not to recommend that the Royal Assent be given.

20   In strict law, the United Kingdom Parliament has full power to pass laws applicable to the Isle of Man but, by constitutional convention, does not in the ordinary course legislate on the Island's domestic affairs, such as penal policy, without its consent. This convention would be followed unless it were overridden by some other consideration, an example of which would be an international treaty obligation.

---

SECTION 2

25 **14.** Judicial corporal punishment of adults and juveniles was abolished in England, Wales and Scotland in 1948 and in Northern Ireland in 1968. That abolition followed upon the recommendations of the Departmental Committee on Corporal Punishment (known as the Cadogan Committee) which issued its report in 1938. The standing Advisory Council on the Treatment of Offenders, in its report of 1960 (known as the Barry report), endorsed the findings of the Cadogan Committee

30 and concluded that corporal punishment should not be reintroduced as a judicial penalty in respect of any categories of offences or of offenders.

**15.** The punishment remained in existence in the Isle of Man. When Tynwald examined the question in 1963 and 1965, it decided to retain judicial corporal punishment, which was considered a deterrent to hooligans visiting the Island as tourists and, more generally, a means of preserving law

35 and order.

In May 1977, by thirty-one votes for and only one against, Tynwald passed a resolution, *inter alia*,

'that the retention of the use of judicial corporal punishment for crimes of violence to the person is a desirable safeguard in the control of law and order in this Island and Tynwald hereby re-affirms its policy to retain the use of judicial corporal punishment for violent crimes to the

40 person committed by males under the age of 21'.

SECTION 3

At the hearing on 17 January 1978, the Attorney-General for the Isle of Man informed the Court that recently a privately organised petition in favour of the retention of judicial corporal punishment had obtained 31,000 signatures from amongst the approximate total of 45,000 persons entitled to vote on the Island.

45 **16.** While under various provisions judicial corporal punishment could be imposed on males for a number of offences, since 1969 its application has apparently been restricted in practice to offences of violence.

During his address to the Court, the Attorney-General for the Isle of Man indicated that the Manx legislature would shortly be considering the Criminal Law Bill 1978 which contained a

50 proposal to limit the use of judicial corporal punishment to young males for certain specified offences only, on the whole the more serious offences of violence. The offence with which the applicant was charged had been omitted from the specified list of offences.

**17.** The name and address of a juvenile sentenced in the Isle of Man, whether to corporal punishment or otherwise, are not published.

55 **18.** According to figures cited before the Court by the Attorney-General for the Isle of Man, judicial corporal punishment was inflicted in 2 cases in 1966, in 4 cases in 1967, in 1 case in 1968, in 7 cases in 1969, in 3 cases in 1970, in 0 cases in 1971, in 4 cases in 1972, in 0 cases in 1973, in 2 cases in 1974, in 1 case in 1975, in 1 case in 1976 and in 0 cases in 1977. The average number of crimes of violence to the person per annum was: between 1966 and 1968 – 35; between 1969 and 1971 – 52;

60 between 1972 and 1974 – 59; and between 1975 and 1977 – 56. In 1975 there were 65 crimes of violence to the person, in 1976 58 and in 1977 approximately 46.

In the three years 1975 to 1977, only one young male was convicted of a crime of violence.

At the 1976 census, the Island's population stood at 60,496.

---

## C  Reading for detail and language study

### 1  *Personal reading comprehension*

You are going to read a section of the text for detailed understanding completely independently. You will choose and study useful vocabulary and language points, then make your own personal reading comprehension exercise on the text and be responsible for the correction of answers yourself.

■ You will study section 1 of the text. Follow the instructions below.

▲ Form groups of three. Each member of the group will study a different section of the text.

■▲ First decide who will study sections 1, 2 and 3, then follow the instructions below.
  i) Work independently. Read your section of the text carefully. Identify the main points and make a note of them. Decide which new words or phrases you need to

understand to follow the main points of the text and use your vocabulary skills to find their meaning – use cognates, word families, the context and logical reasoning and your dictionary.

Are there any other language points which interest you in your section of the text?

ii) Write a few questions (perhaps four or five) about the main points in your section of the text.

Make sure that you know the answers to all your questions.

■ iii) Answer your questions from ii), using your own words where possible.

● When you have finished, compare your work with the example questions and answers given in the key. What differences and similarities are there?

▲ Work in your group of three, starting with the person who has studied section 1. Ask your partners to read the text and answer your questions from ii). Explain any vocabulary they ask you about and correct their answers to your questions.

Point out any language forms of particular interest to the other members of the group.

Do the same with sections 2 and 3 of the text.

iv) In what way do you think the information in section 1 of the text is relevant to the *Tyrer case*?

## 2   Word study

The exercises which follow include vocabulary from sections 1, 2 and 3 of the text. For the words which you have already studied during Exercise C 1 above, compare the *method* you used to understand the words with the method used here. Check that your understanding of the words was correct when you refer to the key.

i) *Word families*

Use your knowledge of root words and word families to decide the probable meaning of the following. Then check that your ideas make sense in the context.

*Example:* Privy Counsellor (line 6)   *Answer: Counsel* is similar to *Council*. Words ending in -or often refer to a person who does an action (e.g. offeror, tortfeasor). A Privy Counsellor is probably someone who acts on the Privy Council – a member of the Privy Council. Does this make sense in the context?

a) juveniles (noun, 25, 53)   b) findings (noun, 29)   c) reintroduce (verb, 30)
● d) safeguard (noun, 38)   e) reaffirm (verb, 39)   f) Manx (adj.) (49)

ii) *Context and logical reasoning*

1) For each word on the left below, two definitions are given on the right. From the context, decide which one you think is correct.

*Example:* consent (22)   (1) agreement   (2) disagreement
a) endorsed (29)   (1) did not support   (2) supported
b) to retain (33, 39)   (1) to keep   (2) to abolish
c) retention (37, 42)   (1) keeping   (2) abolition
d) omitted from (52)   (1) included in   (2) left out of

● *Answer:* (1)

2) Use the context and logical reasoning to decide the probable meaning of the words below in the text. Then check your ideas in your dictionary.

a) thereafter (10)   b) ratification (18)   c) resolution (36)
● d) petition (42)   e) restricted (46)

iii) *Dictionary use*

First try to decide what you think the following words might mean in the text. Decide the grammatical function of each word (noun, verb, etc.). Then find the exact meaning in your dictionary.

a) charged (6)   b) deterrent (34)   c) hooligans (34)
d) hereby (38)   e) address (53)

Which of these words has a different meaning in the text from the one you already know?

iv) *Other words of interest*

    a) Which *Convention*, *hearing* and *Court* are referred to in lines 13, 41, 41 and 48 of the text?

    b) What do you understand by *penal policy* (22)?

    c) Notice the phrase *law and order* (34–5). What do you think it means?

    d) Can you decide the meaning of the Latin phrase in line 36 of the text? It is pronounced /intər ĕiliə/

## 3 Language study

i) *So and such*

What do the following words in the text refer to?

    a) so (10)    b) such (10)    c) such (14)

ii) *Understanding phrases with 'unless'*

Refer to the text and decide which of the two alternatives in the phrase in italics is correct:

    a) UK treaties are not applicable to the Isle of Man if there *is/is not* an express inclusion to this effect. (line 10)

    b) The UK Parliament will legislate on the Isle of Man's domestic affairs without its consent when there *is/is not* a special reason which overrides the constitutional convention. (lines 21–3)

**4** In view of your answers to exercises 2 and 3, check that all the answers to your questions in exercise 1 ii) were correct.

## 5 Multiple choice comprehension check

To check your understanding of the main points, read the whole text carefully and complete each sentence below by choosing the correct alternative from a, b, c and d.

i) The Isle of Man

    a) belongs to the Queen

    b) is totally independent from the UK

    c) has some links with the UK, but mainly governs itself

    d) belongs to the UK.

ii) Since 1950 international treaties applicable to the UK

    a) are automatically applicable to the Isle of Man

    b) are never applicable to the Isle of Man

    c) are applicable to the Isle of Man if there is no provision to the contrary

    d) are only applicable to the Isle of Man if this is expressly stated in the provision.

iii) Domestic legislation for the Isle of Man is generally passed by

    a) Tynwald – the Isle of Man Parliament

    b) the UK Parliament

    c) the Home Secretary and the Privy Council

    d) the Legislative Council.

iv) At the time of the *Tyrer case* judicial corporal punishment existed

    a) in England, Wales, Scotland and the Isle of Man

    b) in the UK

    c) in the Isle of Man

    d) in Northern Ireland and the Isle of Man.

   v) In 1963, 1965 and 1977 Tynwald decided to retain judicial corporal punishment
       a)  to control males under the age of 21
       b)  to prevent crime
       c)  to deter visitors
       d)  to punish hooligans.
  vi) In 1978 the majority of the Isle of Man electorate
       a)  were in favour of keeping judicial corporal punishment
       b)  were entitled to vote for judicial corporal punishment
       c)  were against judicial corporal punishment
       d)  voted in favour of keeping judicial corporal punishment.
 vii) At the time of the *Tyrer case* the Isle of Man Parliament was considering legislation which would
       a)  reduce the use of judicial corporal punishment on young males
       b)  introduce judicial corporal punishment for serious offences of violence
       c)  increase the number of offences for which judicial corporal punishment could be given
       d)  abolish judicial corporal punishment for unlawful assault.
viii) On the Isle of Man, judicial corporal punishment is inflicted
       a)  once a year
       b)  in very few cases, if at all, each year
       c)  for all crimes of violence
       d)  between 35 and 65 times a year.

## 6  Writing a summary II

Write a summary in note form of sections 2 and 3 of the text. Follow the instructions below.
i)   Read sections 2 and 3 of the text carefully and identify the main points.
ii)  Make sure that you understand the main points of the text. Use your vocabulary skills to decide the meaning of any more words or phrases you need to understand for this purpose.
iii) For each group of main points in the text, ask a question. Write the answers to your questions in note form.
     Remember to:
     • include only the main points of the text
     • use your own words where possible
     • cut out all words which are not necessary to the meaning.

## 7  Checking the quality of a summary

i)   To check the quality of a summary, decide:
     • is it brief and concise?
     • is it written in your own words (not copied word for word from the text)?
     • does it contain all the main points of the text and the main points only?
ii)  Check the quality of the following summary of paragraph 14 of the text. Be critical!
     Which two parts of the summary are good? Why are the other two parts bad? Rewrite the bad parts yourself.

### Summary in note form of paragraph 14

(1) Judicial corporal punishment was abolished in the UK in 1948 and 1968.
(2) Reason for abolition: recommendation of Cadogan Committee 1938.

(3) Barry Report 1960 supported Cadogan Committee findings

(4) and concluded that corporal punishment should not be reintroduced as a judicial penalty for any categories of offences / offenders.

▲ Compare your ideas with other members of the class before checking in the key.
●

iii) Check the quality of your own summary of the text in the same way. Can you improve some parts of it?

▲ iv) Exchange the final version of your summary with someone else. Decide if any parts of your partner's summary can still be improved, then discuss your ideas and compare your summaries.

## 8 Oral practice

Use your summary to describe the background to the *Tyrer case*.

▲ Work in pairs, taking turns to describe different aspects of the background of the case.

■ Speak aloud. If possible, record your summary of the case on tape, then listen to your recording.

## D Development: the sentencing of offenders

### 1 Reasons for sentencing

Which phrase on the right completes each of the four sentences beginning on the left? Do you strongly agree or disagree with any of the statements?

A The use of capital punishment for murder was abolished . . .

B Parliament passed a law to reintroduce capital punishment for the murder of police officers . . .

C The infliction of capital punishment was restricted to crimes of terrorism . . .

D The government passed a resolution to retain capital punishment for serious crimes of violence . . .

I . . . on the grounds that life imprisonment of individual offenders was no safeguard against organised groups of criminals.

II . . . as part of their penal policy for the severe punishment of offenders.

III . . . in order to deter criminals from using firearms against members of the forces of law and order.

IV . . . because the Parliamentary Commission found that in most offences of this type it was not an effective deterrent.

●

### 2 Aims of sentencing

a) Which of the following do you think should be the main aim in sentencing offenders?

| | |
|---|---|
| Punishment | – to punish the offender |
| Deterrence | – to deter people from committing crimes |
| Rehabilitation | – to teach the offender to become a normal member of society |
| Protection | – to protect society from criminal behaviour |
| Other | – say what |

● b) Which of these aims applies to each statement from 1 above?

c) Put the different aims in order of importance for you.

d) Refer again to the list of punishments in Section One, Exercise D 2 of this Unit. Which form of punishment do you think is most effective for each of the aims in a)?

▲ Discuss and compare your work and ideas in small groups.

### 3 Talking points

Think about the following points for a few moments:

◆ Which forms of punishment do you think are effective deterrents?

◆ Which punishments can help to rehabilitate the offender?

◆ What do you think are the main aims of the penal system in your country? Do you agree with them?

◆ The Isle of Man Parliament retained judicial corporal punishment on the grounds that it was an effective deterrent to hooligans and a safeguard in the control of law and order. Do you agree?

■ Talk about your ideas. If possible record them on tape, then listen to your recording.

▲ Discuss your ideas in small groups, then compare them with other members of the class.

---

## Section Three: Reading Newspaper Crime Reports

*1* Quickly find the heading below which matches each of the five newspaper articles:

# Home to prison

**Escape charge**

## Heysel case

## Policeman convicted of punching hippy

**Murder charges**

**1**

Three men appeared before magistrates in Hertford accused of murdering PC Frank Mason, who died during an armed hold-up at a bank in Hemel Hempstead. Charles McGhee, 30, of Luton, Perry Wharrie, 28, of Lee, south London, and James Hurley, 26, of Luton, and a fourth man, Robert McFarland, of Luton, accused of disposing of property to impede the arrest of the three, were all remanded in custody for three days.

**2**

A man appeared in Marylebone magistrates court in London yesterday, accused of escaping police custody at a hospital 13 months ago. Alan Knowlden, 36, was also charged with conspiring to commit armed robbery. He was remanded in custody to appear at Lambeth Magistrates Court next Friday.

**3**

BRUSSELS – A convention signed here yesterday should mean that the 26 Britons wanted in Belgium in connection with the 1985 Heysel football riot would be allowed to serve jail sentences in Britain if they are convicted here, **David Usborne** writes.

The accord, signed by 10 states, including Britain and Belgium, guarantees that people convicted in an EC state other than their own will have the right to serve the sentence in their home country.

The Belgian Justice Minister, Jean Gol, confirmed that the convention would apply to the wanted Britons if they are finally tried. 'There would be no problem if these people wanted to do their term in the UK', he said.

A similar convention on the transfer of convicts already exists in the 21-member Council of Europe, but has never been ratified by Belgium.

Belgian efforts to extradite the 26 Britons suffered a serious setback three months ago when the case failed in the High Court because of a legal technicality. Proceedings have now been resumed.

**4**

The trial in Belgium of 26 British football fans on charges arising out of the 1985 Heysel Stadium disaster will open in Brussels today, and be adjourned until the autumn. Belgian defence lawyers will appeal for a suspension because they have not had sufficient access to evidence.

**5**

STEPHEN Syratt, a Wiltshire police sergeant, was found guilty yesterday in Winchester Crown Court of causing actual bodily harm to a member of the 1985 Stonehenge hippy peace convoy. He was sentenced to three months' imprisonment, suspended for 12 months.

The court was told that Syratt, aged 34, of Swindon, who had served for 17 years, had punched a prisoner at Amesbury police station. He would almost certainly be dismissed from his £12,000-a-year job and lose his pension rights, Mr Justice Swinton Thomas said.

Extracts from the *Independent, Guardian* and *The Sunday Times*

**2** Skim the five articles and decide which one(s) report(s):

  a) the suspension of a trial
  b) a preliminary hearing before a magistrates' court
  c) a conviction
● d) an international agreement on serving prison sentences.

**3** Quickly scan the articles and list:
  a) the names of the different courts which are mentioned
● b) the names of the different offences which are mentioned.

  Which of the crimes do you think is the most serious?

## 4 Summary

Choose one of the five articles.
i) Read it carefully and identify the main points.
ii) Use your vocabulary skills to understand any new words or phrases which interest you.
iii) Write a summary in note form of the article. (If necessary refer to Sections One and Two of this Unit for instructions on how to write a summary.)
▲ iv) Work in small groups. Use the notes in your summary to tell the other members of your group about your crime report. Discuss the case, and decide what sentence you would give the offender(s) in question.
■ Use the notes in your summary to describe your crime report. If possible, record the story on tape, then listen to your recording. Decide what sentence you would give the offender(s) in question.

## 5 How serious is the offence?

Draw a word ladder (similar to the one you completed on punishments; see page 150) showing the offences below in personal order of seriousness. Use your dictionary and the glossary to help you decide.
▲ Work together in pairs and try to agree on the same order with your partner.
  ● a parking offence       ● assault
  ● rape                    ● indecency
  ● armed robbery           ● murder
  ● bribery and corruption  ● kidnapping
  ● theft                   ● drunken driving
  ● arson
Which punishment do you think is generally most suitable for each of the crimes?
▲ When you have finished, compare and discuss your results with other members of the class.

## 6 Two cases

Read the two case histories below and decide which offences Jack and Annette have committed:

**Jack Thatcher**   Like his father, Jack Thatcher is a jailbird – at the age of 40 he has spent most of his life in prison for various offences of violence and theft. He comes from a broken home, has had no real education and has never had a job. The only way he knows how to make money is by stealing it. When he came out of prison last week, he decided to rob a village post office. During the robbery, the postmaster tried to ring the alarm, so Jack hit him on the head with his gun. At that moment a customer came into the post office. She screamed. In panic, Jack shouted at her to keep quiet. When she continued to scream, he shot her. Jack thought quickly. He took a box of matches from his pocket and set fire to the building, then escaped with the money.

**Annette Forbes**   Annette Forbes is head of the marketing division of GMC, the computer company. She went to university, has a good job and enjoys a happy family life. She has always been a 'law-abiding citizen'. One day she arrived a little late for work, and had to park her car in a no-parking zone. She took a client out for a business lunch and drank a gin and tonic, half a bottle of wine and a liqueur to celebrate an important new contract. When driving back to work, she was stopped by a policeman, who tested her breath for alcohol. He told her she had drunk too much and would be disqualified from driving for a year. Annette (who needs her car for her job) suggested he might 'forget' about the offence in return for a brand new GMC home computer. That afternoon, Annette remembered that she had no more writing-paper at home. As usual, she took a new packet of paper from the office and a box of six pencils.

- If they are charged and convicted of all their offences, what sentences do you think Jack and Annette will receive?
- In your opinion, what is the most suitable punishment for Jack and Annette?
- Do you think they will commit other offences in future?

▲ Discuss the cases with other members of the class.

## 7   *Vocabulary revision*

Design and complete a vocabulary network on the subject of criminal law.

# UNIT 10
# International Law — Human Rights

Reading the Judgment of a European Court of Human Rights Case

## Section One:    Proceedings before the Commission

### A    Before you read

### 1    Think about the subject

- Remember the facts of the *Tyrer case*. To check your information, refer to the summary on pages 145–6 of Unit Nine.
- At the beginning of Unit Nine you considered the kind of human rights that are generally protected by law. Consider the facts of the *Tyrer case* in relation to this, and decide what you think the proceedings in the case will centre on.
▲ Discuss your ideas with other members of the class.

### 2    Prediction

Look at the title of the text on pages 160–61. What exactly do you suppose it will be about? What kind of information do you think it will contain?

### B    Reading to understand the general themes of a text

1    Quickly skim the text on pages 160–61 to understand what the general themes are, and see if your ideas from Section A above were right or wrong. *Do not* try to understand the text in detail at this stage.

---

*Proceedings before the Commission*

**19.**  In his application, lodged with the Commission on 21 September 1972, Mr Tyrer complained, in particular, that:
5  – his judicial corporal punishment constituted a breach of Article 3 of the Convention;
– such punishment was destructive of family well-being and therefore contrary to Article 8 of the Convention;
10  – no remedies existed to rectify the violation, which was inconsistent with Article 13 of the Convention;

– the punishment was discriminatory within the meaning of Article 14 of the Convention in that
15  it was primarily pronounced on persons from financially and socially deprived homes;
– the violation of Article 3 also constituted a violation of Article 1 of the Convention.
The applicant also claimed damages as well as
20  repeal of the legislation concerned.
**20.**  In its decision of 19 July 1974, the Commission, having considered *ex officio* that the facts of the case raised issues of

---

discrimination on grounds of sex and/or age
25 contrary to Article 14 of the Convention, taken
together with Article 3:
– decided not to proceed further with an
examination of the original complaint under
Article 14 which the applicant had
30 subsequently withdrawn;
– declared admissible and retained those parts of
the application which raised issues under
Article 3, either alone or in conjunction with
Article 14;
35 – declared inadmissible the remainder of the
application.
**21.** In January 1976, the Commission was
notified that the applicant wished to withdraw
his application. However, on 9 March 1976, the
40 Commission decided that it could not accede to
this request 'since the case raised questions of a
general character affecting the observance of the
Convention which necessitated a further

examination of the issues involved'. The
45 applicant took no further part in the
proceedings.
**22.** In its report of 14 December 1976, the
Commission expressed the opinion:
– by fourteen votes to one, that the judicial
50 corporal punishment inflicted on the applicant
was degrading and was in breach of Article 3 of
the Convention;
– that it was not necessary, in view of the
preceding conclusion, to pursue an
55 examination of the issue under Article 14 of
the Convention;
– as regards Article 63 § 3 of the Convention,
that there were not any significant social or
cultural differences between the Isle of Man
60 and the United Kingdom which could be
relevant to the application of Article 3 in the
present case.
The report contains one separate opinion.

*Tyrer case*, 25 April 1978, Series A, No. 26

*2* Decide what each paragraph of the text is about and give each one a suitable heading,
so that you can see the organisation of information in the text clearly when you work
on it in detail later. Make a note of the headings.
*Example:* paragraph 19: Articles of the Convention cited by Tyrer *or:* Mr Tyrer's
● Application

## C Reading for detailed understanding and word study

### 1 *Understanding law terms*

i) Scan the text and note all the words and phrases that you think are law terms.
For example, in his *application, lodged with the Commission* . . . (to lodge an
application with . . .).

▲ ii) Work in small groups and use your shared knowledge, vocabulary skills and a
dictionary to work out the meaning of the words and phrases you have chosen.
Don't be afraid to guess! Compare your work with other groups.

■ Use your own knowledge and vocabulary skills and a dictionary to work out the
meaning of the words and phrases you have chosen. Don't be afraid to guess!

iii) Decide which words and phrases belong specifically to the field of International
Law (e.g. breach of Article 3 of the Convention), and which are also general law
terms that you could also find in the context of domestic law (e.g. to claim
damages). Are these words specific to any particular branch of domestic law? (For
instance, *judicial corporal punishment* is specific to criminal law.)

iv) To help you remember and use the words and phrases you have learnt in future,
organise them into categories of your choice and design and complete a vocabulary
table similar to the one on page 55. As you learn more law terms during this Unit,
write them in the appropriate column in your table.

▲ Compare your table with other members of the class.

### 2 *Cognates and false friends*

i) The words in italics in the exercise overleaf, which also appear in the text, may
look similar to a word in your own language, but is the meaning in fact the same?

Choose the correct alternative from 1 and 2 and compare the meaning of the
English word with the similar word in your own language. Which of the words are
true cognates (the meaning corresponds in both languages) and which are false
friends (the meaning is different)? If you do not speak a cognate language,
complete the exercise anyway to check your understanding of these words. (See
pages 2–3 for more information on cognates and false friends.)

*Example:*   Her *application* was made last week =
1. She presented a request last week (*correct*)
2. She enforced a law last week (*false*)    *Answer:* 1.

a) The results of the survey were
*inconsistent*.
1. There was not enough
information.
2. They did not show a regular
pattern.

b) She comes from a *deprived* family.
1. Her family are poor and needy.
2. Her family are corrupt,
perverted.

c) They *retained* nothing.
1. They kept nothing.
2. They thought nothing.

d) We *affected* their plans.
1. We copied or imitated their
plans.
2. We influenced their plans.

e) That's a case of *discrimination*.
1. An unfair distinction based on
colour, sex, religion etc.
2. A change in the law so that a
criminal act has become legal.

f) Equitable *remedies* exist to
supplement the common law.
1. solutions, cures.
2. means to enforce a right or
compensate a wrong.

ii) Can you translate the words which are false friends in the phrases in i) into your
language? Check your answers carefully in a dictionary.

iii) For practice in using the vocabulary in i) choose the correct form of the
appropriate word to complete the following phrases:
*Example:*   His _application_ for the post of senior legal adviser was not accepted.
a) In many countries a law which is _____ with the constitution is not
valid.
b) The beneficiary of the will _____ the house, but sold everything else.
c) Changes in the law have seriously _____ workers' rights.
d) They were prosecuted under the Race Relations Act for racial _____.
e) It seems that young people from _____ social backgrounds are more
likely to become delinquents.

## 3   Reading for detailed understanding

i) Find the following words and phrases in the text and make a note of where they
occur.
a) family well-being (lines 7–8)
b) rectify (line 10)
c) discriminatory (13)
d) repeal (20)
e) raised issues (23)
f) withdrawn (30)
g) admissible (31)
h) inadmissible (35)
i) remainder (35)
j) accede (40)
k) degrading (51)

ii) Read the text carefully and find the information you need to fill in the first four
columns of the chart on page 163. (You will complete the last column at the end of
this Unit.) As you work, decide which of the words or phrases from i) you need to
understand in order to complete the chart. Where necessary, use your vocabulary
skills to work out the meaning of these key words and phrases. Use cognates, root
words and word families, the general context, logical reasoning and specific

context clues and your dictionary. Don't spend time trying to understand the words you decide are *not* necessary for your reading purpose.

| Article | Issue | Cited by Tyrer | Commission's decision | Court's decision |
|---------|-------|----------------|------------------------|------------------|
|         |       |                |                        |                  |
| 8       | family well-being | Yes | inadmissible |                  |
|         |       |                |                        |                  |
|         |       |                |                        |                  |
|         |       |                |                        |                  |
|         |       |                |                        |                  |

If possible refer to a copy of the European Convention on Human Rights to complete the second column of your chart in your notebook, before checking your information in the key. You will find more information about Article 63 in lines
● 57–62 of the text on p. 161.

### 4 Oral practice

Use the information in your chart from Exercise 3 above to describe the main issues in the *Tyrer case* and the Commission's decision on each issue.
*Example:* 'Mr Tyrer also cited Article 8 of the European Convention on Human Rights, which protects the right to family life. The Commission found that his application was inadmissible on this issue.'
■ Speak aloud. If possible, record your description on tape, then listen to your recording.
▲ Work in pairs. In turn, describe the different points in your chart.

### D Development

Think about the following points:
◆ Consider the Articles of the Convention cited by Tyrer in relation to the facts of the case. Consider the Commission's decision: given the information you have about the case, do you agree with the Commission?
◆ How do you suppose the judgment will continue?

▲ Discuss your ideas with other members of the class.

## Section Two: Judgment and Decision

### A A reading strategy for private study

While studying this book you have learnt and practised many different techniques to help you read with greater understanding. You will now learn a complete reading strategy for private study, which brings together many of these skills. You can use it to study a text of your choice in any language completely independently.

Complete each of the five steps below – Learn about the Text, Question, Read in Detail, Reformulate and Consider – for paragraphs 28–31 of the text on pages 165 and 166. Since you have already studied extracts from the same text, you will already know some of the answers in step 1.

## 1  Learn about the text

i)  Before you read, find out as much as possible about the text. Look at the text and use:
   a) *external information* – decide: what type of text is it?
      When and where was it published? Who by? On what occasion?
      Is it part of a longer publication? If so, what is the relation of this text to the complete text, book, judgment, etc.?
      What, who and where is it about?
   b) *internal information*: titles and subtitles; illustrations, tables and diagrams.
ii) Use your skimming and scanning skills to find key words and phrases in the text, and decide what the main themes are, and how the material is organised. You may like to decide on a heading for each section of the text so that you can see quickly and clearly what it is about.

## 2  Question

Ask yourself the questions you want the text to answer.
• What do you want to know from the text?
• What do you think the text can tell you?
Write your questions, and try to predict some of the answers before you read, if you can.

## 3  Read in detail

Read the text carefully, looking for the answers to your questions and reading to confirm or check your predictions. Note any other important points, too.
Fix the answers in your mind by speaking them out loud, or writing them down.
If working with others, compare your questions and answers with them.
*Vocabulary note*: as you read, use your vocabulary skills to understand **key words and phrases** necessary to answer your questions and follow the main points of the text, but don't spend time on other unknown vocabulary at this stage – this would interfere with your reading.

## 4  Reformulate

Identify the main points of the text and any information that interests you personally, and reformulate this in the form of a summary, chart or diagram for easy future reference.
*Vocabulary note*: study any other vocabulary or language points that interest you now. See Unit 5 for ideas on how to store and process vocabulary, or use your own system.

# 5 Consider

Remind yourself again of what you have learnt, but this time consider the information in relation to your previous knowledge:
- what is the importance of what you have read?
- what are the implications for other things that you already know?
- what is your personal reaction to what you have learnt?

Discuss your ideas with someone else, if you have the opportunity.

---

AS TO THE LAW

## II. ON ARTICLE 3

**28.** The applicant claimed before the Commission that the facts of his case constituted a breach of Article 3 of the Convention which provides:

'No one shall be subjected to torture or to inhuman or degrading treatment or punishment.'

He alleged that there had been torture or inhuman or degrading treatment or punishment, or any combination thereof.

In its report, the Commission expressed the opinion that judicial corporal punishment, being degrading, constituted a breach of Article 3 and that, consequently, its infliction on the applicant was in violation of that provision.

**29.** The Court shares the Commission's view that Mr Tyrer's punishment did not amount to 'torture' within the meaning of Article 3. The Court does not consider that the facts of this particular case reveal that the applicant underwent suffering of the level inherent in this notion as it was interpreted and applied by the Court in its judgment of 18 January 1978 (Ireland v. the United Kingdom, Series A no. 25, pp. 66–67 and 68, §§ 167 and 174).

That judgment also contains various indications concerning the notions of 'inhuman treatment' and 'degrading treatment' but it deliberately left aside the notions of 'inhuman punishment' and 'degrading punishment' which alone are relevant in the present case (ibid., p. 65, § 164). Those indications accordingly cannot, as such, serve here. Nevertheless, it remains true that the suffering occasioned must attain a particular level before a punishment can be classified as 'inhuman' within the meaning of Article 3. Here again, the Court does not consider on the facts of the case that that level was attained and it therefore concurs with the Commission that the penalty imposed on Mr Tyrer was not 'inhuman punishment' within the meaning of Article 3. Accordingly, the only question for decision is whether he was subjected to a 'degrading punishment' contrary to that Article.

**30.** The Court notes first of all that a person may be humiliated by the mere fact of being criminally convicted. However, what is relevant for the purposes of Article 3 is that he should be humiliated not simply by his conviction but by the execution of the punishment which is imposed on him. In fact, in most if not all cases this may be one of the effects of judicial punishment, involving as it does unwilling subjection to the demands of the penal system.

However, as the Court pointed out in its judgment of 18 January 1978 in the case of Ireland v. the United Kingdom (Series A no. 25, p. 65 § 163), the prohibition contained in Article 3 of the Convention is absolute: no provision is made for exceptions and under Article 15 § 2, there can be no derogation from Article 3. It would be absurd to hold that judicial punishment generally, by reason of its usual and perhaps almost inevitable element of humiliation, is 'degrading' within the meaning of Article 3. Some further criterion must be read into the text. Indeed, Article 3, by expressly prohibiting 'inhuman' and 'degrading' punishment, implies that there is a distinction between such punishment and punishment in general.

In the Court's view, in order for a punishment to be 'degrading' and in breach of Article 3, the humiliation or debasement involved must attain a particular level and must in any event be other than that usual element of humiliation referred to in the preceding sub-paragraph. The assessment is, in the nature of things, relative: it depends on all the circumstances of the case and, in particular, on the nature and context of the punishment itself and the manner and method of its execution.

**31.** The Attorney-General for the Isle of Man argued that the judicial corporal punishment at issue in this case was not in breach of the Convention since it did not outrage public opinion in the Island. However, even assuming that local public opinion can have an incidence on the interpretation of the concept of 'degrading punishment' appearing in Article 3, the Court does not regard it as established that judicial corporal punishment is not considered degrading by those members of the Manx population who favour its retention: it might well be that one of the reasons why they view the penalty as an effective deterrent is precisely the element of degradation which it involves. As regards their belief that judicial corporal punishment deters criminals, it must be pointed out that a punishment does not lose its degrading character just because it is believed to be, or actually is, an effective deterrent or aid to crime control. Above all, as the Court must emphasise, it is never permissible to have recourse to punishments which are contrary to Article 3, whatever their deterrent effect may be.

The Court must also recall that the Convention is a living instrument which, as the Commission rightly stressed, must be interpreted in the light of present-day conditions. In the case now before it the Court cannot but be influenced by the developments and commonly accepted standards in the penal policy of the member States of the Council of Europe in this field. Indeed, the Attorney-General for the Isle of Man mentioned that, for many years, the provisions of Manx legislation concerning judicial corporal punishment had been under review.

*Tyrer case*, 25 April 1978, Series A, no. 26

## B  Language study

### 1  Language points

i)  Notice the use of *shall* in Article 3 of the Convention (line 7). *Shall* is often used in formal written laws and regulations. What does it mean, and how would you normally express the same idea in everyday English?

ii)  What do you understand by these expressions from paragraph 31 of the text?
   a)  it might well be that ....     b)  The Court cannot but be ....

### 2  Improve your vocabulary: word-building

i)  The judgment contains many words that possess both a verb and a noun form, e.g. *to deter* (verb) / *deterrent* (noun).

Can you complete each section of the table below in your notebook with the missing verb or noun forms? When you have finished, scan the text to check the words you are not sure of.

ii)  What is the relationship between the verb and noun forms in each section of the table?

*Example*: The verbs in section (1) all end in -T or -TE and form nouns in -TION.

Give each of the eight sections a suitable heading as in the first example.

| (1)  -T, -TE → -TION | | (3) | | (6) | |
|---|---|---|---|---|---|
| convict | *conviction* | | application | assess | argument |
| derogate | *derogation* | | classification | judge | |
| *prohibit* | prohibition | | | imprison | |
| | subjection | (4) | | treat | |
| inflict | | decide | | punish | |
| violate | | provide | | develop | |
| indicate | | | | (7) | |
| | humiliation | (5) | | break | |
| execute | | demand | | believe | |
| legislate | | control | influence | (8) | |
| (2) | | review | | retain | |
| interpret | allegation | | | | |
| | degradation | | | | |

iii) Choose the correct verb or noun form of the words below to complete each of the following statements:

(1) mean     (2) convict     (3) derogate     (4) argue     (5) assess
(6) judge     (7) imprison     (8) prohibit     (9) suffer     (10) provide
(11) deter     (12) interpret

*Example:* In some countries smoking in public places is _ *prohibited* _.
*Answer:* (8)

a) Several different _____ were presented in favour of the plaintiff.
b) The exact _____ of 'torture' in the European Convention was defined in the _____ of *Ireland v. UK* 1978.
c) To _____ damages, the court will consider the exact nature and extent of the injury _____.
d) Some people believe that only the death penalty will really _____ terrorists.
e) He was _____ of murder and sentenced to life _____.
f) International Law _____ that basic human rights shall be protected.
g) The exact effect of a statute depends on the way it is _____ by the judiciary.
h) States must not _____ from their international obligations.


## 3   Connectives

i) As you have seen in previous units, *connectives* are words which are used to connect or join together facts and ideas in a text. A connective indicates the relationship between one part of the text and the next, and in some cases the choice of connective also shows the writer's opinion, or attitude to what s/he is saying.

If you understand the function of a connective, you can use it to help you follow the development of facts and ideas in a text better, and as a guide to understanding difficult sections of the text.

Study the sections of the text that contain the connectives in the box on the left below and choose the function of each one from the list on the right. In particular, notice the type of statement that comes before or after each connective.

*Example:* 'consequently' (*connective*) is used to introduce a consequence or result (*function*).

*Answer:* a / 4

Note that some of these connectives appear more than once in the text. Study all the examples of each one to confirm your original ideas.

| | Connective | Function |
|---|---|---|
| a) | consequently (line 15) | (1) to introduce a contrast |
| b) | accordingly (33, 43) | (2) to intensify a comment or argument, showing |
| c) | nevertheless (34) | strong conviction |
| d) | however (48, 56, 87) | (3) to emphasise the most important point |
| e) | in fact (52) | (4) to introduce a consequence or result |
| f) | indeed (67, 115) | (5) to make a statement more emphatic |
| g) | above all (102–3) | |

ii) Which connectives in i) have similar functions?
Which of the two connectives in each group below gives more emphasis?

    a) *Contrast*         b) *Emphasis*
      however            indeed
      nevertheless       in fact

## 4 Stating facts and expressing personal attitudes

i) Apart from connectives, various other phrases are used in the text to introduce the Court's arguments:

e.g. In the Court's view . . . (line 72). It would be absurd . . . (line 62).

Find more examples of phrases of this type in the text, and decide which ones express plain fact, and which also show a personal attitude towards the information given.

*Example: In the Court's view* . . . simply introduces an opinion or fact

*It would be absurd* . . . shows a feeling of strong conviction or ridicule

ii) Do you think the Court holds a strong view about Tyrer's punishment, or is the judgment just a factual analysis and decision?

● ■ Consider your ideas for a few minutes, then refer to the key.

● ▲ Discuss your ideas with other members of the class, then refer to the key.

iii) What is *your* personal view on the case so far? Do you agree with the Court's attitude towards Tyrer's punishment?

▲ Discuss your ideas in small groups.

5 You are now going to read the rest of the Court's judgment on Article 3 of the Convention. You already know a lot about this text. Read extract (i) to find out how the judgment continues. What is the main theme?

i)

> 1   **32.** As regards the manner and method of execution of the birching inflicted on Mr. Tyrer, the Attorney-General for the Isle of Man drew particular attention to the fact that the punish-
> 5   ment was carried out in private and without publication of the name of the offender.

Use this theme and your background knowledge to formulate some questions that you want the text to answer. (If necessary refer to step 2 of the reading strategy on page 164 to help you write the questions.) Look for the answers to your questions as you read the text. The rest of the judgment has been divided into short sections, each ending with a connective. Use the information in each section, together with the connective, to predict the development of the text. This will help you to follow the Court's reasoning more easily and understand the difficult parts of the text better. Begin by reading extracts ii) and iii) – the first example has been done for you:

ii)

> Publicity may be a relevant factor in assessing whether a punishment is 'degrading' within the meaning of Article 3, but the Court does not
> 10   consider that absence of publicity will necessarily prevent a given punishment from falling into that category: it may well suffice that the victim is humiliated in his own eyes, even if not in the eyes of others.
> 15   The Court notes that the relevant Isle of Man legislation, as well as giving the offender a right of appeal against sentence, provides for certain safeguards. Thus,

*Safeguards* are controls to protect the offender; *thus* (so, in this way) is often used after a general statement to introduce particular examples or a more detailed explanation, so probably the text will continue with particular examples of the controls which exist. Read to check:

iii)

> there is a prior medical examination; the
> 20 number of strokes and dimensions of the birch
> are regulated in detail; a doctor is present and
> may order the punishment to be stopped; in the
> case of a child or young person, the parent may
> attend if he so desires; the birching is carried out
> 25 by a police constable in the presence of a more
> senior colleague.
> **33.** Nevertheless,

Stop to consider how the text will continue, then read to check.

iv)

> the Court must consider whether the other
> circumstances of the applicant's punishment
> 30 were such as to make it 'degrading' within the
> meaning of Article 3.
> The very nature of judicial corporal punish-
> ment is that it involves one human being inflict-
> ing physical violence on another human being.
> 35 Furthermore, it is institutionalised violence,
> that is in the present case violence permitted by
> the law, ordered by the judicial authorities of the
> State and carried out by the police authorities of
> the State. Thus,

Stop to consider how the text will continue, then read to check.

v)

> 40 although the applicant did not suffer any severe
> or long-lasting physical effects, his punishment
> – whereby he was treated as an object in the
> power of the authorities – constituted an assault
> on precisely that which it is one of the main
> 45 purposes of Article 3 to protect, namely a per-
> son's dignity and physical integrity. Neither can
> it be excluded that the punishment may have
> had adverse psychological effects.
> The institutionalised character of this
> 50 violence is further compounded by the whole
> aura of official procedure attending the punish-
> ment and by the fact that those inflicting it were
> total strangers to the offender.
> Admittedly, the relevant legislation provides
> 55 that in any event birching shall not take place
> later than six months after the passing of sen-
> tence. However,

Stop to consider how the text will continue, then read to check.

vi)

> this does not alter the fact that there had been
> an interval of several weeks since the appli-
> 60 cant's conviction by the juvenile court and a
> considerable delay in the police station where
> the punishment was carried out. Accordingly,

Stop to consider how the text will continue, then read to check.

vii)

> in addition to the physical pain he experienced,
> Mr. Tyrer was subjected to the mental anguish

> 65 of anticipating the violence he was to have
> inflicted on him.
> **34.** In the present case, the Court does not
> consider it relevant that the sentence of judicial
> corporal punishment was imposed on the appli-
> 70 cant for an offence of violence. Neither does it
> consider it relevant that, for Mr. Tyrer, birching
> was an alternative to a period of detention: the
> fact that one penalty may be preferable to, or
> have less adverse effects or be less serious than,
> 75 another penalty does not of itself mean that the
> first penalty is not 'degrading' within the mean-
> ing of Article 3.
> **35.** Accordingly,

Stop to consider how the text will continue, then read to check.

viii)

> viewing these circumstances as a whole, the
> 80 Court finds that the applicant was subjected to a
> punishment in which the element of humiliation
> attained the level inherent in the notion of
> 'degrading punishment' as explained at para-
> graph 30 above. The indignity of having the
> 85 punishment administered over the bare post-
> erior aggravated to some extent the degrading
> character of the applicant's punishment but it
> was not the only or determining factor.
> The Court therefore

Stop to consider how the text will continue, then read to check.

ix)

> 90 concludes that the judicial corporal punishment
> inflicted on the applicant amounted to degrading
> punishment within the meaning of Article 3 of
> the Convention.

Did the connectives help you to read the text more easily?
Notice that a connective is also a context clue, which you can use to work out the meaning of unknown key words. We used *thus* in extract ii) to predict the development of the text. Alternatively, it could be used with the information in extract iii) to deduce the meaning of *safeguard*. Given the function of *thus* (see page 168) *safeguard* must be a general term describing regulations designed to protect the offender, of the type described in extract iii).

**6 ●** Use the text to decide the function of the connectives 'furthermore' (extract iv) and 'admittedly' (extract v).

**7 ▲** Did you find the answers to your personal questions as you read the text?
What are the main points in this part of the judgment?
Discuss your answers in small groups.

**8** Choose the appropriate connective from the list below to complete the following summary of the text; use each connective *once* only.

*Choose from:*   a) indeed   b) although   c) furthermore   d) accordingly
e) however

(1) _____ the punishment was inflicted in private and without publicity, it would still be 'degrading' if the victim felt personally humiliated. The execution of the punishment was strictly controlled by law, (2) _____ the Court must still decide if it was degrading in the circumstances. In fact, the violence was institutional violence, consequently because of its official character Tyrer's suffering was not only physical, but also psychological. (3) _____ there was not only the physical pain of the birching, but also the mental suffering caused by the long wait of several weeks before the punishment was given. There was, (4) _____, a long delay at the police station on the day of the whipping. It is not relevant that Tyrer's punishment was imposed for a crime of violence, or that it was given instead of a prison sentence. Thus, the punishment was, in all the circumstances, 'degrading punishment' and was (5) _____ in breach of Article 3 of the European Convention on Human Rights.

## 9 Comprehension check

You have done most of the work on the Court's judgment (paragraphs 28–35) independently. If you wish, use the exercise below to check your understanding of the text. Decide which of the following statements are true, and correct any statements that are wrong.

*Example:* The Court and Commission agreed that Tyrer's punishment was not 'torture'.   *TRUE* [Paragraph 29, lines 17–45.]

a)   They agreed that Tyrer's punishment was not 'inhuman' because he didn't suffer enough.

b)   Criminal conviction is frequently humiliating.

c)   Article 3 of the Convention concerns the execution of the punishment, not the conviction itself.

d)   There are very few exceptions to Article 3.

e)   Judicial punishment is generally humiliating and degrading and therefore contrary to Article 3.

f)   The Court will consider the general context and circumstances to decide if a punishment is degrading.

g)   The Manx population consider judicial corporal punishment degrading.

h)   Even if a punishment discourages people from committing crime, it may still be contrary to Article 3.

i)   In interpreting the Convention, the Court is influenced by the modern penal policy of States belonging to the Council of Europe.

j)   Punishment inflicted in private and without publicity is not degrading.

k)   In some ways official violence is worse than 'private' violence.

l)   Tyrer's punishment constituted a violation of his dignity and physical integrity.

m)  Tyrer suffered both physically and mentally.

n)   Tyrer's punishment was, in all the circumstances, degrading and therefore in breach of Article 3 of the Convention.

## C   Further practice

### 1   Verbs in legal proceedings

You have learnt to understand many verbs which are used in civil, criminal and international court proceedings, but do you know how to *use* each one correctly? To find out, complete the following sentences by choosing the correct verb from the four alternatives. Pay attention to the meaning *and form* of each sentence!

*Example:* The accused was __*charged*__ with arson and murder.

a) submitted     b) sued     c) charged     d) convicted     *Answer:* (c)

i) The plaintiff _____ the defendant for damages for breach of contract.
    a) prosecuted     b) tried     c) sued     d) claimed

ii) The defendant was _____ for theft under the Theft Act.
    a) prosecuted     b) convicted     c) filed     d) sued

iii) The Court _____ that the act was in breach of Article 53 of the Treaty.
    a) claimed     b) held     c) argued     d) charged

iv) The applicant _____ that the defendant State had violated basic principles of International Law.
    a) alleged     b) applied     c) condemned     d) lodged

v) Counsel for the defence _____ that the defendant had acted in self-defence.
    a) defended     b) alleged     c) held     d) submitted

## 2 Reformulation

Use the information in the text to design a chart which shows in detail how Article 3 of the European Convention on Human Rights was applied in the *Tyrer case*. Your chart should illustrate Tyrer's allegations and the Commission's and Court's decisions regarding the different types of treatment or punishment which Article 3 prohibits. For ideas on how to design your chart, refer to the chart on page 163 of this Unit and some of the other charts you have completed in previous units of this book (e.g. pages 41 and 122).

Compare your chart with the one in the key. Does it show the same information?

▲ Compare and discuss your finished work with other members of the class.

## 3 Oral practice

Use your chart from Exercise 2 above to describe and discuss the application of Article 3 of the European Convention on Human Rights in the *Tyrer case*.

▲ Work in pairs.

■ Speak aloud. If possible, record your description on tape, then listen to the recording.

## D Development

*1* The text contains a variety of expressions used to refer to the violation or application of a norm. Write them in your notebook for easy reference. First see how many expressions you can think of without referring to the text. Then scan the texts in Sections One and Two of this Unit to complete these lists.

| *Application of a norm* | *Violation of a norm* |
|---|---|
| in accordance with Article . . . | in breach of Article . . . |
| | |

## 2   *The decision*

i)   Think for a few moments about the *Tyrer case*. In its final decision given at the end of the judgment you have read, the Court gives two rulings on Article 3. Use the cues below to write what you think the decision will say. You can refer to the text you have already read, but don't look at the decision itself yet!
*CUES:*
First ruling: Article 3 / degrading punishment
Second ruling: Violation of Article 3
Write complete sentences, using some of the expressions from your box in Exercise 1 above, and begin your decision with phrases like this:
'The Court holds that . . .'.
'The Court decides that . . .'.

ii)  Read the Court's decision below and decide which of the six rulings correspond to the ones you have written.

■   Compare your decision with the Court's.

▲   Compare your decision with the Court's and with other members of the class.

---

FOR THESE REASONS, THE COURT

**1.** *decides* unanimously not to strike the case out of its list;
**2.** *holds* by six votes to one that the judicial corporal punishment inflicted on Mr. Tyrer amounted to degrading punishment within the meaning of Article 3;
**3.** *holds* unanimously that in the present case there are no local requirements within the meaning of Article 63 § 3 which could affect the application of Article 3;
**4.** *holds* by six votes to one that the said punishment accordingly violated Article 3;

**5.** *holds* unanimously that it is not necessary to examine the question of a possible violation of Article 3 taken together with Article 14;
**6.** *holds* unanimously that it is not necessary to apply Article 50 in the present case.

Done in English and French, the English text being authentic, at the Human Rights Building, Strasbourg, this twenty-fifth day of April, one thousand nine hundred and seventy-eight.

*Signed:* Giorgio BALLADORE PALLIERI
President

---

● *Tyrer case*, judgment of 25 April 1978, Series A, No. 26

*3*  Use the six points of the Court's decision to complete the final column of your chart on
●   page 163.

## 4   *Consolidation*

i)   Choose one or more aspects of the *Tyrer case* that you have studied in Units Nine and Ten from this list:
the facts – the general background – proceedings before the Commission – the Court's judgment on Article 3 – the Court's decision

ii)  Prepare to talk about the aspect(s) of the case you have chosen. Refer to the text and the information you have stored in summaries, charts, etc. in Units Nine and Ten. If you like, take brief notes of what you want to say.

▲   iii) In turn, explain the main facts of the case and discuss any points of particular interest.

■      Describe the aspect of the *Tyrer case* which you have chosen. If possible, record yourself on tape, then listen to your recording. If you prefer to practise writing, write a brief summary of this aspect of the case.

iv)  As you can see, the Court's decision on Article 3 was not unanimous. In fact, the British judge, Sir Gerald Fitzmaurice, dissented. In his separate opinion, he explained that in his view corporal punishment, when inflicted on a juvenile, is no more degrading than any other form of punishment. He remembers that corporal punishment was quite normal when he was at school. In fact, boys preferred it to some other forms of non-violent punishment, and the boy punished did not feel degraded. For these reasons he does not consider that Tyrer's punishment amounted to *degrading punishment* within the meaning of Article 3. What do you think?

THE TYRER CROSSWORD PUZZLE
Can you complete the puzzle on page 175 by solving the clues below?

*CLUES*

1. Tyrer's co-national has no tail! (see drawing) (4,3)
2. This European Convention helps to defend them (5,6)
3. It's illegal to attack someone like this (8,7)
4. The Isle of Man's chief law officer (8,7)
5. A convention or pact (6)
6. The power of a court to hear and decide a case (12)
7. To invoke a law or refer to a precedent (4)
8. The entire *affaire*, as the French would say (4)
9. To submit, to claim (5)
10. One who presents a request to an international court or commission (9)
11. To approve a 5 (see clue 5) (6)
12. In the court's *opinion* (4)
13. A way to compensate a wrong or enforce a right (6)
14. The court _____ that Tyrer's punishment violated Article 3 of the European Convention (4)
15. Shame on the Isle of Man – most modern European States _____ corporal punishment long ago! (9)
16. Not innocent (6)
17. *Violation* of a norm (6)
18. A question the court must consider (5)
19. Anthony – protagonist of our 8 (see clue 5) (5)
20. Just a signatory to a convention – but it sounds like fun! (5)
21. He has broken the law – and may be rude, too! (8)
22. It should convince most people not to break the law (9)
23. It's more expensive, but less painful than corporal punishment! (4)
24. Quite simply: *because* (2,3,7)

# UNIT 11 International Law — Use of Force and Espionage

Reading a Law Review Article

## Section One: The Facts

### A Before you read

### 1 Think about the subject

i) Have you heard of the following? What, if anything, do you know about them?
- Greenpeace
- The *Rainbow Warrior*

▲ Discuss what you know with other members of the class.

ii) Read the passage below to find out about Greenpeace and the *Rainbow Warrior*, and check your ideas from i). Use a dictionary if necessary.

> 'Greenpeace' is the name of an ecology group which is based in Britain. Its members are people of different nationalities who wish to protect the environment we live in. They do research, bring problems to the attention of the public and take non-violent direct action

on many issues related to environmental protection and pollution. One of the issues which particularly concerns Greenpeace is the damage to the environment caused by the use of nuclear bombs in experimental tests..In July 1985 the French planned a series of nuclear tests in the Pacific Ocean. Members of Greenpeace decided to stop the tests if they could, and set off for the area in their boat – the *Rainbow Warrior III*.

Do you know what happened?

French secret agents attacked the boat with explosives while it was moored in Auckland Harbour, New Zealand (Greenpeace supporters were preparing for action in the Pacific). Fernando Pereira, the Greenpeace photographer on the expedition, was killed by drowning in the attack and the *Rainbow Warrior* was sunk.

## B  Reading to understand the general themes and development of the text

### 1  Understanding the general themes of the text

i) Skim the text on page 178 to find out what it is about in general. Do *not* try to read or understand the text in detail for this activity. Find the main themes of paragraphs 1–7 and give each one a suitable heading. Make a note of your headings.

*Example:*  Suitable headings for paragraph A are:
'The conviction and sentencing of Mafart and Prieur'
*or:* 'Legal consequences for French agents involved in the attack'

▲ When you have finished, compare your headings with other members of the class.

ii) Use your headings from i) to decide the correct order of the following themes from the text.
If necessary, refer to the text to check your answer.

*Example:* heading A) ('The role of Europe in resolving the dispute') refers to Paragraph 5.

A) The role of Europe in resolving the dispute
B) The role of the New Zealand Government in the case
C) French economic measures against New Zealand
D) The involvement of the French Government in the attack
E) French liability to the victim's family and Greenpeace
F) The UN Secretary-General's arbitration decision regarding the dispute between France and New Zealand
● G) The conviction and sentencing of French agents involved in the attack

### 2  Describing the development of themes in the text

Use your work from Exercise 1 above to describe the organisation and development of themes in the text. Include any important facts you remember.

*Example: 'The text begins by describing* the conviction and sentencing of two French agents (Mafart and Prieur) for the attack of 10 July 1985 on the *Rainbow Warrior. It then discusses* the involvement of the French Government in the attack and *goes on to describe* . . . . The final part of the text *deals with* . . .'.

To introduce and connect the different themes in the text, use phrases like the ones in italics in the example.

## LEGAL ASPECTS OF THE *RAINBOW WARRIOR* AFFAIR

### A.  Outline of the Facts

Para. 1   Two DGSE agents using false names were arrested in New Zealand on 12 July 1985 and duly charged with passport and related offences. On 23 July they were further charged with conspiracy to commit arson, with wilfully damaging the *Rainbow Warrior* by means of explosives, and with the murder of Fernando Pereira, a crew member who drowned in the incident. They pleaded not guilty and were remanded in custody. In mid-August the French press identified them as Alain Mafart and Dominique Prieur. On 26 July New Zealand police also obtained warrants to arrest agents who had left New Zealand prior to the explosions. On 13 August New Zealand demanded extradition of all those involved, but the French government replied that it could not extradite French nationals. The other agents, including three who reported to the Paris police on 25 August, were never apprehended. The charges against Mafart and Prieur were altered to manslaughter and wilful damage at the hearing on 4 November 1985. The agents pleaded guilty and were sentenced on 22 November to ten years' imprisonment for manslaughter and seven years' for wilful damage, the terms to run concurrently. The French Defence Minister told them that the government would work for their release and on 28 November he urged negotiations for their return to France.

2   An investigation by the French government into the possibility of official involvement, published on 26 August 1985, recognised the identity and affiliation of the agents but found no evidence to indicate that their mission involved anything other than surveillance. On 6 September France notified New Zealand of its concern that Mafart and Prieur should enjoy all the guarantees of international law. After further press revelations France acknowledged on 22 September that the agents had obeyed orders, and protested that they should be exempted from blame.

3   Meanwhile New Zealand had notified France on 6 September that it would take legal steps to secure compensation from the French State. Further, the New Zealand Prime Minister, David Lange, said on 26 September that he had prohibited extradition of the agents and political interference in the legal proceedings. After the convictions he remarked on 16 December that New Zealand would consider repatriating the agents provided they continue to serve their prison sentences. Negotiations between New Zealand and France, which had begun on 23 September 1985, continued intermittently until 19 May 1986 when New Zealand suspended them in protest at continued economic sanctions by France.

4   Early in 1986 France began impeding New Zealand imports. New Zealand formally complained to France on 26 February 1986, and on 4 April the European Community Trade Commissioner upheld the complaint. France did not admit to imposing the trade barriers until 22 April.

5   Other European States were concerned to see the dispute resolved, but efforts at mediation were hardly possible until the facts had been ascertained and the New Zealand proceedings completed. On 12 September 1985 the European Parliament condemned secret service activity against the *Rainbow Warrior* and demanded a full explanation from France. The UK government took little part in the dispute but on 24 September 1985 called on France to settle compensation without delay. During a visit to Europe in June 1986 Lange indicated that various governments had impressed upon him the need for an early resolution of the dispute. Between 31 May and 2 June, Ruud Lubbers, President of the European Council of Ministers and Prime Minister of the Netherlands, explored with the parties a proposal for independent arbitration.

6   France and New Zealand announced on 19 June that they had agreed to refer all matters without precondition to arbitration by the UN Secretary-General. The ruling was completed on 6 July 1986 and signed on 9 July. It required France to apologise and pay a fixed sum to New Zealand; required New Zealand to transfer Mafart and Prieur into French custody; and enjoined France not to impede New Zealand exports to the European Community. The terms were carried out on 22–23 July 1986, and France subsequently abided by the ruling on New Zealand exports.

7   France reached a settlement with the family of Fernando Pereira on 12 November 1985, encompassing a formal apology, compensation totalling 2.3 million francs, and reimbursement of the insurers. France and Greenpeace agreed on 19 December 1985 to negotiate damages – France having admitted legal liability on 10 December. Unable to reach agreement, they referred the matter to a panel of three arbitrators on 10 July 1986. A ruling was still awaited in May 1987.

Michael Pugh, 'Legal Aspects of the *Rainbow Warrior* Affair', *International and Comparative Law Quarterly*, Vol. 36, July 1987

▲  Work in pairs.
■  Speak aloud, or if you prefer, write a brief description of the development of themes in the text.

## C  Reading for detail and language study

### 1  Understanding descriptive phrases

i)  Nouns and adjectives:

*Examples:*  a *prison sentence* (line 27) = a sentence of imprisonment
*passport offences* (line 4) = offence concerning passports

*Prison* and *passport* are both nouns. Like many English nouns, they can also be used with the function of adjectives to describe, or give more information about the noun which follows. When one or more nouns are used in this way (often together with adjectives), the main noun is the last one in the series.

*Examples:*  *secret service activity* (35) = the *activity* of the secret service
            (adj. + noun + main noun)

            *the European Community Trade Commissioner* (31) =
            (adj.        + noun          + main noun)

            the *Commissioner* for trade of the European Community

Explain the following from the text. Use your dictionary if necessary to help you.
a)  Two DGSE agents (line 3)          b)  passport and related offences (4)
c)  a crew member (6)                 d)  the French Defence Minister (15)
e)  the UN Secretary-General (43)     f)  New Zealand exports (47)

ii)  Noun + 's or '
The *noun + 's* or *noun ending in s + '* forms are also used in descriptive phrases.

*Example: ten years' imprisonment* (13–14) = a period of imprisonment *of* ten years
a)  What does *seven years'* (14) refer to?      b)  Why is the main noun missing?

iii)  Clauses:
As you have seen in previous units, a complete clause can be used to give more information about a noun.

*Examples:*  (1)  Two DGSE agents *using false names* (line 3)
            (2)  Fernando Pereira, a crew member *who drowned in the incident*
                (line 6)

These phrases tell us that:
(1)  The two agents were members of the DGSE and used . . .
(2)  Fernando Pereira was a member of the crew and he . . .

iv)  Phrases introduced by a preposition:
Phrases introduced by a preposition after a noun can give more information about the noun.

*Example:*  negotiations *FOR their return to France* (16) tells us that the subject of
            the negotiations is the return to France [of the French agents]
What information is given in the text about the following?
a)  the *secret service activity* condemned by the European Parliament in line 35
b)  the *proposal* which Ruud Lubbers discussed with the parties to the dispute
    (lines 39–41)

## 2 Writing a summary

Use the text on page 178 to write a summary of the facts of the *Rainbow Warrior* affair completely independently. If you prefer, you may choose to summarise the text in the form of a table, chart or diagram. Follow the method you learnt in Unit Nine and refer to page 155 for detailed instructions. For this activity you will be completely responsible for language and vocabulary work which you wish to do on the text. Don't forget to check the quality of your summary (see page 155) when you have finished!

▲ When you have finished, compare your work with someone else's.

## 3 Comprehension check

i) Use your summary of the text to check the facts given in the passage below. Twelve of the facts stated are wrong – can you find the mistakes? You may need to refer to the text for some of the answers – this will depend on the information you chose to include in your summary.

---

**The *Rainbow Warrior* Affair: Summary of the Facts**

**A** *The main events*

July 1985: French secret service agents Mafart and Prieur charged in New Zealand with passport offences, conspiracy to commit arson, wilful damage and manslaughter in connection with *Rainbow Warrior* attack. Pleaded not guilty, remanded in custody.

August '85: French Government agreed to extradite all other agents involved in attack.

September '85: France admitted responsibility for ordering attack. Claimed Mafart and Prieur should therefore not be held liable.

November '85: Mafart and Prieur tried for arson, murder and wilful damage. Pleaded not guilty, convicted, sentenced to life imprisonment. French Defence Minister wished to negotiate their return to France.

**B** *Negotiations between France and New Zealand*

September '85: Negotiations began. New Zealand would take proceedings against Mafart and Prieur for compensation. Insisted on no political interference and refused to extradite agents. In December New Zealand agreed to consider repatriation of agents on condition they served rest of prison sentence in France.

Early '86: France began economic sanctions against New Zealand. New Zealand complaint against sanctions accepted by European Community Commission. France did not admit sanctions.

**C** *Resolution of dispute between France and New Zealand*

September '85: European governments wished to see dispute settled quickly. Attack condemned by European Parliament. UK Government took action to settle dispute.

June–July '86: Dispute referred to UN Secretary-General for arbitration.
Ruling: *France:* apologise, compensate New Zealand, remove economic sanctions.
*New Zealand:* apologise, transfer Mafart and Prieur to French custody.

**D** *Settlement of disputes between France and victims*

November '85: *France to family of dead man:* apology, compensation.
December '85: *France to Greenpeace:* admitted liability, paid damages.

---

ii) Compare your own summary of the facts of the case with the corrected summary in i). In what ways are they similar or different? Compare the style and form, length and basic information they contain.

## 4 Vocabulary consolidation

i) What different crimes were the French agents accused of? Scan the text to check, then add any new offences to the word ladder of crimes you completed on page 150, Exercise 2.

ii) Scan the text for words and phrases connected with criminal law. Add any new vocabulary to the criminal law network you designed and completed at the end of Unit Nine (Section 3, Exercise 7).

iii) Which words and phrases from the text do you particularly want to remember? Make vocabulary cards or lists to store the words, or design a vocabulary table or network showing them in groups and categories of your choice.

▲ Compare your work with that of other members of the class.

## 5 Oral practice

Use all the information you have learnt so far in this Unit to describe the main events of the *Rainbow Warrior* affair. In particular refer to Exercises A1, B1, B2, C2 and C3 for the information you need.

*Start like this:*
'Greenpeace is an organisation for the protection of the environment, which owned a boat called the *Rainbow Warrior III*. In July 1985, the French planned to perform nuclear tests in the Pacific Ocean, so members of Greenpeace . . .'.

▲ Work in pairs. Take turns to describe some of the facts.
■ Speak aloud. If possible, record your description of the facts on tape, then listen to your recording.

## D Development

## 1 International Law and the Rainbow Warrior

i) Work alone or in small groups. On the basis of the facts you have read, consider the following points.
 • What issues of International Law do you think the *Rainbow Warrior* affair involves?
 • In what way(s) do you think France or French agents violated International Law?

ii) **Reading for confirmation**

a) Read the extract below to see if your ideas from i) correspond.

1  *B. Contravention of International Law*

The *Rainbow Warrior* sinking did not have serious consequences for peace. It was an officially inspired military operation with strictly limited intentions. Nevertheless, since the UN Charter was signed international lawyers have increasingly addressed the problem of low-level uses of force. French action clearly

---

5 fell within the broad concept of 'international delinquency' encompassing acts short of belligerency such as 'violation of the dignity of a foreign State, violation of foreign territorial supremacy, or any other internationally illegal act'. The attack and the infringement of New Zealand sovereignty were universally condemned as contrary to international law, and the French government's Memorandum presented to de Cuéllar conceded in section 5 that the abuse of New Zealand sovereignty had been illegal.

10 The French government initially claimed that its agents had merely engaged in 'surveillance'. A more accurate description, given the covert nature of the job, would be 'spying'. Unfortunately, as Richard Falk observed: 'traditional international law is remarkably oblivious to the peacetime practice of espionage'; and while Articles 29–31 of the 1907 Hague Convention deal with spying in wartime, there is no peacetime equivalent. Many jurists, however, would agree with Falk who characterised espionage as illegal but

15 tolerated in many countries. By contrast, Julius Stone argued that spying itself was not illegal – as distinct from the collateral activity such as territorial intrusion. Stone advocated 'reciprocally tolerated espionage' for the superpowers as a kind of confidence-building measure. But such an approach is inappropriate to New Zealand and France for whom, as far as one can tell, reciprocal spying is hardly an assumed aspect of their relationship. In the event the New Zealand authorities ignored the 'surveillance' by French agents and

20 concentrated on the attack itself.

Michael Pugh

### iii) Reading for general understanding

a) What two main issues of International Law does the author identify?
b) Which of the two issues did New Zealand use as basis for their case against France?

### iv) Reading for detailed understanding

Read the extract carefully and answer the following questions.
a) Was the French attack on the *Rainbow Warrior* an example of '*international delinquency*' (line 5) or *belligerency* (line 5)?
b) Which of the following do you think are examples of '*low-level uses of force*' (line 4)?
   (1) the invasion of a foreign State
   (2) a bomb attack on a foreign aeroplane
   (3) a declaration of war on another State
c) Which word in line 7 of the text means a *violation*?
d) What do you suppose is the difference between *surveillance* (10) and *spying* (11)?
e) What other word is used in the text for *spying*?
f) Is peacetime spying legal or illegal?
g) Does the author suppose that France and New Zealand generally spy on each other?
● h) What is the *UN Charter* (line 3) called in your language?

## 2  Test your vocabulary

You have done most of the work on vocabulary in Section One of this Unit completely independently. To check your understanding of some of the key words from the two texts you have read, decide which word from the following list matches each definition in the exercise below.

*Choose from:*

| | | | |
|---|---|---|---|
| (1) belligerency | (2) conspiracy | (3) negotiations | (4) settlement |
| (5) to apologise | (6) arbitrator | (7) concurrently | (8) to extradite |
| (9) manslaughter | (10) delinquency | (11) infringement | |

*Example:*    _settlement_: an agreement or decision which ends an argument or dispute
*Answer:*    (4)

a) _____: to give a person who is suspected of or has committed a crime in another State to the authorities of that State for trial or punishment. It is governed by treaties between the two States and does not apply to political offenders.

b) _____: to say you are sorry.

c) _____: the state of being at war.

d) _____: the crime of unlawful killing in various circumstances, e.g. where death is caused by accident or unlawful act but without the intention to kill necessary for murder.

e) _____: the breach of a law or violation of a right.

f) _____: the discussion of terms and conditions to reach an agreement.

g) _____: criminal behaviour.

h) _____: taking place at the same time, e.g. two prison sentences which take place at the same time.

i) _____: an independent third party who is chosen by both sides involved in a dispute to try to settle it, as an alternative to court proceedings.

j) _____: an agreement between two or more persons to do something which will involve at least one of the parties committing an offence or offences. For example, two people agree that one of them shall steal while the other waits in a car to escape after the theft. The agreement to commit the crime is itself an offence.

● If necessary refer again to the texts to complete the exercise before checking your answers in the key.


## 3  Discussion points

What is your personal moral opinion on the *Rainbow Warrior* affair?

◆ Do you think Greenpeace were right to try to stop France from performing the nuclear tests?

◆ Was the French Government entitled to stop Greenpeace from taking action?

◆ Were the French agents right to follow the orders of their government in the circumstances?

◆ Do you think Mafart and Prieur should be held personally liable for their acts or not? If possible, give a legal opinion on some of the above points, too.
(Section Two of this Unit deals in particular with the law relating to the last point.)

■ Speak aloud. If possible, record your opinions on tape, then listen to the recording.

▲ Discuss your ideas in small groups, then exchange your opinions with the rest of the class.


# Section Two:  The Law

## A  Independent study

You are going to study the text on pages 184 and 185 completely independently. Follow the instructions for the Reading Strategy for Private Study given on pages 164–5, Unit Ten, step by step. Spend as much time as you need on this activity.

## 1 C. State Responsibility and Personal Immunity of Perpetrators for Criminal Acts

Although sovereign States may be obliged to accept the jurisdiction of courts of other States, the con-
5 cept of State criminality, albeit useful in propaganda, is not strongly supported in law. State responsibility for delicts is limited to liability for reparations. It is also an established principle that a State which sends agents to commit an *acta jure*
10 *imperii* abroad is liable rather than the agents who should enjoy immunity from local courts. As de Cuéllar noted, France and New Zealand had great difficulty in reaching an agreement on the fate of the two DGSE agents, Mafart and Prieur, who had
15 been arrested, tried, and sentenced in New Zealand.

M. Fabius, the French Prime Minister, argued that the 'people who merely carried out the act must, of course, be exempted from blame' as they
20 had 'only obeyed orders'. After Mafart and Prieur had been charged with murder and arson but before standing trial the French government admitted responsibility for the act and was willing to apologize. Consequently, so France claimed, the trial in
25 New Zealand was unjustified and contrary to international practice.

At variance with this is the view that individuals are increasingly recognised as subjects of international law, and that agents are liable because
30 they are the means by which acts of State are carried out. On the question of superior orders, precepts of the Nuremburg Charter (adopted by a UN Resolution on 11 December 1946) are commonly regarded as part of positive international
35 law. By their adherence to these precepts both France and New Zealand had accepted the liability of individuals for war crimes and crimes against peace and humanity. Mafart and Prieur had not committed crimes of such magnitude, and the ques-
40 tion of State immunity for lesser acts contrary to international law and crimes against municipal law is considered later. But New Zealand's Memorandum to the Secretary-General cited the IMTs to support the argument that superior orders was no
45 defence, either in international law or in New Zealand law to which the agents were subjected.

*(a) Acts in time of armed conflict.* The legal position is relatively clear regarding status of service personnel during hostilities, at least at the higher levels of
50 conflict. Irrespective of a declaration of a state of war, military personnel who kill foreigners are entitled to 'soldiers' privileges', conditional on obedience to the laws and customs of war which have grown up around the regulations annexed to
55 Convention IV of the 1907 Hague Conventions.

*(b) Acts in time of peace.* At lower thresholds of conflict (sporadic acts of violence, guerrilla activity, so-called 'terrorism', and sabotage), governments 'apply their own criminal law to unpopular cap-
60 tured guerrillas, while granting belligerents' pri-
vileges to popular guerrillas' in accordance with concepts of 'just war'. There was no suggestion that the agents in New Zealand conformed to the requirements for POW status under Article 4 of the
65 1977 Geneva Protocol (I). In the absence of hostilities New Zealand treated the agents as common criminals, not as POWs to be tried for war crimes or crimes against humanity. Although various conventions deal with air piracy, and Protocol I deals with
70 non-international conflict, international law is inadequate to cope with perpetrators of sporadic violence across State boundaries. Indeed, support has been expressed for extending the laws of armed conflict to the lower thresholds of violence.

75 As with low-conflict thresholds the situation regarding State responsibility for covert agents of the State lacks codified legal provision. Jacob Sundberg has suggested that the application of local jurisdiction presupposes that:

80 1. the agent acted clandestinely or on false pretences, rather than, say, as a recognisable serviceman engaged in reconnaissance;
2. officially no connection exists between him and the foreign government benefiting from
85 his espionage and that the foreign government will not come forward and protect him by shifting responsibility to itself.

The principle of agent immunity cannot apply if 'officially' spies do not exist. Sponsoring States
90 typically disown them. In the *Powers* case of 1960 President Eisenhower broke with usual practice and admitted that Powers was spying in plain clothes in a camouflaged U2. American officials justified the espionage, but Powers still stood trial
95 in the Soviet Union.

Yet when a government seeks to protect its agents, whether engaged in spying or other acts, by claiming delictual responsibility for itself, Webster's ruling in the *Caroline* and *McLeod* cases
100 is said to apply. In 1837 McLeod, a British officer, entered the United States to capture the ship which was running men and supplies to assist a rebellion in Canada. A man was killed and McLeod charged with murder. The American Secretary of State
105 ruled that:

> after the avowal of the transaction as a public transaction, authorised and undertaken by the British authorities, individuals concerned in it ought not to be holden personally responsible in the ordinary
> 110 tribunals for their participation in it.

However, in the *Caroline* incident McLeod's presence in American territory was deemed to have been lawfully justified by the doctrine of self-defence.

115 In other situations, including the *Rainbow Warrior* incident, it has been impossible to establish immunity from local jurisdiction for perpetrators and instrumentalities making unauthorised, illegal entries with the official purpose of committing
120 unlawful acts. As the leading case, *The Schooner Exchange v. McFaddon* of 1812 recognised,

immunity from jurisdiction for acts contrary to international law derives ultimately from the consent of sovereign States to territorial access for
125 foreign servants, and warships or aircraft. When a Soviet submarine ran aground inside a Swedish military security area which it had entered without consent on 27–28 October 1981 the local authorities assumed jurisdiction over the vessel and crew with-
130 out Soviet permission – though for political reasons Sweden made only limited use of its rights. Regarding crimes committed by foreign agents against municipal law, as Quincy Wright argued, 'There is no rule of international law which forbids a State to
135 punish individuals who seek to obtain classified documents, who penetrate forbidden areas . . . or who engage in seditious or other activities which it has made illegal', provided the local laws conform to international obligations.

Michael Pugh

## B Language study and comprehension check

In Section A you studied the text on pages 184–5 completely independently. Use some or all of the following exercises to check and consolidate the work you have done on language and vocabulary from the text, and to check your understanding of the text.

## 1 Word study

As you work, compare the method *you* used in Section A to understand some of the following words and phrases from the text, with the method used here.

### i) Dictionary use

First decide what you think the following words could mean in the context. What is the grammatical function of each word (verb, noun etc.)? Then look them up in your dictionary.

- a) reparations (line 8)
- b) perpetrators (71, 117)
- c) thresholds (74, 75)
- d) covert (76)
- e) access (124)
- f) forbids (134)

### ii) Contextual deduction

Use cognates, the context and logical reasoning to decide what the following words and phrases in the text probably mean.

- a) delicts (line 7)
- b) immunity (11, 40, 88, 117, 122)
- c) hostilities (49, 65–6)
- d) privileges (52, 60–61)

### iii) Word families

Use your knowledge of word families, root words, prefixes and suffixes to decide what the following words and phrases from the text probably mean. Check that your ideas make sense in the context before referring to the key.
*Example:* non-international conflict (adj. + noun, line 70) *Answer:* The prefix non- means *not* (e.g. non-contractual obligations = obligations which are not contractual, i.e. which do not derive from a contract). *Probable meaning:* conflict which is not international, i.e. conflict which does not involve more than one State.
Does this make sense in the context?

- a) belligerents (noun, 60)
- b) presupposes (verb, 79)
- c) recognisable serviceman (adj. + noun, 81–2)
- d) disown (verb, 90)
- e) delictual responsibility (adj. + noun, 98)
- f) self-defence (noun, 113–14)
- g) territorial access (adj. + noun, 124)
- h) warships (noun, 125)
- i) forbidden areas (adj. + noun, 136)

iv) **Abbreviations**

a) Which abbreviations used in the text refer to each of the following?
  (1) Members of the armed forces of one State who are captured and taken prisoner by another State in time of war.
  (2) A type of aeroplane used for spying
  (3) International courts with jurisdiction over war crimes

● b) Do you know, or can you guess what the letters of each abbreviation stand for?

v) **Other important words and phrases**

a) Can you give an example which illustrates the meaning of each of the following phrases?
  *Example:* subjects of International Law (28–9)     *Answer:* States are *subjects of International Law* because they have and exercise international rights and duties on the basis of International Law.
  (1) international practice (lines 25–6)
  (2) superior orders (31, 44)
  (3) municipal law (41)
  (4) just war (62)

b) Do you know what each of the following international agreements governs? You will find some clues in the text.
  (1) the Nuremberg Charter (line 32)
  (2) the Hague Conventions 1907 (55)
  (3) the 1977 Geneva Protocol (1) (65)

c) (1) You know that the noun *authority* can mean: a binding precedent; an expert on a particular subject; the power or right to control and command. Does it have any of these meanings in line 128 of the text (*local authorities*)? What are the local authorities called in your country?
  (2) One meaning of *provision* is an individual rule or condition in a statute or contract.
  ● Does it have this meaning in line 77?

## 2   *Language study*

i) **Descriptive phrases**

This exercise will consolidate the work you did on descriptive phrases in Section One C 1 and check your understanding of some key phrases from the text.
What do you understand by the following? Explain each phrase in your own words.
*Example:* State boundaries (72)     *Possible answer:* the lines or limits (boundaries) which divide the territory of one State from another.
a) sovereign States (3)     b) state criminality (5)     c) war crimes (37,67)
d) state immunity for lesser acts contrary to International Law (40–41)
e) soldiers' privileges (52)     f) guerrilla activity (57)
g) the foreign government benefiting from his espionage (84–5)

ii) **Provided**

Study lines 131–39 of the text. Which of the following could be substituted for *provided* to give exactly the same meaning?
● a) when     b) unless     c) on the condition that     d) because

### 3 Comprehension check

i) Without referring to the text again, use your own work from Section A to complete the following summary. Check your understanding of the text by completing the unfinished sentences and choosing the correct alternative from the italicised phrases. When you have finished, refer to the text again to check your summary. The answer to (1) is : *should not*.

---

In the *Rainbow Warrior* affair the French Government claimed that their agents (1) *should / should not* be held liable for their acts on the grounds that (2) *they had only obeyed the orders of the government which had later claimed responsibili*ty.

The French argument was based on (3) *International Law / international practice/ municipal law*.
Both France and New Zealand accepted that under the Nuremberg Charter individuals who commit war crimes against peace and humanity (4) *are / are not* personally liable for their acts. However, Mafart and Prieur (5) *were / were not* accused of crimes against peace and humanity since (6) _____

---
therefore the principles of the Nuremberg Charter (7) *were / were not* applicable in this case. Nevertheless, the New Zealand Government (8) *accepted / did not accept* the argument of superior orders as a defence for Mafart and Prieur.
Liability for acts of violence committed by servicemen in (9) *wartime / peacetime* is clearly regulated by International Law. In fact, soldiers who kill foreigners in wartime (10) _____

---
In peacetime, on the other hand, perpetrators of low-threshold violence are (11) *always / never / sometimes* held liable for their acts, and this depends on (12) _____

---
Mafart and Prieur clearly (13) *had / did not have* P.O.W. status and were therefore treated (14) _____

---
Responsibility for acts of spies (15) *is / is not* clearly regulated by International Law. It seems that agents cannot enjoy immunity from local jurisdiction unless (16) _____

---
In fact, according to the *Caroline* and *McLeod* cases, if a government claims responsibility for the acts of its spies, the agents involved (17) _____
This precedent (18) *only applies / doesn't apply*, however, when the agent's presence in the foreign territory is lawful. Thus, the ruling in *Caroline* and *McLeod* (19) *applies / doesn't apply* in the *Rainbow Warrior* case since (20) _____

---
The reason for this rule is illustrated by the case of the Soviet submarine in Sweden, which shows that (21) _____

---
Under International Law foreign agents (22) *can / cannot* be held liable for illegal acts against municipal law.

---

●■     Compare your completed summary with the one in the key.
▲●     Compare your completed summary with someone else's before referring to the key.

ii) The completed summary of the text in i) contains the author's analysis of the law governing liability for criminal acts of agents abroad. On the basis of this analysis, why were the two French agents held personally liable for their acts in the *Rainbow Warrior* affair?

▲●     Compare your answer with other members of the class before checking in the key.
■●     Check your answer in the key.

## 4  Oral practice

Use your own summary of the text from Section A together with Exercise 3 above and the text to describe the legal position regarding liability for the criminal acts of agents abroad in International Law. Spend a few minutes preparing your description first.
*Include the following aspects:*
- The defence of superior orders
- Liability for acts in time of war: war crimes / soldiers' privileges
- Liability for acts in time of peace: low thresholds of conflict
- Espionage: agent immunity
- When the government accepts liability: lawful entry / unlawful entry / consent.

■  Speak aloud. If possible, record your description on tape, then listen to the recording.
▲  Work in pairs. Take turns to describe some of the main points from the text.


## C  Conclusion

### 1  *The impact of the* Rainbow Warrior *affair*

i)  Think about the following points:
- What is your view of the legal result of the *Rainbow Warrior* affair?
- Do you think the affair will have any positive effects for the future?
- Do you think the affair will have any negative effects?

▲  Discuss your ideas in small groups.

ii)  Read the text below to find the author's view on the impact of the *Rainbow Warrior* affair. Does he think the affair will have positive or negative results in International Law? Does he agree with any of your own ideas from i)?

---

1  *F.  Law and the* Rainbow Warrior

The *Rainbow Warrior* affair bolsters the notion that there is an international doctrine of non-intervention. France was obliged to recognise this, and
5  also to make restitution for contravening the doctrine outlawing armed attack. Further, the case may have a positive long-term benefit in drawing attention to those areas of deficiency, remarked upon by Falk, Lauchterpacht, Crawford and
10  others, in both the substantive rule of international law and its procedures, especially concerning immunity, low-level force, and peacetime espionage. Certainly in government torts the international trend in State practice is to restrict State immunity
15  and assert local jurisdiction, to the extent that it has been said to contribute to the 'demystification of the State as a supreme being'.

Jurists will note that the outcome of the intergovernment dispute was based on an individual's
20  concept of fairness, producing a ruling rather than a legal judgment. De Cuéllar resisted any attempt to imbue the case with theoretical significance or to refer to norms – though no doubt legality as well as practicality formed part of his private deliberations.
25  Yet in so far as the settlement can be considered as an example of State practice, it significantly challenges the principle that either a State or its agents – but not both – are liable for acts contrary to law outside the Geneva Conventions.

Michael Pugh

---

iii)  Read the text again and decide:
a)  Are States *more* or *less* likely to be held liable for torts in International Law now than in the past?
b)  What important point does the author make in lines 18–24 of the text?
●  c)  In what way is the *Rainbow Warrior* settlement new and significant?
iv)  The text above contains both statements of fact and statements of personal opinion. Decide which statements are based on the author's personal opinion.

Which words or phrases in the text help you to decide?

Do you agree with the author's opinions?

▲● Discuss your ideas with other members of the class before referring to the key.

■● Refer to the key to check your ideas.


## D    Development

### 1    Vocabulary consolidation

i)  Scan the texts on pages 178, 181–2 and 184–5 and make a note of all the law terms and any other words or phrases of interest to you. Distinguish between the International Law terms and other law terms, e.g. by using a different colour. Decide which of the words and phrases you have chosen you personally want to remember.
Which ones do you think will be useful to you in the future?

ii) Use one or more of the techniques you have learnt in this book to store the vocabulary you have chosen. You may decide to make vocabulary cards or lists, to put the words into groups and categories of your choice in word tables, to design a word ladder or vocabulary network showing the logical relationship between the words you have chosen, or to store the words in some other personal way.

Remember that *any systematic activity* will help you to learn the new vocabulary! *Example:* The following list of activities is given as an example. If you are interested in studying this group of words, complete some of the activities suggested below. Then work independently on words of your own choice.

a) Scan the text and list all the words and phrases on the theme of *war and force*. The words shown in the box on the right are from the first 55 lines of the text on page 184.

b) Make vocabulary cards or lists: use your dictionary, the glossary and the text and exercises in Section B to help you write the cards.

c) Design and complete a word table by putting the words into related categories of your choice.

*or:* Design and complete a word ladder, showing the words in a logical sequence, e.g. in order of seriousness, or in the order in which they might occur in a real-life situation.

*or:* Design and complete a vocabulary network showing relationships between individual words and / or groups of words.

*or:* Write the name of an event, country or person that you personally associate with each word or phrase. For example, war crimes – the Nuremberg trials; sporadic violence – Northern Ireland; terrorism – the Red Brigade.

| *War and force* |
| --- |
| war crimes |
| crimes against peace and humanity |
| armed conflict |
| hostilities |
| conflict |
| state of war |
| military personnel |
| soldiers' privileges |
| law and customs of war, etc. |


### 2    Oral development: a moot

In Unit Seven you held a moot on a private law case. You are now going to hold an International Law moot.

i)  Choose CASE A or CASE B below. Use the information from the article you have read on the *Rainbow Warrior* affair to decide the legal position of Jane Bond or Captain Kirk under International Law.

CASE A

Jane Bond is a British Intelligence agent who enters Japan as a businesswoman under a false name. While trying to steal an important military secret she kills a Japanese guard. She is arrested and tried for murder by the Japanese authorities. At this point the British Government claims responsibility for the agent's acts. Is she personally liable or not?

CASE B

*HMS Union* is berthed in New York harbour under the command of Captain Kirk of the Royal Navy. British intelligence informs the Admiral of the Fleet that the *Tipperary*, a boat carrying arms for the IRA (the Irish Republican Army, responsible for terrorist attacks against Britain) is about to leave the harbour. The Admiral orders Captain Kirk to take any necessary action to stop the *Tipperary*. Captain Kirk orders his crew to sink the *Tipperary*. Two crew members of the Irish boat are killed in the attack. The Captain is arrested and charged with murder. Is he personally liable or not?

▲  ii) For each case, appoint people to act as counsel for the applicant State and counsel for the defendant State. The other members of the class will act as judges or arbitrators in the case they have chosen.

■       In this activity you are going to play the roles of counsel for the applicant State, counsel for the defendant State and judge or arbitrator.

■ ▲     Prepare your role(s) carefully. Refer to Unit Seven, Section One E 2 and D 4 on pages 131 and 132 to revise some expressions you will need to use in the moot.

iii) Hold the moot, at which first the applicant State, then the defendant State is represented in court. Decide who has won the case and deliver judgment.

iv) Issue a short written judgment.

●       When you have finished, check your arguments and judgment in the key.

## 3  Who's the boss?

i) From the box on the right, choose the name of the person who is the leader or head of each body, organisation, etc. on the left. Some names are used more than once. *Example:* The Secretary-General is the head of the United Nations Secretariat. *Answer:* a / 7

a) The United Nations Secretariat
b) The House of Commons (UK)
c) The British Commonwealth of Nations
d) The International Court of Justice
e) The EEC Commission
f) The UK Government
g) The House of Lords (UK)
h) The European Court
i) The Order of Barristers (UK)
j) The UK
k) The USA
l) The Court of Appeal Civil Division (UK)

(1) the Speaker
(2) the Attorney-General
(3) the British Sovereign
(4) the Master of the Rolls
(5) the President
(6) the Lord Chancellor
(7) the Secretary-General
(8) the Prime Minister

ii) Can you match the following abbreviations to one of the people, organisations, etc.
from i)?
a) AG    b) MR    c) HM QE II    d) LC    e) CA    f) HL
g) PM    h) UN    i) ICJ

iii) Can you give the name of the person who now holds any of the offices in i), or has
done so at some time in the past? You will find several answers in this book.
▲  Compare and discuss your answers with other members of the class before
●  checking in the key.

# Revision and Consolidation, Units 9—11

## Reading an International Court of Justice Judgment

### A  Reading and vocabulary skills; language and structure

In Units 9–11 you have learnt to study a text completely independently. Follow the instructions for each exercise in Part A to see how well you have learnt to use some of the skills practised in this book for the individual study and full understanding of a text.

*Reading skills*

- reading for gist and understanding the development of themes in a text
- reading for general understanding
- reformulation: summarising the main points of a text
- reading for detailed understanding
- understanding the author's attitude to information presented in a text

*Vocabulary skills*

- selecting which unknown vocabulary you need to understand for a particular reading purpose
- using the context to work out the probable meaning of new words in a text
- using root words and word families to work out the meaning of new words in a text

### 1  Learn about the text

i) Before you read, find out as much as you can about the text on page 193 from the title and other information in lines 1–7. Do *not* read the rest of the text yet.
In particular, find out:
What sort of text is it? What is it about? Who was involved? When?
If necessary, use your dictionary to understand these points fully.
Can you predict some of the information the text may contain?
ii) Use your answers to i) to write a few questions of your own that you hope the text will answer.
iii) Quickly skim the whole text on page 193 to find the answers to your questions from ii). As you read, decide what the general themes of the text are.

### 2  Reading for gist and understanding the development of themes in a text (6 points)

Put the main themes of the text (A–G) in the correct order and use them to complete the description which follows of the development of themes in the text. You may need to change or add some words to make correct sentences as in the example. You may refer to the text again, but do *not* spend time reading in detail for this activity.

1
1980
24 May
General List
No. 64

INTERNATIONAL COURT OF JUSTICE
YEAR 1980

**24 May 1980**

# CASE CONCERNING UNITED STATES DIPLOMATIC AND CONSULAR STAFF IN TEHRAN

(UNITED STATES OF AMERICA *v.* IRAN)

**90.** On the basis of the foregoing detailed examination of the merits of the case, the Court finds that Iran, by committing successive and continuing breaches of the obligations laid upon it by the Vienna Conventions of 1961 and 1963 on Diplomatic and Consular Relations, the Treaty of Amity, Economic Relations, and Consular Rights of 1955, and the applicable rules of general international law, has incurred responsibility towards the United States. As to the consequences of this finding, it clearly entails an obligation on the part of the Iranian State to make reparation for the injury thereby caused to the United States. Since however Iran's breaches of its obligations are still continuing, the form and amount of such reparation cannot be determined at the present date.

**91.** At the same time the Court finds itself obliged to stress the cumulative effect of Iran's breaches of its obligations when taken together. A marked escalation of these breaches can be seen to have occurred in the transition from the failure on the part of the Iranian authorities to oppose the armed attack by the militants on 4 November 1979 and their seizure of the Embassy premises and staff, to the almost immediate endorsement by those authorities of the situation thus created, and then to their maintaining deliberately for many months the occupation of the Embassy and detention of its staff by a group of armed militants acting on behalf of the State for the purpose of forcing the United States to bow to certain demands. Wrongfully to deprive human beings of their freedom and to subject them to physical constraint in conditions of hardship is in itself manifestly incompatible with the principles of the Charter of the United Nations, as well as with the fundamental principles enunciated in the Universal Declaration of Human Rights. But what has above all to be emphasized is the extent and seriousness of the conflict between the conduct of the Iranian State and its obligations under the whole corpus of the international rules of which diplomatic and consular law is comprised, rules the fundamental character of which the Court must here again strongly affirm. In its Order of 15 December 1979, the Court made a point of stressing that the obligations laid on States by the two Vienna Conventions are of cardinal importance for the maintenance of good relations between States in the interdependent world of today. 'There is no more fundamental prerequisite for the conduct of relations between States', the Court there said, 'than the inviolability of diplomatic envoys and embassies, so that throughout history nations of all creeds and cultures have observed reciprocal obligations for that purpose.' The institution of diplomacy, the Court continued, has proved to be 'an instrument essential for effective co-operation in the international community, and for enabling States, irrespective of their differing constitutional and social systems, to achieve mutual understanding and to resolve their differences by peaceful means' (*I.C.J. Reports 1979*, p. 19).

**92.** It is a matter of deep regret that the situation which occasioned those observations has not been rectified since they were made. Having regard to their importance the Court considers it essential to reiterate them in the present Judgment. The frequency with which at the present time the principles of international law governing diplomatic and consular relations are set at naught by individuals or groups of individuals is already deplorable. But this case is unique and of very particular gravity because here it is not only private individuals or groups of individuals that have disregarded and set at naught the inviolability of a foreign embassy, but the government of the receiving State itself. Therefore in recalling yet again the extreme importance of the principles of law which it is called upon to apply in the present case, the Court considers it to be its duty to draw the attention of the entire international community of which Iran itself has been a member since time immemorial, to the irreparable harm that may be caused by events of the kind now before the Court. Such events cannot fail to undermine the edifice of law carefully constructed by mankind over a period of centuries, the maintenance of which is vital for the security and well-being of the complex international community of the present day, to which it is more essential than ever that the rules developed to ensure the ordered progress of relations between its members should be constantly and scrupulously respected.

|  | Correct order |
| --- | --- |
| *Themes in the text* | |
| A Seriousness of Iran's violation of fundamental principles of International Law | |
| B Negative consequences of this type of violation for International Law and relations | |
| C Court's finding in the case: Iran in breach of International Law | 1 |
| D Description of Iranian acts constituting breaches of International Law | |
| E Reason for particular seriousness of Iran's conduct | |
| F Reparation | |
| G Fundamental importance of diplomatic rights in international relations | |

**Description of the development of themes in the text**

*Example:* The text begins by stating _the court's finding that Iran is in breach of International Law_ [lines 8–17]

(1) and then considers the question of _____ [17–23]

(2) The Court then goes on to give _____ [24–38]

(3) and comments on _____ [38–51]

(4) and_____ [51–69]

(5) The last paragraph deals with _____ [70–83]

(6) and finally the Court notes _____ [83–99]

## 3  *Vocabulary skills: selecting vocabulary for study (10 points)*

Read lines 8–38 of the text on page 193 in more detail to decide if the following statements are *true* or *false*. As you work, decide which (if either) of the words in capitals you need to understand for this reading purpose. Use your vocabulary skills to understand the words you find necessary. Do *not* spend time on any other unknown words in the text if you can complete this activity.

*Example:* The Court has already examined the merits of the case.  FOREGOING (8) / MERITS (9)

*Answer: True.* Need to understand FOREGOING. Do not need to understand MERITS.

(To decide if the statement is true or false, you need to understand FOREGOING, which describes *when* the Court examined the merits. MERITS will certainly help you to understand exactly the *meaning* and relevance of the statement, but is not necessary to decide if this statement is true or false.)

a) Iran is liable to the USA as a result of treaty obligations, not under principles of general International Law.   SUCCESSIVE (10) / AMITY (13)

b) Iran must make reparation to the USA   ENTAILS (18) / AMOUNT (22)

c) Each Iranian breach of International Law was equally serious.   CUMULATIVE (25) / ESCALATION (27)

d) The Iranian authorities were against the situation created by the militants after 4 November.   PREMISES (31) / ENDORSEMENT (32)

e) During the months of occupation of the Embassy, the Embassy staff were killed.   DETENTION (35) / BOW TO (38)

## 4 Vocabulary skills: word families (6 points)

i) Use your knowledge of root words and word families to decide what the following words probably mean. Give a simple definition for each word. Then check that your ideas make sense in the text.
*Example:* foregoing (adj., 8)   *Answer:* [FORE + GO + -ING] Prefix FORE- often means *before* in time or position, e.g. foreword = a preface or introductory note at the beginning of a book; forejudge = to judge before (e.g. before hearing the full facts); -ING = typical adjectival form.
*Probable meaning:* foregoing = which goes before, previous. Does this make sense in the context?

(1) wrongfully (adverb, 38)   (2) prerequisite (noun, 57)
(3) inviolability (noun, 59,82)   (4) receiving (adj., 83)
(5) irreparable (adj., 89)   (6) ensure (verb, 97)

ii) To show that you understand the words in i), choose the best word to complete the following sentences. Use each word once only, and make any necessary changes (e.g. plural forms).
*Example:* The __*foregoing*__ provisions (see section 1 above) have all been included in the Bill.

a) the Race Relations Act 1976 was passed to _____ fair treatment for people of all races.
b) A good knowledge of French and English is often a _____ for an international lawyer.
c) A _____ order is a court order which places the property of a debtor in the control of a special trustee in bankruptcy cases.
d) It was alleged that the newspaper article had caused _____ damage to the company's good name and professional reputation.
e) The Universal Declaration of Human Rights was made to guarantee the _____ of fundamental rights.
f) The plaintiff claimed damages against his employer because he had been _____ dismissed.

## 5 Vocabulary skills: contextual deduction (6 points)

Use the context and logical reasoning to work out the probable meaning of the following words and phrases in the text.
*Example:* incurred responsibility (16)
*Answer:* Iran has *incurred responsibility* towards the US by committing breaches of International Law.
*Probable meaning:* Iran has *caused itself to be liable / made itself liable.*
*Note:* Your answers should be *similar in meaning* to the answers in the key. They will not be identical and may be in English or your own language.

a) laid upon/on (11, 53)   b) seizure (31)   c) to bow to (38)
d) incompatible with (41)   e) set at naught (77, 81–2)   f) to undermine (91–2)

## 6 Reading skills: reformulation, reading for detail (14 points)

i) Read the whole text carefully and identify the main points. Make a note of them. Work independently and use your vocabulary skills to find the meaning of any unknown words or phrases which you need to understand to follow the main points of the text.

ii) Study the following summary of the text. Use the text to check the quality of the summary and write a comment for each of points 4–17.

*Choose from:*

A  Good: the main points are included in different words and there is no *un*necessary information.

B  Incomplete: not all the main points are included

C  Too long: some *un*important points are included

D  Incorrect: not all the information in the statement is correct

E  Copied: the statement is copied too exactly from the text, it is not expressed in different words.

*Examples:*  see comments on statements (1), (2) and (3) below.

## SUMMARY

*Court's finding*

(1) Court has already examined merits of case. *C – this is not a main point.*

(2) Iran liable to USA for series of breaches of treaty obligations and of principles of general International Law. *B – what kind of obligations and principles has Iran broken?*

(3) Iran must make reparation; form and quantity cannot be determined until breaches stop.

*Description of breaches*

(4) Must consider effect of breaches taken together.

(5) Breaches got worse over a period of time.

(6) Iranian authorities opposed militants' attack on Embassy of 4 November 1979 and seizure of premises and staff.

(7) Later endorsed situation and deliberately maintained occupation of Embassy.

(8) Militants acted on behalf of State for the purpose of forcing the US to bow to certain demands.

*Seriousness of breaches*

(9) Iran guilty of extremely serious violations of fundamental rules of diplomatic and consular law.

(10) In Order of 1979 Court stressed that diplomatic and consular protection given by Vienna Conventions fundamental for modern inter-state relations.

(11) Diplomacy essential for international cooperation and peaceful resolution of disagreements. (ICJ Reports, p. 19).

*Consequences of breaches*

(12) Frequency with which principles of International Law governing diplomatic and consular relations set at naught by individuals or groups is deplorable.

(13) This case especially serious as breaches committed by groups, not individuals.

(14) Court stresses again extreme importance of principles of diplomatic and consular law.

(15) Events of this kind may cause permanent damage to whole structure of International Law and create a risk for security of international community.

(16) It has taken centuries to build this structure of International Law.

(17) It is especially important to respect International Law in complex international community of today.

## 7  *Understanding the author's attitude (8 points)*

i)  From your reading of the whole text, which of the following best describes the Court's attitude towards the seriousness of Iran's breaches of International Law?

a) The Court analyses the facts, expressing a strong opinion, and is very critical of Iran.

b) The Court simply gives a factual analysis of Iran's conduct and the legal situation.

c) The Court analyses the facts and criticises Iran a little.

ii) Which of 1, 2 and 3 below best describes each paragraph? Give reasons for your answers and use each answer once only.

a) Paragraph 90     b) Paragraph 91     c) Paragraph 92

*Choose from:*

(1) expresses strong criticism     (2) gives facts     (3) expresses very strong criticism

## 8 Understanding the logical development of arguments in a text and reading for general understanding; language study: connectives (13 points)

i) Paragraphs 93–4 of the Court's judgment in *USA v. Iran* are reproduced on this page. First skim the text to find the main theme. Do not worry about the missing words!

*Answer:* The main theme of paragraphs 93–4 is _____

---

1 **93.** (1) \_\_*Before*\_\_\_ drawing the appropriate conclusions from its findings on the merits in this case, the Court considers that it cannot let pass without comment the incursion* into the territory
5 of Iran made by United States military units on 24–25 April 1980, an account of which has been given earlier in this Judgment. (2) _____ the United States Government may have had understandable preoccupations with respect to
10 well-being of its nationals held hostage in its Embassy for over five months. (3) _____ the United States government may have had understandable feelings of frustration at Iran's long-continued detention of the hostages, notwithstan-
15 ding two resolutions of the Security Council as well as the Court's own Order of 15 December 1979 calling expressly for their immediate release. (4) _____ in the circumstances of the present proceedings, the Court cannot fail to express its
20 concern in regard to the United States' incursion into Iran. (5) _____, as previously recalled, this case had become ready for hearing on 19 February 1980, the United States Agent requested the Court, owing to the delicate stage of certain
25 negotiations, to defer setting a date for the hearings. Subsequently, on 11 March, the Agent informed the Court of the United States Government's anxiety to obtain an early judgment on the merits of the case. The hearings were (6)

30 _____ held on 18, 19 and 20 March, and the Court was in course of preparing the present judgment adjudicating upon the claims of the United States against Iran when the operation of 24 April 1980 took place. The Court (7) _____ feels
35 bound to observe that an operation undertaken in those circumstances, from whatever motive, is of a kind calculated to undermine respect for the judicial process in international relations; and to recall that in paragraph 47, 1 B, of its Order of 15
40 December 1979 the Court had indicated that no action was to be taken by either party which might aggravate the tension between the two countries.

**94.** At the same time, (8) _____, the Court must point out that neither the question of
45 the legality of the operation of 24 April 1980, under the Charter of the United Nations and under general international law, nor any possible question of responsibility flowing from it, is before the Court. It must also point out that this question can
50 have no bearing on the evaluation of the conduct of the Iranian Government over six months earlier, on 4 November 1979, which is the subject-matter of the United States' Application. (9) _____ \_\_\_\_ the findings reached by the Court in this Judgment
55 are not affected by that operation.

*incursion = a sudden attack on or invasion of hostile territory

---

ii) Read the text again. Follow the logical development of the Court's arguments and put each word or phrase from the list below in the correct position.

*Example:* (1) d

*Choose from:*  a) when     b) however     c) no doubt also     d) before
  e) nevertheless     f) no doubt     g) therefore
  h) accordingly     i) it follows that

### iii) Reading for general understanding

a) Did the Court think the USA was justified in making the incursion into Iranian territory?

b) Why did the Court think the US military operation would 'undermine respect for the judicial process in international relations' (lines 37–8)?

c) Why did the US incursion not affect the Court's findings in the present case?

d) Compare the Court's attitude towards the US incursion in Paragraphs 93–4 with its attitude towards Iran's conduct in the case in Paragraphs 90–92. Is the Court:
   (1) more strongly critical of the USA?
   (2) equally critical of both Iran and the USA?
   (3) more strongly critical of Iran?

## B  Law terms and law

The exercises in Part B will test your knowledge of English law, International Law and law terms that you have learnt in this book and particularly in Units 9–11.

## 1  Law terms I

The word in CAPITALS at the end of each sentence can be used to form a word that completes the sentence. Use your knowledge of word families, word-building and English law terms to fill each blank in this way.

*Example:*  A bilateral treaty is a binding _international_ agreement in
        writing between two States.                                          NATION

a) Experts disagree about the main cause of _____. Does it
   depend mainly on social factors or on the offender's personality and
   physical characteristics?                                                 CRIME

b) When a person who kills has used reasonable force in the
   circumstances to defend himself against attack, he can plead
   _____ to a charge of murder.                                         DEFEND

c) In modern western society serious crimes are generally punished
   with _____.                                                          PRISON

d) All subjects of International Law must respect certain _____
   rules which are universally recognised as fundamental principles of
   International Law.                                                         VIOLATE

e) The defendant admitted that he had published the words
   complained of, but pleaded the _____ that they were true.            JUST

f) Most summary offences must be _____ within 6 months,
   but there is no time limit for _____ on indictment. [2 words]       TRY

g) The DPP (Director of Public Prosecutions) is the public
   _____ in the UK: the government official who brings
   charges against persons accused of crimes.                               PROSECUTE

## 2  Law terms II (8 points)

In this exercise you will find definitions of law terms you have learnt in Units 9–11. Do you know the word or phrase referred to by each definition? The number in brackets [e.g. (8)] refers to the number of letters in each word.

*Example:* A _national_ (8) is a subject or citizen of a State  *Answer:* national

a) When you _____ ___ _____ (5,3,6), you state at the beginning of a trial that you did not commit the offence you are accused of.

b) _____ _____ (5,6) are fundamental rights of man, such as the right to life, the right to freedom of thought and the right to work.

c) _____ (11) is a procedure for the settlement of disputes by one or more independent third parties on a domestic or international level as an alternative to judicial proceedings.

d) A person is _____ (9) of the offence with which they are charged if they are found guilty of it.

e) The _____ (8) is written or spoken statements of facts, or objects which help to prove something at a trial.

f) _____ (9) is legal responsibility for one's actions together with an obligation to repair any injury caused.

g) _____ _____ (5,11) is supreme power in a State: full legislative, executive and juridical powers of a State on its territory.

h) _____ (6) of a law, contract, obligation, etc. means its violation or non-respect.

## 3 Law and law terms (9 points)

Use your knowledge of English law and International Law and law terms to choose the correct alternative and complete each of the sentences below.

*Example:* The defendant's father was charged with ____ *bribery and corruption* ____ for trying to influence the judge by offering him a large sum of money.
  (1) kidnapping    (2) arson    (3) bribery and corruption
  (4) indecency

*Answer:*    (3)

a) Judicial corporal punishment was _____ in England in 1948.
  (1) abolished    (2) endorsed    (3) repealed    (4) ratified

b) The parties continued _____ for several months before a/an _____ to the dispute was finally reached. [Choose two different words.]
  (1) arbitration    (2) negotiations    (3) settlement    (4) reparation

c) The defendant's husband was killed in the accident she had caused. It was found that she was guilty of gross negligence, but had not intended to kill the victim. As a result she was convicted of _____.
  (1) killing    (2) murder    (3) manslaughter    (4) assault

d) The Crown Court sentenced him to _____ for committing assault occasioning grievous bodily harm.
  (1) a suspended sentence    (2) a 2-year probation order
  (3) judicial corporal punishment    (4) 5 years' imprisonment

e) The applicant's punishment was degrading in the circumstances, _____ Article 3 of the European Convention on Human Rights.
  (1) consequently it was in accordance with    (2) accordingly it was contrary to
  (3) nevertheless it constituted a breach of    (4) moreover it was consistent with

f) The UK Government refused to _____ the accused on the grounds that she was a political offender.
  (1) convict    (2) charge    (3) remand    (4) extradite

g) A State may have to make reparations to victims for _____ of its agents abroad.
  (1) infringements    (2) damage caused by criminal acts    (3) espionage
  (4) prosecutions

h) There can be no _____ some of the rights protected by the European Convention of Human Rights.
  (1) derogation from    (2) immunity from    (3) provision for    (4) repeal of

## 4  The law (12 points)

Use your knowledge of English law and International Law to answer the following questions. Give brief, simple answers.

### i)  Unit 9 – public law: criminal law and constitutional law

a)  What is the name of the court which has jurisdiction over offences committed by young people?
b)  Do convicted criminals have the right to appeal against sentence? (Think about the *Tyrer case*)
c)  What is the constitutional position of the Isle of Man with regard to the UK?
d)  Can the UK Parliament legislate for the Isle of Man on domestic matters?

### ii)  Unit 10 – International Law: European human rights

a)  Can individual citizens apply to the European Court of Human Rights if they think their rights have been violated? (Think about the origin of the *Tyrer case*.)
b)  Put the following breaches of human rights from Article 3 of the European Convention in order of seriousness:
inhuman treatment or punishment / torture / degrading treatment or punishment
c)  Why is all humiliating judicial punishment not a violation of human rights?
d)  Will the European Court of Human Rights consider domestic law or policy in States which are signatories to the Convention when reaching a decision?

### iii)  Unit 11 – International Law: use of force and espionage

a)  Who is generally liable for the criminal acts of a State agent committed abroad: the State, the agent, both or neither?
b)  What important principle of International Law was laid down by the Nuremberg Charter of 1945 regarding the defence of superior orders?
c)  Why are soldiers who kill foreigners in a war not guilty of murder?
d)  Can spies enjoy agent immunity for crimes they commit abroad?

*Now check all your answers in the key.*

## C  Word games

## 1  Word association

The following groups of four words are all connected with the same thing or they are examples of the same thing. Write down the missing word or phrase in each group. The number in brackets, e.g. (6), refers to the number of letters in each word.
*Example:*  sentence, punishment, detention, convict (6)
a)  compensation, to recover damages, injured party, to sue (9)
b)  law reports, All E.R., to cite, authority (4,3)
c)  Common Market, directly applicable provisions, Member State, Community law (1,1,1,3)
d)  fine, to deter, penal policy, probation (10)
e)  counsel, barrister, jurist, solicitor (6)
f)  Old Bailey, jury, evidence, indictable offence (5)
g)  General Elections, MP, Speaker, ballot (5,2,7)
h)  Land Law, Tort, Contract, Family Law (7,3)

i) ICJ, treaty, use of force, state sovereignty (13,3)
j) party, hearing, costs, proceedings (10)
k) Hansard, Bill, Queen in Parliament, to enact (11)
l) Law Lord, Master of the Rolls, Your Honour, circuit judge (9)
m) offeree, binding promise, breach, consideration (8)
n) Crown, heir to the throne, Royal Assent, to reign (9)
o) manslaughter, breach of the peace, drunken driving, burglary (7)
p) constitutional convention, custom, common law, legislation (6,2,3)
q) it was laid down that, ruling, decision, to overrule (8)
r) *ratio decidendi*, to bind, *stare decisis*, to distinguish (8,9)

| | | | | | | | | P | R | I | S | O | N | | |
|---|---|---|---|---|---|---|---|---|---|---|---|---|---|---|---|
| | | | | | L | | | B | | | | T | Y | a. |
| | | | | | | C | | S | | | | A | | b. |
| | | | | | | | E | | | | W | | c. |
| | | | | S | | N | | | | C | | N | G | d. |
| | | | | | | | L | | | Y | | R | | e. |
| | | | | | | | T | R | | | | | f. |
| | | U | | O | F | | M | | | | S | g. |
| | | | P | | V | | | | A | | h. |
| | T | R | | T | | | L | A | | i. |
| | | L | | T | G | | | I | O | j. |
| | L | | G | S | | T | I | | k. |
| | | | D | C | | R | Y | l. |
| | | | O | | R | | C | | m. |
| | | S | V | | | G | | n. |
| | | | F | F | | | E | o. |
| | S | | C | O | | W | p. |
| | | J | D | M | | q. |
| U | | C | | P | E | E | E | | r. |

## 2 *Whodunit?*

Johnny, Micky and Sonny have each been accused of a different crime.
The three charges are *murder*, *armed robbery* and *theft*.
Study the *facts* and find the *solution* to the *problem*!

**The problem**

Who was charged with which crime? Who was convicted? Which of the three did *not* go to prison?

**The facts**

The MURDERER was sentenced to life imprisonment.
JOHNNY was charged with a crime of violence.

The man charged with THEFT was convicted.
MICKY was not tried for MURDER.
The man who was not sentenced to imprisonment was not convicted.
SONNY was not accused of THEFT or ARMED ROBBERY.
The man who was not tried for a crime of violence was sentenced to two years' imprisonment.

**The solution**

Johnny _____
Micky _____
Sonny _____

_____ did not go to prison.

# Key

## Introductory Unit

### Exercise C 1

i)  a) degree      b) graduate

ii) a) Where the graduate has obtained the higher degree of Doctor of Philosophy (Ph.D.), s/he is entitled to use the title Doctor (Dr).
    b) English graduates do not use a title in front of their names. They can put letters after their names to indicate the type of degree they have; for example, Ms Amy Wilson B.Sc. (she is a *Bachelor* of *Sc*ience – she has a degree in a scientific subject like mathematics); Mr Ian Jones B.A. (he is a *Bachelor* of *Arts* – he has a degree in an Arts subject like history).
    c) Law graduates can put the letters LL.B. after their names, e.g. Ms Martina Ward LL.B. (she is a *Bachelor* of *Laws*).

iii) An undergraduate is studying for a first degree. A postgraduate is studying for a second or later degree.

iv) Tripos (used for Cambridge University only)

v)  'A'-levels ('A' = Advanced)

### Exercise D 2

(1) C;     (2) A;     (3) D;     (4) B.

### Exercise D 3

a) 3 years     b) 14 subjects (first year – 4; second year – 5; third year – 5)

### Exercise E 1

i)   a) skills (line 7)     b) reasoning (line 8)     c) ethical (10)
ii)  a) read (12, 16)     b) practising (13)     c) to go into (14)
iii) a) papers (24, 32)     b) options (34)
     c) dissertation (44)
iv)  Master of Laws

### Exercise E 2

If any of your answers are wrong, refer to the lines of the text indicated in brackets (...) to find out the reason why.
a) (1) – it is 'academic rather than vocational' (lines 3–4).
b) Interpretation and logical reasoning (line 8).
c) No, it also includes ethical, political and social questions (10–11).

d) The text does not specify this, it simply says that many students intend to practise and many don't (12–15).
e) It doesn't matter, both are equally common (18–21).
f) In the second year, yes; not in the first year (22–32).
g) No, they have a wider choice in the third year (32–5).
h) In the first year students take the four subjects in Group I (22–6);
   in the second year they choose 5 subjects from Groups II and III (26–32);
   in the third year they choose 5 subjects from Groups III and IV (35–42).
i) No, they can do a dissertation instead of an exam in one subject (43–5).
j) 4 (46–7).

### Exercise G 1

i) In general, *private law* is the part of the law which deals with relations between ordinary individuals, and also between individuals and the State in circumstances where the State does not enjoy special rights or powers. In general, *public law* is the part of the legal system which deals with the State and also with relations between the State and ordinary individuals in circumstances where the State enjoys special rights or powers.

ii) Examples of branches of private law are Law of Tort, Law of Contract, Land Law, Family Law. Examples of branches of public law are Constitutional Law and Administrative Law. Criminal Law is sometimes considered a branch of public law and sometimes considered distinct from both public and private law.

iv) No, the distinction is not important or relevant in English law.

vi) a) No, because there is no code of English law.
    b) Yes, it is fundamental.
    c) No, there has been no distinction since 1641.
    d) No.
    e) Many Western European countries such as France, Belgium, Holland, Germany, Spain and Italy; some countries in Africa, the Near East and South America; Japan and Indonesia.
    f) Because this makes it easier to study and explain the law.

# Unit 1

## Section One

### Exercise B 1

A / 2;  B / 6;  C / 3;  D / 4;  E / 1;  F / 5;
G / 7.

### Exercise B 2

a) Written and unwritten sources (lines 1–17).
b) No, only parts of it (lines 18–35).
c) Parliament (41–70).
d) Yes, through interpretation (71–96).
e) (2) (lines 102–23).
f) Yes (194–228).
g) (1) Yes, it was one of the original sources of law
    (229–62).
    (2) No (246–72).
h) On the Continent (298–342).

*Note:* Were most of your answers to exercises B 1 and B
2 correct? If so, you can see that it is possible to
understand what a text is about (B 1) and its general
meaning (B 2) even if you don't understand every word
or phrase.

### Exercise C 1

iii) a) No, only formal enactments are defined as *written
       law.*
    b) Yes – judicial decisions are written, but they are
       defined as *unwritten law* because they are not formal
       enactments.
    c) Yes, many Continental countries have codified a lot
       of their law.
    d) Written.
    e) Judicial precedent.
    f) An area of law (which is part of the Law of Contract)
       which regulates buying and selling products and
       property.
    g) It is an Act of Parliament which regulates the law
       relating to partnership (an area of Company Law).
v) (1) made into a law by a legislative act, e.g. by
       Parliament
   (2) written
   (3) the opposite of enacted law, i.e. law which is not
       enacted
   (4) enacted; answers iii) a and b tell you that ordinary
       words in general English can have a special technical
       meaning in the context of the law. The language of
       the law is very precise.
   (5) codified = made into a code
   (6) the volume of law will probably be larger;
       preponderate over = be greater/larger than
   (7) enacted law, legislation
   (8) goods = products, items of property such as
       manufactured objects; sale of goods is part of the
       Law of Contract.
   (9) Company Law
vi) You probably found that you needed to understand the
    following words from the list in iv) and that the words

indicated in brackets (...) were useful, but not necessary
to answer the questions from iii).
(d), e, f, g, (h), i, k, l, (m), n, p, (q).

### Exercise C 2

1 / c;   2 / h;   3 / b;   4 / d;   5 / e;   6 / g;
7 / a;   8 / f.

### Exercise D 1

i) a) underlined   b) circled

### Exercise D 2

a) (2) (lines 41–59)
b) Delegated legislation is possible in Britain, in fact
   Parliament constantly delegates legislative powers to
   other bodies or individuals (lines 52–4)
c) Yes (56–65)
d) Basic freedoms such as the right to life, liberty or
   property.
e) No. Parliamentary sovereignty in Britain is absolute –
   Parliament can pass any law it wants (57–62).
f) As a member of the EC, Britain has agreed to be subject
   to EC law. This may be considered to limit the power of
   the national parliament.
g) seldom = rarely
h) To show the difficulty of interpreting the exact meaning
   of words (78–85).
i) No, the phrase '*Suppose that* . . .' shows that it is
   imaginary (85).
j) Old King Cole commanded that all dogs in his kingdom
   should be killed (86–7).
k) (1) Jack Sprat (line 88)   It belongs to Jack Sprat.
   (2) the alsatian wolfhound (89)   Jack Sprat wants to
       save his alsatian wolfhound; he asks the court to save
       it.
   (3) the alsatian wolfhound (89)   He says the alsatian is
       a 'hound'; the court must interpret the word 'dogs'.
   (4) the court's decision (92–4)   The court's decision
       will influence the King's command.
   (5) The example shows that courts can influence the
       effect of legislation by their interpretation of the
       words of a law. In the context of sources of law this
       means that courts not only create and develop law
       through judicial precedent (in the common-law legal
       system), but can also influence the effect of enacted
       law.
   (6) The language is typical of legal examples:
       • the phrase '*Suppose that* . . .' introduces the facts
         of the example
       • the simple present tense is used to describe the
         facts: 'Old King Cole *commands* . . .', 'Jack Sprat
         *applies* to the court . . .'
       • the simple future tense is used to introduce the
         legal point: 'the court's decision *will influence* . . .'

### Exercise D 4

a) STATUTE    b) ENACTED LAW
c) LEGISLATIVE ENACTMENT
d) ACT OF PARLIAMENT    e) ENACTMENT

**Exercise E 1**

ii)

| | | ENGLISH LAW | CONTINENTAL LAW |
|---|---|---|---|
| A | TYPE OF LEGAL SYSTEM | common law | civil law |
| B | BASIC CHARACTERISTIC OF SYSTEM | central importance of precedent | central importance of enacted law |
| C | STYLE OF LEGAL REASONING | inductive – reasoning in individual cases leads to general rules | deductive – decisions reached by reasoning from general rules to particular cases |
| D | LEGAL PRINCIPLES | principles are flexible; based on real facts, develop in individual cases | in time fixed principles may not correspond to changing circumstances; general enacted principles are applied to individual cases |
| E | OTHER CHARACTERISTICS | inferior courts must follow decisions of superior courts; central position of judges | original source of principles may be case-law, custom, etc. |

**Exercise E 2**

i) a / 2;  b / 5;  c / 4;  d / 3;  e / 1.
ii) a / 3;  b / 5;  c / 1;  d / 2;  e / 4.
iii) a / 3;  b / 4;  c / 2;  d / 5;  e / 1.
iv) a / 2;  b / 3;  c / 5;  d / 1;  e / 4.

**Exercise E 3**

The basic characteristics, style of legal reasoning and characteristics of legal principles of the systems are divergent (see sections B,C and D of your table from E 1 for details); the central position of judges in the English system is also a distinctive feature.

They are not quite so divergent as might appear, because in practice the original source of codes may be case-law itself, custom (also the original source of judicial precedent) and the opinion of jurists.

**Exercise E 4**

a) No, because the facts of every case are different. There may be more than one similar precedent and the judge must decide which one to follow. Sometimes the judge will have to decide a completely new case.
b) The judge's position is central because s/he makes law in new cases and develops the general principles of the common law through decisions in individual cases.

**Exercise E 5**

a) *True*
b) *False* – in question
c) *False* (note: sometimes *authority* has this meaning, but not in this context in the text) – precedent, precedents
d) *True*
e) *True*
f) *False* (this is the definition for a 'case of first instance' –

case presenting completely new facts for which there is no precedent)
g) *True*
h) *False* – freedom to decide on one's own
i) *True*
j) *False* – legal decisions
k) *True*
l) *False* – disagreements, arguments, controversies

**Exercise E 6**

i) a / 2;  b / 3;  c / 5;  d / 1;  e / 4.
ii) 1 / for;  2 / further;  3 / however;
4 / thus or therefore;  5 / therefore or thus

**Exercise E 7**

If any of your answers are wrong, refer to the lines of the text in brackets (...) to find out why.
i / b (lines 156–66);  ii / a (171–81);  iii / c (194–205);
iv / a (204–14).

**Exercise F 3**

The following are suggestions only.
CASE-LAW: *advantages* – rules are flexible, can change as circumstances change;
*disadvantages* – law can be made by judges, who are not part of the legislative body; the law is made up of separate decisions in individual cases and it may not have a coherent general form or pattern.
CODES: *advantages* – easy to find the law; the law is not a series of separate decisions which are not connected, it has a coherent form and pattern;
*disadvantages* – laws made by theorists, may not relate to actualities of real life.

## Section Two

### Exercise B 1

i) 'common law' has several different meanings, depending on the context.

ii) A (lines 6–9);  B (lines 9–10);  C (6–7); D (22–3).

### Exercise B 2

a) Text D  b) Text E  c) Text C  d) 3

e) the Court of Chancery (Text B, lines 5–6)

f) custom (Text B lines 3–4; Text C 1; Text E 5–6)

g) the US and most Commonwealth countries (Text C 4)

h) comparative law (line 20)

i) Yes (Text D 40–43)

j) it is valid if it does not conflict with US or Californian State law (Text E 22–6)

k) *People v. Rehman* (Text E 12); *Bishop v. US* (Text E 17)

### Exercise B 3

a) 1 – as a source of law, common law is judicial decision as opposed to legislation;

2 – common law is opposed to Equity, the body of law developed by the Court of Chancery;

3 – the common-law legal system contrasts with civil-law legal systems.

b) the common law of England and the colonies before the American revolution (Text E 9–11)

c) law common to all the country, not local law

d) Text E lines 19–21 corresponds to Text D definition 6; Text E lines 1–2 and 13–17 corresponds to Text D definition 7.

### Exercise C 1

d) *TEXT B* line 3 . . . [which was] based . . .

line 2 . . . [which is/was] administered . . .

line 7 . . . [which is] laid down . . .

line 8 . . . [which is] administered . . .

line 12 . . . [which was] crystallised and formulated . . .

*TEXT C* line 1 . . . [which is] based . . .

line 4 . . . [which is] now found . . .

line 5 . . . [which have been] developed . . .

line 6 . . . [which is] derived . . .

### Exercise C 2

i) a) At common law Jones receives money as compensation for the land; in Equity Smith performs the contract, so Jones receives the land itself.

ii) a) breach of contract (line 29)

b) damages (line 30) [*damages* is always plural when it has this meaning]

c) specific performance (line 31)

d) remedies (lines 34, 36), remedy, remedy.

### Exercise D 2

1 / j  they are both words for legislation

2 / o  case-law is written in the law reports

3 / g  equity means fairness, justice

4 / h  they are both used to show a contrast

5 / f  they are both remedies

6 / n  Equity was developed by the Court of Chancery

7 / k  they are both types of legal system

8 / l  they are both used to introduce a consequence

9 / e  they have very similar meanings

10 / m  Parliament is the supreme legislator in the UK

11 / d  jurists write books of authority

12 / c  they have very similar meanings

13 / i  litigation is legal action

14 / b  they have very similar meanings

15 / a  parliamentary sovereignty is a basic doctrine of British constitutional law

# Unit 2

## Section One

### Exercise A

*True:* 1 / a,c,d and e;  2 / a and b;  3 / a; 4 / b;  5 / b.

6 / The United Kingdom of Great Britain and Northern Ireland

*Note:* The UK or the British Isles or the island of Great Britain are often referred to as *Britain* or *England*, but as you can see this is not usually strictly correct.

### Exercise B 1

Possible answers:

Paragraph 2: History of the UK or History of Britain and Ireland

Paragraph 3: Legal systems in the UK or Relationship between UK legal systems.

*Note:* There is no one correct answer for this type of activity. Any heading which identifies the basic topic of the text is good. The act of choosing a heading will help you to define this.

### Exercise C 1

The events are given in the following order in the chart, with corresponding dates:

a) 9 – 1973  b) 2 – 1707  c) 7 – 1937  d) 10 – 1974  e) 3 – about 1707  f) 1 – 1603  g) 8 – 1949 h) 4 – 1800/1801  i) 5 or 6 – 1921 j) 5 or 6 – 1920 and 1922

### Exercise C 2

a / 1  *Clues:* personal *union*

b / 2;

c / (1)  *Clues:* the political *unification* of the two countries took place through the Treaty. This would logically involve *eliminating* separate parliaments and *creating* one parliament.

d / (2)  *Clues:* work and jobs would not make sense in the context. The text goes on to describe the new constitutional *structure* of Northern Irish state organs.

e / (2)  *Rule* can have both meanings in different contexts. *Clues:* here the text does not refer to an individual law, it is general in meaning. About the last 30 lines of this paragraph describe the system of *government* in Northern Ireland.

f / to replace (line 62)

*Note:* As you can see, the key to understanding vocabulary is often in the text, either in a particular word or phrase, or in the general logic of the argument. This means that it is often possible to understand the meaning of words you don't know by putting together pieces of information in the text – you are not just guessing.

## Exercise C 3

i) 'By this Act *provision was made for* Irish
representation . . .                                    (lines 35–6)
'The Irish Treaty *gave* dominion status to . . .     (45–6)
'*Under* the Government of Ireland Act, *as amended by* the Irish Free State Act . . .                    (52–5)
'The Northern Ireland Assembly Act *established* a new constitution . . .                                (58–61)
'The Northern Ireland Act *dissolved* the Assembly . . .
(67–9)
'The Northern Ireland Act *provided that* . . .       (67–9)

ii) a) as amended by
b) abolish = to take away, cancel
establish = to create, set up
give = to pass something to someone
dissolve = to end, bring to an end
*Structure Note:* The Act *provided for Irish representation* (TO PROVIDE FOR + noun)
The Act *provides that a Parliament shall not exceed* five years (TO PROVIDE THAT + subject + verb)

iii) a) provides that     b) (1) By or Under  (2) provision was made for
c) amended          d) (1) abolished  (2) established

## Exercise C 4

ii) The independent kingdoms of England and Scotland *were first linked* . . .                        (lines 20–21)
The political unification of the two countries *was only effected* more than . . .                         (24–6)
By this Act provision *was made* for Irish
representation . . .                                  (35–6)
. . . as provision *had been made* for Scottish
representation . . .                                  (37–8)
. . . the title *was changed* to the present one . . .  (43)
. . . a separate parliament and government . . . *were established* for Northern Ireland . . .          (56–8)
The Northern Ireland Parliament *was replaced* by an elected Assembly . . .                           (63–5)
. . . and the Government [*was replaced*] by an
executive . . .                                      (65–6)
[*Note:* in this case the verb *replaced* (line 65) is not repeated in the text; it is understood from the context.]
. . . the composition of which *was to be agreed* by the Assembly.                                       (66–7)
[*Note:* The use of *to be + infinitive with to* ('was to be agreed' – here with the past participle of the main verb because it is in the passive form) shows that the action was planned, or obligatory. In this case, however, the action never took place.]
. . . a Constitutional Convention *should be held* on the future of N. Ireland.                        (69–71)
*Note:* It is also possible to use modal auxiliary verbs like SHOULD, MUST, MAY, HAVE TO

which give the idea of duty, obligation, possibility, etc. with the passive.]

iii) a) Acts of Parliament are interpreted according to fixed rules of precedent [by the English courts].
b) It is possible that much English law will eventually be codified [by Parliament].
c) Many modern European legal systems have been influenced by Roman law. (Note the complex subject of the passive phrase – 'many modern European legal systems' – there are four adjectives before the noun.)
d) One Parliament for Great Britain was established by the Treaty and Acts of Union of 1706 and 1707.
e) Bigamy is committed by a person who marries a second husband or wife while still legally married to the first one. (Note the complex agent – 'a person who . . . first one').

## Exercise D 1

i) 1) lines 74–87   2) lines 87–91   3) lines 91–4

iii) The following notes are possible, but there is no one correct answer:
*Scotland:* (Relationship) Form and substance very different; different principles, institutions and traditions. Influenced by English law in modern times. No assimilation. (Reasons) Separate evolution. Based on principles of Roman, canon, feudal and customary law.
*Wales:* (Relationship) Fusion of legal systems. (Reasons) English domination of Wales in Middle Ages.
*Northern Ireland:* (Relationship) Basically similar. Administered separately. (Reasons) Not given.

## Exercise E 1

Other systems in the text are: dependency (line 18); independent kingdom (line 20); Dominion (line 46); republic (line 49). Ireland is a republic, the UK is an independent kingdom. Some other systems are: federal state; federal union of states; parliamentary democracy; oligarchy; absolute monarchy; empire. Your examples could be modern or historical.

## Exercise E 2

The following answers are taken from the 1988 *Britannica Book of the Year, World Data* (Encyclopaedia Britannica Inc.) and were correct at the time of writing.
2 / b;   3 / e;   4 / c;   5 / d;   6 / a [all these States are defined as monarchies. Brunei and Oman are sultanates, Bahrain is an emirate]

## *Section Two*

## Exercise C 1

The best answer is: c,e,f,i and j. The other answers are concerned more with history (a,b,d), religion (a,h) and defence (g), rather than the modern *legal* position of the monarchy.

## Exercise D 1

i)  a)  succeeded to the throne (line 24)   Note the difference in style between the two expressions. Which would you use in general conversation?

b)  provision (lines 16, 19)   Note the relation with the verb *to provide* in 'The Act provides that . . .' from exercise C 3, Section 1.

c)  reigns = has the position of monarch (but does not necessarily exercise sovereign power).
rules = governs. The difference is vital because it shows that the monarch is now only a symbol of power, and does not govern the country.

d)  Advice = an opinion or suggestion about what to do, here given by the Prime Minister or another Minister to the Queen to guide her. Normally a person can choose whether to follow advice or not, but here the meaning is slightly different: for constitutional reasons the Queen must accept and follow her ministers' advice, she has no choice.

e)  'To outline' means to give or state the main facts. Here it is used in the passive.

f)  A proposed law – the preliminary version, or *draft* of a new law before it is passed by the legislature. It then becomes enacted law, called an Act of Parliament or statute. In the US a *Bill* becomes an *Act*.

g)  The monarch must give the Royal Assent, that is her/his agreement to a Bill after it has passed through Parliament. This is the last stage in the legislative process, which transforms a Bill into an Act.

i)  The power of the Crown to reduce the punishment or penalty for a crime. The power is exercised for the monarch by the Home Secretary – the Minister responsible for various aspects of the criminal process, e.g. police and prisons. His ministry, the Home Office, is called the Ministry of the Interior in most countries.

ii)  A / 3    B / 1    C / 2

## Exercise D 2

OBLIGATION: a, c. Other expressions:
. . . has to . . .; . . . is compelled to . . .;
. . . is forced to . . .; . . . has a duty to . . .
CAPACITY: b, d, e. Other expressions:
. . . can . . .; has the capacity to . . .;
. . . has the ability to . . . .

## Exercise D 3

a)  No. Since the Act of Settlement 1701, only a Protestant can succeed to the throne. (lines 15–18)

b)  Originally the monarch had absolute power to govern the country, now s/he does not govern in person, but is only a symbol of the authority of the State, which is governed in the monarch's name by the government. (33–6)

c)  The remaining rights, duties and powers of the monarchy. (41–4)

d)  No. Lines 30–36 and 64–7 show this.

## Exercise D 4

Points c,e,f,i and j from exercise C 1 and the following:

● acts on advice of Prime Minister and ministers

● Royal Prerogative includes legislative, executive and judicial rights and duties, e.g. monarch gives Royal Assent to new laws; opens and closes sessions of Parliament

● international role, e.g. signs international agreements; declares war; makes peace, etc.

● appoints people to important public positions, e.g. judges

● exercises most powers through Privy Council

*Note:* there is no one correct answer for an activity of this type. The above notes are only an example.

## Exercise E 2

i)  a)  A member of the British nobility with the right to sit in the House of Lords. A man is called a *peer*, a woman a *peeress*. A hereditary peer inherits the title, which passes to his heirs when he dies, a life peer or peeress holds the title until he or she dies.

b)  Voting, vote

c)  A constituency is an area of the UK for which a representative is elected to the House of Commons.

d)  An election in one or more constituencies during the life of a Parliament, not a General Election in the whole country to elect a new Parliament.

ii)  civil servants (lines 127–8) In the UK civil servants have permanent positions; they do not change when the political party in power changes. The civil service is politically neutral.

iii)  a)  to bind (line 149) In Unit One you saw that a *binding* precedent is one which a judge is *obliged* to follow.

b)  concurrence (154)

c)  to delay (157, 159). *Delay* is also a noun, e.g. the House of Lords caused the delay of the Bill.

d)  treaties (170) (singular: treaty)

## Exercise E 3

ii)  a)  (the residue of discretionary or arbitrary) authority: No. The Royal Prerogative refers to the rights and duties of the Sovereign at any particular time in history.

b)  the Monarch: Yes, only the Monarch has this power.

c)  the body: It advises the Monarch and performs many prerogative and statutory acts for her/him.

d)  the Privy Council: There is a meeting of all its members.

e)  the House of Lords: The House of Lords can delay Bills for a year.

iii)  a)  *Subject* – The European Communities Act 1972 Main verbs and objects – 1) gives the force of law to 2) provides for subordinate legislation

b)  *Basic points:* 1) the European Communities Act gives [certain kinds of] Community law the force of law in the UK.
2) the Act provides for subordinate legislation to give effect to Community obligations and rights.

c) *Relative pronouns:* clause 1) which (line 162) – the
European Communities Act;
clause 2) which (line 170) – (existing and future)
Community law
d) Clause 1) explains the reason for the Act: so that the
UK can perform its Community obligations
Clause 2) describes which kind of Community law is
referred to in b) 1) above: directly enforceable law
(that is, European law which can be applied directly,
without separate enactment by the UK legislature).

## Exercise E 4

i) (2) *legislates* (verb, to legislate) to make law
(3) *legislature* (noun) body with the power to make law
(4) *legislation* (noun) the act of making law, law-making
*Note:* as you know, *legislation* also means *enacted law.*

ii) a) *succession* (noun, 18) right to succeed to the throne
(sometimes act of following in order).
*successor* (noun, 150) somebody or something that
follows another (sometimes person who succeeds to
the throne).
b) *constitutionally* (adverb, 76) referring to the
constitution.
*constitutional* (adjective, 147) referring to the
constitution.
c) *representative* (adjective, 118) based on
representation (of the people); the same word exists
as a noun, meaning somebody or something chosen
to represent others.
d) *disqualified* (verb, to disqualify, 125) not to be able to
qualify. What does the prefix DIS- indicate?
e) *holder* (noun, 128) a person who holds (has,
possesses) something.
f) *judicial* (adjective, 128) referring to the office of
judge or the courts or the administration of justice,
e.g. judicial precedent.
g) *guardian* (noun, 143) person who guards, protects or
watches over something.
h) *supremacy* (noun, 145) the state or condition of being
supreme, supreme authority or power.
i) *membership* (noun, 164) the fact or state of being a
member.
j) *reimposed* (verb, to reimpose, 184) to impose again.
What does the prefix RE- indicate?

## Exercise E 5

a) No, the monarch is also part of the legislature (officially
called the 'Queen in Parliament'. (lines 24 . . . 83 . . .)
b) No, Parliament can legislate for one or more countries,
e.g. only Scotland; only England and Wales, etc. (lines
86–8)
c) Only in part: the House of Commons is, but the House
of Lords is not. (101 . . . 117 . . .)
d) The Lords of Appeal in Ordinary (109). They are senior
members of the judiciary.
e) No, holders of judicial office are disqualified (128 . . .)
f) It has absolute supreme authority to pass any law and
cannot limit the power of future Parliaments to legislate
exactly as they choose. It 'cannot bind its successors'
(149–50 . . .)
g) International obligations, e.g. membership of the
European Communities (161 . . .)

## Exercise E 6

- Queen in Parliament is supreme authority (monarch,
House of Lords, House of Commons)
- composed of two Houses, centrally situated at
Westminster
- House of Commons supreme over House of Lords
- may legislate for all or part of UK
- maximum duration 5 years
- fundamental constitutional rule: Parliament is sovereign,
can pass any law
- *House of Lords:* mainly hereditary. Lords Temporal
(hereditary peers, life peers, Lords of Appeal in
Ordinary) and Lords Spiritual (archbishops and bishops),
Lord Chancellor presides. Can delay passage of a law
(except Money Bills) for one year.
- House of Commons: elected by almost universal adult
suffrage. MPs must be 21 or over, some categories are
excluded. MPs are paid a salary. Speaker presides,
defends rights of House.

## Exercise F 2

a) SPOKES (from SPEAK) + MAN A man (or sometimes
a woman) who speaks, or is chosen to speak for a group.
In modern English *spokeswoman* is often preferred for a
woman, or *spokesperson* can be used for either men or
women.
b) *Head* means chief or leader. *To head* means to lead, to be
the chief of. The minister is the head or chief of the
ministry or department.
*Note:* Like *head*, many English words have more than one
grammatical function (noun, verb, adjective, etc.), but the
same basic meaning. You can improve your understanding
and vocabulary by learning to recognise the use of a word in
all its different forms.
c) President. 'To preside' means to control or to have the
position of authority in an organised body. The Speaker
(Commons); the Lord Chancellor (Lords).
d) A smaller group of people who belong to a larger body,
formed to consider a particular problem together before
reporting to the larger body. Advantages are that more
than one committee can work at the same time; work in
a smaller group may be quicker and more efficient; it
may be possible to specialise more.
e) Departmental. Notice the change in stress, we say:
*dePARTment*, but *departMENTal*. It describes anything
belonging to or related to a department. The opposite is
*non-departmental* (line 231–2).
f) law reform (lines 248, 273)
g) Individual legal principles.
h) civil law (lines 257, 272)

## Exercise F 3

*Title* will usually have meaning 3, especially in the context of
the law of property, but this will not always be true. In line
15, it has meaning 3.
a) line 51–3; line 193–3  d) 1  g) 2
b) 1  e) 133–3; 192–4  h) 2
c) 73–2; 118–2  f) 1  i) 3

## Exercise F 4

a) S/he is the leader of the political party with a majority in
the House of Commons (lines 190–92).

b) The Prime Minister is appointed by the monarch and informs and advises the monarch on government affairs (190, 199).

c) The Cabinet decides government policies, which it presents to Parliament for agreement, discussion, amendment, etc. (213 . . .).

d) The Cabinet decides what to do. The department or ministry does it (212 . . .; 221 . . .).

e) They include legislative, executive and judicial acts (241 . . .). What does this tell you about the theory of the Separation of Powers in the UK?

f) There is no Ministry of Justice. The judicial system is administered by the courts, the Lord Chancellor and the Home Secretary (266 . . .).

### Exercise F 5

• Head of government is the Prime Minister, leader of majority political party in Commons

• post of Prime Minister regulated by constitutional conventions

• Ministers appointed by Crown on Prime Minister's recommendation

• *Prime Minister:* presides over Cabinet meetings; member of Commons; advises monarch; government spokesman; recommends important public appointments

• *Cabinet:* most important ministers, about 23; decides government policy; meetings private and secret, no vote; collective responsibility for all decisions

• *Government departments and ministries:* each department run by a minister; give effect to government policies.

### Exercise G 2

ii) Points to consider when referring to foreign institutions in your language:

1. Does a close equivalent exist in your system, with the same basic function? E.g. *Bill* – a proposal of law before Parliament. If so, direct translation is generally possible, using the equivalent term. Of course the exact characteristics of a UK Bill will be different, and it may sometimes be necessary to explain this.

2. Is there no real equivalent in your system? For instance, *Lord Chancellor.* S/he presides over the House of Lords and so may be similar to the president of the Senate or Upper House in some States, but s/he has many other important functions which probably will not correspond to one particular figure. Use the English term 'Lord Chancellor', and explain his/her functions and position in your language, perhaps making comparisons where possible.

*Note:* Take care with terms which seem to be equivalent, but are not really. For example, *Prime Minister.* There may be a figure with a similar name in your system, but are his/her functions basically similar, too?

3. Does the concept exist in your system? For instance, *by-election* – an election in one or more constituencies when an MP dies, etc., during the life of a Parliament. In some systems, a parliamentary representative who dies is replaced by the candidate who came after them at the last General Election. If a concept does not exist you will need to explain it briefly in your own language. Only give the English term, too, if it is important, like *Lord Chancellor.*

4. Does the same term refer to the same thing? For example, *Community Law* – in the context of Western Europe this refers to the law of the European Communities. It might refer to something else in a different community. If so, it will be necessary to define the term more exactly in your own language.

*Note:* Use the same principles when speaking about your own system in English. NB It is better to use terms which are not specific to only one particular system, but are international or 'neutral', where possible. For instance, *proposal of law, draft,* rather than the specifically English or American *Bill; Lower House, Lower Chamber,* rather than *House of Commons.*

iii) It is not always possible or correct to translate a law term into another language. Very often concepts and institutions do not correspond in different legal and state systems. Don't be afraid to use the original term and give an explanation in the other language where this seems best. Use this method in particular when you need to be very accurate.

### Exercise G 4

i) Lines 5, 122 – individual laws. Lines 147, 168 – law as a system.

ii) *Similar:* convention and practice; a rule and a law; an Act of Parliament and a legal enactment (also a statute. *Note:* these refer to individual laws); statute law and legislation (also enacted law. *Note:* these are general terms).

*Quite different from all the others:* Bill; provision.

iii) (1) Bill
(2) a legal enactment
(3) an Act of Parliament
(4) provisions
(5) rules
(6) law
(7) statute law / legislation
(8) practices
(9) conventions

## Unit 3

### *Section One*

### Exercise A 3

a, d and e

### Exercise B 1

a) Lord Hailsham (see dates in lines 4–5).

b) Yes (lines 5–9).

c) Custom (10).

d) To make sure that the House of Commons, and therefore the nation, was supreme (10–13).

e) The sovereignty of Parliament has passed to the House of Commons and then to the government (14–17).

f) Because it controls the party system and the civil service (17–18).

g) That the different components of government no longer control each other because one part has gained too much power (18–22).

h) does not control (21–3).

i) Yes (2–27).

j) He asks this question, but does not give an answer here (28–9).

## Exercise B 2

a) 3 – citizenship   b) 7 – partnership   c) 5 – leadership   d) 1 – membership   e) 8 – ownership

The suffix *–ship* can be used for a condition, state or quality (e.g. citizenship = the condition of being a citizen; ownership = the state of owning something); it can also be used for a group or association (e.g. leadership = a group of leaders; partnership = an association of partners).

## Exercise B 3

a) No, it means the individual or body with sovereign power in a State (in this case, the House of Commons). When Sovereign refers to the monarch it is generally written with a capital 'S'.
b) An MP in the House of Commons or a peer in the House of Lords appointed to organise the members of his or her party in parliamentary procedures and in particular to make sure that party members participate in votes and debates and support their party's policies.
c) A political party or parties seen as a working structure.
d) (1) Yes  (2) No  (3) The balance of power has changed, so that the different components of government no longer control each other because one part has gained too much power.
e) The body of rules and laws which regulate how elections are held.

## Exercise B 4

Diagram A: 1 / c;   2 / b;   3 / e;   4 / a;   5 / d.
Diagram B: 1 / f;   2 / g;   3 / b;   4 / d or e [note that 'which . . . controls the party whips' etc. (lines 17–18) refers to the *government* (line 17)];   5 / d or e;   6 / a;   7 / c.

## Exercise C 1

a) He is clearly against them. The following words and phrases from the text should help you to decide.
*dictatorship* (line 19) – in a democracy a dictatorship is always considered a bad thing; '. . . the government, which *in addition to its influence in Parliament controls the party whips, the party machine and the civil service*' (lines 16–18 – this long list, with the phrase *in addition to its influence* and the verb *controls* suggest criticism;
*machine* (line 18);
*predominant influence* (21–2);
*the government controls Parliament and not Parliament the government* (22–3) – the wording of this phrase suggests that the situation is the wrong way round.

b) No, not at this stage. He only says which problems must be considered to decide this.

## Section Two

### Exercise B 1

the Labour Party (lines 25, 39, 50)
the Social Democratic Party or SDP (line 44)
the Conservative Party (50)
the Liberal Party (69)
the Scottish National Party (76)

- the Social Democratic and Liberal Alliance (also called 'the Alliance' (line 74) is not a separate party. The name was used during the period when the Social Democratic Party and Liberal Party worked together.
- The political situation changed after the June 1987 General Election. A section of the Social Democratic Party joined together with the Liberal Party to form the Social and Liberal Democrats (later called the Liberal Democrats). As a result the Liberal Party no longer exists as a separate party. The Social Democratic Party continued to exist as a smaller separate party.
- Referring to Exercise A 2: the Republican, Royalist and Socialist Parties do not exist in Britain (the British socialist party is called Labour); the Green Party and Communist parties exist, but do not have members in the UK Parliament at the time of writing.

## Exercise B 2

He thinks it is unfair. Some reasons are:
- the way in which the country is divided into constituencies [electoral areas] (lines 13–29);
- the way parties choose candidates (30–42);
- the way parties are financed (44–54);
- the way MPs are elected (55–78).

## Exercise C 1

i) 2 / sovereignty (Text One: lines 5, 14, 15, 16, 26)
3 / sovereign (Text One: line 7)
4 / imprisonment (3)
5 / prisoner
6 / electorate (22)
7 / electoral (4, 20, 54, 56, 81)
8 / register (9)   9 / register (5, 11)
10 / representation (11)
11 / representative (Text One: 6, 8, 29, 31)
12 / residence (6)
13 / resident
14 / recommendation (14, 18, 26)
15 / approval (15)
16 / vote (58)
17 / voter (32, 34, 35, 82)
18 / expenditure (45)
19 / expensive (47)
20 / prefer

ii) a) the verb
b) some typical noun endings are -ship (dictatorship); -ty (sovereignty); -ment (imprisonment); -ate (electorate); -tion (representation); -ence (residence); -al (approval). Can you think of at least one other noun with each of these endings? For example partner*ship*.
c) -or (elector, dictator); -er (prisoner, voter).
d) -ive (elective); -ed (registered); -ing (voting).

iii) a) an *election* is the process of choosing candidates for an office by vote
the *electorate* is the group of all the people who have the right to vote in an election.
b) the *sovereign* is the individual or body with sovereign power in a State
*sovereignty* is supreme power and authority in a State
c) a *prison* is a building where criminals are kept to punish them by taking away their liberty

*imprisonment* is the state of being kept in prison

d) a *register* is an official list or record of things
   *registration* is the act of recording something on a register

e) *expenses* are sums of money which you spend while doing something
   *expenditure* is the total amount of money spent on something

iv) a / 6;  b / 4;  c / 5;  d / 1;  e / 7;  f / 3.

v) a) Representatives    b) electorate
   c) (1) registrar (2) registers    d) sovereign
   e) (1) voters (2) electoral    f) (1) spent (2) expenses
   g) a prison    h) resident    i) (1) approved
      (2) recommendation/s
   j) elections

## Exercise C 2

i)  a / 2;    b / 5;    c / 4;    d / 6;    e / 3;    f / 1.

ii) A process by which candidates are selected for a second time, or again. The prefix RE- often indicates that an action is repeated.
   (1) act of considering something again
   (2) organisation in a new or different form
   (3) to state in a new or different form
   (4) to write something again
   (5) to arrange something in a new or different way
   (6) to marry again
   a / 4 rewrite    b / 6 remarried    c / 5 rearranged
   d / 1 reconsideration    e / 3 re-stated

iii) a) as (line 18)
   c) Whichever = any one or any number from a group of things or persons. Here it is singular (whichever *candidate*). You could also say 'the candidate who obtains most votes is elected'.
   d) The number of votes and seats do not correspond.

iv) a) No [*unsuccessfully* – they did *not* have success in the case] (lines 24–9)
   b) (1) Yes (2) No [*Unlike* – the UK system is *not* like the US system] (35–8)
   c) This can happen when a party does not have the same amount of support in different areas of the country. It may win seats by a large majority in some areas and so have more than 50 per cent of the total votes in the country, but lose by a small number of votes in many other areas, and so not obtain more than 50 per cent of the seats. [*unevenly* – support is *not* distributed evenly in the country] (64–6)
   d) No [*unlikely* – it would *not* be likely (probable)] (96–100)

## Exercise C 3

i)  c

ii) a) The Boundary Commissions
   b) (1) recommendations    (2) Boundary Commissions
   c) A smaller party which has even support in the country, but not enough to come first in individual constituencies.
   d) Because they have a lot of support in particular parts of the country, so they are able to win seats there.

iii) a) so that (line 83)    b) Thus (86)
   c) i.e. (Latin *id est* meaning *that is*) (89, 91, 99)
   d) No – he says '*if* this system *were adopted . . . it would be* very unlikely that either of the two main parties *would win* an overall majority of seats . . .' (lines 96–9)
   The choice of conditional tense shows that he does not think it probable. Cf. '*If* this system *is adopted . . . it is* very unlikely that either of the two main parties *will win* an overall majority of seats . . .'. In this case the speaker thinks the system will probably or very possibly be adopted.

## Exercise C 4

If your answer is wrong, carefully study the parts of the text indicated by the line references in brackets (...) and try to decide why, as in the example on page 69.
a) (3) the Boundary Commissions make recommendations (they do not *decide*); their recommendations are sometimes *controversial* and have even been challenged in court (lines 14–29)
b) (2) 'each party has its own method for choosing candidates' (37–8)
c) (4) 'election law puts strict limits on expenditure during an election campaign' (45–6)
d) (1) for example, the Labour Party is financed mainly by the trade unions, the Conservative Party by industry (50–52)
e) (4) s/he obtained most votes (57–60)
f) (4) this can happen when a party comes second in many constituencies (62–7)
g) (3) people want a different system because of the 'lack of correlation between votes and seats' (79–96)

## Exercise D 1

The vote is valid – it is marked with a cross in the right place and only one candidate is indicated.

## Exercise D 2

i)  e

ii) *Facts and arguments:* he has chosen those aspects of the electoral system which can be considered unfair, e.g. the fact that parties are financed in different ways; the fact that a party can obtain many votes and few seats. He presents these facts in a negative way through his arguments
   *Vocabulary:* his choice of vocabulary emphasises the negative aspects of the system, e.g. the Boundary Commission's recommendations are *highly controversial*; the way boundaries are drawn *profoundly affects* the electoral prospects of a party; parties with no strong financial base *suffer a considerable electoral disadvantage*.
   *Style:* the style of writing also emphasises the negative aspects of the system, e.g. each paragraph (except the first) starts with criticism – *Their main disadvantage* is the British electoral system . . .; It is this *lack of correlation between seats and votes* . . .

iii) It is clear that the author thinks the UK electoral system is unfair and does not provide representative government. It therefore seems likely that he agrees with Lord Hailsham's view that the British constitution

has become an 'elective dictatorship', not with Dicey's
view that it is a model of representative government.

# Unit 4

## Exercise A 2

2 points for each correct answer. Maximum 8 points.
A / 3 (paragraph 819);  B / 2 (para. 818);
C / 4 (para. 820);  D / 1 (para. 817)

## Exercise A 3

½ point for each different name from the lists below.
Maximum 5 points. The line reference in brackets (…)
shows where each name is given for the first time in the text.
a) Crown (line 10); Sovereign (line 36); Queen (65)
b) Lords (10) or House of Lords (53); Commons (10) or
House of Commons (14); Houses of Parliament (26–7).
c) Cabinet (11); ministers (36); Prime Minister (37);
ministry (11); departmental minister (46–7); Minister
for the Civil Service (85–6).

## Exercise A 5

½ point for each correct answer in i). ½ point for each
correct answer in ii). Maximum 8 points.
i) Your answers should be similar in meaning to the
following, but will not be identical.
   a) [Dissolve + -tion] -tion is a typical noun ending.
   *Answer:* the dissolving or ending [of Parliament].
   b) [Remove + -al] -al is a typical noun ending.
   *Answer:* (act of) removing, taking away.
   *His removal* (line 52) = removing him, taking him
   away.
   c) [Impartial + -ly] -ly is a typical adverb ending.
   *Answer:* in an impartial way.
   d) [Director + -ships] The suffix -ship indicates a state,
   quality, position or office (e.g. leadership,
   membership). *Answer:* positions as director.
   e) [Fundamental] -al is a typical noun ending;
   -s indicates a plural noun. *Answer:* fundamental
   points or issues.
   f) [Dis- + approve + -al] The prefix dis- has a negative
   meaning; -al is a typical noun ending. *Answer:* (act
   of) not approving.
   g) (Ill- + defined] ill- (adverb) = in a bad or wrong
   way. *Answer:* defined badly or wrongly.
   h) [Prime + Minister + -ial] -ial is a typical adjectival
   ending. *Answer:* relating to the office of Prime
   Minister.

ii) a) directorship    b) dissolution
    c) impartially     d) prime-ministerial
    e) ill-defined     f) removal
    g) disapproval     h) fundamentals

## Exercise A 6

1 point for each correct answer. Maximum 9 points.
a) The Cabinet must not be *hampered* in their action by
lack of funds or inability to pass legislation (lines 12–13).
Lack of funds or inability to pass legislation would
*obstruct* or *block* Cabinet action. *Answer:* obstructed,
blocked.

b) The purpose of the *Opposition* is to give the electorate a
*choice* of ministry; the Opposition's job is to criticise the
ministry (line 20). The Opposition is a check on the
ministry's power and may defeat the Government at the
next General Election (78–9). Therefore the Opposition
must be an organised body which criticises and controls
the power of the Government and may replace the
Government in an election. *Answer:* an organised body
opposed to the Government in power. [In Britain the
Opposition is the parliamentary party in the Commons
which is second in number to the majority party which
forms the Government.]
c) The Opposition's job is to persuade the electorate that it
is better qualified to govern *in [the Government's] stead*
(20–21). The Opposition must persuade the electorate
that it is better qualified to govern *in place of* the
Government. *Answer:* in place of, instead of [the
Government].
d) There is no authoritative source which you can refer to
to *ascertain* whether a convention exists and what it is
(32–3). You would refer to a source to *find out / learn*
whether a convention exists and what it is. *Answer:* to
find out, to learn.
e) The Sovereign must act on the advice *tendered* to her by
her ministers (36). The Prime Minister must *tender* the
resignation of the ministry in certain circumstances
(41–3). Ministers *offer/give* advice to the Sovereign. The
Prime Minister must *offer/present* the resignation of the
ministry. *Answer:* to tender = to offer, give, present.
f) The membership of committees must *afford* proper
party representation (62). Presumably membership of
committees must *provide / give* proper party
representation. *Answer:* provide, give.
g) Each House of Parliament has *standing orders*. By
convention some of them cannot be abolished or
substantially changed. The examples in the text show
that standing orders regulate parliamentary procedure
(63–5). *Answer:* rules which regulate procedures in the
House of Commons or House of Lords.
h) Members of a ministry should *relinquish* company
directorships which might influence their conduct as
ministers (71–2). If a directorship might influence a
minister s/he should *give it up*. *Answer:* give up.
i) If government measures are unpopular, the Opposition
will defeat [beat] the Government at the next General
Election and *supplant* them in their control of the
executive (79–81). If the Opposition defeats the
Government by winning a General Election, the
Opposition will take control of the executive by *taking
the place of* the Government. *Answer:* take the place of.

## Exercise A 7

½ point for each correct part of an answer. Maximum 10
points. For instance, in the example, *which* refers to
conventional usages (½ point; conventional usages have the
force of customary law (½ point).
a) They = the rules and principles embodied in these
conventional usages (line 10); the rules and principles
embodied in conventional usages (i.e. constitutional
conventions) should make sure the country is controlled
by 'a ministry . . . chosen by the electorate'.
b) which = the ministry and Cabinet (line 11); the ministry
and Cabinet remain responsible to the electorate.
c) which = the party or combination of parties (14); no,

the Cabinet may belong to a combination of parties, i.e. more than one.

d) it = the Opposition (20) ⎫ (1) the Opposition
e) its = the ministry's (21) ⎰ (2) the ministry i.e. the
　　　　　　　　　　　　　　　　　　　present Government
f) who = that member of the House of Commons (37); no, only the one who can gain the confidence of the House can be appointed Prime Minister.
g) he = the Prime Minister (39); the Prime Minister can recommend the dissolution of Parliament.
h) that = any bill (40); the Sovereign must assent to a bill when it has passed both Houses of Parliament (or in certain cases only the House of Commons).
i) her = the Sovereign's (45); because even if ministers act in the name of the Sovereign, this is only a formality, since she must always follow her ministers' advice.
j) those = the standing orders (64); standing orders define the procedure for legislation by private bill.

## Exercise A 8

1 point for each correct *True/False* answer. Maximum 10 points. If your answer is wrong, refer to the line references in brackets (...) to understand why.
a) *True* (lines 2–4, 8–10)
b) *False* (4–5) Today, *as in the past*, much of the practical workings of the constitution depends on conventional usages.
c) *True* (13–15)
d) *True* (18–21)
e) *False* (26–8) In some cases it is only a matter of definition whether something is a convention or a rule of law.
f) *True* (29) There may be doubt as to whether something is only a practice or a convention, but true conventions are always binding.
g) *False* (32–4) There is no *authoritative source* which explains whether a convention exists and what it is. To find this information you need to refer to different sources such as constitutional law books, history books, etc.
h) *False* (75–8) The *Cabinet* exercises control over both legislative and executive functions.
i) *True* (78–81)
j) *True* (76–7, 82–7)

## Exercise A 9

iv) 1 point for each of the following conventions. Maximum 10 points. Your answers should be similar in content to the following, but will probably be expressed in different words.

*The Sovereign*
● must appoint ministers recommended by Prime Minister to ministry and Cabinet
● must accept Prime Minister's recommendation to dissolve Parliament
● must give Royal Assent to bills approved by Parliament

*The Executive*
● ministers always politically responsible to Commons for their acts
● ministerial responsibility is personal and collective
● civil servants not responsible to Commons

● civil servants must obey departmental minister's instructions
● civil servants must be politically neutral, cooperating with government in power
● civil servants cannot be removed because ministry changes

*The Legislature*
● Speaker must be impartial in controlling debate in Commons
● Speaker does not lose office if his party loses power
● membership of committees must give fair representation to each party
● some standing orders cannot be abolished or substantially changed

## Exercise B 1

1 point for each correct answer. Maximum 10 points.
a / 4; 　　b / 1; 　　c / 3; 　　d / 2; 　　e / 1; 　　f / 4;
g / 3 [*a safe seat*]; 　　h / 2; 　　i / 4;
j / 1 [*a General Election*]

## Exercise B 2

1 point for each correct answer. Maximum 8 points.
a) judicial precedent or judicial decision
b) Equity
c) constitutional monarchy
d) Land Law or the Law of Property
e) Parliamentary sovereignty
f) the judiciary
g) law reform
h) Royal Prerogative

## Exercise B 3

1 point for each correct answer. Maximum 10 points.
a / 4　It's the only word which is not connected with the Sovereign.
b / 1　Parliament *passes*, *enacts*, and *amends* laws, and uses legislation to *abolish* things, but not to *recommend* things.
c / 4　It's the only word which is not connected with nationality.
d / 5　It's the only political party which is not active in the UK.
e / 2　It's the only one which is not a source of English law.
f / 3　It's the only one which is not connected with elections.
g / 2　Its the only one which is not a branch of English law or a separate subject for study.
h / 1　It's the only one which is not part of the Government.
i / 3　It's the only one which is not connected with the doctrine of judicial precedent.
j / 4　It's the only one which is not connected with the House of Lords.

## Exercise B 4

1 point for each correct answer. Maximum 12 points. Your answers should be similar in content to the ones below, but will not be identical. The parts in brackets (...) are extra

pieces of information, which you may give, but which are not necessary to have a point.

i)  a)  The main source of law in a civil-law country is written or enacted law (in the form of codes); the main source of law in a common-law country is unwritten or unenacted law (in the form of judicial decision).

b)  Judges must follow previous decisions in similar cases according to rules of binding precedent; (where a case is completely new they must follow general common-law principles).

c)  • a Common-law legal system is one based on the English common law and is contrasted with civil-law systems based on Roman law.
    • Common law (the rules and principles developed by the common-law courts) is contrasted with Equity (the rules and principles developed by the Court of Chancery).
    • (Originally) the common law was the law common to the whole of England, not local law or custom.

If you have different answers from those above, check that they are correct by referring to the dictionary definitions of common law given on page 29.

d)  Equity developed to give justice in particular cases where the common-law rules and remedies were too rigid. (It adds to or supplements the common law.)

ii)  a)  Ulster (Northern Ireland)    b)  Scotland

c)  The position of the Sovereign (who is the Head of State) is only symbolic because s/he does not in fact govern the country (the Government governs the country through Parliament).

d)  It is part of the UK Parliament and legislature (and is composed of unelected members. It is the upper chamber of Parliament. It also has judicial functions as a court of appeal – see Unit Six).

iii)  a)  The power, or sovereignty of Parliament has been transferred first to the House of Commons, then to the Government.

b)  Because the House of Commons is an elected body, but in Lord Hailsham's opinion the Government has gained too much influence and is not effectively controlled by the other components of the system. It therefore acts as a dictator.

c)  No, there are some exceptions (e.g. peers, people serving prison sentences).

d)  In each constituency the candidate who gains more votes than any other candidate is elected.

## Exercise C

# Unit 5

## Section One

### Exercise A 2

i)  a) EEC Treaty  b) Common Market
    c) National courts
    d) Community law (*Note:* The European Communities
       is a collective term for the European Atomic Energy
       Commission (Euratom), the European Coal and
       Steel Community (ECSC) and the EEC. They are
       legally distinct, but closely connected. 'Community
       law' refers to the law of the three Communities.)
    e) Directly applicable

ii) a) enactment    b) legislator   c) to pass a law
    d) provisions   e) under        f) parliamentary
    g) UK Government

iii) a) construe    b) application  c) counsel
     d) judgment

### Exercise B 1

i)  To help the reader to understand the text more easily by
    dividing it into shorter parts.

ii) The headings show clearly what material the text
    contains and state exactly what each section is about.
    Each section of this text will probably give details about
    a particular rule of statutory interpretation, e.g. what
    the rule is, when it is applied.

vi) The following are only a guide to some possible
    questions and answers on the text. Your own work from
    iii) may be different.

    i) The literal rule (Answers to example questions given
    in iii)
    a) The rule that the words of a statute must be
       interpreted in their ordinary, literal or grammatical
       meaning.
    b) Yes.
    c) It must be applied before any other rule of
       interpretation.
    d) Yes, if the literal interpretation of the words gives an
       absurd, inconsistent or ambiguous meaning.

    ii) The golden rule (Possible completed example
    questions from iii) and answers)
    a) *Question:* What is the golden rule?
       *Answer:* The rule that the literal meaning of words
       may be modified to give a meaning which is not
       absurd or inconsistent.
    b) *Q:* When is the golden rule applied?
       *A:* When the literal rule gives an absurd or
       inconsistent meaning.
    c) *Q:* Are there any exceptions to the golden rule?
       *A:* The text doesn't specify this, but it seems that it
       is always possible to modify the literal interpretation
       of words where this gives an absurd or inconsistent
       meaning.

    iii) Consider the whole enactment (Possible questions
    and answers)
    a) *Q:* What is the rule?
       *A:* The court may look at the whole enactment to

understand words or phrases which seem absurd if
considered on their own.
b) *Q:* Can the court always consider the whole
   enactment?
   *A:* No, only when the golden rule is applied and it is
   necessary to modify the literal meaning of the
   words.
   *Q:* Are there any exceptions to the rule?
   *A:* The text doesn't specify this.

iv) The history of the enactment (Possible questions and
answers)
a) *Q:* What is meant by the 'history' of the enactment?
   *A:* It has two meanings: (1) debates and discussions
   in Parliament when the enactment was made; (2)
   previous Acts of Parliament and the general legal,
   social and political background when the Act was
   passed.
b) *Q:* What is the rule?
   *A:* The court may use previous enactments and the
   general background to interpret an enactment, but
   not debates and discussions in Parliament when the
   enactment was made.
c) *Q:* When is the rule applied?
   *A:* The text doesn't specify this, but it seems that it
   can look at the history of the enactment when it is
   necessary to modify the literal interpretation of the
   words of a statute (applying the golden rule).

### Exercise C 1

b) (line 22) 'so as to avoid absurdity or inconsistency'
   *Main action:* modify the construction of the words of the
   enactment
   *Purpose:* to avoid absurdity or inconsistency

   (lines 42–3) 'in order to discover the true intention of the
   legislators'
   *Main action:* consider discussions and debates in
   Parliament
   *Purpose:* to discover the true intention of the legislators

   *Other ways of expressing purpose:* the infinitive with 'to',
   e.g. the courts may modify the literal meaning of words
   *to avoid* absurdity or inconsistency.

### Exercise C 2

ii) *Obligation* – MUST: the grammatical sense of the words *is
   to be adhered to* (lines 12–14); the literal rule *is to be
   applied* (14–15).
   MUST NOT: Hansard *is not to be cited* (51).
   *Grammar note:* the construction is: [subject + correct
   part of verb 'to be' + infinitive with 'to'] The examples
   are in the passive form, so we have the correct part of the
   verb 'to be' + the infinitive of the verb 'to be' + past
   participle of the main verb (adhered, applied, cited).
   This form is often used to express obligation in the
   formal style of legal English.
   *Possibility* – CAN: we *may cite* . . . (10); the grammatical
   sense of words *may be modified* (20–21); *it is permissible
   for the court to consider* the history . . . 60–62).
   CANNOT: the court *is not entitled to construe* . . . (lines
   6–7); history in this sense *may not be referred to* (47–8);
   *there is to be no recourse to* the statutes consolidated (68;
   the complete italicised phrase means *it is not possible to
   refer to* the statutes).

## Exercise C 3

a) From the construction of the phrase we understand that *'travaux préparatoires'* and 'history in this sense' refer to the same thing. The definition of 'history' is given at the beginning of the phrase (the genesis of the enactment: its progress through Parliament, debates and discussions in Parliament). *Travaux préparatoires* = the progress of the enactment through Parliament, including debates and discussions.

b) The phrase in brackets explains the meaning. Consolidating statute = a statute which brings together a series of previous enactments.

## Exercise C 4

a) the principal, main or most important rule
b) first (literally 'first appearance' – Latin)
c) so (line 4)
d) inconsistency (line 6)
e) construction (line 8). It means 'interpretation'.
f) to construe them loosely or fancifully (line 7)

## Exercise C 5

a) Yes (lines 1–4, 12–14)
b) No (6–9)
c) They can apply the golden rule (17–23)
d) Interpretation must be strict, but if it is absolutely necessary the courts can modify the grammatical and ordinary sense of the words in order to avoid an absurd, ambiguous or inconsistent meaning (23–6).
e) Yes, this method of interpretation can be used when it is necessary to modify the literal interpretation of the words (28–33).
f) No (36–48)
g) No (36–46)
h) Yes (36–45)
i) Yes (52–62) (*Note:* only when the golden rule is applied and it is necessary to modify the literal interpretation of the words)
j) Yes (52–62) (*Note:* as i) above) In the case of a consolidating statute this is only possible when the words are ambiguous (61–8).

## Exercise D 1

ii) public assembly (line 10); public place (11); public procession (21); racial hatred (24); dwelling (29); recording (36); written material (40).
v) You may notice that the definitions are very detailed.

vi) a) Yes (the town square is a public place open to the air, more than 20 people are present).
b) No (a theatre is not wholly or partly open to the air).
c) Yes (a road is a highway).
d) Yes (the public has access to the stadium for a match on payment and with permission).
e) Yes (they are a group of people in Britain defined by ethnic and national origins).
f) Yes (they are a group of people in Britain defined by nationality).
g) Yes (a tent is defined as a 'structure' and it is occupied as their home).
h) No (it is part of a structure occupied as a home, but it is not so occupied).

i) They must use the definition given in section 21(2) (of the Public Order Act 1986).
j) Yes (it is a sign or visible representation).

## Section Two

### Exercise A

Some possible ideas are given below. Your own work may be different.

i) A • UK: judges look at the literal meaning of words in a statute. They can only modify the literal interpretation (e.g. by looking at the whole enactment, at previous enactments, at the legal, social and political background) if it gives an absurd or inconsistent meaning.
*Europe:* judges look at the general intent of the legislator, at the spirit of the enactment. They can refer to *travaux préparatoires*.
• Yes, possibly. Because it is so different from their own method.

B • It seems that the Court of Appeal applied the literal rule of interpretation. 'Restrictions' are limitations. The literal meaning of 'quantitative restrictions' is limitations in quantity. A limitation means *less* of something, not *none* of it. Therefore, looking at the literal meaning of the words, the phrase 'quantitative restrictions' does not include 'total exclusion'. A UK statute (which gives very small detail) would specify both 'quantitative restrictions' and 'total exclusion' separately, if both meanings were intended.
• The purpose of the Article was to allow free trade. Limitations in quantity and total exclusion are both against free trade. Therefore, using the European style of interpretation (looking at the spirit of the enactment and the general intent of the legislator), 'quantitative restrictions' includes total exclusion.
• It illustrates the difficulty an English court may have in using the Continental style of statutory interpretation. (The House of Lords said it showed the dangers of applying English rules of construction to the EEC Treaty.)

C • In Parliament is sovereign, must it accept EC legislation which it does not agree with? If Parliament passes a later law which conflicts with EC law, which law is valid? You will find the solution which the UK Parliament has chosen at the end of this Unit (Exercise D 3).

### Exercise B 1

a) *Macarthys Ltd v Smith* (line 1)
b) Court of Justice of the European Communities; Court of Appeal, Civil Division (lines 3, 7)
c) Lord Denning MR, Lawton and Cumming-Bruce LJJ (8, also 18, 64, 65) (*Note* Lord Denning is one of the most famous English judges of the twentieth century, whose work has profoundly affected the development of some areas of English law. He is a highly respected and often controversial legal figure.
d) a woman (10–11, 20–23)
e) Equal Pay Act 1970; Sex Discrimination Act 1975;

European Communities Act 1972 (12, 13, 22, 40, 59–60, 71, 75)
f) 119 (13, 30, 31, 32, 36, 38, 39, 77, 79)
g) Yes (64, 65)
h) 17 April 1980 (9)

### Exercise B 2

a) 20–23    b) 38–42; 70–72    c) 47–9; 58–63
d) 74–9

### Exercise B 3

(1) Equal pay for men and women employed to do comparable work
(2) Who shall pay the costs of the action
The most interesting legal issue is possibly the question of what happens when EC and UK law conflict.

### Exercise B 5

a) Ltd (line 1)    b) MR (8, 18)    c) LJ (64, 65)
d) LJJ (8)    e) All ER (73)

### Exercise C 1

b) a person who makes an application (to the court)
c) [to require, -ment] something which is necessary ('there was no requirement' = it was not necessary)
d) [consistent, inconsistency, in-] not consistent (i.e. *in conflict with* Article 119)
e) [when, ever] every time that
f) [over, rides (to ride)] is more important than, takes priority over
g) [here, after] after this
h) [to cost, (the) cost] the money which the court case costs (note that this refers to the expense of litigation, not equal pay for Mrs Smith)
i) [parliament, -ary, draft, man/men] people who draft (draw up) Bills going before Parliament
j) [mis-, understand, -ing] understanding badly or wrongly

### Exercise C 2

The information from the text and reasoning which may help you to decide the meaning of each word and phrase is given in square brackets [. . .].
i) a) [Mrs Smith did not receive equal pay (lines 20–22). She *took proceedings* under the Equal Pay Act: she did this under the Act because she did not receive equal pay.) *Meaning:* she took legal action.
   b) [In the court case *she claimed* that her pay should be equal to his: this is what she said in the case, and what she wanted.] *Meaning:* she stated, demanded as her right
   c) [The statute did not apply in the case of *successive employment*, it only applied when the man and woman were employed at the same time: successive = not at the same time.] *Meaning:* when one person is employed after the other has left
   d) [The majority of the court *held* that the objection was well-founded: this was the court's decision.] *Meaning:* gave the decision (as a judgment in a court case)

e) [The applicant was right. She *was entitled to* be paid the same as a man/£60 (line 48): the court found that this was her right.] *Meaning:* had/has the right to
f) [The applicant was right. She was entitled to be paid the same as a man. The appeal that the employers brought to this court must therefore be *dismissed*: the employers lost the appeal.] *Meaning:* rejected, not accepted
g) [The argument before us today was *as to* costs: this was the subject of the argument.] *Meaning:* about, regarding
h) [It was argued at the *hearing* before the tribunals and before this court . . .: this argument was presented to the tribunals and court when they examined the case.] *Meaning:* examination of a case before a court
i) [The *party* who loses has to pay costs. The employers should pay all the costs: the employers were one of the two sides involved in the dispute.] *Meaning:* one of the persons or sides involved in a legal dispute
j) [In the case of inconsistency European law *will prevail over* municipal legislation: either European law or municipal law will have priority. Correct answer: European law will have priority (this is confirmed in other parts of the text, e.g. lines 37–42.] *Meaning:* will have priority over
k) [Solicitors: Bailey, Shaw and Gillett (for the employers); John L. Williams (for the applicant): Bailey, Shaw and Gillett and John L. Williams are names of *solicitors*. They did something *for* the employers and applicant relating to the case) *Meaning:* lawyers acting for the parties to the case
*Note:* In the UK the legal profession is divided into two branches: 'the Bar' or barristers (also called counsel when conducting a law case) and solicitors. A solicitor advises clients and may represent them in the lower courts. A barrister represents litigants in the superior courts and can normally only deal with clients through a solicitor. (This distinction may be changed by law reform in preparation at the time of writing.) In Scotland barristers are called 'advocates'. Sumra Green (line 83) is the name of the barrister who wrote the law report for *Macarthys Ltd v. Smith*, not one of the barristers who represented the parties in court.

ii) a) are entitled to    b) took proceedings
(*Note:* 'claimed against' would be used for an insurance claim, not a lawsuit)    c) hearing    d) parties
e) claimed

### Exercise C 3

a) Because she discovered that a man employed to do the same job before her was paid £10 a week more than her (lines 20–23).
b) Under the Equal Pay Act 1970 (as amended by the Sex Discrimination Act 1975) the man and the woman were only entitled to the same pay if they were employed at the same time. Therefore under English law Mrs Smith was not entitled to equal pay (23–9).
c) Because they were not sure about the interpretation of Article 119 of the EEC Treaty. They asked the European Court to decide whether Article 119 applied in the case of successive employment (36–7).

d) Article 119 applies even when the man and the woman are not employed at the same time (43–4).

e) Under national law the man and the woman were only entitled to equal pay if they were employed at the same time; under European law they were entitled to equal pay even in the case of successive employment (24–6, 43–4).

f) European law. Because under the European Communities Act 1972 EC law is part of English law and provisions of the EEC Treaty have priority over an English statute when the two are inconsistent (40–42, 70–72).

g) The issue of who should pay costs (51).

h) Because the employers thought they were entitled to look only at the English statute and in fact under the Equal Pay Act they would have won the case, and would therefore not have had to pay costs (51–7).

i) The employers had no right to look only at the English statute. EC law is part of our law; therefore, as in any other case, the party who loses (the employers) must pay costs (58–63).

### Exercise C 4

ii) . . . under Article 119 there was no requirement that the man and the woman *should be employed* contemporaneously . . . (lines 32–3)
. . . it *must be made* plain . . . (38)
. . . the man and the woman *need not be employed* at the same time . . . (43)
That interpretation *must* now *be given* . . . (45)
The appeal . . . *must* therefore *be dismissed*. (50)
. . . the court had to decide which *had to be given* priority. (61)

a) In such a case the costs have to be paid by the party who loses.

b) All the costs of the appeal to this court should be paid by the employers.

c) But the meaning of the English statute cannot be affected by such a judgment in Luxembourg.

d) The majority of this court took the view that there was no ambiguity about the words of the Equal Pay Act 1970 which had to be construed. *Note:* 'which' is the object of the active phrase. It remains unchanged as subject of the passive phrase.

### Exercise C 5

i) consistent; inappropriate; legal; unlawful; valid; unambiguous; irrelevant; satisfactory. *Negative prefixes:* un- in- ir- (before 'r') il- (before 'l')
*Note:* 'lawful' and 'legal' have the same meaning. 'Lawful' is more formal in style and is used principally in legal language as opposed to general English. It is used for the names of many specific offences, e.g. unlawful possession of drugs.

ii) a) unlawful   b) unambiguous   c) illegal
d) inconsistent   e) inapplicable

### Exercise C 6

ii) A   Under the Equal Pay Act 1970 (as amended by the Sex Discrimination Act 1975) Ms Jones is entitled to £150 a week, the same pay as Mr Adams, since they are both employed at the same time to do the same job. (Article 119 EEC gives the same result.) Employers pay costs.

B   Under the Equal Pay Act 1970 (as amended by the Sex Discrimination Act 1975) Mr Wilson is not entitled to equal pay with Ms Felps since she left her job before he was employed by Brain and Co., and the provisions of the English statute do not apply in cases of successive employment. However, under Article 119 of the EC Treaty Mr Wilson is entitled to equal pay, since that Article provides that a man and a woman are entitled to equal pay for the same work even if they are not employed at the same time (*Macarthys Ltd. v. Smith*). Under the European Communities Act 1972, when EC law conflicts with a UK statute, EC law prevails. Therefore Mr Wilson is entitled to £160 a week. Employers pay costs.

### Exercise D 2

Note that the following solutions are only suggestions.
Network (1): a / 9;  b / 1;  c / 2;  d,e,h / 3,6,10;  g / 7; j,k / 5,11; i,f /8,4.
Network (2):

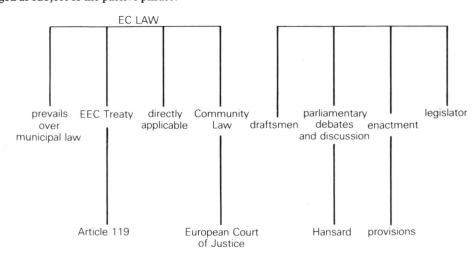

## Exercise D 3

- Because under the European Communities Act 1972, EC law is part of UK law, and that Act provides that in cases of conflict EC law has priority (40–42).
- Yes. He explains that EC law is part of UK law and is given priority by a statute enacted by the UK Parliament (the European Communities Act). Therefore the question of conflict between law enacted by the UK Parliament and law imposed on the UK Parliament by another body without the consent of Parliament is avoided.
- Yes (65, 70–72).
- They looked at the meaning of the English Act and European law separately. Cumming-Bruce LJ explains that the court did not use the EEC Treaty to help interpret the Equal Pay Act because the words of the Equal Pay Act were not ambiguous. (Therefore according to English rules of construction it was correct to apply the literal rule of interpretation and look only at the words of the statute itself) (74–7).

# Unit 6

## Section One

### Exercise A 2

i)   A / 3;     B / 5;     C / 1;     D / 2;     E / 4.

### Exercise B 1

The following headings are suggestions only.
Paragraph B: The Court of Appeal
Paragraph C: The High Court – civil jurisdiction
Paragraph D: The High Court – criminal jurisdiction
Paragraph E: The Crown Court
Paragraph F: The Central Criminal Court
Paragraph G: County courts
Paragraph H: Magistrates' courts

### Exercise B 2

(1) House of Lords
(2) Court of Appeal (Civil Division)
(3) Court of Appeal (Criminal Division)
(4) High Court (Family, Chancery and Queen's Bench Divisions)
(5) High Court (Queen's Bench Division)
(6) County courts
(7) Crown Court
(8) Magistrates' courts
Numbers 1–5 and 7 are superior courts; numbers 6 and 8 are inferior courts.

### Exercise B 4

a)   civil and criminal (here 'civil' refers to private law as opposed to criminal law)
b)   The House of Lords, magistrates' courts and the Queen's Bench Division of the High Court
c)   The House of Lords, Court of Appeal, High Court and Crown Court.
d)   The House of Lords
e)   The Queen's Bench Division

f)   Three (from the magistrates' court to the High Court, to the Court of Appeal, to the House of Lords)
g)   Four (from the magistrates' court to the Crown Court, to the High Court, to the Court of Appeal, to the House of Lords)
h)   No, some are dealt with by magistrates' courts, and appeals from there go directly to the High Court.

*Note:* The text you have read is full of specialised law terms. However, you probably found that you could complete the diagram showing the basic organisation of the courts and answer the above questions *without* understanding many words in the text.

### Exercise C 1

iii) *Example:* sitting (65) = *a division, section or branch (of a court).* This shows that a dictionary may not contain the correct definition of a word in a particular context. For this reason it is important to think about the meaning of a word *before* you refer to a dictionary, and use your own ideas and the context to help you decide what a word means – sometimes these will be more complete and accurate than a dictionary.

1   lay [definition 6 (adjective) 2] *non-professional, not expert, (with reference to the law) Note:* use the part of speech at the beginning of each definition (e.g. v – verb, n – noun, adj. – adjective) to find the meaning you want more quickly, and scan the definitions and examples for law terms. (Here: law, lawyer.)

2   hear [definition 3] *(of a judge in a law court) try (a case) Note:* as soon as you decide a particular definition is not the right one (e.g. definition 1) use the numbers to move on and look quickly for the definition you want.

4   jury [definition 1] *body of persons who swear to give a decision on issues of fact in a case in a court of justice*

5   justice [definition 4] *Justice of the Peace* (abbr. JP) *magistrate Note:* you may need to refer to the word 'magistrate' to understand this meaning of 'justice'. There are three definitions of 'justice' as a law term (2, 3 and 4) – you will need to read the definitions and study the text carefully to choose the right one.

6   magistrate [the only definition] *civil officer acting as a judge in the lowest courts; Justice of the Peace.*

7   sentence [definition 1] *(statement by a judge, etc. of) punishment*

8   *indictable [adj.] indictable offences, that may be tried by jury Note:* 'indictable' is not a separate headword in this dictionary so you need to use the root word 'indict' to find it. This is often true of adjectives and adverbs. You also need to consider the word in its complete context and read the examples in the dictionary. In this case it is the phrase 'indictable offences' in both the text and dictionary which gives the correct definition.

9   summarily *Note:* this is not a separate headword (see note to 8 above). Definition 2 contains other law terms (justice, punishment) but does it make sense in the context? Is it probable that the magistrates' court tries cases without delay and *without attention to small matters?* In fact, as with 'sitting' (65) the correct definition is not given in

this dictionary. 'Summarily' here means *without a jury*, the opposite of 'on indictment'. You may need to use a law dictionary to find this definition.
*General Note:* A dictionary can help you to understand the meaning of words if you use it carefully together with your own vocabulary skills, knowledge and intelligence. Sometimes you may need to use a law dictionary to find a definition or more complete explanation of law terms. (See page 239 for list of dictionaries.)

## Exercise C 2

i) a) *appeal* (1) a smaller specialised body (committee) which hears appeals; (2) jurisdiction over appeals
   b) *division* (1) a smaller section or branch (division) of a court which itself acts as a court
   c) *statute* (1) jurisdiction granted to the court by statute; (2) offences defined by statute (as opposed to common law)

ii) proceedings which deal with matters of Family Law, e.g. divorce, adoption

iii) a) defendant (92) *Note:* the party who defends a civil action is also called the defendant
    b) No, here it simply means 'to choose'.
    c) No, in the context of the law it means 'to examine and decide a criminal or civil case before a court'. Trial (92) – the hearing of a civil or criminal case before a court

iv) a) lines 44–50
    b) *habeas corpus* (46, an order to bring a person who is held in custody before a court to make sure that s/he is not being held illegally); *mandamus* (49, an order to perform a public duty, e.g. hold an election, hear an appeal); prohibition (49, an order to prevent an act by a court or body against the rights of an individual); *certiorari* (50, an order used to review or cancel ('quash') decisions of inferior courts, tribunals, etc.).

## Exercise C 3

If your answer is wrong, refer to the text to understand why.
a) *True* (lines 4–11)
b) *False* (not for criminal cases in Scotland (2, 16–21)
c) *True* (29–33)
d) *True* (44–50)
e) *False* (not for appeals and sentencing decisions sent from magistrates' courts (57–63)
f) *True* (64–8)
g) *False* (they only hear civil cases, their jurisdiction is *granted by* statute, 73–5)
h) *False* (lay magistrates called justices of the peace can sit in magistrates' courts, 78–81)
i) *True* (87–9)
j) *True* (84–7)
k) *False* (the defendant can choose, not the court (87–93)

## Exercise D 1

i) a / 3;    b / 8;    c / 9;    d / 1;    e / 4;    f / 5;
   g / 2;    h / 6;    i / 10;    j / 7.

ii) English judges, especially in the higher courts, have

great social and professional prestige, as their titles show (Sir/Dame/Lord). They are very well-paid, e.g. at about the same period the Prime Minister's salary was £58,650 a year, while the rest of the Cabinet except peers earned £47,020. In fact the highest-paid member of the government is the Lord Chancellor, who then earned £79,400. However, a successful barrister or company director would earn more. You may notice that there are no female titles for judges sitting in the Court of Appeal and House of Lords. The old Act of Parliament creating these offices was passed at a time when women did not hold such positions. As a result women judges in these courts are called 'Lord', not 'Lady', e.g. Lord Butler Schloss, the first woman judge ever to be appointed in the Court of Appeal.

## *Section Two*

### Exercise A 1

- Judicial precedent is the doctrine by which decisions of courts in previous cases are considered as a source of law which will influence or bind courts in later similar cases.
- Because it is one of the principal sources of English law. The common-law system is based on the application and development of legal rules through judicial precedent.
- A binding decision is one which future courts must follow when deciding similar cases.
- An authority is a judicial decision cited (e.g. in a later case) as a statement of the law. A binding authority is one which the court must follow, a persuasive authority is one which influences but does not bind the court.

### Exercise B 1

i) a) 19–22    b) 2–7    c) 22–6

ii) a) Lord Gardiner, LC (line 9)
    b) 26 July 1966 (9)
    c) as a judicial body (the statement was made 'before judgments were given' and was made on behalf of Lord Gardiner, LC and the Lords of Appeal in Ordinary, lines 8–11)
    d) *Halsbury's Laws* (37–8) (short for *Halsbury's Laws of England*)

### Exercise B 2

ADVANTAGES: to decide what the law is and how to apply it to individual cases / certainty of the law, so people know how to act / basis for orderly development of the law
DISADVANTAGES (if applied too rigidly): injustice in particular cases / restricts proper development of the law.

### Exercise B 3

a) Previous decisions of the House of Lords are normally binding, but the House may 'depart from a previous decision when it appears right to do so' (lines 22–6).
b) (1) House of Lords decisions are no longer binding on the House itself *in all cases* (22–6).
   (2) The rules of precedent in lower courts are not changed (33–5).
c) The answer is not clear from the words of the statement. In fact, the phrase 'depart from' suggests (1). However,

later practice of the House of Lords showed that (2) was intended – the new decision becomes the precedent for future cases.

d) In the Law of Contract and Property, Tax and Criminal Law – in these areas it is especially important for the law to be certain, so that people can act accordingly (27–32).

## Exercise B 4

a) *Stare decisis* (line 3) Literally, to stand by things decided. It expresses the basis of the doctrine of precedent – the principle that previous decisions are authoritative and binding.

b) The Lord Chancellor.

c) 'Their Lordships' (12, 19) [also 'the Lords of Appeal in Ordinary' (11)].

d) However. It expresses contrast (between the freedom of the House of Lords to depart from previous decisions and the fact that the doctrine of precedent is an indispensable foundation of the law (3–7); between the advantages and disadvantages of judicial precedent (19–22)).

## Exercise C 1

i) a) *dicta* (lines 11, 14, 17, 20)   b) *obiter dicta* (17)
   c) *ratio decidendi* (1, 4, 5, 10, 20)

ii) *Ratio decidendi:* the reason for the decision, the principle on which the decision is based. *Dicta:* statements made by judges which are not necessary to the decision. The *ratio decidendi* constitutes binding precedent.

iii) a) No (14–15)
   b) Judicial *dicta* – these are carefully considered judicial opinions, not just simple comments (16–20).

## Exercise C 2

i) Paragraph 579 (Divisional Court decisions) refers to High Court decisions. (A Divisional Court consists of two or three judges of the Queen's Bench, or Chancery, or Family Divisions of the High Court.)

## Exercise C 3

i) b / 1;   c / 5;   d / 4;   e / 2.

ii) The first and last; the second and third.

iii) a) are bound     b) is bound to     c) is not binding
    d) do not bind / are not binding on

iv) a) No (this is confirmed by lines 67–9 of the text).
    b) No (this is confirmed by the phrase 'it is desirable', line 70)
    c) . . . a decision of the House of Lords . . . should be regarded as applicable . . . [72–4]
       . . . interpretations should be avoided which result in one meaning in one country and one in another [84–6].
    d) *Should* and *ought to* both express the idea of obligation or duty. They are used to indicate a correct or sensible action and to give advice, but they do not express authority to impose an obligation. (Cf. must, bound to, have to – an obligation is *imposed*).

*Compare:* The Court of Appeal must follow decisions of the House of Lords (a strict obligation is imposed on the Court of Appeal; it has no choice).

Scottish courts ought to follow decisions of the House of Lords (a duty or obligation exists, but it is not imposed on Scottish courts – they are free to choose).

## Exercise C 4

i) Legal meaning: the *case* before it (line 44); which *case* to follow (45).
   'in which case' (lines 44, 46–7) means 'and when this happens' or 'in these circumstances'.

ii) a) [weak, -en, -ed] to weaken = to make weak; weakened = made weak.
    b) [over, rule, -d] to overrule = to decide a case using a different principle from that used in an earlier case (thus creating a new precedent). The previous case is 'overruled'.
    c) [mis-, applied, mis-, understood] answer (3) the prefix *mis-* = bad or badly, wrong or wrongly. Examples: misfortune, to misbehave, misinformed.
    d) [guide, lines] guidelines are rules or advice which instruct or guide in how to do something.

## Exercise C 5

Below is one possible diagram. Your own work may be different.

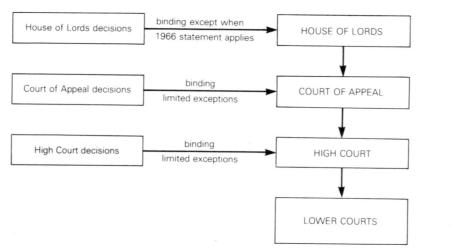

## Exercise C6

i) a) 2     b) 2     c) 1     d) 1     e) 1     f) 2

ii) d) to determine     e) to sentence     f) to patent

iii) a) patent     b) determined     c) proper
d) sentenced

## Exercise D 1

a) No, it can depart from its previous decision (lines 2–9)
[i.e. overrule it, applying the new rule from the 1966
statement].

b) No, only Parliament can correct a wrong decision on a
question of law (16–18).

c) Yes, since the Court of Appeal is inferior to the House of
Lords (21–3).

d) The House of Lords precedent (33–6).

e) Yes (31–3).

f) No (38–40).

g) If it is a civil case, yes; if it is a criminal case, no (29–40,
50–55).

h) Yes (63–6).

i) Yes (24–7).

j) No, the High Court ought to follow the Scottish
decision, but it is not bound to do so (67–9, 78–86).

k) No, the US decision may influence the English court,
but it is not bound to follow it (87–9, 100–105).

# Unit 7

## Section One

## Exercise A 2

1 / d     2 / g     3 / f     4 / e     5 / c     6 / h     7 / a
8 / i     9 / b

## Exercise A 3

a) v. = *versus*, used in the title of civil and criminal cases.
In spoken English we say 'versus', 'against' or 'and'.
Most lawyers would call this case 'Carlill and the
Carbolic Smoke Ball Co.'
Co. = Company

b) QB = the Queen's Bench Division of the High Court

c) It is probably a civil case, as most criminal cases have R.
or sometimes A.G. in the citation e.g. *R. v. Jones* (see
Unit 3, Section Two, Exercise C 2). The case involves a
private person (Carlill) acting against a company. The
case is about 100 years old. However, due to the
operation of the doctrine of precedent it is still an
important authority which is cited today in modern
contract cases and textbooks. The style and content of
the language used in the judgment have changed very
little in this period.

## Exercise B 1

i) lines 1–11     ii) lines 12–41     iii) lines 42–3
iv) lines 44–5     v) lines 46–77

## Exercise B 2

So that it is easy for practising lawyers (who often need to
refer to case-law) to see what point(s) of law the case
established.

## Exercise B 3

J. (lines 12, 42) Justice, the title of an English High Court
judge.

l. (18, 24, 43) pound sterling.

s. (33, 34) shilling: before the introduction of the decimal
system in 1971, a shilling was worth 12 pence and there were
20 shillings (240 pence) in 1 pound. Shillings do not exist
any more and there are now 100 pence in 1 pound. Today
10s. = 50 pence.

LJ (44, 46) Lord Justice, the title of a Court of Appeal
judge.

## Exercise C 1

a) a lady – Mrs Carlill (line 37 and title)

b) The proprietors and vendors of the carbolic smoke ball –
The Carbolic Smoke Ball Co. (13–15 and title)

c) Mrs Carlill, the plaintiff (42–3)

d) The Carbolic Smoke Ball Co. (43) (In the appeal they are
called the *appellants* and Mrs Carlill is the *respondent*,
although in fact Bowen, LJ continues to use the terms
*plaintiff* and *defendants*.)

## Exercise C 2

a) Disease = illness

b) A verb used when you put money in a bank. To deposit
= to put a sum of money in a bank account. Deposited
= put in a bank account.

c) Something which acts against disease, the disease was
not contracted. Preventives = things that stop a person
from catching a disease.

d) The judge decided that the plaintiff had the right to the
100l.; the defendants objected to this because they had
to pay this money. Recover = a verb, to get money from
someone as the result of a favourable judgment in a
lawsuit.

*Note:* The use of context clues guides you to understand the
general meaning of an unknown word or phrase so that you
can continue to read with understanding. If you need to
know the exact meaning with 100 per cent accuracy, you
may need to use a dictionary to check your ideas, but in fact
this kind of accuracy is generally not necessary.

## Exercise C 3

a) A medical preparation called the carbolic smoke ball
(lines 13–15).

b) To stop people from catching flu or colds (19–21, 26–8).

c) Yes, always – the disease was contracted in 'no
ascertained case' during the last epidemic (28–30).

d) No, they are described as 'the cheapest remedy in the
world' – they lasted a long time and only cost 10 shillings
(30–33).

e) To anyone who caught flu, a cold, etc. after using the
smoke ball in a specified way (18–23).

f) To show that the offer was sincere, or serious (24–25).

g) Because she had seen the advertisement and believed it
(37–9).

h) Yes, she did (37–40).

i) No, she caught flu after using the smoke ball for nearly
two months (39–41).

j) Presumably to sell more smoke balls, and so make more
money.

### Exercise C 4

Not i)   She sued to recover the £100 reward, not for damages.

Not iii)  The plaintiff won the case of first instance, it was the defendant company that appealed against that decision.

ii)      Correct answer.

### Exercise D 1

No, it was only an offer (lines (50–51).

### Exercise D 2

ii)  2 . . . the terms are very wide (they include people who used the ball *before* the advertisement was published);
3 . . . it is an offer to the world in general;
4 . . . it is not a definite offer (because there is no way of checking the experiment).

iii)  (3) c – specifying   d – explaining   e – asserting
f, g and h – specifying
(5) The offer is not definite because the terms are too vague (because no time limit is fixed) and therefore it is not possible that the company seriously intended to pay the reward (to anyone who caught flu at any time after using the smoke ball).

### Exercise D 3

i)  PART A: It is not a definite offer, because there is no time limit. / It is too vague regarding the persons involved. It is an offer to the world in general. / It is not a definite offer because there is no chance of checking the experiment. / It is not a serious promise intended to form the basis of a contract. / No contract is intended because the advertisement is too vague.

ii)  It is too vague to be a definite offer (no time limit, etc.).
It is an offer to the general public, not a particular person.
It is not a serious offer.

### Exercise D 4

i)  'It was urged that . . .' (lines 59–60)
'It is also contended that . . .' (71–2)
Other phrases: The defendants argue / submit / claim that . . .
It is argued / submitted / claimed that . . .
Note the use of the impersonal form: '*it is submitted / contended*, etc.'.

### Exercise E 1

ii)  (1) k – solicitor, a – client
(2) d – executor, m – testator
(3) q – tortfeasor, b – injured party
(4) f – vendor, o – purchaser
(5) e – trustee, g – beneficiary, e – trustee, g – beneficiary
(6) n – offeree, c – offeror
(7) p – employer, j – employee
(8) i – landlord, r – tenant

iii)  -EE indicates the object of an action. Example, an employee is someone who is employed, an offeree is someone who receives an offer.

## Section Two

### Exercise A 2

The following is only a guide. Your own description will not be exactly the same. ' . . . the protection of the smoke ball should last. He then considers whether the advertisement was intended as a serious offer, and discusses the argument that it is a contract made with all the world. Finally, he considers the question of consideration – he defines the concept and decides whether there is consideration in the present case.'
[*Note:* the judge gives his decision in the case immediately (line 46, Section One text '*I am of the same opinion*'). He then gives a reasoned analysis of the case and reasons for the decision itself, which is not explicitly repeated.)

### Exercise B 1

i)  a) *True*   b) *False*   c) *True*   d) *True*

ii)  a) *False* (they are intended to make people *use* the smoke ball, lines 5–12)
b) *False* (it only includes people who catch flu after having read the advertisement, 12–25)
c) *False* (it should be used regularly for 2 weeks, 23–4)
d) *True* (he does not accept the other possible construction, that it should last during the epidemic, 25–41)
e) *True* (42–7).

### Exercise B 2

ii)  ' . . . if you could not check or superintend his manner of using it.'
unless = if + not

iii)  a) 'It was also said that the contract was made with all the world . . . *It is not a contract made with all the world*. There is the FALLACY of the argument. *It is an offer made to all the world*.' The argument is that the contract is made with all the world. The argument is wrong. FALLACY = fault in an argument, wrong argument.
b) ' . . . and why should not *an offer be made to all the world* which is to RIPEN INTO *a contract with anybody who comes forward and performs the condition*?' The offer becomes a contract when someone performs the condition. RIPEN INTO = become, change into.
c) '*It is an offer to become liable to anyone who, before it is* RETRACTED, *performs the condition*.' The offeror only becomes liable if the offeree performs the condition *before* the offer is RETRACTED, i.e. while the offer is still valid – before the offeror has changed his mind and taken back the offer. RETRACTED = taken back.
d) 'Any act of the plaintiff from which the defendant derives a BENEFIT *or advantage*' 'But I think also that the defendants received a BENEFIT from this user . . . *because the use of the smoke balls would promote their sale*.' It is listed together with 'advantage' – it must be something similar to an advantage, something good; promoting the sale of the smoke balls was a good thing for the defendants. A BENEFIT = something which helps a person, a good thing.

e) '. . . *any labour*, DETRIMENT *or inconvenience . . . suffered* by the plaintiff . . .'.
It is listed together with 'labour' and 'inconvenience', it is 'suffered' – it must be a bad thing. A DETRIMENT = harm, damage, loss.

f) 'Can it be said that if *the persons . . . applies . . . the carbolic smoke ball to his* NOSTRILS . . . he is doing nothing at all . . .'. The person using the smoke ball (which we know is for diseases like colds and flu) applies it to his NOSTRILS. NOSTRILS must be a part of his body; it is plural. NOSTRILS = the two passages of the nose.

v) a) retracted  b) warranted  c) fallacy
d) benefit  e) fulfilled  f) detriment

## Exercise B 3

a) Yes (there is no reason in law why it should not be binding). (lines 52–5)
b) Because it would give them some advantage (promoting the use and sale of the smoke ball). (lines 53–4)
c) Because it does not apply in this case – the defendants did not make a contract with the whole world (they only made an offer to the world). (lines 56–61)
d) When any person who, on the faith of the offer and before the offer is withdrawn, performs the conditions specified in the offer. (lines 61–4)
e) With those people who accept the offer (by performing the condition specified in the offer). (lines 63–4)
f) No (it is possible to accept an offer by the act of performing a specified condition). (lines 62–4)
g) It is too late – no contract is created. (lines 61–2)
h) A benefit to the offeror (in this case the defendant) or a detriment to the offeree (the plaintiff). (lines 68–71)
i) There was a benefit to the defendants – the sale of the smoke ball was promoted, and a detriment to the plaintiff, who suffered the inconvenience of using the ball. (lines 79–83)

## Exercise B 4

Yes – Lindley, Bowen and Smith LJJ all agreed to dismiss the appeal.

## Exercise B 5

| Summary of PART A | PART B |
|---|---|
| 1 Only an offer, not a contract | True, it is only an offer, which becomes a contract on acceptance. |
| 2 Not definite, no time limit | The smoke ball gives protection while in use. |
| 3 Vague regarding persons involved | It applies to persons who used the smoke ball after the advertisement was published. |
| 4 Vague – offer to world in general | It is possible to make an offer to the world in general, which becomes a contract with individuals who accept the offer by performing the conditions specified. |
| 5 Not definite – no way of checking the experiment | The promise may be extravagant for this reason, but this is no reason in law why it should not be binding. |
| 6 Not a serious promise | The fact that 1000ℓ was deposited at the bank shows that it was a serious offer. |
| 7 No contract intended because advertisement too vague | Bowen LJ construes the advertisement as ordinary people would read it and according to what is reasonable. He uses the words of the advertisement to decide what the defendants intended, so that the terms of the offer become clear. |

## Exercise B 6

i) Points 1, 2, 3 and 6 from Exercise B 5 above apply only to the particular facts of *Carlill*. Points 4, 5 and 7 contain general legal principles.
The *rationes decidendi* are contained in point 4:
● It is possible to make an offer to the world in general which becomes a contract with individuals who accept the offer.
● It is possible to accept an offer by the act of performing the conditions specified in it if the offer is in the form of a promise in return for an act.

ii) The second and third points (Section One text, lines 7–11) correspond to the *rationes decidendi* above.

iii) '. . . if a person chooses to make extravagant promises . . . the extravagance of the promises is no reason in law why he should not be bound by them.' (lines 52–5)
'. . . the law does not require us to measure the adequacy of the consideration . . .' (77)
'Inconvenience sustained by one party at the request of the other is enough to create a consideration.' (78–9)

iv) The Court of Appeal, High Court and all courts of first instance are bound by the decision. The principles could be overruled only by the House of Lords or changed by Act of Parliament.

v) He refers to case-law (*Laythoarp v. Bryant*, line 67) and a work of authority cited in that case (Selwyn's *Nisi Prius*, 66). He also applies general common-law principles without referring to their original source (e.g. 'Inconvenience sustained by one party at the request of the other is enough to create a consideration', lines 78–9).

*Note:* The judgment is a typical example of judicial reasoning. The judge reaches his decision by a process of logical reasoning based on a detailed examination of the facts of the case approached from the point of view of the ordinary person and of what is reasonable, applying the principles of the common law.

## Exercise C 1

| | | | | | | |
|---|---|---|---|---|---|---|
| 1 / p | 2 / b | 3 / m | 4 / g | 5 / u | 6 / n | 7 / q |
| 8 / e | 9 / v | 10 / c | 11 / f | 12 / h | 13 /l | |
| 14 / r | 15 / a | 16 / s | 17 /k | 18 /i | 19 / v | |
| 20 / o | 21 / t | 22 / j | 23 / d | | | |

## Exercise C 2

*Note:* only information from the text is used in the following arguments and decisions.

*CASE A*

FOR THE PLAINTIFF: The advertisement was a definite offer. It was an offer to the public in general which the plaintiff accepted by fulfilling the conditions specified (*Carlill v. Carbolic Smoke Ball Co.*) – finding and returning the defendant's cat. In consideration for the promise of £100 the plaintiff suffered the inconvenience of finding and returning Miaow. The offer was not revoked and remained valid for a reasonable period of time.

FOR THE DEFENDANT: The advertisement was not a contract. It was an offer to the world in general, not to a particular person. It was not a definite offer, it was vague regarding the time limit. There was no consideration for the promise to pay £100. In any case, Y did not accept the offer.

JUDGMENT: for the plaintiff (adopting the arguments for the plaintiff, above). It was held that the plaintiff was entitled to recover the £100 reward on the grounds that by her act of finding and returning the defendant's cat she had performed the conditions specified in the offer, thus accepting the offer and creating a legally binding contract with the defendant.

*CASE B*

FOR THE PLANTIFF: The defendant company intended the advertisement to be read as a serious offer, which would encourage people to use the new product, so promoting their sales. People reading the offer would understand that it was serious because the product was expensive and the advertisement specified that users must follow the instructions on the packet carefully. The plaintiff bought the product on the basis of the advertisement. By his act of buying and using the product as instructed he fulfilled the conditions specified in the offer, thus creating a contract with the defendant company (*Carlill v. Carbolic Smoke Ball Co.*). There was double consideration since there was a benefit to the offeror in the promotion of their sales and a detriment to the offeree in the inconvenience of using the product.

FOR THE DEFENDANTS: The advertisement was only an extravagant promise, it was not a serious offer intended to form the basis of a legally binding contract and members of the public who read it would not construe it that way. The case must be distinguished from *Carlill v. Carbolic Smoke Ball Co.* since in *Carlill* the defendant company stated that they had deposited money with the bank for the purpose of paying the reward and it was this fact which showed the sincerity of their intention to contract. It was vague – there was no way of checking the experiment. It was an offer to the world in general, not to a particular person. There was no consideration for the promise.

JUDGMENT: for the defendants. It was held that the plaintiff was not entitled to recover the cost of the product on the grounds that the advertisement was not a serious offer intended to form the basis of a legally binding agreement. The case must be distinguished from *Carlill* on the grounds submitted by counsel for the defendants. Normally advertisements of this kind are not intended to create legal relations and there is nothing in the facts of the present case to show that the offer was so intended.

# Unit 8

## Exercise A 1

1 point for each correct answer. Maximum 8 points. The information in brackets (. . .) is extra and is not necessary to have a point.

a) (Ordinary) Shares.
b) Rolls Royce plc.
c) 170p (p = pence).
d) No (at two different times).
e) The Secretary of State for Trade and Industry.
f) 3 May 1987
g) Purchasers must pay the second part of the price of the shares.
h) Line 27 to end of this document, and in the Prospectus (referred to in lines 19–20).

## Exercise A 2

1 point for each correct ½ of an answer e.g. a) lines 14 (1 point) – 21 (1 point). Maximum 10 points.
a) lines 14–21    b) 25–6    c) 41–5    d) 46–56
e) 67–73

## Exercise A 3

ii) 1 point for each correct answer. Maximum 6 points.
   b) verb, definition 1: *cancel, withdraw* (in the text *cancelled, withdrawn*)
   c) noun, respect 1, definition 3: *reference, relation* (in the text *in respect of* = *in relation to*, not *as regards* from definition 4)
   d) verb, definition 3: *cause to be* (line 68 in the text: *cause* the previous payment *to be* liable)
   e) adjective, definition 2: *be subject to*
   f) noun: *-ure n*[U] *-ing* refer to the definition of the verb *forfeit* for the meaning: (*have to*) *suffer the loss of something as a punishment or consequence, or because of rules* [in the text *liable to forfeiture* = liable to be lost as a consequence (of the terms of the contract]
   g) adjective, due 1, definition 2: *proper, at the right and proper time*

## Exercise A 4

1 point for each correct answer. Maximum 6 points.
a) '. . . *both this document and the Prospectus, which together* GOVERN *your rights and obligations* . . .'. The contractual rights and obligations are specified, laid down in this document and the Prospectus. GOVERN = regulate, lay down, determine.
b) '*Offer for Sale by Samuel Montagu and Co. Limited* ON BEHALF OF *the Secretary of State for Trade and Industry* . . . *of Ordinary Shares* . . . *at 170p per share of which 85p is payable on application* . . .' Samuel Montagu is the vendor, selling shares in Rolls Royce to people who make an application on the basis of the advertisement (not to the Secretary of State). ON BEHALF OF = for, as the representative of.
c) '. . . *you* . . . *offer to purchase* . . . *the number of shares specified on your application form* . . . and agree that *you will accept such shares as may be* ALLOCATED *to you* . . .' ALLOCATED = set apart, given (to you) as your share (of the total number of shares).
d) '. . . the Secretary of State [agrees] that he will not . . . *offer any of the Shares to any person other than by means of* one of the PROCEDURES *referred to in the Prospectus* . . . . *By means of* refers to a method, a way of doing something. The Prospectus contains detailed

information about the offer. PROCEDURES = methods, ways (of offering the shares).

e) '. . . if you are requested to do so . . . *you will DISCLOSE in writing to the person making [the request] the names . . .*'. DISCLOSE = tell, make known.

f) '. . . *to pay . . . the second INSTALMENT of 85p per share . . .*'.
'. . . *each sale of shares* is conditional on *the due prior payment of the second INSTALMENT . . .*'.
INSTALMENT = one of the parts of a payment which is divided into more than one part.

## Exercise A 5

2 points for each correct answer. Maximum 16 points.

a) The Secretary of State (for Trade and Industry) [lines 42, 46].
b) No (he has agreed to accept the number of shares which are allocated to him) [lines 43–4].
c) Yes [17–19, 44–5].
d) No [46–50].
e) The Secretary of State agrees not to offer any of the shares to any person except by following one of the procedures specified in the Prospectus, before 11 May 1987 [46–50].
f) Yes, it constitutes a detriment to the offeree (the Secretary of State).
g) Yes – he has broken one of the terms of the collateral contract [51–6].
h) The Secretary of State may keep Joe's previous payment as a forfeit, and consider the contract at an end. He is entitled to recover full compensation for all loss and damage suffered as a result of the breach [64–73].

## Exercise A 6

½ point for each correct answer in i), ½ point for each correct answer in ii). Maximum 6 points.

i) Your answers should be similar in meaning to the following, but will not be identical.
(1) [JUR(Y) + -OR] Suffix -OR often refers to a person who performs an action – the agent. Answer: person who acts as a member of the jury.
(2) [IN- + CAPABLE] Prefix IN- often indicates the negative form of an adjective. Answer: not capable.
(3) [UN- + CONDITION + -AL + -LY] UN- = negative prefix; -AL = typical adjectival form; -LY = typical adverb ending. Answer: (adverb) without any condition(s) being attached.
(4) [MIS- + TRIAL] Prefix MIS- often means wrong, bad. Answer: a bad or false trial (i.e. one which is not valid because of a fundamental defect).
(5) [REQUIRE + -MENT] -MENT is a typical noun ending. Answer: something which is required, needed.
(6) [PROMIS(E) + -EE] Suffix -EE often refers to the person who is the object of an action e.g. offeree. Answer: person who receives a promise.

ii) a) unconditionally    b) jurors    c) mistrial
d) promisee    e) requirement    f) incapable

## Exercise B 1

1 point for each correct answer. Maximum 10 points.
a / 11 (are not always entitled to)    b / 1    c / 8
d / 6    e / 3    f / 4    g / 7    h / 9    i / 2
j / 10

## Exercise C 1

1 point for each correct answer. Maximum 6 points.
a) lay peers
b) cases of first instance
c) court of civil jurisdiction / civil court
d) the EEC Treaty
e) construe
f) rules of (binding) precedent

## Exercise C 2

1 point for each correct answer. Maximum 10 points.
a / 4    b / 6 (cited)    c / 2 (ruled)    d / 11 (to issue)
e / 3    f / 7    g / 5    h / 9 (sittings)    i / 10
j / 1 (to recover)

## Exercise C 3

1 point for each correct answer. Maximum 10 points.
a / 1    b / 3    c / 4    d / 1 (the *ratio decidendi*)    e / 3
f / 2    g / 4    h / 3    i / 1    j / 4

## Exercise C 4

1 point for each correct answer. Maximum 12 points. Your answers should be similar in content to the following, but will not be identical. The information in brackets (. . .) is extra, and is not necessary to have a point.

i) a) The literal rule of interpretation: courts must construe the words of a statute in their literal, ordinary and grammatical meaning.
b) (1)
c) It should refer the question to the European Court of Justice.
d) An English statute (the European Communities Act 1972) provides that EC law is part of UK law and prevails in cases of conflict.

ii) a) Civil and criminal.
b) • They may be members of a jury, *or*
• they may be justices of the peace (lay magistrates in a magistrates' court).
c) It is the final court of appeal.
d) It is the doctrine by which courts are bound by decisions of earlier courts in similar cases (each court in the hierarchy is generally bound by its own past decisions, and is always bound by decisions of courts superior to it).

iii) a) No (there is no time limit to the binding authority of a precedent; a case continues to bind future courts until it is overruled or becomes inconsistent with the decision of a higher court – or in the case of the House of Lords by the House itself – or until it is changed by statute).
b) No (in the case of a promise in return for an act, the offeree can accept by performing the conditions specified in the offer, as in *Carlill*).
c) No (the court will construe the offer in detail to decide whether the advertiser seriously intended to make a legally binding promise – would an ordinary person understand the offer as serious or not?).
d) No (a contract can also be made in a special written form called *under seal*).

## Exercise D 1

i) b, e, a, g, d, c, f.

ii)  d, b, g, a, h, c, i, f, j, e.
*Answer:* The plaintiff won the case.

## Exercise D 2

b) UNANIMOUS    c) RATIO DECIDENDI
d) IT WAS HELD    e) SENTENCE
f) DAMAGES    g) INJURED PARTY
h) CONSTRUE    i) TRIAL    j) ISSUE
k) OFFEROR    l) NATIONAL COURTS
The first letters of every word spell *JURISDICTION.*

# Unit 9

## Section One

### Exercise A 1

a / 8    b /1    c / 3    d/ 3, 9    e / 4    f / 6, 6
g / 2    h / 7

### Exercise A 2

iii) Convention

### Exercise B 1

iii) b)  25 April 1978 (line 2)
c)  An application to the European Commission of Human Rights which the Commission then referred to the court (lines 25–6).
d)  A UK citizen, Mr Anthony M. Tyrer, against the UK (28–32).
e)  Punishment which the applicant had received (34–73)
f)  Paragraph 9: the facts – Tyrer's crime, conviction and appeal.
Paragraph 10: Tyrer's punishment.
Paragraph 11: the law governing Tyrer's sentencing and punishment.

### Exercise C 1

ii)  Question (3): What was the sentence? (lines 46–8)
(4): Did Tyrer appeal against conviction or sentence? (50)
(5): Why did he lose the appeal? (52–6)
(6): In what circumstances was the punishment given? (56–70)
(7): Was Tyrer injured by his punishment? (72–4)

The following notes are a guide only.

iii) [Question 2] Committed unlawful assault occasioning actual bodily harm to pupil at his school because punished after victim reported him to teachers. Pleaded guilty.
iv) [Question 3] Sentenced to three strokes of the birch.
[4] Appealed against sentence (to Isle of Man High Court of Justice).
[5] Lost appeal because crime very serious and court saw no reason to change sentence.
[6] Punishment given (after medical examination and long wait) by three policemen in presence of doctor and father.
[7] Punishment hurt, but did not injure applicant.

### Exercise C 3

a)  (1) later in this document, statement
(2) according to which
b)  PRISON – to be imprisoned = to be put in prison
c)  Any act which causes harm to a person or (in their presence) to their property, or which causes fear of harm through assault, riot or some other disturbance is a 'breach of the Queen's peace'. Language or behaviour which offends or threatens other people or which is or seems violent may cause (or may itself be) a breach of the peace.
d)  No – a fixed period of time
e)  (1) – the law normally fixes the *maximum* punishment for a crime.
f)  (1) a child    (2) a young person
(3) a young person (he was 15)
(4) in the order mentioned

### Exercise C 4

a)  The Petty Sessions and Summary Jurisdiction Act 1927.
b)  A fine, imprisonment, whipping.
c)  Yes, the court can sentence an offender to a fine and whipping or to imprisonment and whipping.
d)  No, 'language or behaviour tending to a breach of the peace' can also be punished by whipping.
e)  No, only a male child or young person, i.e. a boy aged 10–16.
f)  Yes, it is regulated in detail by the Summary Jurisdiction Act 1960 (see lines 97–118).

### Exercise C 5

Your answers should be similar in content to the following, but will not always be identical.
(2) European Commission of Human Rights
(3) the UK    (4) 1978    (5) 15    (6) the Isle of Man
(7) unlawful assault occasioning actual bodily harm
(8) juvenile court    (9) a pupil    (10) school
(11) three other boys    (12) assault    (13) victim
(14) reported them for taking beer to school
(15) Petty Sessions and Summary Jurisdiction
(16) three strokes of the birch    (17) sentence
(18) High Court of Justice of the Isle of Man
(19) dismissed    (20) very serious
(21) there was no reason to interfere with the sentence
(22) Summary Jurisdiction    (23) medical
(24) punishment    (25) three policemen
(26) his father and a doctor    (27) control
(28) policemen

### Exercise D 1

ii)  C, H, E/A (in Criminal Law a *charge* is an accusation), D, G (at the trial), F, B.
iii) 1 – after being charged with an offence and especially during the trial.
2 – at any time after conviction.
3 – before being arrested and charged.
4 – after conviction and especially during the period of punishment.
5 – (as a general term) at any time after committing a crime; (as a law term) after conviction.
6 – after being charged and during the trial.

v) (1) arrest/charge   (2) criminals   (3) arrested
(4) charged   (5) accused / defendants
(6) convicted   (7) sentenced

## Section Two

### Exercise B 1

Section 1 – B
Section 2 – C
Section 3 – A

### Exercise C 1

iii) *Question 1:* Is the Isle of Man part of the UK? (lines 2–3)
ANSWER: No, it is a dependency of the Crown and has its own state organs and legal system.
*Question 2:* What is the role of the Crown with regard to the Isle of Man? (3–7, 15–19)
ANSWER: The Crown (acting through the Privy Council and in particular the Home Secretary) is responsible for the good government of the island, and the Queen in Council ratifies legislation passed by the Isle of Man Parliament.
*Question 3:* Do international treaties which apply to the UK also apply to the Isle of Man? (8–11)
ANSWER: Yes, but since 1950 only if the Isle of Man is expressly included.
*Question 4:* Does the European Convention on Human Rights apply to the Isle of Man? (11–14)
ANSWER: Yes.
*Question 5:* Can the UK Parliament pass domestic legislation for the Isle of Man without its consent? (20–24)
ANSWER: Not normally, because of a constitutional convention to this effect.

### Exercise C 2

i) a) A *juvenile court* is a special court for young people. *Juveniles* are young people.
b) [FIND -INGS] Related to the verb *to find*. *Answer: findings* are things which are discovered or learnt as the result of an (official) enquiry.
c) [RE- INTRODUCED] The prefix RE- often means *again* (e.g. restatement, rewrite). Reintroduced = introduced again, brought back.
d) [SAFE GUARD] A safeguard is something which protects or guards against a risk, danger, etc.
e) [RE-AFFIRM] (See c above) to reaffirm = to affirm, declare again.
f) [MAN] Adjective. Manx = of the Isle of Man.

ii) 1) a / 2   b / 1   c / 1 (*Note:* retention is the noun related to the verb *retain* from b) above)   d / 2
2) a) *Thereafter* is in direct contrast to *Prior to* (line 8). *Answer:* after that, from that time on.
b) Tynwald legislation requires *ratification* by the Queen in Council: the Royal Assent is necessary before it becomes valid law. *Answer:* official confirmation or approval.
c) The *resolution* was a statement of policy which was voted on and passed by the Manx Parliament. *Answer:* a formal statement of

opinion agreed on by an organised body, usually by vote.
d) 31 000 people signed the *petition*, which was in favour of retaining judicial corporal punishment. *Answer:* a written request or demand (to a government or other body) signed by many people.
e) In law, judicial corporal punishment could be given for many offences, but in practice it was *restricted* to offences of violence. *Answer:* limited.

iii) a) The following words have different meanings.
*charged* (verb) – the Home Secretary is *given as a duty or responsibility* (prime responsibility for Isle of Man affairs), he is not *accused of a criminal offence*.
e) *address* (noun) – the Attorney-General made *a formal speech* to the Court, he did not give *details of where he lives*.

iv) a) The European *Convention* on Human Rights, the *hearing* before the European Court of Human Rights, the European *Court* of Human Rights
b) Policy relating to punishment for crimes. *Note:* the adjective *penal* generally refers to punishment, not to crime itself. For example, *the penal system* is the system of punishments relating to different crimes. Cf. *Criminal Law* – the law relating to crime itself.
c) A state of peace in a society where the law is respected.
d) Among other things.

### Exercise C 3

i) a) as extending, in the absence of contrary provision, to the Isle of Man
b) such treaties = international treaties applicable to the UK
c) such territories = territories for whose international relations [the UK Government] were responsible

ii) a) is not   b) is

### Exercise C 5

If your answer is wrong, refer again to the parts of the text indicated to understand why.
i – c (lines 2–7, 20–24)
ii – d (8–11)
iii – a (15–19, legislation is passed by Tynwald, then ratified by the Queen in Council)
iv – c (25–6, 32)
v – b (32–40)
vi – a (41–44)
vii – d (48–52, Tyrer was whipped for unlawful assault)
viii – b (55–61)

### Exercise C 7

ii) (1) – bad:
● *does not give all main points:* important to state that judicial corporal punishment was abolished for both juveniles and adults.
● *Not exact enough:* specify which countries abolished judicial corporal punishment in which year.
● *Not concise:* cut out '*was* abolished in *the* UK.'
*Correct version of (1):* Judicial corporal punishment of

juveniles and adults abolished: England, Wales, Scotland – 1948, Northern Ireland – 1968.

(2) and (3) – good: give main facts using different words, are brief and concise.

(4) – bad:

- *not concise*
- *not in own words:* long sentence copied word for word from original text.

*Corrected version of (4):* concluded: judicial corporal punishment should not be brought back for any types of offences / offenders.

### Exercise D 1

A / IV     B / III     C / 1     D / 11

### Exercise D 2

b)   A / IV – deterrence     B / III – deterrence
     C / I – protection     D / II – punishment

## Section Three

### Exercise 1

1 Murder charges     2 Escape charge     3 Home to prison
4 Heysel case     5 Policeman convicted . . .

### Exercise 2

a / 4     b / 1, 2     c / 5     d / 3

### Exercise 3

a)   Magistrates' courts (articles, 1, 2); the High Court
     (article 3); the Crown Court (article 5).
b)   Murder, armed robbery, disposing of property to
     impede arrest (article 1).

Escaping police custody, conspiring to commit armed robbery (article 2).

(Assault) occasioning actual bodily harm (article 5).

*Note:* Articles 3 and 4 both refer to the same case – the Heysel football riots in Belgium in which 39 football fans were killed by British supporters. In Britain the Public Order Act 1986 (see Unit 5) was passed largely to deal with the problem of football violence.

### Exercise 6

*Jack:* armed robbery, assault occasioning actual or grievous bodily harm, murder, arson.
*Annette:* a parking offence, drunken driving, bribery and corruption, theft.

# Unit 10

## Section One

### Exercise B 2

The following headings are examples only.
Paragraph 20: The Commission's decision on which Articles of the Convention to examine
Paragraph 21: Tyrer's request to withdraw his application
Paragraph 22: The Commission's opinion on Articles 3, 14 and 63

### Exercise C 2

i)   a / 2     b / 1     c / 1     d / 2     e / 1     f / 2

iii) a) inconsistent     b) retained     c) affected
     d) discrimination     e) deprived

### Exercise C 3

All the information in the chart below comes from the text on pages 160–61.

| Article | Issue | Cited by Tyrer | Commission's decision |
|---|---|---|---|
| 3 | degrading punishment | YES | admissible – in breach of Art. 3 |
| 8 | family well-being | YES | inadmissible |
| 13 | existence of remedies to rectify violations | YES | inadmissible |
| 14 | discrimination (e.g. for social status, age, sex) | YES | not to proceed separately, to consider with Art.3; not necessary to examine issue |
| 1 | | YES | inadmissible. |
| 63 | social or cultural differences | NO | no significant differences between Isle of Man and UK |

*Extra information:* Article 1 provides that the parties to the Convention 'shall secure to everyone within their jurisdiction the rights and freedoms' defined in the Convention. Article 63 provides that the Convention may be extended to apply to territories for whose international relations a member state is responsible, 'with due regard to local requirements' (e.g. social or cultural differences).

## Section Two

### Exercise B 1

i) 'No one must be . . .'

ii) a) 'It is quite possible/likely that . . .'
  b) 'The Court must necessarily be . . ./The Court cannot help being . . .'

### Exercise B 2

i) and ii)

|   (1)   -T, -TE → -TION   |   |   (3)   -Y → -ICATION   |   |   (6)   + -MENT   |   |
|---|---|---|---|---|---|
| convict | conviction | apply | application | argue | argument |
| derogate | derogation | classify | classification | assess | assessment |
| prohibit | prohibition | **(4)   -IDE → -ISION** | | judge | judgment |
| subject | subjection | | | imprison | imprisonment |
| inflict | infliction | decide | decision | treat | treatment |
| violate | violation | provide | provision | punish | punishment |
| indicate | indication | | | develop | development |
| humiliate | humiliation | **(5)   NO CHANGE** | | **(7)   CONSONANT CHANGE** | |
| execute | execution | demand | demand | break | breach |
| legislate | legislation | control | control | believe | belief |
| **(2)   + -ATION** | | influence | influence | **(8)   OTHER** | |
| interpret | interpretation | review | review | | |
| allege | allegation | | | retain | retention |
| degrade | degradation | | | | |

*Note:* When a suffix is added, a final -e is generally lost e.g. argue, argument.

iii a) 4 arguments  b) 1, 6 meaning, judgment
  c) 5, 9 assess, suffered
  d) 11 deter  e) 2, 7 convicted, imprisonment
  f) 10 provides
  g) 12 interpreted  h) 3 derogate

### Exercise B 3

i)  b / 4  c / 1  d / 1  e / 5  f / 2  g / 3

ii) 'consequently' and 'accordingly'; 'nevertheless' and 'however'; 'in fact' and 'indeed'
  a) nevertheless  b) indeed

### Exercise B 4

i) The following phrases simply introduce statements of opinion or fact:
  lines 17–18 'The Court shares the Commission's view that . . .'

19–20 'The Court does not consider that . . .'
38–9 '. ... the Court does not consider on the facts of the case that . . .'
40–41 '. . . it therefore concurs with the Commission that . . .'
46  'The Court notes first of all that . . .'
56–7 '. . . as the Court pointed out in its judgment . . .'
90–91 '. . . the Court does not regard it as established that . . .'

The following phrases show personal conviction:
lines 99  '. . . it must be pointed out that . . .'
102–3 'Above all, as the Court must emphasise . . .' (strong conviction)
107  'The Court must also recall that . . .'

ii) The judgment begins with a series of plain statements of fact and opinion, but as it continues the choice of expressions shows that the Court holds a strong view about the matters discussed.

### Exercise B 6

FURTHERMORE: the phrase before 'Furthermore' gives an argument against judicial corporal punishment. The phrase introduced by 'Furthermore' gives another argument against it. *Furthermore = in addition, moreover.* It is used to give additional information and may reinforce a statement or argument.

ADMITTEDLY: The sections before and after the sentence beginning 'Admittedly' state negative aspects and effects of the punishment. 'Admittedly' introduces a positive aspect of the relevant legislation, in contrast with the general tone of the text. *Admittedly = it must be admitted.* It is used to introduce a statement or fact that contrasts with the speaker's general opinion, or with the general tone of an argument.

### Exercise B 8

1 / b  2 / e  3 / a  4 / c  5 / d

**Exercise B 9**

If your answer is wrong, refer to the parts of the text indicated to understand why.

a) *True* (paragraph 29, lines 34–43)
b) *True* (paragraph 30, lines 46–55)
c) *True* (paragraph 30, lines 48–52)
d) *False* – there are no exceptions (paragraph 30, lines 56–62)
e) *False* – it is generally humiliating, but in order to be 'degrading' within the meaning of Article 3 there must be more than the usual element or degree of humiliation (paragraph 30, lines 46–55, 62–77)
f) *True* (paragraph 30, lines 77–82)
g) *Don't know* – the Court thinks it is quite likely; however, it is not certain from the evidence (paragraph 31, lines 83–97)
h) *True* (paragraph 31, lines 97–106)
i) *True* (paragraph 31, lines 107–14)
j) *False* – if the victim feels humiliated, a punishment may still be degrading even if there is no publicity (paragraph 32, lines 1–14)
k) *True* (paragraph 33, lines 32–53)
l) *True* (paragraph 33, lines 39–46)
m) *True* (paragraph 33, lines 39–66)
n) *True* (paragraph 35, lines 78–93)

**Exercise C 1**

i / c    ii / a    iii / b    iv / a    v / d

**Exercise D 2**

ii)  Rulings 2 and 4

**Exercise D 3**

| | Court's decision |
|---|---|
| Article 3 | in breach of Art. 3 |
| Article 8 | not considered |
| Article 13 | not considered |
| Article 14 | not necessary to examine Art. 14 |
| Article 1 | not considered |
| Article 63 | no local requirements which could affect application of Art. 3 |

**Exercise C 2**

The following table is an example only.

| Article 3 | Applicant's allegations | Commission's findings | Court's decision |
|---|---|---|---|
| Torture | Yes | No | No – not the required level of suffering |
| Inhuman treatment | Yes | No | No – not relevant |
| Inhuman punishment | Yes | No | No – not the required level of suffering |
| Degrading treatment | Yes | No | No – not relevant |
| Degrading punishment | Yes | Yes | Yes – in all the circumstances the level of humiliation was such that Tyrer was subjected to 'degrading punishment' |

**Exercise D 1**

| APPLICATION OF A NORM | VIOLATION OF A NORM |
|---|---|
| . . . in accordance with Article . . . | . . . in breach of Article . . . |
| . . . within the meaning of Article . . . | . . . was inconsistent with Article . . . |
| . . . raised issues under Article . . . | . . . constituted a violation of Article 3 . . . |
| . . . there can be no derogation from Article 3 . . . | . . . in violation of Article 3 . . . |
| . . . under Article 14 . . . | . . . in breach of the Convention . . . |
| . . . the application of Article 3 . . . | . . . the violation of Article 3 . . . |
| | . . . constituted a breach of Article 3 . . . |
| | . . . contrary to Article . . . |

# The Tyrer crossword puzzle: solution

Across and down entries (crossword grid):

- 3. UNLAWFUL ASSAULT
- 7. CITE
- 8. CASE
- 9. ARGUE
- 11. RATIFY
- 12. VIEW
- 14. HELD
- 16. GUILTY
- 17. BREACH
- 18. ISSUE
- 19. TYRER
- 22. DETERRENT
- 24. ON THE GROUNDS

Down:
- 1. MA...
- 2. H
- 5. T R E S...
- 6. J
- 10. APPLY
- 13. RS
- 15. A
- 20. PARRY
- 21. OFFENDER
- 23. FINE

# Unit 11

## Section One

### Exercise B 1

ii)  A/5;  B/3;  C/4;  D/2;  E/7;  F/6;  G/1.

### Exercise C 1

i)  a)  Two agents working for the DGSE (Direction Générale de la Sécurité Extérieure – the French Secret Service)

b)  offences concerning passports and other related offences

c)  a member of the crew

d)  the Minister for Defence of France

e)  the Secretary-General of the United Nations

f)  exports from New Zealand

ii)  a)  A period of imprisonment of 7 years.

b)  Because in the context of crime and sentencing we understand that a number of years refers to years of imprisonment, so this is not always specified. In this text it is especially clear because 10 years' *imprisonment* has already been specified (lines 13–14).

iii)  (1) . . . false names  (2) . . . drowned in the incident

iv)  a)  The secret service activity which the European Parliament condemned was directed against the *Rainbow Warrior*.

b)  Ruud Lubbers' proposal was that the parties should refer the case to independent arbitration.

### Exercise C 3

i)  There are 12 mistakes. The line references show the parts of the text on page 178 which contain the relevant information. Refer to the text to check any of your answers which are wrong.

*Section A*

July 1985 – they were charged with *murder*, not manslaughter (line 5)

August '85 – the French Government *refused* to extradite the agents (line 10)

November '85 – they were *not* tried for arson and they were tried for *manslaughter*, not murder (lines 11–13); they pleaded *guilty* (13); they were sentenced to *10 years'* for manslaughter and 7 *years'* for wilful damage, *not* to life imprisonment (13–14).

*Section B*

September '85 – New Zealand would take proceedings against *the French State*, not their agents (lines 23–4).

Early '86 – New Zealand complaint accepted by European Community *Trade Commissioner*, not Commission (31–2); France *admitted* sanctions (in April '86) (line 32).

*Section C*

*September '85* – UK Government *did not take action*, they 'took little part in the dispute' and only 'called on France' to settle compensation (36–7).

June–July '86 – New Zealand did *not* have to apologise, they only had to transfer the agents (44–5).

*Section D*

December '85 – France *did not pay damages* in December '85; they could not agree on the amount of damages and referred the question to arbitration in July '86 (49–52).

### Exercise D 1

iii)  a)  (1)  violation of New Zealand sovereignty (attack involving low-level use of force) (described in first paragraph)

(2)  spying (second paragraph)

b)  the first: violation of New Zealand sovereignty

iv)  a)  international delinquency: it fell 'short of belligerency', i.e. was not serious enough to be classed as belligerency (line 5)

b)  Only (2). (1) and (3) are both acts of war (belligerency).

c)  infringement

d)  *surveillance* means simply watching or observing, *spying* means watching or observing *secretly*.

e)  espionage (lines 12, 14, 16)

f)  The answer is not clear. According to Falk (line 14) it is illegal but tolerated; according to Stone (lines 15–16) it is not illegal in itself, but may involve illegal acts.

g)  No (lines 17–19)

### Exercise D 2

a/8;  b/5;  c/1;  d/9;  e/11;  f/3;  g/10;  h/7;  i/6;  j/2.

## Section Two

### Exercise B 1

i)  Check that the dictionary definitions you have found correspond to the following in meaning.

a)  (noun, plural) (in International Law) compensation for injuries or breaches of international obligations

b)  (noun, plural) people who commit acts (which are often crimes)

c)  (noun, plural) levels

d)  (adjective) secret

e)  (noun) right to enter [the territory of a State]

f)  orders [a State] not to [punish individuals]; does not allow [a State] to [punish individuals]

ii)  Check that your own ideas correspond to the following in meaning. Your answers will probably not give as much detail.

a)  intentional breaches of International Law (by a subject of International Law)

b)  non-liability [*for* acts; *in respect of* jurisdiction/local courts]

c)  state of war (between States or parties)

d)  special rights (granted to a particular person or class of persons)

iii)  a)  people who are at war [*belligerency* = the state of being at war]

b)  supposes or requires as a preliminary condition [pre- + suppose]

c) a man who can be recognised or identified as a member of the services (armed forces) [recognise + able; service + man]
d) refuse to accept [them] as their own, say they have no connection with [dis + own]
e) responsibility regarding delicts [delict + -ual]
f) the right to defend oneself (in International Law against the actions of another State) [self + defence]
g) access to [the] territory [of a State] [territory + -ial]
h) ships for use in war (for fighting) [war + ship]
i) area where one is not allowed to go [forbid + -en]

iv) a) (1) POWs (line 67)   (2) U2 (93)   (3) IMTs (43)
b) (1) *Prisoners of War*
(3) *International Military Tribunals* (two of these were created after the Second World War – the Nuremberg and Tokyo IMTs)

v) a) The following are definitions only. Any real or imaginary examples of your own are acceptable.
(1) a general practice of International Law which is not yet accepted as obligatory and has therefore not yet become a rule of customary International Law
(2) orders given by a superior in a hierarchical organisation, e.g. the army
(3) the internal law of an individual State, as opposed to International Law
(4) war which is just, e.g. because it is based on self-defence or national liberation
b) (1) defines crimes against peace, war crimes and crimes against humanity
(2) concern the conduct of war, use of force and peaceful resolution of conflicts
(3) is additional to the Red Cross Conventions of 1949 concerning the treatment and recognition of POWs and regulating the use of some kinds of arms
c) (1) No, in line 128 it means the persons or bodies with the power to control affairs in a particular area, in this case Sweden. In the context of domestic law the local authorities are responsible for various aspects of government in a particular part of the country.
(2) No, in line 77 it means *regulation* – responsibility for covert agents is not *regulated* by law.

**Exercise B 2**

i) a) States which exercise sovereignty, independent States
b) criminal behaviour on the part of a State
c) crimes which violate the laws and customs of war
d) the non-liability (immunity) of a State in respect of less serious acts which violate International Law
e) special rights granted to soldiers [in wartime, e.g. immunity from liability for killing]
f) methods of fighting used by guerrillas
g) the foreign government which gains some advantage (benefits) from [the agent's] spying

ii) c

**Exercise B 3**

i) The line references show the parts of the text which

contain the information for each answer. Refer to the text to check any of your answers which are wrong.
(3) international practice (lines 25–6)
(4) are (lines 31–8)
(5) were not (lines 35–9)
(6) they had not committed such serious crimes (38–9)
(7) were not (31–9)
(8) did not accept (42–6)
(9) wartime (47–50)
(10) are not liable for their acts provided they have obeyed the laws and customs of war (50–55)
(11) sometimes (56–62)
(12) whether they are popular or unpopular guerrillas (56–62)
(13) did not have (62–5)
(14) as ordinary criminals (65–8)
(15) is not (75–7)
(16) the foreign government accepts responsibility for the agents' acts (77–87)
(17) should not be held personally liable (96–110)
(18) only applies (111–25)
(19) doesn't apply (115–19)
(20) the agents had entered New Zealand territory illegally with the official purpose of committing unlawful acts (115–20)
(21) immunity from local jurisdiction for unlawful acts in International Law derives from the consent of sovereign States to territorial access for foreigners (120–25)
(22) can (131–9)

ii) The agents had only obeyed orders and the French Government had accepted responsibility for their acts. However, since their presence on New Zealand territory was unlawful they were not entitled to agent immunity because the doctrine derives from the consent of the sovereign State to territorial access for foreigners.

**Exercise C 1**

ii) He thinks it may have the positive effect of showing the need for clear rules of International Law regarding immunity, low-level force and peacetime espionage (lines 6–13)

iii) a) More likely – the trend is to restrict state immunity (lines 13–17)
b) That the Secretary-General's arbitration decision does not have the force of a legal judgment. It is only a single ruling reached by an individual in a particular case.
c) Because both the State *and* its agents were held liable for the agents' unlawful acts (lines 26–9).

iv) Personal opinions: the author's prediction about the positive long-term benefits of the case (lines 6–13), 'may have' (line 7) shows that this is not a certain fact, only a prediction; the comment that De Cuéllar probably considered both the the practical and legal position in reaching his decision (lines 21–4), 'no doubt' shows that this is a personal opinion, not a statement of fact.

**Exercise D 2**

*Note: only* information from the text is used in the following arguments and decisions.

*Case A*
*For the applicant State (Japan)*
Jane Bond's presence in Japan was unlawful. Per the *Schooner Exchange v. McFaddon* case agent immunity derives from consent to territorial access for foreigners. Since there was no consent in this case, Jane Bond is personally liable for her acts.

*For the defendant State (UK)*
Jane Bond was a government agent and only obeyed orders; the UK Government has accepted full responsibility for her acts; therefore per the *Caroline* and *McLeod* cases and international practice, she should not be held personally liable, but enjoy agent immunity.

*Judgment:* (Adopting the arguments of the applicant State) Jane Bond is personally liable.

*Case B*
*For the applicant State (US)*
Individuals are increasingly recognised as subjects of International Law. Agents are liable because they are the means by which State acts are carried out. Superior orders is no defence. He is not entitled to soldiers' privileges, which only apply in wartime, not for single acts of aggression.

*For the defendant State (UK)*
Captain Kirk was a recognisable government serviceman who was engaged in State business and followed superior orders. He should therefore enjoy agent immunity. In any case Captain Kirk is a member of the armed forces and is entitled to soldiers' privileges, and is therefore not liable for killing foreigners. It is true that individuals are liable for war crimes and crimes against peace and humanity (per the Nuremberg Charter, adopted by UN Resolution of 11 December 1946 and generally regarded as part of positive International Law), but the sinking of the *Tipperary* and death of the two crew members does not fall into this category. For all these reasons he should not be held personally liable for his acts.

*Judgment:* Captain Kirk is not entitled to soldiers' privileges in the absence of hostilities. However, adopting the other arguments of the defendant State, he is not personally liable.

### Exercise D 3

i) a / 7;    b / 1;    c / 3;    d / 5;    e / 5;    f / 8;
    g / 6;    h / 5;    i / 2;    j / 3;    k / 5;    l / 4.

ii) a) Attorney-General     b) Master of the Rolls
    c) Her Majesty Queen Elizabeth II     d) Lord Chancellor     e) Court of Appeal     f) House of Lords     g) Prime Minister     h) United Nations
    i) International Court of Justice

## Unit 12

### Exercise A 2

½ point for each correct answer. Maximum 6 points.
i) A / 4;    B / 7;    D / 3;    E / 6;    F / 2;    G / 5.
   (1) . . . reparation.
   (2) . . . a description of Iranian acts constituting breaches of International Law
   (3) . . . the seriousness of Iran's violation of fundamental principles of International Law

   (4) . . . the fundamental importance of diplomatic rights in international relations.
   (5) . . . the reason for the particular seriousness of Iran's conduct
   (6) . . . the negative consequences of this type of violation for International Law and relations.

### Exercise A 3

1 point for each *True/False* answer. Maximum 5 points.
½ point for each correct vocabulary answer, maximum 5 points. e.g. (in the example) need to understand *FOREGOING* = ½ point; do not need to understand *MERITS* = ½ point.

a) *False*: Iran is liable as a result of both treaty obligations *and* principles of general International Law (lines 10–17). Do not need to understand *successive* or *amity*.
b) *True* (lines 17–20). Need to understand *entails*. Do not need to understand *amount*.
c) *False*: there was an *escalation* of breaches – they got progressively worse (lines 25–38). You can understand the answer by studying the list of breaches in lines 28–38, but it is helpful to understand *escalation*. Do not need to understand *cumulative*.
d) *False*: the Iranian authorities gave their *endorsement* (approval) of the situation (32–3). You can understand the answer from the fact that the authorities *maintained* the occupation (34–5), but it is helpful to understand *endorsement*. You do not need to understand *premises*.
e) *False*: the text refers to the *detention* of the staff – they were held prisoner – but not killed (35). Need to understand *detention*. Do not need to understand *bow to*.

### Exercise A 4

½ point for each correct answer. Maximum 6 points. Your answer should be *similar in meaning* to the one in the key, but will probably not be identical.

i)   (1) [WRONG + FUL + LY] Suffix -FUL is a typical adjectival form – WRONGFUL = wrong or unjust; suffix -LY is a typical adverbial form. WRONGFULLY = in a way which is wrong or unjust.
   (2) [PRE- + REQUISITE] Prefix PRE- = before; REQUISITE is a noun related to the verb REQUIRE; PREREQUISITE = something which is required or necessary before another thing (as a preliminary condition).
   (3) [IN- + VIOLATE + -ABLE + -ITY] Prefix IN- gives a negative meaning; VIOLABLE [VIOLATE + ABLE] = which can be violated; -ITY = typical noun ending which indicates a state or quality. INVIOLABILITY = quality or state of not being capable of violation.
   (4) [RECEIVE + ING] -ING = typical adjectival form. RECEIVING = which receives (the *receiving State* (line 83) is the one *which receives* the foreign embassy on its territory).
   (5) [IR- + REPAIR + ABLE] IR- = negative prefix used before 'r'; -ABLE = suffix meaning *which can be*; REPARABLE = which can be repaired. IRREPARABLE = which cannot be repaired.
   (6) [EN- + SURE] Prefix EN- = to make, cause to

become e.g. enable, enact. ENSURE = to make something sure or definite (*to make* the ordered progress of relations between its members *sure* – lines 97–8).

ii)  a / 6;  b / 2;  c / 4;  d / 5;  e / 3;  f / 1.

## Exercise A 5

1 point for each correct answer.
a)  The Vienna Conventions (etc.) have *laid* these obligations *upon* Iran/States – a convention *places* or *imposes* obligations *on* a party. *Answer:* placed on/ imposed on.
b)  After their *seizure* of the Embassy and staff, the militants maintained the occupation – before maintaining occupation, they must *take/gain possession* of the Embassy. *Answer:* taking/gaining possession of (by force).
c)  Iran wanted to force the US to *bow to* their demands – they wanted the US to *accept/submit to* their demands. *Answer:* to accept/submit to.
d)  The conditions described (lines 38–41) are *incompatible* with the UN Charter and human rights law – they are clearly *contrary to/not consistent with* the Charter, etc. *Answer:* contrary to/not consistent with.
e)  The relevant principles of International Law (etc.) are *set at naught* by Iran or those who behave like Iran in the present case – they are *regarded as of no value* by Iran. *Answer:* regarded as of no value.
f)  Events of this kind cause irreparable harm and *undermine* the structure of International Law – they *seriously damage/weaken* the structure of the law. *Answer:* seriously damage/weaken.

## Exercise A 6

ii)  1 point for each comment which corresponds to the following. Maximum 14 points.
(4) A   (5) A   (6) D – Iranian authorities did not oppose attack on Embassy.   (7) A   (8) E
(9) B – also guilty of serious breaches of human rights law and UN Charter.   (10) A   (11) C – it is not necessary to give the ICJ page reference.   (12) E
(13) D – this case especially serious because breaches committed by government of receiving State, not only by private individuals or groups.   (14) A   (15) A
(16) C – this piece of information is not important.
(17) A

## Exercise A 7

i)  2 points for the correct answer: a)

ii)  1 point for each correct answer and 1 point if you have given the correct reason (maximum 6 points).
a/2 – gives factual information only. Describes Court's decision and the question of reparation.
b/1 – uses strong forms (adjectives, adverbs and verbs) to give emphasis to statements criticising Iran's conduct, examples: what has *above all* to be *emphasized* (line 45); the Court must . . . *strongly* affirm (50–51); *manifestly incompatible* (41); *stressing* (52–3); *cardinal importance* (54), etc.
c/3 – uses very strong forms (adjectives, adjectives + nouns) to give strong emphasis to statements

criticising Iran's conduct, examples: *deep regret* (line 70); *essential* (73); *deplorable, unique, very particular gravity* (78–9); *irreparable harm* (89–90), etc.

## Exercise A 8

1 point for each correct answer. Maximum 13 points.

i)  . . . the US military incursion into Iranian territory of 24–25 April 1980.

ii)  2 / f;   3 / c;   4 / e;   5 / a;   6 / h;   7 / g;  8 / b;   9 / i.

iii)  Your answers should be similar in content to the following, but will not be identical. The parts in brackets (. . .) are extra pieces of information, which you may give, but which are not necessary to have a point.
a)  No (the Court could understand why the US might be worried and frustrated (lines 8–17) but clearly did not think the attack was justified) (19–42).
b)  Because the ICJ hearing had already taken place and the Court was actually preparing its judgment at the time of the attack (the US had even asked for an early judgment which the Court had tried to give). Choosing to settle the dispute by force in those circumstances shows that the US did not believe in the power of the Court to settle the dispute (19–42).
c)  Because this question was not before the Court and in any case could not change the legal impact of Iran's behaviour 6 months before (43–55).
d)  3 (the Court is critical of the US attack, but does not use the very strong emphatic language noted in Paragraphs 91 and 92 of the text – see answer to Exercise A 7 ii).

## Exercise B 1

1 point for each correct answer. Maximum 8 points.
a) criminality   b) self-defence   c) imprisonment
d) inviolable   e) justification   f) tried, trial
g) prosecutor

## Exercise B 2

1 point for each correct answer. Maximum 8 points.
a) plead not guilty   b) Human rights
c) Arbitration   d) convicted   e) Evidence
f) liability   g) State sovereignty   h) Breach

## Exercise B 3

1 point for each correct answer. Maximum 9 points.
a / 1;   b / 2, 3;   c / 3;   d / 4;   e / 2;   f / 4;
g / 2;   h / 1.

## Exercise B 4

1 point for each correct answer. Maximum 12 points. Your answers should be similar in content to the ones below, but will not be identical. The parts in brackets (. . .) are extra pieces of information which you may give, but which are not necessary to have a point.
i)  a)  The juvenile court
    b)  Yes (as Tyrer did).
    c)  It is not part of the UK; it has a special relationship

with the UK. (It is a dependency of the Crown and has its own government, legislature and courts, etc. The Crown is responsible for good government on the Isle of Man.)

d) In strict law, yes. In practice it does not do so without the Isle of Man's consent (because of a constitutional convention to this effect).

ii) a) No, individuals apply to the Commission, which can then refer the case to the Court.
   b) 1) torture (most serious)
      2) inhuman treatment or punishment
      3) degrading treatment or punishment
   c) Because by its very nature all judicial punishment involves humiliation, therefore there must be some other factor to make it a violation of human rights.
   d) Yes. (In the *Tyrer case* the Court said that modern penal policy in member States of the Council of Europe was relevant in considering the legal status of judicial corporal punishment.)

iii) a) The State, the agent enjoys immunity.
    b) The defence of superior orders does not apply to some particularly serious acts (such as war crimes and crimes against peace and humanity).
    c) Because they enjoy special rights called soldiers' privileges (provided they have not violated the laws and customs of war).

d) Only if their government accepts responsibility for their acts *and* their presence on foreign territory is lawful (since the principle of immunity derives from consent to territorial access for foreigners).

ADD UP YOUR TOTAL SCORE OUT OF 100!

## Exercise C 1

a) LIABILITY   b) CASE-LAW   c) EEC LAW
d) SENTENCING   e) LAWYER   f) TRIAL
g) HOUSE OF COMMONS   h) PRIVATE LAW
i) INTERNATIONAL LAW   j) LITIGATION
k) LEGISLATION   l) JUDICIARY
m) CONTRACT   n) SOVEREIGN
o) OFFENCE   p) SOURCE OF LAW
q) JUDGMENT   r) JUDICIAL PRECEDENT

## Exercise C 2

Johnny was charged with armed robbery. He was not convicted.
Micky was convicted of theft and sentenced to two years' imprisonment.
Sonny was convicted of murder and sentenced to life imprisonment.
Johnny was the only one who did not go to prison.

# Glossary

*Note*: the words in this glossary are defined only with the meaning(s) they have as law terms in this book. Many words also have meanings in general or legal English which are not given here. For a complete list of general meanings refer to a good mono- or bilingual dictionary of the English language; for a complete list of legal meanings and a more complex explanation of terms which particularly interest you refer to a good law dictionary or work of legal reference. Some suggestions are given below.

### Some monolingual dictionaries for learners of English

*Collins COBUILD English Language Dictionary* (Collins, 1987)

*Collins COBUILD Essential English Dictionary* (Collins, 1988)

*Longman Dictionary of Contemporary English*, 2nd edition (Longman, 1987)

*Longman Active Study Dictionary of English* (Longman, 1983)

*Oxford Advanced Learner's Dictionary of Current English*, 4th edition (Oxford University Press, 1989)

*Oxford Student's Dictionary of Current English*, 2nd edition (Oxford University Press, 1988)

### Some English law dictionaries and reference books

*A Concise Dictionary of Law* (Oxford University Press, 1986)

*A Dictionary of Law*, 2nd edition, by L.B. Curzon, M & E Professional Dictionaries (Pitman, 1983)

*Osborne's Concise Law Dictionary*, 7th edition, by Roger Bird (Sweet and Maxwell, 1983)

*The Oxford Companion to Law*, by David M. Walker (Oxford University Press, 1980)

*Black's Law Dictionary*, 5th edition (West Publishing Company, 1979) [for English and American law terms]

*Halsbury's Laws of England*, 4th edition (the most complete and complex work of reference) (Butterworth, 1979)

## How to use this Glossary

Each term that is explained (headword) is printed in **bold** type. This is followed by the pronunciation, then the kind of term or phrase (i.e. what part of speech) it is, thus:

| | |
|---|---|
| *v.* | verb |
| *n.* | noun (*pl.n* = plural noun) |
| *a.* | adjective |
| *adv.* | adverb |
| *conj.* | conjunction |
| *prep.* | preposition |
| *past participle* | |
| *art.* | article |
| *abbrev.* | abbreviation |

The definition follows, then in brackets ( ) collocations, fixed phrases, exemplification of usage and derived forms. Words which also appear in the glossary as headwords are printed in *italics*. Closely connected terms which also appear in the glossary are introduced by the words 'See also'.

---

**abolish** /ə'bɒlɪʃ/, *v.* To bring to an end by *law*. (*Corporal punishment* was abolished in England in 1948; abolition (n.))

**accuse** /ə'kju:z/, *v.* To state that someone is *guilty* of a *crime*, to *charge* someone with a crime. (They were accused of *conspiracy*.)

**accused** /ə'kju:zd/, *n.* The accused is the person in a *criminal trial* who is *accused* of a *crime*, the *defendant*. (The accused was found *guilty* and *fined* £500.)

**Act** See *Act of Parliament*

**action** /'ækʃn/, *n.* An action is a lawsuit; *legal proceedings* before a *civil court* in which a *party sues* for a legal right. (If you take legal action you proceed against someone in a *court* of *law*.)

**Act of Parliament** /,ækt əv 'pɑ:ləmənt/, *n. + prep. + n.* A written *law* made by the *Queen in Parliament* which states or changes *legal* rules on a particular subject. (The Equal Pay Act 1970; the Law of Property Act 1925)
See also *enactment*; *statute*

**administer** /əd'mɪnɪstə/, *v.* To apply, put into operation. (The *courts* administer the *law*; administration (n.), the administration of *justice*)

**Administrative Law** /əd'mɪnɪstrətɪv ,lɔ:/, *a. + n.* Administrative law is the area of *law* relating to the functions and powers of *government* organisations (not the supreme *executive* and *legislature*) and how they operate in practice to *administer* government policy.
See also *Constitutional Law*

**admissible** /əd'mɪsəbl/, *a.* That can be allowed or considered by a *court*, *tribunal*, etc. (The court *held* that the application was admissible only in part; opposite: inadmissible)

**AG** /eɪ 'dʒi:/, *abbrev.* The Attorney-General (*AG v Hopkins* ['Attorney-General against Hopkins'] is the name of a *criminal case* of particular importance in which the Attorney-General conducts the *prosecution* for the *Crown*.)
See also *Attorney-General*

**allege** /ə'ledʒ/, *v.* To claim or state (usually in *evidence*) that something is true. (The *prosecution* alleged that the *accused* had planned the *robbery* some time before. alleged (a.); allegation (n.))

**All ER** /æl i: 'a:/, *abbrev*. The All England Law Reports, one of the main collections of reports of English *cases*.
See also *law reports*

**amend** /ə'mend/, *v*. To make changes in a rule, document, *law*, etc. (The *Act* was amended to include *nationals* of *EEC States*; the Equal Pay Act 1972 (as amended by the Sex Discrimination Act 1975))

**appeal** /ə'pi:l/, *n*. An appeal is an *application* to a higher *court* or *body* to examine again a *case* decided by a lower court or body and possibly give a different decision. (court of appeal; appeal court; She won the appeal.)

**appeal** /ə'pi:l/, *v*. If you appeal against the decision of a *court* or *body* you *apply* to a higher court or body to examine the *case* again and possibly give a different decision. (He appealed against *conviction*.)

**appellant** /ə'pelənt/, *n*. A person who makes an *appeal*.
See also *appeal*

**appellate** /ə'pelɪt/, *a*. Relating to *appeals*. (appellate *jurisdiction* [see jurisdiction]; the Appellate Committee of the *House of Lords*)
See also *appeal*

**applicant** /'æplɪkant/, *n*. A person who makes a formal request ('application') to a *court*. (applicant *State*: a State which makes an application to a court)

**apply** /ə'plaɪ/, *v*. To put into operation; to have an effect; to make a formal request. (The *courts* interpret and apply the *law*; the rules of *International Law* apply to all *States*; he applied to the court for an order of *specific performance*; applicable (a.); application (n.))

**arbitration** /ˌa:bɪ'treɪʃn/, *n*. Arbitration is the process of *settling* a *dispute* by referring it to one or more independent third parties for decision as an alternative to *court proceedings*. (The dispute was referred to arbitration.)

**arbitrator** /'a:bɪtreɪtə(r)/, *n*. An arbitrator is an independent third party who is chosen to *settle* a *dispute* as an alternative to *court proceedings*. (The Secretary-General of the *UN* acted as arbitrator in the dispute.)

**arrest** /ə'rest/, *v*. To take away the freedom of a person suspected of a *crime* by *legal authority*. (They were arrested for *unlawful* possession of drugs; arrest (n.))

**arson** /'a:sn/, *n*. Arson is the *crime* of *unlawfully* damaging or destroying property by fire with the intention to do so, or not caring if this is the consequence of your act.

**article** /'a:tɪkl/, *n*. An article is a complete, separate section or rule in a document such as a *contract*, *treaty*, etc. (Article I of the US Constitution defines the composition and powers of Congress; Art. (abbrev.))

**assault** /ə'sɔ:lt/, *n*. An *unlawful* physical attack against another person or an act which makes them fear immediate physical violence. (*unlawful* assault; assault occasioning actual bodily harm: assault which causes physical injury to a person; assault occasioning grievous bodily harm (GBH): assault which causes very serious physical injury)

**assault** /ə'sɔ:lt/, *v*. To make an *unlawful* physical attack against another person, or do something which makes them fear immediate physical violence.

**Attorney-General** /ə,tɜ:nɪ 'dʒenrəl/, *n*. The Attorney-General (usually a member of the *House of Commons*) is the chief *law officer* and principal *legal* adviser of the *Crown* in England and Wales and leader of the English *Bar*. S/he sometimes acts as *counsel* for the Crown.

See also *law officer*

**authority** /ɔ:'θɒrətɪ/, *n*. An authority is a *judicial decision* cited (e.g. in a later *case*) as a statement of the *law*; an authority is an official organisation or *government* department with the power to act and make decisions; authority is the right or power to act, command, judge, etc. (binding authority [see *binding precedent*]; persuasive authority – one which influences but does not *bind* the *court*; the local authorities are responsible for social services; *Parliament* has authority to pass any law it wants.)

**ballot paper** /'bælət ˌpeɪpə(r)/, *n. + n*. A paper used by a voter in an *election* to register his or her (secret) vote. Also 'voting paper'.

**Bar** /ba:/, *n*. The Bar is the profession of *barrister*, and a collective term for all barristers (in the US all *lawyers*). Barristers are 'called to the Bar' when they are admitted to practise before the *court*.
See also *barrister*

**barrister** /'bærɪstə/, *n*. A barrister (in Scotland 'advocate') is a member of the *legal* profession who has been 'called to the Bar': s/he may represent *litigants* in both inferior and superior *courts* and can normally only deal with clients through a *solicitor*.
See also *Bar*; *counsel*; *solicitor*

**beneficiary** /ˌbenɪ'fɪʃərɪ/, *n*. A beneficiary is a person for whose benefit or advantage property is held in *trust*; also, a person who receives something under a *will*.
See also *trust*, *will*

**bigamy** /'bɪgəmɪ/, *n*. You *commit* the *crime* of bigamy if you marry another person when you are still *lawfully* married to someone else.

**Bill** /bɪl/, *n*. A Bill is a proposed *law* – the preliminary version or draft of an *Act of Parliament*, which is put before the *legislature* for discussion and approval.
See also *Act of Parliament*

**bind** /baɪnd/, *v*. To place a person or persons under *legal* obligation; to place a *court* under legal obligation to act in accordance with (a) previous *judicial decision(s)*. (The *contract* binds the *parties* to share the cost of transport equally; *High Court judges* are bound by decisions of the *Court of Appeal*.)

**binding precedent** /ˌbaɪndɪŋ 'presɪdənt/, *a. + n*. A binding precedent is a *judicial decision* which future *courts* must *follow* when deciding similar *cases*; under the *doctrine* of binding precedent decisions of courts in previous cases are considered as a *source of law* which will influence or *bind* courts in later similar cases.
See also *judicial precedent*; *stare decisis*

**body** /'bɒdɪ/, *n*. A body is an organised group of people working as a unit, often in an official capacity. (a *government* body; a *legislative* body)

**bound** /baʊnd/, *past participle*. See *bind*.

**branch of law** /ˌbra:ntʃ əv 'lɔ:/, *n. + prep. + n*. A separate area or subject of *law*. (*Family law* is a branch of *private law*.)

**breach** /bri:tʃ/, *n*. A breach is the act of breaking a *law*, agreement, etc., a violation. (in breach of *Article* 24; a breach of *International Law*)
See also *breach of contract*

**breach of contract** /ˌbri:tʃ əv 'kɒntrækt/, *n. + prep. + n*. The breaking of an obligation imposed on a *party* by a *contract*.
See also *contract*

**breach of the peace** /ˌbriːtʃ əv ðə ˈpiːs/, *n. + prep. + art. + n.* Any act which causes harm to a person or (in their presence) to their property, or which causes fear of harm through *assault*, riot or some other disturbance is a 'breach of the Queen's peace'.

**bribery and corruption** /ˌbraɪbəri ənd kəˈrʌpʃn/, *n. + conj. + n.* Bribery and corruption is the *crime* of offering or giving money, a favour, etc. to a person in order to influence them in their duty.

**burglary** /ˈbəːrgləri/, *n.* Burglary is the *crime* of entering a building without the permission of the owner, with the intention of stealing, causing grievous bodily harm (see *assault*), etc. (burglar (n.) – a person who *commits* burglary)

**by-election** /ˈbaɪ ɪˌlekʃn/, *n.* A by-election is an *election* in one or more *constituencies* during the life of a *Parliament*, for example because a *Member of Parliament* has died. See also *General Election*

**Cabinet** /ˈkæbɪnət/, *n.* The Cabinet is the *body* of senior *Ministers* of the *Crown* presided over by the *Prime Minister* which formulates *government* policy and initiates *legislation*. It is the supreme *executive* in the British *constitution*. See also *executive*

**canon law** /ˈkænən ˌlɔː/, *n. + n.* A *body* of *codified* Roman ecclesiastical (church) *law*; in England, the law of the Church of England.

**capital punishment** /ˌkæpɪtl ˈpʌnɪʃmənt/, *a. + n.* The *sentence* of death imposed as punishment for a *crime*. (Capital punishment for *murder* was *abolished* in the UK in 1965. Also called 'the death penalty', 'the death sentence'.)

**case** /keɪs/, *n.* A *legal* action or *trial*; a set of legal circumstances; a written report of an action including the opinions of the *judge(s)* who decided the *dispute*. A case of first impression is one which presents a completely new set of facts. See also *case-law*; *first instance*

**case-law** /ˈkeɪsˌlɔː/, *n. + n.* Case-law is the body of *law* contained in previous *judicial decisions* as opposed to *statute law*. See also *judicial precedent*; *law reports*

**Central Criminal Court** /ˌsentrəl ˈkrɪmɪnəl ˌkɔːt/, *a. + a. + n.* The section of the *Crown Court* for London, often called the 'Old Bailey'. See also *Crown Court*

**certiorari** /ˌsəːtɪəˈrɑːrɪ/, *(Latin).* *Certiorari* is an order from the *High Court* used to review and cancel decisions of inferior *courts*, *tribunals*, etc. See also *judicial review*

**Chancellor of the Exchequer** /ˌtʃɑːnsələ(r) əv θɪ ɪksˈtʃekə(r)/, *n. + prep. + art. + n.* The Chancellor of the Exchequer is the *Cabinet Minister* who is political head of the Treasury and is responsible for the control of national finances, e.g. public spending and tax.

**Chancery Division** /ˈtʃɑːnsəri dɪˌvɪʒn/, *n. + n.* A division of the *High Court of Justice*, presided over by the *Lord Chancellor* with *jurisdiction* over *cases* concerning the *law* of property, *trusts*, etc.

**charge** /tʃɑːdʒ/, *n.* A charge is a formal accusation of a *crime*, usually made by the police. (He faces six charges of *theft*.)

**charge** /tʃɑːdʒ/, *v.* To accuse someone formally of a *crime*. (She was arrested and charged with criminal damage.)

**charter** /ˈtʃɑːtə(r)/, *n.* A charter is a document stating the principles, functions and organisation of a *body*. (the UN Charter)

**circuit judge** /ˈsəːkɪt ˌdʒʌdʒ/, *n. + n.* Circuit judges *hear civil* and *criminal cases* in the *county courts* and *Crown Court* of a district of England and Wales called a circuit and may sit as *High Court judges* if asked by the *Lord Chancellor*.

**citation** /saɪˈteɪʃn/, *n.* A reference to previous *judicial decisions* or authoritative writings; the title by which a judicial decision is known, e.g. *R. v Smith*.

**cite** /saɪt/, *v.* To refer to a previously decided *case* of *legal authority* in support of an argument. (*Counsel* for the *plaintiff* cited *Carlill v Carbolic Smoke Ball Co.* in her submission to the *court*.)

**citizen** /ˈsɪtɪzən/, *n.* A person who has the nationality of a *State*, involving duties toward the *State* and the right to protection by it. (A foreign national who marries a British citizen does not gain British *citizenship*.)

**citizenship** /ˈsɪtɪzənʃɪp/, *n.* The status of a *citizen*. (British citizenship can be gained by registration.) See also *citizen*

**civil** /ˈsɪvl/, *a.* Relating to *private law* as opposed to *Criminal Law* and *Administrative Law*. (a civil *case*) See also *private law*

**Civil Division** /ˈsɪvl dɪˌvɪʒn/, *a. + n.* A branch or section of the *Court of Appeal* that exercises the *civil jurisdiction* of the Court. See also *Court of Appeal*

**civil law** /ˈsɪvl ˌlɔː/, *a. + n.* *Roman Law* or a legal system based on Roman Law as distinct from the English system of *common law*; *private law* as opposed to *Criminal Law* and *Administrative Law*. See also *common law*; *private law*

**civil servant** /ˌsɪvl ˈsəːvənt/, *a. + n.* A civil servant is a person employed in the *Civil Service*. See also *Civil Service*

**Civil Service** /ˌsɪvl ˈsəːvɪs/, *a. + n.* The Civil Service is the body of persons employed by the branches of *government* administration which are not *legislative*, *judicial* or military, e.g. the administrative and executive staff of government departments. See also *civil servant*

**code** /kəʊd/, *n.* A systematic, written collection of *laws* on a particular subject or area of law. (Code Napoléon; civil code; codify (v.); codification (n.))

**collective responsibility** /kəˌlektɪv rɪˌspɒnsəˈbɪlətɪ/, *a. + n.* The *doctrine* of collective responsibility is a *constitutional convention* according to which all members of the British *Cabinet* are responsible together for Cabinet decisions.

**Commercial Law** /kəˈməːʃl ˌlɔː/, *a. + n.* Commercial Law is not a distinct *branch of law* in the English *legal system*. It is a general term which includes various aspects of different branches of law such as the *Law of Contract* and of Property, which are relevant to business and commerce.

**commit** /kəˈmɪt/, *v.* To do (something wrong or *illegal*.) (They committed *murder*. She has committed a *tort*.)

**common law** /ˈkɒmən ˌlɔː/, *a. + n.* Common law is the body of *law* based on *custom* which is *administered* and developed by the *courts* in *judicial decisions*. It contrasts with *statute law*, *Equity* and *civil law*. A common-law *legal system* is one based on the English common law as opposed to one based on the civil law of Rome. See also *civil law*; *Equity*; *statute*

**Common Market** /ˌkɒmən ˈmɑːkɪt/, *a. + n.* See *EEC*

**Commons** /ˈkɒmənz/, *pl.n.* See *House of Commons*

**Commonwealth** /'kɒmənwelθ/, *n*. The Commonwealth is the association of *States* formed by the United Kingdom and self-governing nations which were once part of the British Empire. The British *Sovereign* is the head of the Commonwealth, whose members are equal in status.

**Community law** /kə'mju:nətɪ ˌlɔ:/, *n. + n*. See *EC Law*.

**community service order** /kə'mju:nətɪ ˌsɜ:vɪs ˌɔ:də(r)/, *n. + n. + n*. A community service order is a *court* order to a person *convicted* of a *crime* to do a certain number of hours of work without pay in the local community instead of another form of punishment.

**Company Law** /'kʌmpənɪ ˌlɔ:/, *n. + n*. Company Law is the area of law relating to businesses organised as companies. It includes the formation and ending of companies, their legal status and the duties of their members.

**comparative law** /kəm'pærətɪv ˌlɔ:/, *a. + n*. Comparative law is the study of *law* which compares (aspects of) *different legal systems*.

**condemn** /kən'dem/, *v*. To state the punishment of a person found *guilty* in a *criminal trial* (especially a severe punishment). (The *judge* condemned the terrorist to life *imprisonment*.)
See also *sentence (v.)*

**Conflict of Laws** /'kɒnflɪkt əv ˌlɔ:z/, *n. + prep. + n*. Conflict of Laws is the area of *law* of each *legal system* which regulates how to deal with *cases* involving a foreign element. Also called private international law or international private law.
See also *International Law*

**consideration** /kənsɪdə'reɪʃn/, *n*. A *doctrine* of the English *Law of Contract*: if a *contract* is not in a special written form, there must be consideration, i.e. something which is given in return for the promise (an advantage to one *party*, or a disadvantage to the other).
See also *under seal*

**conspiracy** /kən'spɪrəsɪ/, *n*. Conspiracy is the *crime* of agreeing with one or more other persons to do something which will involve at least one of the *parties committing* an *offence* or offences, e.g. two people agree that one of them shall steal while the other waits in a car to escape after the *theft*.

**conspire** /kən'spaɪə(r)/, *v*. To agree with one or more other persons to do something which will involve at least one of the *parties committing* an *offence* or offences. (The three men conspired to rob the bank.)
See also *conspiracy*

**constituency** /kən'stɪtjuənsɪ/, *n*. A constituency is an area of the UK for which a *representative* is *elected* to the *House of Commons*. (constituent (n.))

**constitution** /ˌkɒnstɪ'tju:ʃn/, *n*. The constitution of a *State* is the political and *legal* structure of *government*. It defines the composition, powers and relations of the *head of state*, *legislature*, *executive* and *judiciary*. (constitutional (a.); constitutionally (adv.))
See also *Constitutional Law; convention*

**Constitutional Law** /ˌkɒnstɪ'tju:ʃənl ˌlɔ:/, *a. + n*. Constitutional Law is the *law* relating to the *legal* structure of *government* in a *State*. It defines the principal *organs* of government and their relationship to each other and to the individual.
See also *constitution*

**construction** /kən'strʌkʃn/, *n*. Interpretation of the meaning of words, or of a document, *statute*, etc.

**construe** /kən'stru:/, *v*. To interpret the meaning of words, or of a document, statute, etc.

**contract** /'kɒntrækt/, *n*. A legally *binding* agreement between two or more *parties*. (contract /kən'trækt/ (v.); contracting /kən'træktɪŋ/ (a.); contractual /kən'træktʃuəl/ (a.))
See also *breach of contract; Law of Contract*

**contract** /kən'trækt/, *v*. To form a legally *binding* agreement. (They contracted to build a new swimming-pool.)

**convention** /kən'venʃn/, *n*. A convention is a *treaty* between *States*; a convention of the *constitution* is a rule or practice which regulates the conduct of the *Crown* and *state organs* where there are no formal *legal* rules. (The *European Convention on Human Rights*; by convention *Parliament* must be *summoned* at least once a year; conventional (a.))

**Conveyancing Law** /kən'veɪənsɪŋ ˌlɔ:/, *n. + n*. Conveyancing Law is the area of *law* relating to the practical transfer of property, especially *land*.
See also *Land Law*

**convict** /'kɒnvɪkt/, *n*. A convict is a person who has been found *guilty* of a *crime* in a *court* of *law*.

**convict** /kən'vɪkt/, *v*. To find an *accused* person *guilty* of a *crime* in a *court* of *law*. (He was convicted of *theft*; convicted (a.))

**conviction** /kən'vɪkʃn/, *n*. The finding that an *accused* person is *guilty* of a *crime* in a *court* of *law*. (He had six previous convictions.)

**corporal punishment** /ˌkɔ:pərəl 'pʌnɪʃmənt/, *a. + n*. Punishment which consists of causing a person to feel physical pain, e.g. by whipping. (*judicial* corporal punishment)

**costs** /kɒsts/, *pl.n*. Costs are the expenses of legal *proceedings*. The *party* which loses usually has to pay costs for both sides.

**Council of Europe** /ˌkaʊnsl əv 'jʊərəp/, *n. + prep. + n*. The Council of Europe is a *body* of European *States* which aims to create greater unity between its members, discusses and forms agreements on economic, social, scientific, *legal* matters, etc. and promotes *human rights*.
See also *European Convention on Human Rights*

**counsel** /'kaʊnsl/, *n*. Counsel is the term for a *barrister* or barristers conducting a *law case*. (Counsel for the *prosecution*)
See also *barrister*

**county court** /'kaʊntɪ ˌkɔ:t/, *n. + n*. county courts are the main *civil courts* with limited *jurisdiction* to *hear cases* in *tort* and *contract* or relating to *land*, *trusts*, divorce, etc. in a certain area of England or Wales.

**court** /kɔ:t/, *n*. A court is a person or group of persons with *authority* to *hear* and decide *disputes* by interpreting and *applying* rules of *law*. Also the place where *cases* are heard. (A *civil* court hears only civil cases. A *criminal* court hears only criminal cases. A court of *appeal* hears *appeals*.)

**Court of Appeal** /ˌkɔ:t əv ə'pi:l/, *n. + prep. + n*. The Court of Appeal is second to the House of Lords in the hierarchy of the English *courts*. It has *civil* and *criminal jurisdiction* (exercised by the Civil and Criminal Divisions) to hear *appeals* from lower courts.

**Court of Chancery** /ˌkɔ:t əv 'tʃɑ:nsərɪ/, *n. + prep. + n*. The Court of Chancery was the *court* of *Equity* (which also had *common-law jurisdiction*) presided over by the *Lord Chancellor*. Its jurisdiction is now exercised by the *Chancery Division* of the *High Court of Justice*.

**crime** /kraɪm/, *n*. Crime is *illegal* conduct for which a person may be *prosecuted* and punished by the *State*. A crime is a single illegal act for which a person may be prosecuted and punished by the State.

**criminal** /'krɪmɪnl/, *a. Illegal*; of or relating to *crime* or *Criminal Law* as opposed to *Civil Law* (a criminal act; a criminal *case*)
See also *Criminal Law*

**criminal** /'krɪmɪnl/, *n.* A criminal is a person who has committed a crime. (criminality (n.); criminally (adv.))
See also *crime*

**Criminal Division** /'krɪmɪnl dɪ,vɪʒn/, *a.* + *n.* The branch or section of the *Court of Appeal* that exercises its *criminal jurisdiction*.
See also *Court of Appeal*

**Criminal Evidence** /,krɪmɪnl 'evɪdəns/, *a.* + *n.* Criminal Evidence is the area of *law* which regulates the presentation of *evidence* in *proceedings* before a *court*. Also called the 'Law of Evidence' or 'Evidence'.
See also *evidence*

**Criminal Law** /'krɪmɪnl ,lɔː/, *a.* + *n.* Criminal Law is the *law* relating to *crime*, i.e. *illegal* conduct for which a person may be *prosecuted* and punished by the *State*.
See also *crime*

**Criminal Procedure** /,krɪmɪnl prə'siːdʒə(r)/, *a.* + *n.* Criminal Procedure is the area of *law* which regulates the way in which *legal proceedings* are conducted in *criminal cases*. Cf. *civil* procedure for civil cases.

**Criminology** /,krɪmɪ'nɒlədʒɪ/, *n.* Criminology is the study of *criminal* conduct in society, including the causes of criminal conduct and the general pattern of *crime* in society.
See also *crime*

**Crown** /kraʊn/, *n.* The Crown is the *monarch* or *monarchy* in the capacity of *head of state* or an institution of *government*; in a general sense, the *State*.

**Crown Court** /'kraʊn kɔːt/, *n.* + *n.* The superior English *criminal court*, which *hears* all *cases tried* by *jury* and *appeals* from *magistrates' courts*. It sits in major towns in England and Wales.

**custody** /'kʌstədɪ/, *n.* The state of being kept under guard or in prison. (She was held in police custody.)

**custom** /'kʌstəm/, *n.* In English *law* a custom is a practice which has been followed for so long that it has the force of law; custom is the original *source* of the *common law*. In *International Law* a custom is a general practice, followed for a substantial period of time, accepted as law; custom is an important source in the development of International Law. (Laws and customs of war; customary (a.); customary law)
See also *common law*

**damages** /'dæmɪdʒɪz/, *pl.n.* A sum of money which the *court* orders the *defendant* to pay to the *plaintiff* as compensation for a *breach of contract* or a *tort*. (The court awarded the plaintiff £5000 in damages.)

**defence** /dɪ'fens/, *n.* The defence is the lawyer(s) who represent the *defendant* in a *civil* or *criminal* case; the *legal* argument used by the defendant to oppose the accusations made by him or her.

**defendant** /dɪ'fendənt/, *n.* In *criminal proceedings* the defendant is the person *accused* of a *crime*; in *civil* proceedings *legal* action is taken (by the *plaintiff*) against the defendant. (The defendant was found *guilty* and fined £200; the plaintiff *sued* the defendant for *damages* for *breach of contract*; the defendant *state* [in *International Law* proceedings])

**delegate** /'delɪgeɪt/, *v.* To give part of one's powers or rights

to another person or *body* of a lower grade. (delegated (a.); delegation (n.))

**delegated legislation** /'delɪ,geɪtɪd ,ledʒɪˌsleɪʃn/, *a.* + *n.* *Legislation* made by a person (e.g. a *Minister*) or body (e.g. a local *authority*) under authority *delegated* by *Parliament*. Also called 'subordinate legislation'.

**delict** /dɪ'lɪkt/, *n.* A delict is an intentional *breach* of *International Law* by a *subject* of International Law. (delictual (a.))

**delinquency** /dɪ'lɪŋkwənsɪ/, *n. Criminal* behaviour; see also *delinquent*. (*State* delinquency)

**delinquent** /dɪ'lɪŋkwənt/, *n.* A person (especially a young person called a juvenile delinquent) who *commits* minor *crimes*. (delinquency (n.); Juvenile delinquency is a major problem in many British cities.)

**dependency** /dɪ'pendənsɪ/, *n.* A dependency (or 'dependent territory') is a region outside the British Isles which does not belong to the British *Crown*, but which is subject to British *jurisdiction* and is represented in relation to other foreign countries by the UK.

**derogate** /'derəgeɪt/, *v.* To act against an obligation. (*States* must not derogate from their international obligations; derogation (n.))

**deter** /dɪ'tɜː(r)/, *v.* To persuade or encourage someone not to do something because of unpleasant consequences. (Does the death penalty really deter people from *committing murder*? Many *criminals* are not deterred by severe *sentencing*; deterrent (n.), the death penalty is a strong deterrent; deterrence (n.), one of the aims of sentencing is deterrence)

**dicta** /'dɪktə/, (*Latin*). *Dicta* are statements about the *law* in a *judgment* which are not necessary to the *judge's* decision in the *case*. (*Obiter dicta* /'oubitə 'dɪktə/ are simple comments; judicial *dicta* are carefully considered judicial opinions.)

**dismiss** /dɪs'mɪs/, *v.* A *court* dismisses an *appeal* when, after *hearing* the *case*, it refuses to change the decision of the previous court. (Appeal dismissed.)

**dispute** /'dɪspjuːt/, *n.* An argument, disagreement, controversy. (The *International Court of Justice hears* disputes relating to *International Law*.)

**dissolve** /dɪ'zɒlv/, *v.* To end the life of a *Parliament* by public announcement of the *Sovereign*, leading to a *General Election*. (Parliament was dissolved after four years.)

**distinguish** /dɪ'stɪŋgwɪʃ/, *v.* To recognise a difference between a *case* and a previously decided case so that the *court* is not *bound* by the previous decision. (The case must be distinguished from *R. v Summers* on the grounds that the *defendant* in that case did not act under the influence of alcohol.)

**division** /dɪ'vɪʒn/, *n.* The separate sections of the *High Court* and the *Court of Appeal* are called divisions.
See also *Court of Appeal*; *High Court*

**divisional court** /dɪ'vɪʒənl ,kɔːt/, *a.* + *n.* A court consisting of two or three *judges* of the *Queen's Bench*, or *Chancery*, or *Family Divisions* of the *High Court*.
See also *High Court*

**doctrine** /'dɒktrɪn/, *n.* A doctrine is a general principle of *law* formulated by *judges* and *jurists*. (The doctrine of *binding precedent*, a doctrine of *International Law*.)

**domestic** /də'mestɪk/, *a.* Domestic *law* is the national law of a *State*, as opposed to *International Law* (also called 'municipal law'); domestic *proceedings* are proceedings relating to *Family Law* matters.

See also *Family Law*

**dominion** /də'mɪnjən/, *n.* Some *Commonwealth* countries which were UK colonies (e.g. Canada, Australia) were called dominions when they became fully independent from Britain.
See also *Commonwealth*

**drunken driving** /ˌdrʌŋkən 'draɪvɪŋ/, *a.* + *n.* Drunken driving is the *crime* of driving a car, motorcycle, etc., with more than the *legal* limit of alcohol in the blood, or driving while not able to drive properly because of the influence of alcohol.

**EC** /iː 'siː/, *abbrev.* The three European Communities, which are legally distinct, but closely connected: the European Atomic Energy Commission (EURATOM); the European Coal and Steel Community (ECSC) and the European Economic Community (EEC). A group of Western European States including the UK and Republic of Ireland are members of the EC.
(ar. EC *State* – a State which belongs to the European Communities)
See *EC Law*, the *EEC*
See also *Community law*

**EC Law** /iː 'siː ˌlɔː/, *abbrev.* + *n.* EC Law is the system of *law* created by the European Communities. Also called Community Law.
See also *EC*

**EEC Treaty** /iː ˌsiː 'triːtɪ/, *abbrev.* + *n.* The Treaty of Rome, 1957, which first created the *European Economic Community*. Art. 59 EEC – Article 59 of the EEC Treaty.
See also *EC*, *EEC*

**EEC**, *abbrev.* The EEC is the European Economic Community, whose members have agreed to develop economic activity in the Community together by creating a common market. Also called the 'Common Market'. The wider term EC is now in general use. (EEC Law – the system of law created by the EEC) See also *EEC Treaty*, *EC*

**elect** /ɪ'lekt/, *v.* To choose a candidate for an *office* (usually political) by vote. (He was elected president by a large majority; elective (a.); electoral (a.), electoral system; elector (n.))

**election** /ɪ'lekʃn/, *n.* An election is the process of choosing candidates for an *office* (especially a political office) by vote. (The Conservatives won the election; election campaign)
See also *by-election*; *General Election*

**electoral roll** /ɪˌlektərəl 'rəʊl/, *a.* + *n.* The electoral roll is a register of all the people in an area of the UK who have the right to vote in local or national *elections*. Also called 'register of electors'.
See also *election*

**electorate** /ɪ'lektərət/, *n.* The electorate is the group of all the people who have the right to vote in an *election*.
See also *election*

**enact** /ɪ'nækt/, *v.* A *legislative body* such as *Parliament* enacts a *law* when it makes a law following the correct procedure. (enacted (a.))

**enactment** /ɪ'næktmənt/, *n.* An enactment is a written *law* made by *Parliament* or another *legislative* body or a part of such a law, e.g. an *Act of Parliament*.

**enforce** /ɪn'fɔːs/, *v.* To cause or force people to obey (a *law*, etc) (The police enforce the law.)

**enforceable** /ɪn'fɔːsəbl/, *a.* A *law* etc. is enforceable when it is possible to cause or force people to obey it. (Would a law to stop people drinking alcohol before going to football matches be enforceable? Opposite: unenforceable)

**entitle** /ɪn'taɪtl/, *v.* You are entitled to something if you have a *legal* right to it. (In Britain men and women are entitled to equal pay for equal work.)

**entrenched** /ɪn'trentʃt/, *a.* When rights are entrenched they are specially protected by *law* so that it is very difficult to change them.

**equitable** /'ekwɪtəbl/, *a.* Of or relating to *Equity*, valid in Equity. (Equitable rights and *remedies*)
See *Equity*

**Equity** /'ekwɪtɪ/, *n.* Equity is a special area of English *law* which was first created by the *Lord Chancellor*, then developed by the *Court* of Chancery (now called the *Chancery Division* of the *High Court*). It consists of rules and *remedies* which supplement the *common law* when this is necessary for *justice* in a particular *case*.

**European Commission of Human Rights** /ˌjʊərəˌpɪən kə'mɪʃn ˌhjuːmən 'raɪts/, *a.* + *n.* + *prep.* + *a.* + *pl.n.* The European Commission of Human Rights is a *body* created by the *European Convention on Human Rights* to investigate complaints of *breaches* of the Convention and where possible reach a friendly *settlement*.
See also *European Convention on Human Rights*

**European Community** /ˌjʊərəˌpɪən kə'mjuːnətɪ/, *a.* + *a.* + *n.* See *EC*

**European Convention on Human Rights** /ˌjʊərəˌpɪən kən'venʃn ɒn ˌhjuːmən 'raɪts/, *a.* + *n.* + *prep.* + *a.* + *pl.n.* The European Convention on Human Rights is a *convention* in force since 1953 for the protection of the *human rights* of all people in the *Member States* of the *Council of Europe*.
See also *Council of Europe*

**European Court** /ˌjʊərəˌpɪən 'kɔːt/, *a.* + *n.* The Court of Justice of the European Communities, with *jurisdiction* over questions of *Community law*.
See also *Community law*

**European Court of Human Rights** /ˌjʊərəˌpɪən kɔːt əv ˌhjuːmən 'raɪts/, *a.* + *n.* + *prep.* + *a.* + *pl.n.* The European Court of Human Rights is the *court* created by the *European Convention on Human Rights*, which has *jurisdiction* over *cases* brought under the Convention.
See also *European Convention on Human Rights*

**European Economic Community**, see *EEC*

**European Parliament** /ˌjʊərəˌpɪən 'paːləmənt/, *a.* + *n.* The European Parliament is an *organ* of the three European Communities with advisory and supervisory functions, composed of directly *elected* members from each *Member State*.
See also *Community law*

**evidence** /'evɪdəns/, *n.* In *Criminal Law* the evidence is everything (objects, statements, documents) which helps to show how a *crime* happened.
See also *Criminal Evidence*

**executive** /ɪg'zekjʊtɪv/, *n.* The executive is the branch of *government* which puts into effect the policy and *laws* formulated by the *legislature*; in the UK, the *Crown* and *Ministers* (also part of the legislature), the *Civil Service* and local *authorities*. (executive (a.))

**executor** /ɪg'zekjʊtə(r)/, *n.* An executor is a person appointed by a *will* to *administer* the property of the person who made the will, and give effect to his or her wishes.
See also *will*

***ex parte*** /ˌeks 'paːtɪ/, *Latin*; *R. v Smith ex parte Jones* is the name of a *case* in which the *Crown* represents the *State*

against Smith in *criminal proceedings* and the application to the *court* was made by an individual called Jones.
See also *citation*; *R*.

**extradite** /'ekstrədaɪt/, *v*. To give a person who is suspected of or who has *committed* a *crime* in another *State* to the *authorities* of that State for *trial* or punishment. It is regulated by *treaties* between the two States and does not apply to political *offenders*. (The French *Government* refused to extradite the two French *nationals*; extradition (n.))

**Family Division** /'fæməlɪ dɪ,vɪʒn/, *n. + n*. A Division of the *High Court* with *jurisdiction* over *cases* relating to *Family Law* and the transfer of property on death.
See also *Family Law*; *High Court*

**Family Law** /'fæməlɪ ,lɔ:/, *n. + n*. Family Law is the area of *law* relating to the organisation of the family and the *legal* relations of its members.

**feudal law** /'fju:dl ,lɔ:/, *a. + n*. The *land law* of the feudal system, a political and social system found all over Europe in medieval times.

**fine** /faɪn/, *n*. A fine is a sum of money which a person is ordered to pay as punishment for a *crime*. (A £100 fine)

**fine** /faɪn/, *v*. To order someone to pay a sum of money as punishment for a *crime*. (He was fined £20 for a parking *offence*.)

**first instance** /,fɔ:st 'ɪnstəns/, *a. + n*. A *case* of first instance is one which is before a *court* for the first time, not an *appeal*; a court of first instance is one which *hears* cases of first instance.

**follow** /'fɒləʊ/, *v*. To apply the principles contained in a *precedent* and so act in accordance with it. (The *court* followed *Carlill v Carbolic Smoke Ball Co*.)

**French Law** /'frentʃ ,lɔ:/, *a. + n*. French Law is the system of *law* developed in France.

**General Election** /,dʒenrəl ɪ'lekʃn/, *a. + n*. A General Election is an *election* in the whole of a country to *elect* a new *Parliament*.
See also *by-election*

**government** /'gʌvənmənt/, *n*. Government is the process and method of governing a *State*; the government is the *body* of people who are responsible for governing a State; in the UK the Government is the *executive* generally or in *Parliament* the political party in power. (Democratic government; the Italian Government; a cut in government spending; the Government was almost defeated in the *Commons* yesterday; govern (v.))
See also *executive*

**grant** /gra:nt/, *v*. To give something formally or *legally*. (The *convict* was granted a pardon under the *prerogative of mercy*.)

**guilty** /'gɪltɪ/, *a*. A person is guilty of an *offence* if s/he has *committed* it. (He was found guilty of *murder* and *sentenced* to *life imprisonment*. Opposite: not guilty)

**habeas corpus** /,heɪbɪəs 'kɔ:pəs/, *(Latin)*. The *writ* of habeas corpus is an order from the *High Court* to bring a person who is held in *custody* (e.g. in prison) before a *court* to make sure that s/he is not held *illegally*.

**Hansard** /'hænsa:d/, *n*. Hansard is the name of the official report of debates in the UK *Parliament*.

**head of State** /,hed əv 'steɪt/, *n. + prep. + n*. The head of state is the person who acts as the formal head of a *State* and represents it in *International Law*. S/he may have wide executive powers (e.g. the President of the United States) or be only a symbol of power (e.g. the British *monarch*) depending on the *constitution* of the State.

**hear** /hɪə(r)/, *v*. To *try* a *case*.

**hearing** /'hɪərɪŋ/, *n*. A hearing is an occasion on which a *case* is examined and decided before a *court*, *tribunal* etc., a *trial*. (The hearing is next Monday at the *Central Criminal Court*.)

**heir** /eə(r)/, *n*. An heir is a person with the *legal* right to receive property, a title, etc., when the owner or holder (usually an older member of the same family) dies. (Heir to the throne; he is heir to a large fortune; heiress (for a woman or girl))

**High Court** /'haɪ ,kɔ:t/, *a. + n*. The High Court of Justice consists of the *Queen's Bench*, *Family* and *Chancery Divisions*. It has mainly *civil jurisdiction* to *hear* cases of *first instance* and appeals. It is third in the hierarchy of *courts* in England and Wales after the *House of Lords* and *Court of Appeal*.

**hold** /həʊld/, *v*. To decide (in a *judgment*). (It was held that a valid *contract* had been made.)
See also *judgment*

**Home Secretary** /,həʊm 'sekrətrɪ/, *a. + n*. The Home Secretary is the British *Government Minister* who is head of the Home Office, the *ministry* which deals with internal affairs in England and Wales. S/he is responsible for the general administration of the *Criminal Law*, police and prisons, nationality and immigration, and advises the *Sovereign* on the exercise of the *prerogative of mercy*.

**House of Commons** /,haʊs əv 'kɒmənz/, *n. + prep. + n*. The House of Commons is the Lower, but more powerful House of the UK *Parliament*. It is a *representative body* which consists of 650 *elected* members. Its main functions are representation of the people, control of finance and policy and *legislation*. Also called 'the *Commons*'.
See also *House of Lords*; *Member of Parliament*

**House of Lords** /,haʊs əv 'lɔ:dz/, *n. + prep. + n*. The House of Lords is the Upper House of the UK *Parliament*. It is not a *representative body* and consists of the *Lords Spiritual* and the *Lords Temporal*. Its main parliamentary functions are debate on matters of public interest and *legislation*, which it has power to delay. As a *judicial* body it is the Supreme *Court* of *Appeal* in the UK. *Cases* are *heard* by an *Appellate* Committee which usually consists of five or three *Law Lords*. Also called 'the *Lords*'.
See also *House of Commons*; *Lords Spiritual*; *Lords Temporal*

**Houses of Parliament** /,haʊzɪz əv 'pa:ləmənt/, *pl.n. + prep. + n*. The buildings in Westminster, London, where the UK *Parliament* sits; the *House of Commons* and the *House of Lords*.
See also *House of Commons*; *House of Lords*; *parliament*

**human rights** /,hju:mən 'raɪts/, *a. + pl.n*. Fundamental rights of all human beings (such as the right to life, the right to freedom of thought and the right to work) which are generally protected by *law*. (*UN* Universal Declaration of Human Rights; human rights law)

**ICJ** /aɪ si: 'dʒeɪ/, *abbrev*. See *International Court of Justice*

**illegal** /ɪli:gl/, *a*. Not *legal* – it is illegal to do something which is against the *law*. (Opposite: *legal* (a.); illegally (adv.))

**immunity** /ɪ'mju:nətɪ/, *n*. Freedom from a legal obligation or consequence such as *prosecution* for *crimes*. (*State* immunity: foreign States are not subject to the *jurisdiction* of national *courts* in other States.)

**imprison** /ɪm'prɪzn/, *v*. To put in prison. (He was imprisoned

for six months.)
See also *imprisonment*

**imprisonment** /ɪm'prɪznmənt/, *n.* Imprisonment is the state of being kept in prison. It is a method of punishing *criminals* by taking away their liberty. (A term of imprisonment is the period which a person has to spend in prison; life imprisonment is the longest possible prison *sentence*, but is not necessarily for the rest of a person's life. Imprison (v.); imprisoned (a.))

**indecency** /ɪn'di:sənsɪ/, *n.* Indecency is the *crime* of doing something which the average person would find shocking or disgusting in that it offends public moral values, e.g. homosexual acts in public.

**indictable offence** /ɪndaɪtəbl ə'fens/, *a. + n.* An offence which could be tried by *jury* in the *Crown Court*, now called a 'notifiable offence'.

**indictment** /ɪn'daɪtmənt/, *n.* A person is *tried* on indictment when s/he is tried by *jury* in the *Crown Court* for an *indictable offence*. The indictment is a formal document of accusation which is read out in *court*.
See also *indictable offence*

**injured party** /ˌɪndʒəd 'pa:tɪ/, *a. + n.* In a *civil case* the injured party is the person who has suffered harm, damage or a wrong.

**International Court of Justice** /ˌɪntə,næʃnəl ,kɔ:t əv 'dʒʌstɪs/, *a. + n. + prep. + n.* The International Court of Justice is the main *judicial organ* of the United Nations Organisation and has power to *hear disputes* relating to *International Law*. (ICJ (abbrev.))

**International Law** /ˌɪntə'næʃnəl ,lɔ:/, *a. + n.* International Law is the system of *law* which regulates relations between *States*. It is a special system of *legal* rules which is not part of any national system of law. Also called public international law. (Not related to private international law – see *Conflict of Laws*.)

**international practice** /ˌɪntə'næʃnəl ,præktɪs/, *a. + n.* A general practice of *International Law* which is not yet accepted as obligatory and has therefore not yet become a rule of *customary* International Law.

**issue** /'ɪʃu:/, *n.* An issue is a point of *dispute* or matter for consideration in a *court case*. (The main issue in the present case is who should pay *costs*.)

**issue** /'ɪʃu:/, *v.* To give out officially. (The *court* issued a *writ* of *habeas corpus*.)

**J** /dʒeɪ/. *abbrev.* Justice, the *title* of an English *High Court* judge. (Smith, J. – Mr Justice Smith)

**judge** /dʒʌdʒ/, *n.* A judge is a person with *authority* to *hear* and decide *disputes* brought before a *court* for decision. (judge (v.))

**judgment** /'dʒʌdʒmənt/, *n.* The judgment is the *legal* reasoning and decision of a *court* in a *case* brought before it.

**judicial** /dʒu:'dɪʃl/, *a.* Of or relating to *courts* of *law* or the administration of *justice* or the *office* of a *judge*. (judicial appointments; *judicial decision*)

**judicial decision** /dʒu:,dɪʃl dɪ'sɪʒn/, *a. + n.* See *judicial precedent*

**judicial precedent** /dʒu:,dɪʃl 'presɪdənt/, *a. + n.* Judicial precedent is the *doctrine* by which decisions of *courts* in previous *cases* are considered as a *source of law* which will influence or *bind* courts in later similar cases. A judicial precedent is an earlier *judicial decision* which influences or binds courts in later similar cases.
See also *authority*; *binding precedent*

**judicial review** /dʒu:,dɪʃl rɪ'vju:/, *a. + n.* Judicial review of administrative action is the power of the *High Court* to make sure that the acts and decisions of inferior *courts*, *tribunals* and administrative *bodies* are *legal* and valid. The Court may *grant* the 'prerogative orders' of *certiorari*, *mandamus* and *prohibition*.
See also *Queen's Bench Division*

**judiciary** /dʒu:'dɪʃərɪ/, *n.* The judiciary is a collective term for all *judges*. (In the UK, the *Sovereign* is head of the judiciary.)

**jurisdiction** /ˌdʒʊərɪs'dɪkʃn/, *n.* The power of a *court* to hear and decide a *case*. (*civil* jurisdiction: jurisdiction over civil cases; *criminal* jurisdiction: jurisdiction over criminal cases; *appellate* jurisdiction: jurisdiction to hear appeals)

**Jurisprudence** /ˌdʒʊərɪs'pru:dəns/, *n.* Jurisprudence is the science or philosophy of *law* – the study of fundamental questions of law in general, not the explanation, criticism or application of the law of a particular system.

**jurist** /'dʒʊərɪst/, *n.* A jurist is a great expert in the *law* who is normally an academic *lawyer*, writer or consultant (but may also be a *judge* or practising lawyer).

**jury** /'dʒʊərɪ/, *n.* A body of persons (usually 12) who decide the facts of a *case* (usually *criminal*) and give a decision of *guilty* or *not guilty* called a verdict. The *judge* directs the jury on matters of *law*.

**justice** /'dʒʌstɪs/, *n.* Justice is the moral ideal of being right, just; a justice is a *judge*. (Opposite: injustice)

**justice of the peace** /ˌdʒʌstɪs əv ðə 'pi:s/, *n. + prep. + art. + n.* A justice of the peace is a *judicial* officer who is not a professional *lawyer* who exercises judicial functions mainly in the *magistrates' courts*. Also called a *lay magistrate*.
See also *magistrates' courts*

**juvenile court** /'dʒu:vənaɪl ,kɔ:t/, *n. + n.* A special branch of a *magistrates' court* which *hears criminal cases* against children and young persons under 17 and deals with other matters relating to children.

**kidnapping** /'kɪdnæpɪŋ/, *n.* Kidnapping is the *crime* of stealing or taking a person away by force, fear etc., without their consent.

**Labour Law** /'leɪbə ,lɔ:/, *n. + n.* Labour Law is the area of *law* relating to the employment of workers. It includes their *contracts* and conditions of work, trade unions and the *legal* aspects of industrial relations. Also called Industrial Law.

**land** /lænd/, *n.* In *law*, land is the part of the earth's surface which it is possible to own. It generally includes the air above it, soil below it, trees, buildings, etc. on it.
See also *Land Law*

**Land Law** /'lænd ,lɔ:/, *n. + n.* Land Law is the area of *law* which deals with rights and interests related to owning and using *land*. Land is the most important form of property, so the name Land Law is often used for the Law of Property in general.
See also *Conveyancing Law*; *land*

**landlord** /'lændlɔ:d/, *n.* A landlord is a person who owns or holds *land* which someone else pays to use and possess under a *contract* called a *lease*.
See also *lease*; *tenant*

**law** /lɔ:/, *n.* The law is the body of rules with *authority* to govern the actions and relations of people in an organised political community or among *States*. A law (*plural*: laws) is one of the rules in a system of law, which deals with a particular subject. (You must obey the law; a new law on education comes into force next month.)

**law-abiding** /'lɔː əbaɪdɪŋ/, *a.* A law-abiding citizen is someone who obeys the *law*.

**law and order** /,lɔː ənd 'ɔːdə(r)/, *n. + conj. + n.* A state of peace in a society where the *law* is generally respected. (The forces of law and order: those responsible for the administration of justice, e.g. the police and *courts*)

**Law Commission** /'lɔː kə,mɪʃn/, *n. + n.* The Law Commission is a *body* created in 1965 to review the *law* and prepare programmes for its systematic *reform*, development and modernisation. Two separate Commissions exist for the English and Scottish *legal systems*.

**lawful** /'lɔːfʊl/, *a.* Within the *law*, *legal*; recognised by law. (lawful practice; his lawful wife; lawfully (adv.))

**Law Lords** /'lɔː lɔːdz/, *n. + pl.n.* See *Lord of Appeal in Ordinary*

**Law of Contract** /,lɔː əv 'kɒntrækt/, *n. + prep. + n.* The Law of Contract (also Contract Law, Contract) is the *law* relating to *contracts*, i.e. legally *binding* agreements.
See also *contract*

**law officer** /'lɔː ,ɒfɪsə(r)/, *n. + n.* The Law Officers of the Crown are the *Attorney-General* and the *Solicitor-General* (for England and Wales), the Lord Advocate and Solicitor-General for Scotland (for Scotland). They are the *legal* advisers and *representatives* of the *Sovereign* and *Government*.

**Law of Tort** /,lɔː əv 'tɔːt/, *n. + prep. + n.* The Law of Tort (also called Tort, Tort Law, the Law of Torts) is the *law* relating to *torts*, i.e. *civil* wrongs independent of *contract*.
See also *tort*

**law reform** /'lɔː rɪ,fɔːm/, *n. + n.* Law reform is the process of revising and changing the *law* to make it better.

**law reports** /'lɔː rɪ,pɔːts/, *n. + n.* The law reports are written reports of decisions of the superior *courts* published for the information of the *legal* profession. (the All England Law reports)

**lawyer** /'lɔːjə(r)/, *n.* A general term for a member of the *legal* profession, e.g. a *judge*, *barrister*, *solicitor*, *law* teacher.

**lay** /leɪ/, *a.* Not expert (in the *law*), not a professional (*lawyer*). (lay peer; lay magistrate)

**lay down** /leɪ 'daʊn/, *v. + prep. [lay, laid, laid]* To decide as a *legal* principle in a *judgment* (In *Carlill v Carbolic Smoke Ball Co.* it was laid down that an offer may be made to a particular person or to the world in general.)

**LC** /el 'siː/, *abbrev.* See *Lord Chancellor*

**lease** /liːs/, *n.* A lease is a *contract* between the owner or holder of property and a person or persons who usually agree to pay money for the use and possession of the property for a fixed period of time.
See also *landlord*; *tenant*

**legal** /'liːgl/, *a.* Of or relating to the *law*; allowed by law, not contrary to law. (The English *legal system*; is it legal to smoke marijuana in your country?) (legally /'liːgəlɪ/ (adv.), legality /,liː'gælətɪ/ (n.))

**Legal History** /,liːgl 'hɪstərɪ/, *a. + n.* Legal History is the study of the origins and historical development of a particular *legal system* or of legal systems, principles and institutions in general.

**legal system** /'liːgl ,sɪstəm/, *a. + n.* All the institutions, bodies of *laws* and principles, ideas, methods, procedures, traditions and practices which together form an organised system for the application of law in a *State* or community. (the English legal system)

**legislate** /'ledʒɪsleɪt/, *v.* To pass a *law* or laws, *enact* into law. (legislative (a.), legislative body, legislative powers)

**legislation** /,ledʒɪs'leɪʃn/, *n.* Legislation is all or part of a country's written *law*, *statute law*; also the process of making written law.
See also *statute*

**legislator** /'ledʒɪsleɪtə(r)/, *n.* One who *legislates*, a member of the *legislature*.
See also *legislate*

**legislature** /'ledʒɪsleɪtʃə(r)/, *n.* The legislature is the supreme *body* with responsibility and *authority* to *legislate* for a political unit such as a *State*.
See also *legislate*

**liability** /,laɪə'bɪlətɪ/, *n.* *Legal* responsibility for one's actions together with an obligation to repair any injury caused. (She admitted liability for the accident.)

**liable** /'laɪəbl/, *a.* Subject to a *legal* obligation; *legally* responsible for one's acts. (*Offenders* are liable to a £50 *fine*; an employer may be liable for the *torts* of his employee.)

**litigant** /'lɪtɪgənt/, *n.* A litigant is a *party* in a *civil action*.
See also *action*; *litigation*

**litigation** /,lɪtɪ'geɪʃn/, *n.* Litigation is the process of proceeding against someone in a *court action*.

**LJ** /el 'dʒeɪ/, *abbrev.* See *Lord Justices of Appeal*

**LL.B.** /el el 'biː/, *abbrev.* Letters used after the name of a Law graduate, short for 'Bachelor of Laws'. (Martina Ward, LL.B.)

**LL.M.** /el el 'em/, *abbrev.* Letters used after the name of a person with a Master's degree in Law, short for Master of Laws.

**Lord Chancellor** /,lɔːd 'tʃɑːnsələ(r)/, *n. + n.* The Lord High Chancellor is the chief *judicial* officer in the British *Constitution*. S/he is a *peer* and *Cabinet Minister*, *Speaker* of the *House of Lords*, president of the Supreme Court and of the House of Lords sitting as a final *court* of *appeal*. S/he appoints *magistrates*, recommends people for high *judicial office*, and has responsibility for the administration of the courts, *law reform*, etc. (LC (abbrev.))

**Lord Chief Justice** /,lɔːd ,tʃiːf 'dʒʌstɪs/, *n. + n. + n.* The Lord Chief Justice of England is the President of the *Queen's Bench Division* of the *High Court* and the *Criminal Division* of the *Court of Appeal*. S/he is a *peer* and the second most important member of the *judiciary* after the *Lord Chancellor*. (LCJ (abbrev.))

**Lord Justice** /,lɔːd 'dʒʌstɪs/, *n. + n.* See *Lord Justice of Appeal*

**Lord Justice of Appeal** /,lɔːd ,dʒʌstɪs əv ə'piːl/, *n. + n. + prep. + n.* The *title* of an ordinary *judge* of the *Court of Appeal*, referred to in *legal* books as Smith LJ or Smith and Jones L.JJ. (LJ (abbrev.); Lords Justices /'dʒʌstɪsɪz/ of Appeal (plural); L.JJ. (plural abbrev.))

**Lord of Appeal in Ordinary** /,lɔːd əv ə,piːl ɪn 'ɔːdɪnərɪ/, *n. + prep. + n. + prep. + a.* The *title* of a *judge* with a life *peerage* who exercises the *judicial* functions of the *House of Lords*. (Lords of Appeal in Ordinary (plural), also called the 'Law Lords')

**Lords** /lɔːdz/, *pl.n.* See *House of Lords*

**Lords Spiritual** /,lɔːdz 'spɪrɪtʃʊəl/, *pl.n. + a.* The Lords Spiritual are 26 senior members of the Church of England (the archbishops of Canterbury and York and certain bishops) who have the right to sit in the *House of Lords*.
See also *House of Lords*; *Lords Temporal*

**Lords Temporal** /,lɔːdz 'tempərəl/, *pl.n. + a.* The Lords Temporal are men and women who have the right to sit in the *House of Lords* because they are hereditary or life *peers* or *Lords of Appeal in Ordinary*.
See also *House of Lords*; *Lords Spiritual*

**magistrate** /'mædʒɪstreɪt/, *n.* A *lay* magistrate is a *justice of the peace*; a stipendiary magistrate has greater powers and receives a salary.
See also *justice of the peace*

**magistrates' courts** /'mædʒɪstreɪts ,kɔ:ts/, *n.* + *n.* The lowest *courts* of *first instance* with limited *civil* and *criminal jurisdiction*, generally composed of 2–7 *lay justices of the peace*. All criminal *prosecutions* begin here.
See also *justice of the peace*

**mandamus** /,mæn'deɪməs/, *n. Mandamus* is an order from the *High Court* to a *tribunal*, public official, etc., to perform a public duty, e.g. hold an *election*, *hear* an *appeal*.
See also *judicial review*

**manslaughter** /'mænslɔ:tə(r)/, *n.* Manslaughter is the *crime* of *unlawful* killing which is not *murder*, but is not an accident, e.g. killing by negligence or when the killer does not have full mental responsibility for his or her acts.
See also *murder*

**Master of the Rolls** /,ma:stə(r) əv ðə 'rəʊlz/, *n.* + *prep.* + *art.* + *pl.n.* The Master of the Rolls is the President of the *Civil Division* of the *Court of Appeal*, the most important civil *judge* in England outside the *House of Lords*.

**Member of Parliament** /,membə(r) əv 'pa:ləmənt/, *n.* + *prep.* + *n.* A Member of Parliament is a person *elected* by voters in a UK *constituency* to represent them in the *House of Commons*. (MP (abbrev.); Members of Parliament (plural))

**Member State** /'membə steɪt/, *n.* + *n.* A Member State is a *State* which is a member of an international organisation. (Member States of the EC)

**MEP** /em i: 'pi:/, *abbrev.* An MEP is a Member of the *European Parliament*. (MEPs (plural))
See also *European Parliament*

**Minister** /'mɪnɪstə(r)/, *n.* A Minister of the Crown is a member of the *House of Commons* or *House of Lords* who holds one of the chief political offices in the UK *government*, e.g. as head of a Government Department.
See also *Cabinet*

**ministry** /'mɪnɪstrɪ/, *n.* A ministry is a *government* department which has a *Minister* as its head; the Ministry is the whole group of Ministers who form a government. (the Ministry of Defence; The Ministry must resign if it loses the confidence of the *Commons*.)

**moot** /mu:t/, *n.* A moot is an imaginary *case* argued by *law* students for practice in presenting *cases* in court.

**monarch** /'mɒnək/, *n.* King or Queen in a *monarchy*.
See also *monarchy*

**monarchy** /'mɒnəkɪ/, *n.* Monarchy is the system of *government* in which a single person called King or Queen holds the *office* of *head of state* for life, usually by hereditary right; a monarchy is a *State* governed by such a system. (In an absolute monarchy the monarch *rules* the country personally; in a constitutional monarchy s/he has no real power to govern.)

**money Bill** /'mʌnɪ ,bɪl/, *n.* + *n.* A *Bill* which, in the opinion of the *Speaker* of the *House of Commons*, relates only to taxation and public spending.

**MP** /em 'pi:/, *abbrev.* See *Member of Parliament*. (She is an MP; there are 650 MPs in the *House of Commons*.)

**municipal law** /mju:'nɪsɪpl ,lɔ:/, *a.* + *n.* The national *law* of a *state*, as opposed to *International Law*. Also called 'domestic law'.

**murder** /'mɜ:də(r)/, *n.* Murder is the *crime* of *unlawful* killing *committed* with the intention to kill or seriously injure. (murder (v.); murderer (n.))

**national** /'næʃnəl/, *n.* A national is a person who is a *citizen* of a *state*. (Foreign nationals must register with the immigration *authorities*; nationality (n.))
See also *citizen*

**norm** /nɔ:m/, *n.* A rule.

**offence** /ə'fens/, *n.* A crime. You *commit* an offence if you do something which is against the *law*. (A *common-law* offence is one which is defined by rules of common law; a *statutory* offence is one which is defined by *statute*; a parking offence is the offence of parking your car in a place where it is *illegal* to park; offender (n.))
See also *crime*; *indictable offence*; *summary*

**offender** /ə'fendə(r)/, *n.* An offender is a person who has *committed* a crime.
See also *crime*; *offence*

**offeree** /,ɒfə'ri:/, *n.* In the *Law of Contract* the offeree is the person who accepts an offer to form a *contract*.

**offeror** /'ɒfərə(r)/, *n.* In the *Law of Contract* the offeror is the person who makes an offer to form a *contract*.

**office** /'ɒfɪs/, *n.* Public position of *authority*, especially as part of the *government*. (the office of president; the last *Lord Chancellor* held office for seven years.)

**Old Bailey** /,əʊld 'beɪlɪ/, *a.* + *n.* The Old Bailey is the popular name for the *Central Criminal Court*.
See also *Central Criminal Court*

**organ** /'ɔ:gən/, *n.* An official organisation or *body* which has a special purpose. (*state* organ; *judicial* organ; Parliament is the main *legislative* organ.)

**overrule** /,əʊvə'ru:l/, *v.* A *court* overrules a decision in an earlier *case* when it uses a different principle to decide a later case, so creating a new *precedent*. The earlier decision is overruled. (Compare: a decision which is changed on *appeal* is 'reversed'.)

**ownership** /'əʊnəʃɪp/, *n.* Ownership is the state of being an owner; the exclusive right to use, possess and dispose of property. (own (v.); owner (n.))

**parliament** /'pa:ləmənt/, *n.* A parliament is a national *body* which represents the people of a *state* and has supreme *legislative* powers within the state; Parliament is the *legislature* of the UK, consisting of the *Sovereign*, the *House of Lords* and the *House of Commons*. (parliamentary (a.))

**parliamentary sovereignty** /,pa:lə,mentrɪ 'sɒvrəntɪ/, *a.* + *n.* The basic *doctrine* of British *Constitutional Law* according to which Parliament is *sovereign* and has unlimited *legislative* power.

**party** /'pa:tɪ/, *n.* Each of the sides involved in a *legal dispute* is a party to the *case*.

**patent law** /'peɪtənt ,lɔ:/, *n.* + *n.* The *law* relating to the exclusive right to make and sell an invention.

**peer** /pɪə(r)/, *n.* A peer has a *title* of nobility *granted* by the *Crown* such as Baron or Duke, which gives him the right to sit and vote in the *House of Lords*. (life peer; hereditary peer; peeress (for a woman))
See also *Lords Temporal*

**peerage** /'pɪərɪdʒ/, *n.* A peerage is a *title* of nobility which may be *granted* by the *Crown*; the peerage is the collective term for all *peers*. (She was granted a peerage for her life's work in education; few of the peerage regularly attend sittings of the *House of Lords*.)

**penal** /'pi:nl/, *a.* Relating to punishment (for *crime*). (Penal policy; the penal system)

**per incuriam** /'pɜ:r ɪn'kjʊərɪæm/, *(Latin).* A decision of a *court* is made *per incuriam* if the court does not *apply* a relevant *law* or *follow* a *binding precedent*.

**plaintiff** /ˈpleɪntɪf/, *n.* The plaintiff is the person who takes *legal* action against somebody (called the *defendant*) in a *civil case*. (The plaintiff *sued* the defendant for *breach of contract*.)

**plead guilty** /ˌpliːd ˈɡɪltɪ/, *v.* + *a.* You plead guilty when you state at the beginning of a *trial* that you *committed* the *crime* you are *accused* of. (Opposite: plead not guilty)

**precedent** /ˈpresɪdənt/, *n.* See *judicial precedent*

**prerogative of mercy** /prɪˌrɒɡətɪv əv ˈmɜːsɪ/, *n.* + *prep.* + *n.* The prerogative of mercy (part of the *Royal Prerogative*) is the power of the *Crown* to excuse a *criminal offence* or reduce a punishment on the advice of the *Home Secretary*.

**Prime Minister** /ˌpraɪm ˈmɪnɪstə(r)/, *a.* + *n.* The Prime Minister (usually the leader of the political party with a majority in the *House of Commons*) is the head of the UK *Government*. S/he chooses and presides over the *Cabinet*, is leader of all government policies and is chief adviser to the *Sovereign* on matters of government.

**private law** /ˈpraɪvɪt ˌlɔː/, *a.* + *n.* In general, private law is the part of the *law* which deals with relations between ordinary individuals, and also between individuals and the *State* in circumstances where the State has no special rights or powers.
See also *public law*

**Privy Council** /ˌprɪvɪ ˈkaʊnsəl/, *a.* + *n.* The Privy Council is a council of the British *Sovereign* composed of persons who hold or have held high political, *legal*, or ecclesiastical *office*, and including the Royal Family. Its functions are mainly formal. The *Judicial* Committee of the Privy Council mainly *hears appeals* from *Commonwealth* countries and colonies. (Privy Counsellor [a member of the Privy Council])

**probation** /prəˈbeɪʃn/, *n.* If a person *convicted* of a *crime* is put on probation, instead of punishment s/he must behave well for a period of 1–3 years and accept the instructions of a social worker called a probation officer. If s/he is convicted of another crime while on probation s/he will also be punished for the original crime.

**procedure** /prəˈsiːdʒə(r)/, *n.* Procedure is the way business is conducted in an official meeting etc.; the formal manner of starting and conducting *legal* action in a *civil* or *criminal court*. (parliamentary procedure; the procedure of the *High Court* is mainly regulated by the Rules of the Supreme Court.)

**proceedings** /prəˈsiːdɪŋz/, *pl.n.* The act or process of proceeding against someone by *legal* action in a *civil* or *criminal court*, a lawsuit. (He took proceedings against his employer; criminal proceedings)

**prohibition** /ˌprəʊhɪˈbɪʃn/, *n.* Prohibition is an order from the *High Court* to prevent an act by a *court* or administrative *body* against the rights of an individual.
See also *judicial review*

**promulgate** /ˈprɒmlɡeɪt/, *v.* To bring a *law* into effect by official public announcement. (promulgation (n.))

**prorogue** /prəˈrəʊɡ/, *v.* To bring a *session* of *Parliament* to an end.

**prosecute** /ˈprɒsɪkjuːt/, *v.* To take *criminal proceedings* against someone. (The police decided to prosecute the two men for criminal damage.)

**prosecution** /ˌprɒsɪˈkjuːʃn/, *n.* Prosecution is the process of preparing and presenting the *case* against a person *accused* of a *crime*, taking *criminal proceedings* against someone; the prosecution is the person or *body* that *prosecutes*, including the *lawyers* who act against the accused person. (In some countries homosexuals face prosecution; the *defendant* was questioned carefully by the prosecution.)

**prosecutor** /ˈprɒsɪkjuːtə(r)/, *n.* The person who presents the *case* in a *criminal court* against a person *accused* of a *crime*.

**provide** /prəˈvaɪd/, *v.* To set down as a rule or condition in a *statute*, *contract*, etc. (The Parliament Act 1911 provides that a *Parliament* shall not last for more than five years.)

**provision** /prəˈvɪʒn/, *n.* A provision is a rule or condition in a *statute*, *contract*, etc. (under the provisions of the Theft Act 1968)

**public Bill** /ˈpʌblɪk ˌbɪl/, *a.* + *n.* A *Bill* relating to matters of general concern which normally *applies* to all the UK and is introduced in *Parliament* by a *government Minister*. Compare a 'private Bill', which only concerns a particular person, *body* or place.
See also *Bill*

**public law** /ˈpʌblɪk ˌlɔː/, *a.* + *n.* In general, public law is the part of the *legal system* which deals with the *State* and also with relations between the State and ordinary individuals in circumstances where the State has special rights or powers.
See also *private law*

**QB** /kjuː ˈbiː/ or **QBD** /kjuː biː ˈdiː/, *abbrev.* The *Queen's Bench Division* of the *High Court*.
See also *Queen's Bench Division*

**Queen in Council** /ˌkwiːn ɪn ˈkaʊnsəl/, *n.* + *prep.* + *n.* The *Sovereign* and the *Privy Council*.
See also *Privy Council*

**Queen in Parliament** /ˌkwiːn ɪn ˈpɑːləmənt/, *n.* + *prep.* + *n.* The Queen in Parliament is the title of the UK *legislature*, composed of the *Sovereign* and both *Houses of Parliament*.

**Queen's Bench Division** /ˌkwiːnz ˈbentʃ dɪˌvɪʒn/, *n.* + *n.* + *n.* A Division of the *High Court* with *civil* and *criminal jurisdiction*, which is also responsible for *judicial review*. (QB or QBD (abbrev.))
See also *High Court*; *judicial review*

**R.** /ɑː(r)/, *abbrev.* Regina or Rex, Latin for Queen or King. *R. v Smith* is the name of a *case* in which the *Crown* represents the *State* in *criminal proceedings* against Smith. We say 'The Crown against Smith'.
See also *citation*

**rape** /reɪp/, *n.* The crime of having sex with a woman or girl without her consent, e.g. by force, fear or deception.

**ratify** /ˈrætɪfaɪ/, *v.* To confirm or approve an agreement, *treaty*, etc. officially so that it becomes valid. (*Legislation* passed by the Isle of Man *Parliament* must be ratified by the *Queen in Council*; ratification)

***ratio decidendi*** /ˌreɪʃɪəʊ desɪˈdendɪ/, (*Latin*). The *ratio decidendi* is the reason for a *judicial decision*, the principle on which it is based. It is the part of the decision which is *binding* as a *precedent*. (*rationes decidendi* (plural))
See also *binding precedent*

**recover** /rɪˈkʌvə(r)/, *v.* To get money from someone as compensation as the result of a favourable *judgment* in a *civil action*. (The *plaintiff* recovered £5000 in *damages*.)

**rehabilitate** /ˌriːhəˈbɪlɪteɪt/, *v.* To make a person (e.g. a *criminal*) able to live a normal life in the community again by education, training, etc. (rehabilitation (n.))

**remand in custody** /rɪˌmɑːnd ɪn ˈkʌstədɪ/, *v.* + *prep.* + *n.* If a person *accused* of a *crime* is remanded in custody s/he is sent back from a *court* to prison to wait for *trial* at a later date, e.g. while the police continue to investigate the *case*.

**remedy** /'remədɪ/, *n.* A remedy is a method which the *law* gives to prevent, put right or compensate a wrong. (*Damages* and *injunctions* are *civil* remedies.)

**remit** /rɪ'mɪt/, *v.* To free someone from a punishment; to cancel part of a prison *sentence*; to refer a *case* to another *court* for consideration. (His *sentence* was remitted; the *case* has been remitted to the *Crown Court*.)

**reparation** /ˌrepə'reɪʃn/, **reparations** /ˌrepə'reɪʃnz/, *n.*, *pl.n.* (In *International Law*) compensation for injuries or *breaches* of international obligations.

**repeal** /rɪ'piːl/, *v.* To cancel a *law* officially so that it is no longer valid. (The Corn Laws were repealed in 1846 after years of protest.)

**representative** /ˌreprɪ'zentətɪv/, *a.* A representative *body* is one that consists of *elected* members chosen by voters to represent them. (The *House of Lords* is not a representative chamber. Representative government: a system of government in which the people and their opinions are represented.)

**representative** /ˌreprɪ'zentətɪv/, *n.* A representative is a person chosen by another or others to represent them; a Representative is a member of the House of Representatives, the Lower House of the US Congress.

**robbery** /'rɒbərɪ/, *n.* Robbery is the *crime* of using force or causing fear of force in order to steal (*commit theft*).
See also *theft*

**Roman Law** /'rəʊmən ˌlɔː/, *a.* + *n.* Roman Law is the system of *law* developed at Rome and in the Roman Empire.
See also *civil law*

**Royal Assent** /ˌrɔɪəl ə'sent/, *a.* + *n.* The approval by the British *Sovereign* of a *Bill* which has been passed by both *Houses of Parliament* so that it becomes *law* as an *Act of Parliament*. (By *convention* the Royal Assent is never refused.)

**Royal Prerogative** /ˌrɔɪəl prɪ'rɒgətɪv/, *a.* + *n.* The special powers and rights which still belong to the British *Crown* and are exercised today by the *Sovereign* in person or by *government Ministers*. (The Sovereign *dissolves Parliament* under the Royal Prerogative.)

**rule** /ruːl/, *v.* To govern a *state*; to give an official decision e.g. in a *court action*. (Henry VIII ruled the country for 38 years; the *judge* ruled in favour of the *defendant*; rule (n.): government)
See also *ruling*

**ruling** /'ruːlɪŋ/, *n.* A ruling is a decision made by a *judge*, *tribunal*, etc. (The committee's ruling was in favour of the *applicant*.)

**sanction** /'sæŋkʃn/, *n.* In *International Law* a sanction is a measure taken against a *State* to force it to obey International Law or as punishment for breaking it. (Economic sanctions against South Africa.)

**seat** /siːt/, *n.* A *parliamentary constituency*; a place as a member of an official *body*. (Safe seat, marginal seat; he was candidate for a London seat; she won a seat in the Commons.)

**self-defence** /ˌself dɪ'fens/, *n.* In *Criminal Law* self-defence is the right to use reasonable force to defend oneself or another person against attack. It is a *defence* to a *charge* of *murder* or other *crimes* of violence. In *International Law* self-defence is the right of a *State* to defend itself against armed attack.

**sentence** /'sentəns/, *n.* The *judgment* of a *criminal court* stating what punishment is to be given to a person convicted of a *crime*; the punishment which a person convicted of a *crime* receives. (She *appealed* against sentence; he is serving a three-year sentence for *theft*; sentencing (n.))

**sentence** /'sentəns/, *v.* To state in the *judgment* of a *criminal court* what punishment is to be given to a person *convicted* of a *crime*. (The *judge* sentenced her to life *imprisonment*.)

**session** /'seʃn/, *n.* A period of time during which a *legislative* or *judicial body* meets; a meeting of a legislative or judicial body. (The life of a *Parliament* is divided into sessions, normally of one year each. Silence! The *court* is in session.)

**settlement** /'setlmənt/, *n.* An agreement or decision which ends an argument or *dispute*. (The *parties* reached a private settlement; settle (v.))

**sitting** /'sɪtɪŋ/, *n.* A *session* during which a *court of law* hears *cases*; a division, section or branch of a court. (sit (v.))

**solicitor** /sə'lɪsɪtə(r)/, *n.* A solicitor is a member of the *legal* profession who advises clients and may represent them in inferior *courts*. Solicitors instruct *counsel* and deal with *conveyancing*, *wills*, *trusts*, commercial work, *litigation*, etc.
See also *barrister*

**Solicitor-General** /səˌlɪsɪtə 'dʒenrəl/, *n.* + *n.* The Solicitor-General (usually a member of the *House of Commons*) is the second *Law Officer* of the *Crown* in England. S/he acts as deputy to the *Attorney-General*.
See also *Attorney-General*; *law officer*

**source of law** /ˌsɔːs əv 'lɔː/, *n.* + *prep.* + *n.* A source of law is something which gives origin to valid rules of *law*. (*Judicial precedent* is an important source of English law.)

**sovereign** /'sɒvrɪn/, *a.* Having supreme authority. (*Parliament* is sovereign in the UK *constitution*; sovereign power; a sovereign *State*)
See also *State sovereignty*

**sovereign** /'sɒvrɪn/, *n.* King or Queen, the *head of state* in a *monarchy*; a *body* with *sovereign* power.

**sovereignty** /'sɒvrəntɪ/, *n.* Sovereignty is supreme authority in an independent political society.
See also *parliamentary sovereignty*; *State sovereignty*

**Speaker** /'spiːkə(r)/, *n.* The Speaker is the chief officer of the *House of Commons*, who is *elected* by its members to preside over the House; the Speaker of the *House of Lords* is the *Lord Chancellor*, who presides over the House.

**specific performance** /spəˌsɪfɪk pə'fɔːməns/, *a.* + *n.* When the *court grants* an order of specific performance it orders a person to perform his or her obligations under a *contract*. It is an *equitable remedy*.
See also *Equity*

**stare decisis** /ˌstaːreɪ de'siːsɪs/, (*Latin*). The principle that decisions of *courts* in previous *cases* must be *followed* in later similar cases.
See also *judicial precedent*

**State** /steɪt/, *n.* A State is an independent, politically organised community of people living in a fixed part of the world under the *authority* of a *sovereign government*; the State is the government as opposed to the ordinary people of a country. (The USA is a federal State; a *crime* is an *illegal* act which is *prosecuted* and punished by the State).

**State sovereignty** /ˌsteɪt 'sɒvrəntɪ/, *n.* + *n.* Supreme power in a *State*: full *legislative*, *executive* and juridical powers of a State on its territory. (A *sovereign* State is a State which exercises State sovereignty – an independent, self-governing State.)

**statute** /'stætʃuːt/, *n.* A statute is an *Act of Parliament*;

statute law is the body of *law* contained in Acts of Parliament as opposed to *case-law*. (statutory (a.))
See also *Act of Parliament*

**subject** /'sʌbdʒɪkt/, *n.* Every *citizen* of a *State*, except the *Sovereign*, is a subject; States, organisations of States and international bodies such as the *UN* are subjects of *International Law*, with rights and duties under it.
See also *citizen*

**subordinate legislation** /sə'bɔːdɪnət ledʒɪs,leɪʃn/, *a. + n.*
See *delegated legislation*

**sue** /suː/, *v.* To take *legal action* against someone in a *civil case*. (They sued the company for £1000 *damages*.)

**suffrage** /'sʌfrɪdʒ/, *n.* Suffrage is the right to vote in an *election*. (universal adult suffrage: the right of all adults to vote)

**summarily** /'sʌmərəlɪ/, *adv.* A person is *tried* summarily if s/he is tried for a minor *offence* (called a 'summary offence') without a *jury* in a *magistrates' court*.

**summary** /'sʌmərɪ/, *a.* Relating to the right to *try* a minor *offence* without a *jury* in a *magistrates' court*. (summary jurisdiction, conviction, offence)

**summon** /'sʌmən/, *v.* The *Sovereign* summons *Parliament* when s/he calls for the *election* of a new Parliament after the old one has been dissolved; a *court* summons a person when it gives them an official order (called a *summons*) to appear in court.

**suspended sentence** /sə,spendɪd 'sentəns/, *a. + n.* A suspended sentence is a prison *sentence* of less than two years which does not take effect unless the *convicted* person *commits* another *crime* during the period specified by the *court*.

**tenant** /tenənt/, *n.* A tenant is a person who pays for the use and possession of another person's *land* under a *contract* called a *lease*.
See also *landlord; lease*

**term** /tɜːm/, *n.* A term is a rule or condition in an agreement such as a *contract*. (terms and conditions; Under the terms of the contract the *offeror* is responsible for transport.)

**testator** /te'steɪtə(r)/, *n.* A man who makes a *will*. (testatrix /te'steɪtrɪks/: a woman who makes a will)
See also *will*

**theft** /θeft/, *n.* Theft is the *crime* of stealing: dishonestly taking permanent possession of property which belongs to someone else.

**title** /'taɪtl/, *n.* Title is a person's *legal* right to *property*; a title is a word used before a person's name to show their status, profession or *office*. (She has no title to the house; English *lawyers* do not have a special title.)

**tort** /tɔːt/, *n.* A tort is a *civil* wrong which is not only a *breach of contract*, for which the person who suffers harm can obtain *damages* in a civil *court*. (tortious (a.))
See also *injured party; Law of Tort; tortfeasor*

**tortfeasor** /,tɔːt'fiːzə(r)/, *n.* A tortfeasor is a person who has *committed* a *tort*.
See also *tort*

**treaty** /'triːtɪ/, *n.* A treaty is an international agreement in writing between two or more *States*.

**trial** /'traɪəl/, *n.* A trial is the process of examining and deciding a *civil* or *criminal case* before a *court*. (The case was sent for trial at the *Crown Court*.)

**tribunal** /traɪ'bjuːnl/, *n.* General: a person or *body* of persons with power to decide claims or *disputes*. Modern Britain: usually composed of *laymen*, simple informal procedure, decisions based on discretion, experience, etc. Cf. *court*: usually composed of professional *judges*, formal *procedure*, decisions according to rules of *law*. (industrial tribunal)

**trust** /trʌst/, *n.* A trust is a type of property arrangement under which property is transferred to one or more *trustees* who become the *legal* owner(s) of the property, which they must hold and *administer* in *Equity* for the benefit or advantage of another person or group of persons or for a specific purpose. (A trust may be for the benefit of individuals or for a purpose such as helping the poor.)
See also *beneficiary, Equity, trustee*.

**trustee** /trʌ'stiː/, *n.* A trustee is the *legal* owner of property which s/he holds in *trust* and must *administer* for the benefit or advantage of another person or group of persons.
See also *beneficiary; trust*

**try** /traɪ/, *v.* To examine and decide a *criminal* or *civil case* before a *court*; to *hold* a *trial* of somebody. (The case was tried in the *Crown Court*; she was tried for *murder*.)

**UN** /juː 'en/, *abbrev.* See *United Nations Organisation*

**under seal** /,ʌndə 'siːl/, *prep. + n.* A *contract* under seal is one which is made in a special written form. (Most contracts for *land* must be made under seal.)

**unenacted** /,ʌnɪ'næktɪd/, *a.* Not formally made into *law* by a *legislative body*. (unenacted law)

**United Nations Organisation** /juː ,naɪtɪd 'neɪʃnz ,ɔːgənaɪ,zeɪʃn/, *a. + pl.n. + n.* An organisation created in 1945 to maintain international peace and encourage cooperation between *States*, based on the *sovereign* equality of all its members (most States in the world). (The UN (abbrev.))

**unlawful** /ʌn'lɔːfʊl/, *a.* Not *lawful*, against the *law*. (unlawfully (adv.))

**v.** /viː/, *abbrev.* Versus = against. Used in the title of *civil* and *criminal cases*. (Smith v Jones, R. v Smith. We say 'Smith against Jones' or 'Smith and Jones'
See also *citation; R.*

**vest** /vest/, *v.* To place *authority*, power, etc. in the control of a person or *body*. (The police are vested with wide powers to investigate *crime*.)

**voting paper** /'vəʊtɪŋ ,peɪpə(r)/, *a. + n.* See *ballot paper*

**war crimes** /'wɔː ,kraɪmz/, *n. + pl. n.* Crimes which violate the *laws* and *customs* of war.

**warrant** /'wɒrənt/, *n.* A warrant is an official document which gives *authority* to do a specified action, e.g. a warrant signed by a *magistrate* which orders a person to be *arrested* and brought before the *court*.

**wilful** /'wɪlfʊl/, *a.* Intentional, not by accident. (wilful damage)

**will** /wɪl/, *n.* A will is a *legal* document in which a person states how s/he wants to dispose of his or her property when s/he dies. (the last will and testament of Adam Smith)

**writ** /rɪt/, *n.* A document issued by a *court* in the name of the *Sovereign*, which orders a person to do or not to do a particular act.

# Index

Page numbers in brackets refer to extra information given in the key.